GAME TESTING
ALL IN ONE

D1174712

CHARLES P. SCHULTZ
ROBERT BRYANT
TIM LANGDELL, PH.D.

THOMSON
————————————
COURSE TECHNOLOGY
Professional ■ Trade ■ Reference

1-11

ISBN: 1-59200-373-7

Library of Congress Catalog Card Number: 2004090735

Printed in the United States of America

04 05 06 07 08 BH 10 9 8 7 6 5 4 3 2 1

Publisher and General Manager:
Stacy L. Hiquet

Associate Director of Marketing:
Sarah O'Donnell

Marketing Manager:
Heather Hurley

Manager of Editorial Services:
Heather Talbot

Acquisitions Editor:
Mitzi Koontz

Senior Editor:
Mark Garvey

Marketing Coordinator:
Jordan Casey

Developmental Editor:
Dave Astle

Project Editors:
Sean Medlock and Jenny Davidson

Technical Reviewer:
Robert Bryant

PTR Editorial Services Coordinator:
Elizabeth Furbish

Copy Editor:
Kim Cofer

Interior Layout Tech:
Shawn Morningstar

Cover Designer:
Mike Tanamachi

CD-ROM Producer:
Brandon Penticuff

Indexer:
Sharon Shock

Proofreader:
Kezia Endsley

Thomson Course Technology PTR,
a division of Thomson Course Technology
25 Thomson Place
Boston, MA 02210
http://www.courseptr.com

REFERENCES

PUBLISHED WORKS

Bartle, Richard A. *Hearts, Clubs, Diamonds, Spades: Players Who Suit MUDs*. <http://www.mud.co.uk/richard/hcds.htm> (29 January, 2005). [Chapter 12]

Bolton, Michael. *Sample Test Plan Template*. DevelopSense, 2003. <http://www.developsense.com/testing/TestPlanOutline.doc> (January 30, 2005). [Chapter 7]

Caminos, Rob and Stellenbach, Tim. *Cross-Platform User Interface Development*. 2004. http://www.gamasutra.com/gdc2004/features/20040326/caminos_01.shtml> (29 January, 2005). [Chapter 6]

Crosby, Philip. *Quality is Free*. Signet, 1980. [Chapter 6]

Diaz-Marino, Rob. *Super Street Racer Game Design Document*. 2004. <http://cpsc585.draggor.com/docs.asp#gamedesign> (29 January, 2005). [Chapter 4]

Edwards, Betty. *Drawing on the Right Side of the Brain*. Chapter 3. Tarcher/Perigee, 1989. [Chapter 14]

Finney, Kenneth C. *3D Game Programming All In One*. Premier Press, 2004. [Chapter 4]

Fristrom, Jamie. *Manager in A Strange Land: Churning*. 2003. <http://www.gamasutra.com/features/20031212/fristrom_01.shtml> (29 January, 2005). [Chapter 16]

Janis, Irving Lester. *Victims of Groupthink*. Houghton Mifflin, 1972. [Chapter 14]

Kearney, Greg, Larry Mellon and Darrin West. *Testing The Sims Online*. GDC, 2003. <http://serious-code.net/moin.cgi/AutomatedTestingInMmpGames> (29 January, 2005). [Chapter 16]

Neumann, Peter G. *Computer Related Risks*. Addison Wesley, 1994. [Chapter 2]

Orr, Bonnie. *High Concept*. SCREENTALK, 2002. <http://www.screentalk.biz/art043.htm> (30 January 2005). [Chapter 5]

Peterson, Ivars. *Fatal Defect: Chasing Killer Computer Bugs*. Vintage, 1996. [Chapter 2]

Silvester, Niko. *Writing Fiction: A Beginner's Guide*. Part 8: Form and Structure. <http://teenwriting.about.com/library/weekly/aa111102h.htm> (30 January, 2005). [Chapter 5]

Sudman, Seymour and Wansink, Brian. *Consumer Panels*. South-Western Educational Pub., 2002. [Chapter 14]

Wairy, Louis Constant. *Memoirs of Constant*. Volume III, Chapter IX. New York, The Century Company, 1907. <http://www.napoleonic-literature.com/Book_11/V3C9.html> (29 January, 2005). [Chapter 3]

Yarborough. *007 Insider Update #1*.007 Insider 06.12.2003. <http://www.eagames.com/official/007/everythingornothing/us/insider.jsp?newsID=i2> (30 January, 2005). [Chapter 5]

"Black Pendant." *Yu-Gi-Oh!* Card image. [Chapter 13]

A Note on the Hotfix. January 23, 2001. <http://classic.zone.msn.com/asheronscall/news/ASHEletterJan2.asp> (29 January, 2005). [Chapter 2]

Dark Age of Camelot Test Version 1.70ak Release Notes. June 28, 2004. <http://www.gamebanshee.com/news/static/EpIIulklVZaoBsRXef.php> (30 January, 2005). [Chapter 3]

Free MBTI Personality Test. 2005. <http://www.boomspeed.com/zsnp/mbti.htm> (29 January, 2005). [Chapter 2]

I'm Afraid We Must Talk About…Panic Underwater. The Why Files™. <http://whyfiles.org/sports/scuba> (January 29, 2005). [Chapter 1]

Ingres® Project C Coding Standard. Computer Associates®. 2004 <http://opensource.ca.com/projects/ingres/documents/technical/ C_Coding_Standard.pdf> (29 January, 2005). [Chapter 6]

More Questions and Answers about Panic Underwater… The Why Files™. <http://whyfiles.org/sports/scuba/scubaq4.html> (January 29, 2005). [Chapter 1]

Nyko® Speakercom™. 2004. <http://www.nyko.com/nyko/products/?i=27#> (29 January, 2005). [Chapter 15]

Ocean's Eleven. Warner Brothers, 2001. [Chapter 8]

Onboard Sound Menu Crash Update. 2003. <http://www.codemasters.com/downloads/?downloadid=12431> (29 January, 2005). [Chapter 2]

Quality Assurance Plan Template. Teraquest. <http://www.teraquest.com/resource/ documents/SQAPlanTemplateOne.doc> (29 January, 2005). [Chapter 6]

Sega Dreamcast Page Two. IEEE Micro. <http://www.computer.org/micro/articles/dreamcast_2.htm> (29 January. 2005). [Chapter 15]

Table for DPMO to Sigma. Mulbury Consulting. <http://www.eurosixsigma.com/sixsigma/sigma_table.htm> (29 January, 2005). [Chapter 6]

SPC for MS Excel. SPC for Excel. <http://www.spcforexcel.com/software.htm> (29 January, 2005). [Chapter 6]

Spinal Tap. MGM, 1994. [Chapter 6]

Star Trek®: Elite Force II v1.1 Patch. Activision, 2003. <http://www.fileplanet.com/131329/130000/fileinfo/ Star-Trek:-Elite-Force-II-v1.1-Patch> (29 January, 2005). [Chapter 15]

Unreal Engine and Game Code Overview. Unreal Wiki, 2001. <http://wiki.beyondunreal.com/wiki/ Unreal_Engine_And_Game_Code_Overview> (29 January, 2005). [Chapter 15]

Vanish. Allakhazam's Magical Realm. <http://camelot.allakhazam.com/ability.html?cabil=73> (29 January, 2005). [Chapter 3]

Vermont HighTest™ User's Guide. Version 4.02. Vermont Creative Software, Inc., 2002. <ftp://ftp.vtsoft.com/pub/ hightest/download/patch/40/hightestmanual402.zip> (29 January, 2005). [Chapter 17]

Yu-Gi-Oh! The Eternal Duelist Soul Prima's Official Strategy Guide. Prima Games, 2002. [Chapter 13]

SOFTWARE TITLES

Alien Hominid™. the Behemoth, 2004. [Chapter 5]

American Idol™. Codemasters. [Chapter 2]

Asheron's Call®. Turbine Entertainment Software Corporation, 1999. [Chapter 2]

Astrosmash™. Intellivision Products, Inc., 1981. [Chapter 8]

Battle Realms™. Crave Entertainment, Inc., 2001. [Chapter 14]

Battlefield 1942™. Electronic Arts™, 2004. [Chapter 4]

Britney's Dance Beat™. THQ, 2002. [Chapter 4]

Castle Wolfenstein: Enemy Territory™. Activision. [Chapters 3, 8]

Dance Dance Revolution Ultramix™. Konami. [Chapter 4]

Dark Age of Camelot™. Mythic Entertainment, Inc., 2001. [Chapter 3]

Dead or Alive® 3. TECMO, LTD., 2001. [Chapters 2, 10]

DevTrack™. Tech Excel, Inc. [Chapter 2]

Dr. Blob's Organism™. Digital Eel, 2003. [Chapter 4]

ESPN NFL 2K5. Sega®, 2004. [Chapters 4, 10]

Final Fantasy Tactics® Advance. Square Enix Co, Ltd., 2003. [Chapters 5, 13]

Flanker. SSI. [Chapter 14]

GameSpy Arcade. ©IGN Entertainment. [Chapter 8]

Grand Theft Auto. Rockstar Games. [Chapter 5]

Grand Theft Auto: Vice City. Rockstar Games. [Chapter 4]

HALO. ©Microsoft Corporation. [Chapters 5, 10, 12, 15]

James Bond 007™: Everything or Nothing™. Electronic Arts, 2003. [Chapter 5]

LoadRunner. Mercury Systems. [Chapter 16]

Metal Gear Solid. Konami. [Chapter 5]

"Microsoft® Excel." Microsoft Corporation. [Intro]

Microsoft® *Minesweeper.* Copyright © 1981-2001 Microsoft Corporation. [Chapter 17]

"Microsoft® Outlook." Microsoft Corporation. [Chapter 2]

"Microsoft® Windows® CE." Microsoft Corporation. [Chapter 2]

"Microsoft® Word." Microsoft Corporation. [Intro]

Midnight Club II. Rockstar Games. [Chapter 4]

Mortal Kombat. Midway. [Chapter 5]

MVP Baseball™ 2004. EA Sports. [Chapter 4]

NBA Street Vol. 2. Electronic Arts. [Chapters 2, 3]

NCAA Football 2005. Electronic Arts. 2004. [Chapter 3]

Neverwinter Nights Gold. Atari. [Chapter 2]

"Nintendo® GameCube™." Nintendo. [Chapter 5]

"PalmOS™." [Chapter 2]

SimCity™. Electronic Arts. [Chapter 5]

SimCity 3000™. Electronic Arts. [Chapter 4]

The Sims™. Electronic Arts. [Chapter 14]

The Sims Online™. Electronic Arts. [Chapter 16]

"SmartDraw 6" [Chapter 11]

"Snowblind." Official Xbox Magazine. Issue 34.

Spider-Man 2. Activision. [Chapter 16]

Star Trek® Elite Force II. Activision. [Chapter 15]

Star Wars: Knights of the Old Republic. Lucas Arts. 2003. [Chapters 2, 3, 4, 5]

StarCraft. Blizzard. [Chapter 14]

Tekken. Namco. [Chapter 14]

Tony Hawk's Underground. Activision. [Chapter 15]

True Crime: Streets of LA. Activision. [Chapters 2, 4, 5]

Unreal Tournament. Atari. [Chapters 3, 4, 8, 11]

Unreal Tournament 2004. Atari. [Chapters 3, 5, 11, 15] (screenshots in CH. 11)

"Vermont HighTest™." Vermont Creative Software, Inc. [Chapter 17]

Warhammer 40,000: Dawn of War™. ©Games Workshop Ltd 2004. [Chapters 13, 17]

Wario Ware, Inc. Nintendo. [Chapter 5]

World of Warcraft. Blizzard. [Chapter 16]

Yu-Gi-Oh! The Eternal Duelist Soul™. Konami. [Chapter 2]

Zoo Tycoon. Microsoft. Blue Fang Games. [Chapter 5]

"Dreamcast." Sega.

Madden Football. Electronic Arts. [Chapter 4]

Pokémon. Nintendo. [Chapter 4]

"PlayStation®2." Sony.

"PS2®." Sony.

"Xbox®." Microsoft.

To my mother, father, and grandmother, for the sacrifices they made.
—Charles Schultz

To my wife Lisa, whose patience is boundless.

—Robert Bryant

For Cheri, Melissa, Sebastian, Sybil, Ted, and Jenny.

—Tim Langdell

ACKNOWLEDGMENTS

Charles Schultz

To start, I must acknowledge the work of the staff at Course PTR. You would not be reading my words if Mitzi Koontz had not taken time to chat with me at GDC 2004 and subsequently given me the opportunity to author this, my first book. Jenny Davidson and Brandon Penticuff also deserve special mention for polishing my work and taking my inputs at all hours of the day and night.

Many thanks to Dave Astle for his feedback, his encouragement, and for providing a home for the book's Web page at testbook.gamedev.net.

There is a special place in my heart for Schultz's Subalterns—the people who have worked for me over the course of many years at Motorola, putting my testing ideas into practice. I appreciate all of the hard work and skill they have applied under my leadership. Their labor and their candid feedback have made the test methods in this book more effective and easier to use.

I would also like to thank my fellow game fanatics James Dusek, Danny Sanchez, and Ted O'Hare. As I was writing this book they acted as sounding boards for my ideas, logged multiplayer time with me, and provided me with new games to try.

My work at Motorola continues to be exciting and challenging due to the efforts of Arnie Pittler and Jacques Meekel. I appreciate their trust in my abilities and the new challenges they continue to provide me.

Nothing has changed my perspective on software testing the way the Orthogonal Defect Classification (ODC) has. My thanks go out to Ram Chillarege who invented ODC and has shared his wisdom with me on a number of occasions.

Most of all, I thank my wife, Mirta, for giving up many nights and meals we should have spent together so I could work on the book.

Robert Bryant

For my small part, I'd like to dedicate this book to Don DeLucia, who taught me what a bug is, and to Ray Boylan, who taught me how to fight to get it fixed. Also to Mark Burke, for picking me out of the chorus, and to John Bloodworth and Tuan Trinh, from whom I continue to learn every day. Finally, to my wife Lisa, whose patience is boundless.

Tim Langdell

My contribution to this book could not have been written without the kind support and assistance of several people. I wish to thank Anthony Borquez, Director of the USC Information Technology Program for his kind support. Thanks, too, to all my industry colleagues, just a few of whom I name here: John Hight of Atari; Michael Gilmartin, head of game testing at Blizzard Entertainment; Michael Gonzalez, head of games testing at Universal Vivendi Games; Shannon Studstill of Sony; Bing Gordon, Steve Anderson, and Neil Young of Electronic Arts; and Will Wright of Maxis. Last, but not least, my work would not be possible without the incredible support of my wife, Cheri, and of my ceaselessly amazing children Sebastian and Melissa.

About the Authors

CHARLES P. SCHULTZ is an Operations Manager for Motorola's Global Software Group, working on software testing and mobile gaming. He has more than 20 technical publications to his credit and has spoken at industry conferences in the areas of personal robotics, software quality, and software testing. Charles has also developed and taught computing classes at various levels, ranging from children's programs at the Miami Museum of Science to graduate level university courses.

ROBERT BRYANT is currently Studio Director at videogame publisher Crave Entertainment, where he has also served as QA Manager and Executive Producer of such games as *World Championship Poker*, *Pinball Hall of Fame*, *Future Tactics: the Uprising*, *Mojo!*, *Tokyo Xtreme Racer 3*, and *Intellivision Lives!*. He began his games career in the interactive division of Mattel, Inc., where he was lead tester on dozens of projects and co-designed *Nick Click Digital Camera* and *CD-ROM*. He is a frequent speaker on the subjects of game testing methods and management. He holds a BA from Washington and Lee University and an MFA from the University of Southern California.

TIM LANGDELL, a veteran of the game industry, is full-time faculty in the USC Viterbi School of Engineering's Information Technology Program where he chairs the Game Curriculum Sub-Committee, and teaches game design and game testing. Tim is also Chairman of EDGE Games, which he founded in 1979—one of the top games brands well-known for innovative games, games magazines, and games hardware. Tim has produced more than 180 games (including *Garfield*, *The Punisher*, *Fairlight*, and the hit 1980s cult classic *Brian Bloodaxe*) and written several books on computer game programming, including *The Spectrum Handbook*. He is an innovator of games education: In 1992 he devised the first curriculum course in interactive entertainment at USC's Film School where he taught for several years. Tim co-founded the Academy of Interactive Arts & Sciences, is a member of the IGDA, a member of the Writer's Guild of America, and a member of both BAFTA and BAFTA/LA (where he served on the Board of Directors).

Contents

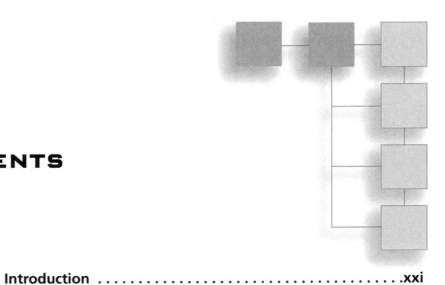

PART III: TESTING FUNDAMENTALS 103

INTRODUCTION

In this book you will learn about the roles and responsibilities of a game tester, including how to best apply software test engineer methodologies to the game industry. This knowledge can be applied by testers to help create staffing plans and schedule test tasks, as well as generate thorough and effective test cases for games. Topics include how games are made, how testing fits into the production cycle of a game, testing fundamentals, test automation, and how to test different game genres.

References to many different game types and titles are spread out among the topics and methods taught in this book. It's okay if you haven't played all of these games yet. In each case the games and features illustrate specific concepts which will be explained to you in the text and illustrated in examples. Please don't get angry if one or more of your favorite games are not mentioned. It's up to you to go and test them using what you learn from this book.

How the Book Is Organized

This book is divided into five parts, each consisting of multiple chapters. The parts and chapters are organized to provide a logical progression to increase your knowledge and develop new skills. As the book title indicates, all aspects of game testing are pulled together into this one volume. However, if you want to target one or more specific parts or chapters to address an immediate need in your job, you will find that each one stands on its own to provide the full range of information for its topic. Furthermore, each chapter concludes with a summary and exercises, making it possible to use this book as a college level textbook in a Computer Science or Game Development curriculum. While it provides all the topics you need for a stand-alone course on game testing, it can also supplement game software development, game development process, and game development practicum classes. Even if you are not a classroom student, do the exercises and check your answers with those provided in the appendices to cement and expand your understanding of this subject matter.

Part I "About Game Testing" introduces the reader to game testing in terms of culture, philosophies, and the contribution testing makes to the final game release that everyone (hopefully!) rushes out to buy. If all goes well, the users will let you know.

Part II "Making Games" reveals how an individual contributes to the overall game project. This includes the different kinds of roles and responsibilities that are required of testers through various stages of the development and production of game software.

Part III "Testing Fundamentals" introduces testing concepts and practices from a formal software engineering approach. These practices will boost your testing IQ. Tools and files included on the book's CD will help you quickly produce useful test documents, capture important data, and analyze the measurements described in this section.

Part IV "Testing Techniques" is a set of tutorials on different methodologies for producing tests for your game. Each can be used by itself, or in combination with the others. They are good for testing any portion of your game at any stage of development. A portion of Chapter 12, "Cleanroom Testing," relies on the techniques taught in the two chapters preceding it, so keep that in mind if you try to flip over to read that one on its own.

Links to test tools are included on the book's CD to help you learn and practice these methods. In addition to the tools, there are some template files that will make it easier for you to produce your tests by "filling in the blanks" rather than starting from an empty sheet. Information about how to use the templates is provided in the chapters and appendices.

Part V "More Effective Testing" addresses ways to make the most out of your limited time and resources to reach new heights in the quantity and quality of the test you can produce and run. Again, tool links are included on the CD for this book to help you learn and practice the methods described in this section.

The appendices contain answers to chapter questions, details about the CD contents, and supplemental information for the testing techniques covered in Part IV.

Who Should Read This Book?

This book is for people looking to start a career in game testing, current software testers interested in moving into games, and current game testers who want to learn new techniques to improve their testing skills and results. It will also prove beneficial for small game team members who are involved in game testing as well as their main responsibility, such as programming or artwork. Current or aspiring test leads and project managers will also gain from reading this book.

If you are already an experienced game tester, I recommend you read through Chapter 1 and then skim Chapters 2 and 3, and all of Part II before focusing your attention on Parts III through V. Then go and apply what you learn in Parts IV and V in your real-life job. If you are a test lead, then apply the contents of Part III to your job, and get your testers to start using what's in Parts IV and V on your projects.

Experienced testers who have not been involved in the game industry may want to skim or skip Chapter 3, but otherwise should read the rest of the book and do the exercises. You will benefit from putting the techniques in Parts IV and V to work in your current job, but also try to put in some hours on your own doing the same for some games you own.

If you are looking to break into the game industry as a tester, then you have the most work to do. Read everything in the book, do all the exercises, and while you're job hunting, practice the techniques in Parts IV and V. You can do that as a Beta tester (see especially chapters 4 and 14), or just by picking some of your favorite games to test on your own.

If you are a game project manager who wants to better understand the testing side of your projects, STOP SPYING ON US! But seriously, that's a great thing to do! You can skip Part II if you'd like, but otherwise dig in to the other parts of the book. The following table summarizes the suggested uses of this book:

Role	Ch.1	Ch.2	Ch.3	Part II	Part III	Part IV	Part V
Game Tester	R	S	S	S	R	A	A
Other Tester	R	R	S	R	R	A	A
Future Game Tester	R	R	R	R	R	A	A
Game Test Lead	R	S	S	S	A	R	R
Game Project Mgr.	R	R	R	S	R	R	R

R = Read and do exercises
S = Skip or Skim, optionally doing exercises
A = Apply to your job after reading and doing exercises

Using This Book

The CD

Companion files are arranged into folders for each chapter. Some of the files require you to install other software which you may not have, and those are provided in the Tools folder on the CD. Many tools on the CD are demo or shareware versions, so if you are satisfied with them and intend to use them in your work, please honor your licensing and purchasing obligation. If you want tools that do more than what's been included here, see if the tool companies provide more advanced versions of what you have right now. Otherwise, check with some colleagues or search the Web to find what you are looking for. More details about the CD contents are provided in the "What's on the CD" appendix at the back of this book.

Your Tools

Microsoft Excel and Word are the only software you are expected to already have in order to use files provided on the CD. When installing the executable programs referenced on the CD, choose the installation options best suited for your machine, or consult the program's Web site for other download options or versions.

Support Web Site

You will find a Web site for this book at http://testbook.gamedev.net. This site will include errata, new or updated examples, documents, templates, and helpful information. Stop by every now and then to see what's new and maybe you'll find something interesting there.

Now go put what you read in this book into practice, and have a productive, satisfying, and exciting career in the game industry.

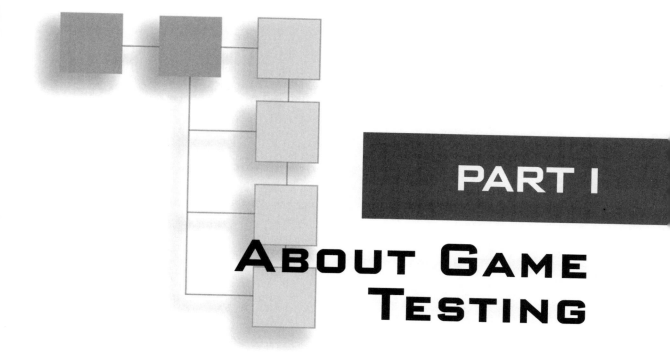

PART I

ABOUT GAME TESTING

CHAPTER 1

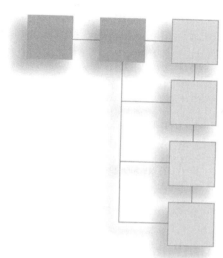

TWO RULES OF GAME TESTING

Whenever I start a new test team or bring a new tester into the group, I give them these two rules:

Rule 1: Don't Panic

Rule 2: Trust No One

Don't Panic

In a game project, panic is a bad thing. The person panicking did not choose to panic, and may not realize it is happening. It is an irrational reaction to a set of circumstances, and it can lead a tester to cause harm to the project. When I sense that a tester is reacting inappropriately to some unreasonable request, I will indirectly remind him not to panic by asking "What's rule one?"

Scuba divers put themselves in a situation similar to what game testers might face: limited resources (the equipment you bring with you), time constraints (air supply), rules to follow (rate of descent/ascent), and other surprises (unexpected sea visitors). According to Dr. William Morgan, episodes of panic or near-panic may explain many recreational diving accidents and deaths. The panic attack was often spurred by something that a non-diver would deem serious—entanglement, an equipment malfunction, or the sight of a shark. But the attacks don't make things better, Morgan says—they can lead to irrational and dangerous behavior.[1] Even scuba divers with many years of experience sometimes experience panic for no apparent reason.[2]

1. "I'm Afraid We Must Talk About…Panic Underwater." The Why Files™
   <http://whyfiles.org/sports/scuba> (January 21, 2005)

2. "More questions and answers about Panic Underwater…" The Why Files™
   <http://whyfiles.org/sports/scubaq4.html> (January 21, 2005)

Testing the wrong build, failing to notice an important defect, or sending developers on a wild goose chase after a non-existent bug shouldn't end up getting you physically hurt, but there will be a price to pay in extra time, extra money spent, and/or loss of sales and reputation.

Game project panic happens when you are

- Unfamiliar
- Unprepared
- Under pressure
- Unrested
- Nearsighted

Unfamiliar

As a member of a game team, you might be asked to do something you've never had to do before. You might be given someone else's tests to run, be thrown into the middle of a different game project, or told to take someone else's place at the last minute to do a customer demo. In situations like these, rely on what you know, stick to basics, and pick up any new or different ways of doing things by watching the people who have already been doing it.

You may even be asked to accomplish something you've never done before, such as achieve 100% automation of the installation tests, or write a tool to verify the foreign language text in the game. Maybe *no one* has ever done this before. Don't make a commitment right away, don't make stuff up, and don't try to be a hero. If you are unfamiliar with a situation, you act based on your best judgment, but it still may not be right. This requires good "radar" on your part to know when to get help, and also a dose of humility so you don't feel like you have to take on everything yourself or say "yes" to every request. You don't need to lose any authority or "street cred." Find someone who's "been there, done that" and can steer you toward some working solutions. Stay away from responses that are known to fail. You can even search the Internet to see if anyone else has been through it and lived to tell about it.

Note

Chapter 8, "The Test Process," shows you how to define and follow a set of activities that will give you consistent test throughput and results, even when you're in unfamiliar territory.

Unprepared

Nobody expects the Spanish Inquisition, and a lot of unexpected things will happen on your project. Expect the unexpected! Many parts of the game need to be tested at various points in the game's life cycle. Behind the scenes, many different technologies are at work—3D graphics, audio, user interfaces, multithreading, and file systems to name a few. If you are not ready for a variety of test assignments and don't have the skills needed to perform them successfully, then you will stumble rather than star.

Study, practice, and experience are ingredients for good preparation. During the course of the project, try to get to know more about the game code. Keep up with the industry so you are also aware of what the next generation of games and technologies will be like. Become an expert in the requirements and designs for the parts of the game you are responsible for testing, and then get familiar with the ones you *aren't* responsible for. When you least expect it, you may need to take on a different position, fill in for another tester, or grow into more responsibility. Be ready when it happens.

Note

The information in Chapter 5, "The Game Production Cycle," gives you a heads up on preparing yourself to succeed as a game tester, as well as covers what kinds of environments, projects, roles, and jobs you might find yourself in someday.

Under Pressure

Pressure can come from any of three directions:

- Schedule (calendar time to complete the project)
- Budget (money to spend on the project)
- Headcount (the quantity and types of people assigned to work on the game)

There's nothing to prevent one or more of these resources from shrinking at any time during the project. As a tester, these factors won't be under your control. Usually they are determined by business conditions or project managers. In any case, you will be impacted. Figure 1.1 shows the resources in balance with the scope of the project.

Moving in any one of these points on the triangle squeezes the project, creating pressure. Sometimes a game project starts out with one of these factors being too small, or they can get smaller anytime after the project has launched. For example, money can be diverted to another game, developers might leave to start their own company, or the schedule gets pulled in to release ahead of a newly announced game that competes with yours. Figure 1.2 shows how a budget reduction can cause pressure on the game project's schedule and headcount.

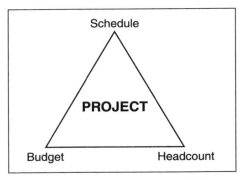

Figure 1.1 Resources balanced with project scope.

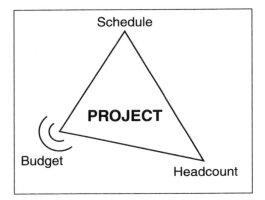

Figure 1.2 Budget reduction causes pressure.

Another way to cause pressure within this triangle is to try to stuff more into it than was originally planned for. This demand could be internally driven, such as adding more levels or characters, or scrapping the old graphics engine for a new one to take advantage of some newly announced hardware. Other unplanned changes might be made to support more game platforms than originally planned or to keep up with newly announced games in terms of number of levels, characters, online players supported, and so on. Figure 1.3 illustrates how increasing the scope of a project can put pressure on the budget and headcount if they are not increased.

When there is pressure on the project, you can expect it to get passed on. Someone demands something from you, and uses phrases like the following:

- I/we need … immediately
- I don't care…

- That was then, this is now
- Figure out how to do it
- Make it happen
- Deal with it
- We can't afford to…
- Nothing else matters but…

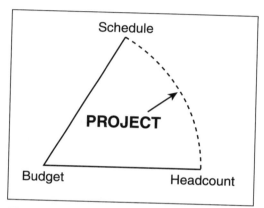

Figure 1.3 Budget and headcount pressure caused by project scope increase.

It's likely that you will get more than one demand at a time, and from different people to boot. Examine the schedule, budget, and headcount available to you. Achieve the request by then scaling down what you would normally do so that it fits in your new triangle. Do the things that will have the most impact on meeting the request to the greatest extent possible. Then in the next release, take care of the stuff that didn't fit this time around.

Note

Chapter 2, "Being a Game Tester," introduces you to what's expected of you in your role as a tester, and how to make an impact on the quality of the game.

Chapter 5, "The Game Production Cycle," describes how goals and expectations change as the game progresses from being a concept to hitting the shelves, and how this affects the tester's job along the way.

Unrested

Running long tests after staying up for 30 hours straight or working 100+ hours a week is not the best approach to finding defects. It is, however, a good way to introduce them! When developers do this, they keep testers in business, but it doesn't help get the game released. It's just as bad for the project when testers make mistakes.

Reporting a problem that doesn't really exist (for example, tested the wrong build, didn't do the setup or install properly, and so on) will send the developers on a wild goose chase and waste precious time. If you absolutely have to do testing late at night or at the end of a long week, make a checklist to use before and after the testing. If there's another tester around, have her check your stuff and you can check hers when she does her testing. Also, by writing down some of the information as you go along, you won't be prone to mistakes later on if you have to rely on your tired memory. It's kind of like a pre-launch checklist for the space shuttle. If something is wrong, stop the countdown. Go back and make it right—like it says in the test instructions. After testing is done, record pertinent results and facts. The next page includes an example checklist that you can start with and expand on to fit your own game projects.

In addition to putting practices into place for checking mistakes, look for ways to prevent them in the first place. Depending on your game platform and test environment, automation may be a viable option to make your work repeatable at any time of the day. Automated tasks can even go to work while you're at home resting.

Note

Chapter 16, "Game Test Automation," and Chapter 17 "Capture/Playback Testing," describe techniques and tools you can use to make the best use of your testing *and* resting time.

Nearsighted

Panic symptoms can include too much focus on the near term. Many game projects take months, so make that a factor in deciding what to work on today and how to do it. A question I will ask a tester to put him back in the right frame of mind is "Will this be our last chance to test this?" If the answer is "no," then we discuss how to approach the present situation in the context of an overall strategy of repeated testing, feedback from test results, budgeting resources, and so on.

Successful sports teams know how to avoid panic. When they are losing, they're confident that they can come back from behind and win the game because they are a) familiar with the situation, b) prepared to deal with it from practice, film study, and in-game experience, c) rested, and d) don't feel pressure to make up the deficit immediately. Teams that have a losing record often lack one or more of these ingredients.

Late Night Testing Checklist

Pre-Test

Do you have the right version of the test?

Test version: _____

Are you using the right version of the build?

Build version: _____

Are you using the right hardware configuration/settings?

Describe: _____

Are you using the right game controller and settings?

Describe: _____

Which installation options did you use (if any)?

Describe: _____

Is the game in the right initial state before running the test case?

Describe: _____

Post-Test

Did you complete all of the test steps in order?

Did you document the completion of the tests and the test results?

Did you record all of the problems you found?

If you reported a problem, did you fill in all of the required fields?

N o t e

Chapter 7, "Test Phases," shows you what kinds of testing should be done along the way as the game code matures. This helps you test appropriately for a particular situation and also know that you can rely on the additional testing you will do later in the game.

Trust No One

On the surface this sounds like a cynical approach, but the very fact that testing is built into the project means that something can't be trusted. You'll read more about this in Chapter 3, "Why Testing Is Important," and in Chapter 5. The very existence of testers on a game project is a result of trust issues, such as the following:

- The publisher doesn't trust that your game will release on time and with the promised features, so they write contracts that pay your team incrementally based on demonstrations and milestones.
- The press and public don't trust that your game will be as good and fun and exciting as you promise, so they demand to see screen shots and demos, write critiques, and discuss your work in progress on bulletin boards.
- Project managers don't trust that the game code can be developed without defects, so testing is planned, funded, and staffed. This can include testers from a third-party QA house and/or the team's own internal test department.
- The publisher can't trust the development house testers to find every defect, so they may employ their own testers or issue a beta release for the public to try it out and report the defects they find.

Don't take it personally. It's a matter of business, technology, and competition. Lots of money is on the line and investors don't want to lose it on your project. The technologies required to produce the game may not even have been available at the time development started, giving your team the opportunity to create the kind of game no one has ever done before. By trying to break the game, and failing, you establish confidence that it will work. Games that don't come out right fall victim to rants and complaints posted on the Internet. Don't let this happen to you!

Balancing Act

Evaluate the basis of your testing plans and decisions. Hearsay, opinions, and emotions are elements that can distract you from what you should really be doing. Using test methods and documenting both your work and results will contribute to an objective game testing environment.

Measuring and analyzing test results—even from past games—gives you data about your game's strengths and weaknesses. The parts that you trust the least—the weak ones—will need the most attention in terms of testing, retesting, and analysis. This relationship is illustrated in Figure 1.4.

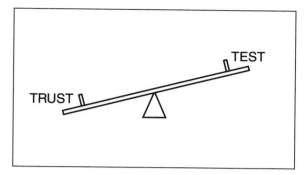

Figure 1.4 Low trust means more testing.

The parts you can trust the most—the strong ones—will require the least attention from you, as illustrated in Figure 1.5. These should still be retested from time to time to re-establish your trust. Chapter 5 helps you determine what kind of testing to do, and when to do it. Chapter 8 gives you specific strategies and criteria for planning, choosing, and revisiting testing.

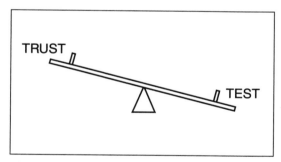

Figure 1.5 More trust leads to less testing.

Note

Chapter 6, "Software Quality," introduces you to some basic principles for evaluating the trustworthiness of your game code. Chapter 9, "Testing by the Numbers," describes measurements that you can compile from the test data you normally collect and explains how to analyze those measurements to zoom in on specific problem areas.

Word Games

It's useful to be wary of advice you get from outside the test team. Well-meaning people will suggest shortcuts so the game development can make better progress, but you won't remove bugs from the game by simply not finding them. Don't trust what these people are telling you. At the same time, don't cross the boundary from being distrustful to turning hostile. The whole team is working to deliver the best game it can, even when it doesn't seem that way to a tester.

A general form of statements to watch out for is "X happened, so (only/don't) do Y." Here are some examples:

- "Only a few lines of code have changed, so don't inspect any other lines."
- "The new audio subsystem works the same as the old one, so you only need to run your old tests."
- "We added foreign language strings for the dialogs, so just check a few of them in one of the languages and the rest should be okay too."

And some variants:

- "We only made small changes so don't worry about testing <insert feature name here>."
- "You can just run one or two tests on this and let me know if it works."
- "We've gotta get this out today so just …."

Tip

You'll be surprised how many bugs you will find by behaving opposite from the advice you get from other people about what should and should not be tested.

Don't equate a "trust no one" attitude with a "don't do anything you're asked to do" attitude. If a test lead or the project manager needs you to meet goals for certain kinds of testing to be done, be sure you fulfill your obligation to them before going off and working on the stuff you don't trust. The difference is between being a hero ("I finished the tests you wanted, and also managed to start looking at the tournament mode and found some problems there. We should do more testing on that next time around") or a zero ("I didn't have time to do the tests you wanted because I was getting some new tests to work for the tournament mode").

Note

In Chapter 4, "The Game Team," you learn something about what the other people on the game project are doing, and how your testing affects their work and impacts the progress of the game.

Last Chance

Examine your own tests and look for ways you can improve so you gain more trust in your own skills in finding defects. Just never let that trust turn into arrogance or the belief that you are perfect. Leave room to mistrust yourself just a little bit. Remain open to suggestions from managers, developers, other testers, and yourself. For example, if you're in the middle of running a test and you're not sure you are testing the right version—check it! You may have to go back and start over, but that's better than reporting the wrong results and wasting other people's time too.

As game development progresses, management and developers want to feel comfortable about the quality of the game and its readiness for the next milestone and, ultimately, final release. As a tester, you should not be lulled into complacency. I often re-energize my team by instructing them to "Treat this release like it's our last chance to find problems." Conflicts will arise about whether or not to introduce new tests, and you'll hear complaints about why important problems are found so late in the project. There are many reasons for late defects showing up that have nothing to do with incompetent testing. Here are some you will run into:

- The defects were introduced late, just before you found them.
- Bugs from earlier rounds of testing kept you from getting to the part of the game where the late defect was hiding.
- As you spend more time testing the game you become more familiar with where the defects are coming from, so it is perfectly natural that especially subtle problems might not be found until late in the project.

In any case, even if the bugs were there from the very first release, they were not put there by the testers. Somewhere there is an imaginary world where game testers get to hear "Thank you for finding this important defect right before we shipped it!" but don't count on that happening in our world (refer to Figure 1.6).

Note

Chapter 12, "Cleanroom Testing," and Chapter 14, "Play Testing and Ad Hoc Testing," give you methods to use for testing the game based on your testing intuition and insight.

Trust Fund

You can get a head start on knowing what not to trust in a couple of ways. Sometimes the developers will tell you, if you just ask...

Tester: "Hey Bill, is there anything you're particularly concerned about that I should focus on in my testing?"

Bill: "Well we just redid the logic for the *Fuzzy Sword* quest, so we definitely want that looked at."

Figure 1.6 Our world (left) and the tester loving world (right).

You can get more clues by mentioning parts of the system and seeing how people react. Rolling eyes and pauses in response are giveaways that there is some doubt as to how good that new weapon will work or if multiplayer will work as well as it did before the latest changes.

Note

In Chapter 3, you find out why testing is important to the health of the game. It covers many factors that contribute to making things go wrong and how you, the game tester, should deal with them.

Give and Take

If you've been paying close attention up to this point—and you should as an aspiring or working game tester—you would have noticed an apparent contradiction between the testing approach to counteract panic ("don't treat this release like it's the last one"), and the "trust no one" approach of treating each release like it *is* the last one. A sports analogy might illustrate how these concepts can co-exist.

In baseball, one batter can't step up to the plate with bases empty and put six runs on the board. Instead, batter by batter and inning by inning, the team bats according to the situation, producing the most runs it can. The batters and base runners succeed by being patient, skilled, and committed to their manager's strategy. If every batter tries to hit a home run, the team will strike out a lot and leave the opposing pitcher fresh for the next inning.

At the same time, when each player is at bat or on base, he is aggressively trying to achieve the best possible outcome. He is fully analyzing the type and location of each pitch, executing his swing properly, and running as fast as he can once the ball is hit. He knows that it contributes to the team's comeback and that his one run or RBI could mean the difference between a win and a loss for the team.

So, as a tester, you can do *both at once* by following this advice:

- Know your role on the team based on the responsibilities assigned to you
- Execute your tasks aggressively and accurately
- Do the most important tests first
- Do the tests most likely to find defects often
- Make emotion-free and objective decisions to the best extent possible

Note

Chapter 15, "Defect Triggers," describes how testing causes defects to appear so you can cover those possibilities in your testing. These also help you decide which tests will be the most important ones to run and which ones should be run the most often.

The Rest of the Story

The rest of this book equips you to apply the two rules to your game testing. Don't feel like you have to incorporate everything at once to be successful. You may already consider yourself an effective tester. Use new insights from this book to refine your existing skills and add the techniques you learn in Chapters 10–17 where it makes the most sense for your projects.

You should also apply the two rules to what you read in this book. Don't trust that what you read here will work every time for everything you do. If you get results that don't make sense, find out why. Try something, and then measure or evaluate it to decide whether to go on using it and refining it, whether to try something new, or whether to go back to what you were doing in the first place. But do try it before passing judgment. I would just caution you not to trust yourself too much before you make sure you are applying the technique properly. Then you can decide if it works for you. These methods are good—trust me.

Remember, as a game tester, everyone is trusting in you to find problems before the game ships. Don't give them cause to panic!

Note

Chapter 10, "Combinatorial Testing," Chapter 11, "Test Flow Diagrams," and Chapter 13, "Test Trees," introduce you to three important game testing methods. Use them to understand the game software early in development and systematically explore the game's features and functions throughout the project.

Summary

In this chapter you learned two important rules for game testing, and how they relate to the remaining chapters of this book. Panic and trust are counter-productive to game testing. You can beat the system by remembering and applying the two rules.

Panic results in

- Poor judgment and decision making
- Unreliable test results
- Too much emphasis on the short-term

Panic costs the project in

- Unnecessary rework
- Wasted effort
- Loss of confidence and credibility

Avoid panic by

- Recognizing when you need help, and getting it
- Preparing for the unexpected
- Relying on procedures
- Getting sufficient rest

Don't trust

- Hearsay
- Opinions
- Emotions

Rely on

- Facts
- Results
- Experience

Test each game release as if

- It's not the last one
- It is the last one

Exercises

1. What is Rule 1?

2. Give two or three examples where you could have applied this rule but did not, and describe how results might have been different if you did apply it in one of those situations.

3. What is Rule 2?

4. Give two or three examples where you could have applied this rule but did not, and describe how results might have been different if you did apply it in one of those situations.

5. Which of the following puts pressure on a game project?

    a) New funding

    b) Taking people away to have them work on another game

    c) A requirement to add more levels to be comparable to a competitor's recently announced title

    d) b and c

6. EXTRA CREDIT: Name the two science fiction games that feature the phrases "Don't Panic" and "Trust No One."

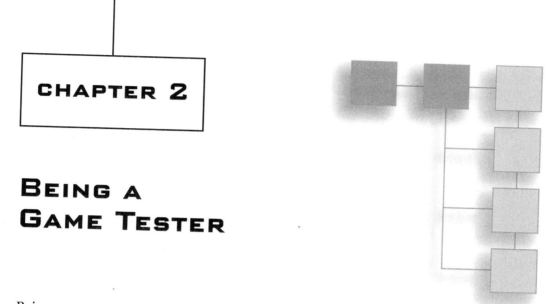

CHAPTER 2

BEING A GAME TESTER

Being a game tester starts with being a game player. This is the part that seems to attract most people to the profession. Just imagine—getting paid to play games! For the most part you don't get to test (play) whatever you feel like on any given day. You are given assignments that you're expected to complete thoroughly and on time—even if it means you have to stay late to get them done. The tests and the hours will pile up anytime you get near to a major release.

But just playing the game isn't enough to be a good tester. Sure, you need to have a knack for finding problems, but you also need to do a good job at other things such as documenting and reporting bugs, reporting test progress, and helping developers find and fix your bugs. These tasks are done over and over again until the game ships. Think of the acronym "PIANo TV"—**P**lay, **I**dentify, **A**mplify, **N**otify, and **o**ptionally, **T**estify and **V**erify. Figure 2.1 illustrates this sequence of activities.

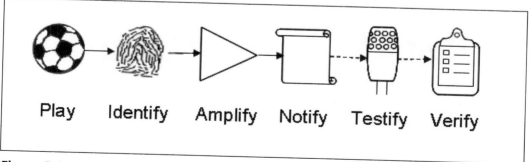

Figure 2.1 Game testing activities.

Playing Games

At home, you play games to have fun. You get to choose what to play, when to play, and how to play it. Testing games can still be fun, but you have fewer choices about what, when, and how to play. Everything you do when you play is for a purpose—either to explore some area of the game, check that a specific rule is being enforced, or look for a particular kind of problem.

Your job begins by running a series of tests that are assigned to you. Some of the tests are very specific and consist of step-by-step instructions. These rely on your keen observations and attention to details. This is a good format for user interface (UI) testing. Here's a short example for testing a portion of the character selection UI in *Star Wars: Knights of the Old Republic* for Xbox:

1. Select New Game from the Main Menu.
   - ■ Check that the Male Scoundrel picture and title are highlighted (see Figure 2.2).
   - ■ Check that the scoundrel character description is displayed correctly.

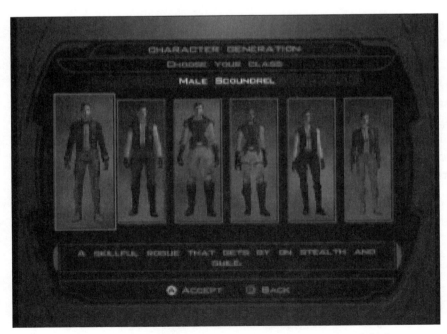

Figure 2.2 *Knights of the Old Republic* character selection screen initial state showing Male Scoundrel.

2. Scroll to the left using the D-Pad.
   - Check that the Female Scoundrel picture and title are highlighted.
   - Check that the scoundrel character description is unchanged.

3. Scroll to the right using the D-Pad.
   - Check that the Male Scoundrel picture and title are highlighted.
   - Check that the scoundrel character description is unchanged.

4. Scroll to the right using the LEFT analog stick.
   - Check that the Male Scout picture and title are highlighted.
   - Check that the scout character description is displayed correctly.

5. Scroll to the left using the LEFT analog stick.
   - Check that the Male Scoundrel picture and title are highlighted.
   - Check that the scoundrel character description is displayed correctly.

6. Scroll to the right using the RIGHT analog stick.
   - Check that the Male Scoundrel picture and title are unchanged.
   - Check that the scoundrel character description is unchanged.

7. Press the X button.
   - Check that the Male Scoundrel picture and title are unchanged.
   - Check that the scoundrel character description is unchanged.

8. Press the Y button.
   - Check that the Male Scoundrel picture and title are unchanged.
   - Check that the scoundrel character description is unchanged.

9. Press the B button.
   - Check that the Main Menu screen is displayed with "New Game" highlighted.

So you see, you are given specific operations to perform and details to check for at each step. This can become tedious over the course of a long test case, especially when doing many of these tests one after the other. To keep subtle problems from slipping past you, maintain concentration and treat each item as if it's the first time you've seen it.

Other test assignments involve more open-ended directives, and may be in checklist or outline form. These tests rely more on your own individual game knowledge, experience, and skills.

A situation in which you might run into a checklist is testing special moves in a fighting game. For example, the following checklist is to test Tina Armstrong's special attacks in *Dead or Alive 3*. To successfully and efficiently complete this testing, you must be able to perform the game controller button presses with the right timing and in the right fight situation.

- ☐ Machine Gun Missile
- ☐ Triple Elbow
- ☐ Combo Drop Kick
- ☐ Turn Uppercut
- ☐ Dolphin Uppercut
- ☐ Knee Hammer
- ☐ Leg Lariat
- ☐ Front Step Kick
- ☐ Crash Knee
- ☐ Short Range Lariat
- ☐ Elbow Suicide
- ☐ Front Roll Elbow
- ☐ Front Roll Kick
- ☐ Flying Body Attack

Whereas the checklist tends to be focused on verifying a narrow set of game behaviors, an outline can be used to test a broader range of results without worrying much about the detailed steps to take to reach that goal. For example, in *NBA Street Vol. 2*, you have the ability to unlock special player jerseys by achieving certain results during a game or a series of games. Imagine having to define or follow a button-by-button series of steps to complete an entire game! So you, the tester, need to know the game well enough to pick the right players for your team and then play the game well enough to reach the goals that unlock each of the jerseys. An outline like the one that follows is sufficient for this purpose.

Unlock Special Jerseys

> Bill Russell
>
> > Beat all teams in the Northwest Region without losing
>
> Bill Walton
>
> > Score over 1,000,000 trick points in a game

Connie Hawkins

> Get 20 blocks in a game and win the game

Elgin Baylor

> Shut out the opposing team

James Worthy

> Beat all teams in the Northeast Region without losing

Jerry West

> Win a game without getting any of your shots blocked

Oscar Robertson

> Beat all teams in the Southwest Region without losing

Walt Frazier

> Beat all teams in the Central Region without losing

In addition to running these tests, you may also find yourself writing tests for you or other testers to run. Later in this book you learn some formal methods for designing tests, but that option may not always be available to you. In an informal testing situation, choose step-by-step, checklist, or outline form to describe the testing you want done, or to record any undocumented testing you may have completed.

Identifying Bugs

Game testing has two purposes. The first is to find defects that are in the game code or design. The second is to demonstrate which parts of the game are working properly. When the test doesn't find any problems, it "Passes." When a test finds a problem, it "Fails."

Another possible outcome of a test is "Blocked," which means an existing problem keeps you from getting to other parts of the test—such as when the PC version of the *American Idol* game crashes after you reach the final 10 (see the following sidebar). This blocks you from doing any testing on the final rounds of the contest.

The test could also be "Not Available," meaning the part you are supposed to test has not been included in the version of the game you were given to test. It might be because the developers are still in the process of getting all the game elements put together, so a level, item, function, or character is intentionally left out of the test release. It could also be that the game version for the platform you are testing does not include what you are trying to test—such as *True Crime: Streets of LA* multiplayer modes, which are only available for the PC.

Title > Onboard Sound Menu Crash Update

Date Uploaded > 28th November 2003

Description > To solve the problems with the *American Idol* game crashing back to the Windows desktop when navigating the menus at the start of the game OR once the player is through to the final 10 of contestants.

http://www.codemasters.com/downloads/?downloadid=12431

Here Comes the Judge

Not every tester will notice the same defects when testing the same part of a game. Likewise, not every tester will run the same test in the same way. Psychology may have an explanation as to why this happens, in the form of the Myers-Briggs Type Indicator (MBTI). One of the categories in this indicator rates a person as either a Judger or a Perceiver.

Judgers like to be scheduled, organized, and productive.

If you are a Judger, you prefer a structured, ordered, and fairly predictable environment, where you can make decisions and have things settled*. You are serious and formal. You like to make decisions. You like to organize and make plans. You pay attention to time. You use schedules and timetables as a guide. You like to work first, play later. You like to finish projects best. You are settled, decisive, routinized, and predictable. You dislike surprises and need advanced warnings. You need issues settled. You get things done as soon as possible. Others may see you as concise, focused, and hard-working. You tend to use the directive communica-tion style. (e.g. "Ask Jerry for specific instructions on balancing the budget.") You want to arrange things to happen as you want them to happen. You are planning for the future. You are good at listing tasks and developing timelines. You see the need for most rules.*

Perceivers like to be flexible, curious, and nonconforming.

If you are a Perceiver, you prefer to experience as much of the world as possible. You like to keep your options open and are most comfortable adapting. *You are playful and casual. You like to postpone some decisions, if you can. You like to keep plans flexible. You like to wait-and-see. You are less aware of time or late. You do whatever comes up. You like to play first, work later. You like to start projects best. You are flexible, spontaneous, unpredictable, and tentative. You are more carefree, leisurely, and disorganized. You enjoy surprises and spontaneous happenings. Others may see you as verbose and scattered. You don't like anything unalterable. You tend to use the informative communication style. (e.g. "Jerry has some information that might help you balance the budget.") You are interested in watching things unfold. You question the need for many rules.*

http://www.boomspeed.com/zsnp/mbti.htm

Note

Not sure if you are more of a Judger or Perceiver? You can take the temperament test at www.personalitytest.net/cgi-bin/q.pl to find out.

The tendency toward one of these behaviors versus the others will manifest itself in the way you approach testing, and the kinds of defects you tend to find. For example, a Judger is good at following step-by-step instructions, running through a lot of tests, and finding problems in game text, the user manual, and anywhere the game is inconsistent with historical facts. The Perceiver tends to wander around the game, come up with unusual situations to test, report problems with playability, and comment on the overall game experience. Judgers will verify the game's "authenticity" and Perceivers will verify its "fun-ticity."

Conversely, there are things Judgers and Perceivers may not be good at. A Judger may not do steps or notice problems that aren't in the written tests. A Perceiver may miss seeing problems when running a series of repetitive tests. Although testing without written tests provides more freedom, Perceivers may not always have good documentation of how they got a bug to show up.

You are probably not 100% of one type, but you most likely have a tendency toward one or the other. Don't treat that as a limitation. Use that knowledge to become more aware of areas you can improve so you can find more bugs in the games you test. Your goal should be to use both sets of qualities at the appropriate times and for the right purpose. When you see a bug that someone else found and it makes you think "Wow!

I never would have tried that," then go and talk to that person and ask her what made her think of doing that. Do this often and you can start to find those same kinds of bugs by asking yourself "How would Linda test this?". Make sure you share your own "bug stories" too. A couple of books on software defects that can give you some more insight are: *Computer Related Risks*, by Peter G. Neumann, and *Fatal Defect*, by Ivars Peterson.

Table 2.1 shows some of the ways that each personality type affects the kinds of bugs testers will find and what kinds of testing are best used to find them.

Table 2.1 Tester Personality Comparison

Judger	Perceiver
Runs the tests for…	Finds a way to…
Conventional game playing	Unconventional game playing
Repetitive testing	Testing variety
User manual, script testing	Gameplay, usability testing
Factual accuracy of game	Realistic experience of game
Step-by-step or checklist-based testing	Open-ended or outline-based testing
May rely too much on test details to see defects	May stray from the original test purpose
Concerned about game contents	Concerned about game context

Amplifying Problems

Normally the word "amplify" makes you think of something getting bigger or louder. In this case, "amplifying" your defect will narrow it down for the developers, make it more likely the defect will be fixed right the first time, and reduce the overall time and cost spent on the problem.

If you found a way to crash the game by performing basic operations, there's not much else you need to do to draw attention to your defect to get it fixed. If the way to cause the crash is obscure, or you find it late in the project, or if it seems difficult to pinpoint and repair, your defect will likely take a back seat to other ones. In both cases, there are some specific ways that you can amplify the defects to maximize their "fixability."

Early Bird

Find defects *early* by testing the following items as soon as they become available. If you don't know how to get the information you need, ask the development team or build engineer if you can get some kind of report of the changes in each build.

- New levels, characters, items, cut scenes, and so on as soon as they are introduced
- New animations, lighting, physics, particle effects, and so on
- New code that adds functionality or fixes defects
- New subsystems, middleware, engines, drivers, and so on
- New dialog, text, translations, and so on
- New music, sound effects, voice-overs, audio accessories, and so on

Places Everyone

You may have found a defect in some deep, dark corner of the game, but that might not be the only place it shows up. If you stop looking there and hurry to log your bug and move on to the next test, you may have overlooked a more common place or scenario in the game where the same bug shows up. It would be nice if all game bugs were fixed before the product shipped, but there are reasons why that's not done. A defect that only happens in an obscure place might get left in the game that ends up on the store shelves.

Find defects in *more places* within the game by looking for the following:

- All of the places in the game where the same faulty behavior can be activated
- All of the places in the code that call the defective class, function, or subroutine
- All of the game functions that use the same defective item, scene, and so on
- All of the items, levels, characters, and so on that have a shared attribute with the faulty one (for example, character race, weapon type, levels with snow, and so on)

And then, use this two-step process to increase the *frequency* of the defect:

1. Eliminate unnecessary steps to get the defect to appear.
2. Find more frequent and/or more common scenarios that could include the remaining essential steps.

Notifying the Team

Once you've found the problem and can describe all the ways in which it affects the game, you need to record that information and notify the developers about it. Typically, project teams will use software tools to help with this. DevTrack is one of the defect tracking and management tools used in the game industry. Although you don't have to be concerned about the installation and management of this kind of tool, you should become familiar with how to best use it to record your defects and get them closed. This is not meant to be a full-blown tutorial—just an initial exposure and discussion of the following:

- Using a defect tracking system
- Information essential to good defect reports
- Some typical mistakes and omissions
- Extra things you can do to help get your bug looked at and fixed

Figure 2.3 shows the new defect entry window of the DevTrack tool. The main elements of this window are the function selection along the top, the view selection at the left, and the data viewing/entry screen on the right.

In general, this function and the view selection choices are very similar to using an email program like Microsoft Outlook. You can see which things need your attention, browse through them, and add information to them if you need to.

The data entry screen is where you make your contribution, so the following sections explore some of the key fields you need to work with. To learn more about using other functions of DevTrack, you can explore the demo at www.techexcel.com.

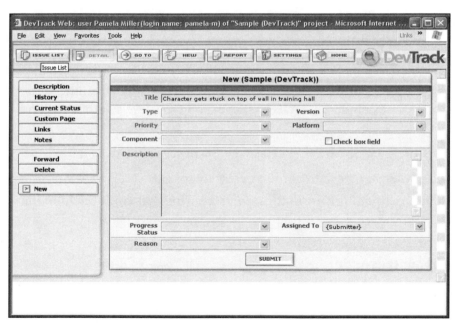

Figure 2.3 DevTrack's new defect window.

Describe

Start your entry with a descriptive title. Generic or broad descriptions like "Had to restart game" or "Problem in training hall" do not sufficiently describe the problem to get the attention of the people who need to go after the problem and fix it. Imagine picking up a newspaper and reading headlines like "Some Crime Happened" or "A Team Won"—it might leave you scratching your head. Instead, provide one or two details that help narrow down the problem.

Take a cue from the Sports page. If a team beats another under no special circumstances, you might see a headline like "Yankees Beat Red Sox." But if something else noteworthy happens, there might be more detail, like "Marlins Shutout Yankees to Win Series." Think of your bug as a noteworthy event that will be competing for the reader's attention.

Figure 2.4 has a title and a description for a problem found while playing *Neverwinter Nights Gold*. In this case the title mentions *what* happened and *where* it happened. Always include the "what" and then add one or two of the distinctive "who," "where," "when," or "how" factors.

In the description, be sure to include all of these details: who (Fighter character), what (on top of interior wall), where (in training hall), when (after visiting spell trainer), how (jump). Then, describe how you were able to remedy the situation, if at all, and add any things that you tried to do that would not reverse or undo the effects of the problem. This serves two purposes. First, it helps the project leaders evaluate the importance of fixing the bug. Second, it gives the developers clues about how the problem happened and how they might go about fixing it. It also establishes the minimum criteria for your testing later on when you need to verify that this bug was properly fixed.

Another way to describe your defect in detail would be to provide a step-by-step description of how you found it. Don't start from when you turned the computer on, but include the steps that are relevant to reproducing the problem. So, an alternative description for the *Neverwinter Nights* bug would be:

> Create a Fighter character. Go to the training hall and visit the spell trainer. Leave the spell trainer's room and jump up onto the wall across from his door. The character can move around along the wall but cannot jump down to resume playing the game.

You should also include information about any additional places you looked for the problem where it *didn't* show up.

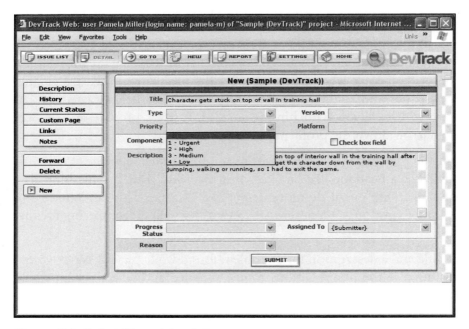

Figure 2.4 Defect title and description.

Prioritize

Depending on the "rules of engagement" for your project, you may also be required to classify the defect priority (or "severity") and/or type. Figure 2.5 shows an example pull-down menu of choices for assigning an initial priority to this defect.

The names and meanings of the priority choices may be different for your project, but the concept is the same. Rank the defect according to its importance, as defined for each choice. For example, "Urgent" may be defined as a defect that stops or aborts the game in progress without any way to recover and continue the game. This kind of bug probably also causes some of the player's progress to be lost, including newly won or discovered items. If your character was frozen in a multiplayer game, this could also result in player death and its associated penalties after the evil horde you were fighting continued happily pummeling you until your health reached 0.

A "High" priority bug may be a problem that causes some severe consequence to the player, such as not getting a quest item after successfully completing the quest. This priority could also be used for an "Urgent" type of defect that happens under obscure circumstances. You should be stingy about making that kind of a downgrade when you first log the bug, especially in a multiplayer game, because nefarious players may be able exploit that bug to their advantage or your disadvantage if the obscure cir-

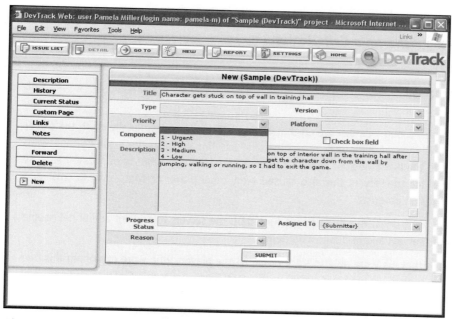

Figure 2.5 Defect priority selection.

cumstances are discovered in the released game and subsequently publicized. An example of this kind of misuse happened in the *Asheron's Call* PC-based online game where players would kill their character and then intentionally crash the game server. Once the server was back up, they were able to retrieve a duplicate of a rare item from their corpse. See the following sidebar for the developers' response to this defect when it occurred in January of 2001.

"Medium" defects cause noticeable problems, but probably do not impact the player in terms of rewards or progress. The difference between "High" and "Medium" may be the difference between getting your bug looked at and fixed, put aside to be fixed in a post-release patch, or left in the game as it is. When in doubt, unless otherwise directed by your project leads, assign the "High" priority so it will be fairly evaluated before being downgraded. Be careful not to abuse this tactic, or the defects you find will not be taken as seriously as they should.

The "Low" priority is normally for very minute defects that don't affect gameplay, those that occur under impossible conditions, or those that are a matter of personal taste. For example, in the GBA game *Yu-Gi-Oh! The Eternal Duelist Soul*, when Yami Bakura is defeated for the 10th time, the dialog box refers to the "Great Sheme of Things" instead of the "Great Scheme of Things."

A Note on the *Asheron's Call* Hotfix

January 23, 2001

We wanted to thoroughly explain the cause of today's hotfix, and what impact it will have on you, the players.

Late Monday night, a bug was discovered that allowed players to intentionally crash the server their characters were on. Additionally, a person could use this bug and the resulting time warp (reverting back to the last time your character was saved to the database) to duplicate items. By intentionally crashing the servers, this also caused every other player on that server to crash and time warp, thus losing progress.

We were able to track down this bug and we turned off the servers to prevent additional people from crashing the servers and/or duplicating items.

The good news is that we were able to track down all the players who were exploiting this bug and crashing the servers. As we have stated in the past: Since *Asheron's Call* was commercially released, it has been our policy that if players make use of a bug that we did not catch or did not have time to fix before releasing the game, we would not punish them for our mistake, instead directing our efforts toward fixing those bugs as soon as possible. ***The exceptions to this are with those bugs that significantly affect the performance or stability of the game***.

The players who were discovered repeatedly abusing this bug to bring down the servers are being removed from the game. While we dislike taking this type of action, we feel it is important that other players know that it is unacceptable to disrupt another player's game in such a fashion.

We deeply regret this bug, and sincerely apologize for the consequences this has had on our players.

— The *Asheron's Call* Team

http://classic.zone.msn.com/asheronscall/news/ASHEletterJan2.asp

---

In many game companies, an additional "severity" rating is used in conjunction with a "priority." In these cases, the severity field describes the potential impact of the bug on the player, while the priority field is used by the team to establish which defects are determined to be the most important to fix. These categories can differ when a low impact (severity) defect is very conspicuous, such as misspelling the game's name on the Main Menu, or when a very severe defect is not expected to occur in a player's lifetime, such as a crash that is triggered when the console's date rolls over to the year 3000. The ability of a player to recover from a defect and the risk or difficulty associated with fixing a defect are also factors in determining the priority apart from the severity. In this arrangement, severities are typically assigned by the person who logs the defect and the priority gets assigned by the CCB or the project manager.

Pick a Type

The defect Type field is also important for routing and handling of your defect. Figure 2.6 shows the list provided in the DevTrack demo.

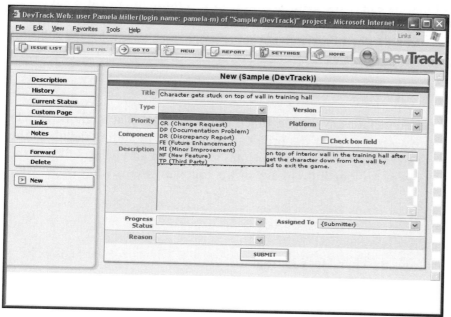

Figure 2.6 Defect type selection.

Not everything you find as a tester is a bug in the sense that something doesn't work as planned. You will find things that could be improved or added to the game to make it better. These kinds of issues would be classified as "Minor Improvement" or "New Feature," respectively.

Likewise, you can enter a "Future Enhancement" for such things as

An idea for the sequel

An optimization to make for the next platform you port the game to

Adding support for a brand new type of controller

A feature or item to make available for download after the game ships

Another function of the game tester is to check the documentation. You could be looking for consistency with how the actual game functions, important things that are left out, or production errors such as missing pages, mislabeled diagrams, and so on. These would fall into the "Documentation Problem" type.

The "Third Party" type could be problems introduced by software or hardware that your team does not produce. For example, a particular brand of steering wheel controller doesn't give force feedback to the user, whereas three other brands work fine.

For the kinds of defects where the game is simply not working the way it is supposed to, the "Discrepancy Report" type would be specified, while the "Change Request" choice might be used for something that has a larger scope, such as redoing the collision detection mechanism in the game.

Be Helpful

Finally, make sure you include any other artifacts or information that might be of help to anyone trying to assess or repair the problem. In addition to adding details to the description, with DevTrack you can use the Notes function to add helpful files to the defect record. Attach or provide links to any of the following items you can get your hands on:

- Server logs
- Screen shots
- Transcripts from the character's journal
- Sound files
- Saved character file
- Videotape recording (including audio) of the events leading up to and including the bug
- Traces of code in a debugger
- Log files kept by the game platform, middleware, or hardware
- Operating system pop-ups and error codes
- Data captured by simulators for mobile game environments, such as BREW®, Java, Palm OS™, or Microsoft® Windows® CE

Note

Not all defect tracking systems you use will be structured this way or look exactly like DevTrack. Just pay attention to getting the basics right and ask the other testers or your test lead what else is expected of you when reporting a bug. For example, you may be expected to send an email to a special mailing list if the defect tracking system you are using does not do that automatically, or you may be using a shared spreadsheet instead of a tool specifically designed for defect tracking. For an online list of some other defect tracking tools, see http://www.aptest.com/bugtrack.html.

Pass or Fail

Tests that fail are good from your perspective, but it's also important for the project to know which tests passed. You will probably be expected to record the completion and results of your tests by indicating which passed and which failed. Other status types might include "Blocked" or "Not Available," where "Blocked" indicates that an existing problem is preventing you from executing one or more steps in the tests, and "Not Available" indicates that a feature or capability that is part of the test is not available in the version of the game you are testing. For example, a multiplayer scenario test is "Blocked" if a defect in the game prevents you from connecting to the multiplayer server. A test that can't be run because the level hasn't been added to the game yet would be classified as "Not Available."

Usually this information goes to the test lead and it's important to provide it in a timely manner. It might just be a physical sheet of paper you fill out and put on a pile, or an electronic spreadsheet or form you send in. This information can affect planning which tests get run for the next release, as well as the day-to-day assignments of each tester.

Note

In the course of testing, keep track of which version of the game you are running, which machine settings you're using, peripherals, and so on. It's also a good idea to make and keep various "save" files for the game so you can go back later to rerun old tests, or try new ones without having to play through the game again. I also recommend that you keep your own list of the bugs you have found so that you can follow up on them during the project. I have personally been the victim of bug reports that were "lost" or "moved," even though the bugs themselves were still in the software. Just make sure you have a way to identify each save file with the game version it was made for. Otherwise, you can get false test results by using old files with new releases or vice versa.

Testify to Others

As much as you may become attached to the defects you find, you may have very little to say directly about whether or not they get fixed. Your precious defects will likely be in the hands of a merciless Change Control Board (CCB). This might go by some other name in your company or project team, but the purpose of this group is to prioritize, supervise, and drive the completion of the most necessary defects to create the best shipping game possible when the project deadline arrives. This implies that defects are easier to get fixed when they are found early in the project than when they are found later. The threat of messing up the rest of the game and missing the shipping deadline will scare many teams away from fixing difficult defects near the end of the project. This is why you want to find the big stuff early!

The CCB generally includes representatives from development, testing, and project management. On a small game team, everyone might get together to go over the bugs. On larger productions, the leads from various groups within the project will meet, along with the project manager and the configuration manager—the person responsible for doing the builds and making sure the game code files are labeled and stored properly in the project folder or other form of code repository. Your defects will be competing with others for the attention of the CCB. The defect type and priority play an important role in this competition. Also, if you were diligent in providing details about how to reproduce the bug and why it is important to fix, your bugs will get more attention.

Different strategies for determining the "final" priority of a defect can produce different results for the same defect. If only a single individual, like the head of the CCB, gets to decide on the priority, then the tendency will be for defects to have a lower average priority (meaning less "severe") than if people with different perspectives, such as producers, designers, developers, and testers, each give a score and the average score is used.

Also keep in mind that if your project has a particular goal or threshold for which kind of defects are allowed to be released in the game, then anything you submit will be under pressure to get de-prioritized below that threshold. This is where amplifying the defect helps you make a stronger case for why something should be considered high priority versus medium, for example.

One of the difficulties some testers have is balancing "ownership" of the defect with knowing when to "let go." You are expected to find stuff and report it. Other people on the project are usually designated to take responsibility for properly processing and repairing the defect. Don't take it personally if your defect doesn't get fixed first, or other people don't get as excited about it as you do.

Verify the Fix

As a tester your involvement doesn't end after the bug is found and reported. You can expect to help developers reproduce the bug, run experiments for them, and re-test after they think the bug is fixed. Sometimes you will run the test on a special build that the developer makes and then you will need to re-run it after the fix is inserted into the main version of the game release.

Summary

Use your knowledge of your Judger/Perceiver traits to get better at finding a wider variety of defects and get more testing done. This includes reading and thoroughly knowing the rules of the game. At the same time, take on positions, assignments, or roles that make the most out of your tendencies.

Once you've seen a bug, identify it, try to make it show up in more places, and try to make it show up more frequently. Then you're ready to document the bug in the defect tracking system. Use a specific title and provide a detailed description. Include files that provide evidence of the problem and could help reproduce and track down the defect. A poorly documented bug costs CCB time, developer time, and *your* time in reprocessing the same defect instead of moving on to find more bugs.

When you do your testing, have the tape running, so to speak, so that when the defect happens you have all the evidence to include in the bug report.

Expect to spend a portion of your time writing up defects, reporting your results, and going back over your issues with developers and re-running your tests on one or two experimental builds before a good fix makes it into a general release to the team.

Exercises

1. What is Rule 2?

2. Identify each of the following as Judger (J) or Perceiver (P) behaviors:
   a. Noticed a misspelling in the user manual
   b. Created a character with all skills set to 0 just to see what would happen
   c. Reported that the AK-47 doesn't fire at the correct rate
   d. Found a way to get his skater off the map

3. Which of the following is an appropriately detailed defect title?
   a. Game crashes
   b. Found a bug in multiplayer mode
   c. Can't drive Fastkat vehicle into the hallway south of the main chamber
   d. Character dies unexpectedly

4. Which of the following should be in the defect description?
   a. Where the defect happened
   b. How the defect happened
   c. Who in the game caused the problem
   d. What the defect did to the game
   e. All of the above

5. Your first assignment for Gamecorp is testing a first-person shooter game. Your character, a cyborg wearing heavy armor, is on the second level carrying a knife and ammo for the megazooka weapon. You find an empty megazooka, pick it up and try to fire it, but it doesn't shoot because it's reading 0 ammo. You know from your project meetings that the weapon is supposed to automatically load any ammo you are carrying for it. What are some things you should do to "amplify" this defect?

6. What are some of the kinds of problems you might find by running the step-by-step test example from the "Playing Games" section of this chapter?

7. Rewrite the step-by-step test in outline form. What are some advantages of doing this? What are some disadvantages?

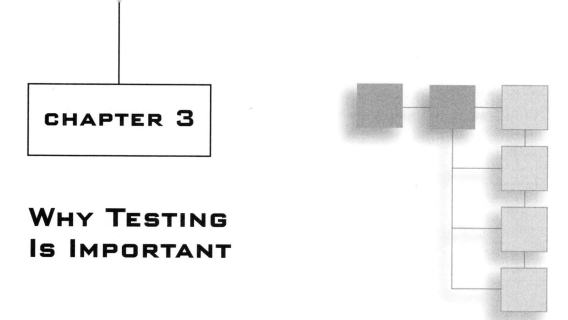

CHAPTER 3

WHY TESTING
IS IMPORTANT

Writing this chapter led to this big list of answers to the question of "Why is testing important?"

- It's easy for game software to go wrong
- There are many opportunities for making a mistake
- Game software is complex
- People write game software and people make mistakes
- Software tools are used to produce games and these tools are not perfect
- There is a lot of money at stake for games to succeed
- Games must work on multiple platforms with a variety of configurations and devices
- People expect more out of every game you make
- It better work right if you are going to have 100,000 people playing at the same time online and expect them to pay a monthly fee for that privilege
- Critics are standing by ready to rate your game in print and on the Internet
- Games have to be fun, meet expectations, and get released on time

The short and simple answer, which summarizes everything in this list, is "Because games get made wrong." If you can identify mechanisms or patterns that describe *how* games get made wrong, you can relate that back to what kinds of problems your tests should look out for and anticipate as you follow your path to becoming a top-notch game tester. *[Jedi Persuade]The patterns you seek are not here.* Maybe the people who care the most about game testing can help you understand.

Who Cares?

Testing must be important to game publishers because of all the trouble they go through to staff and fund testers and then organize and manage the rounds of beta testing that precede the official game release. It's important to console providers because they require certain quality standards to be met before they will allow a title to ship for their box. Mobile game testing is important to handset manufacturers and wireless carriers in order to get approved for their devices and networks.

Testing is important to the development team. They rely on testers to find problems in the code. The testers bear the burden of getting blamed when serious defects escape their notice. If defects do escape, someone wonders why they paid all that money for testing.

Testing is important because of the contractual commitments and complex nature of the software required to deliver a top-notch game. Every time someone outside of your team or company is going to get a look at the game, it is going to be scrutinized and publicized. If all goes well, it might get canonized. If not, then your sales and profits could vaporize.

Despite all of the staffing, funding, and caring, games still get made wrong.

Defect Typing

Let's leave the people behind for a minute and look at the software. Software can fail in a variety of ways. It is useful to classify defects into categories that reveal how the defect was introduced and how it can be found or, even better, avoided in the future. The Orthogonal Defect Classification (ODC) system, developed by IBM, was developed for this purpose. This system defines multiple categories of classification, depending on the development activity that is taking place. This chapter explores the eight defect type classifications, and examines their relevance to game defects. The defect type classifies the way the defect was introduced into the code. As we go along, keep in mind that each defect can be either the result of incorrect implementation or of code that is simply missing. The defect types listed next summarize the different categories of software elements that go into producing the game code:

Function

Assignment

Checking

Timing

Build/Package/Merge

Algorithm

Documentation

Interface

N o t e

If you have trouble remembering this list, try remembering the acronym "FACT BADI."

Defect examples in this section are taken from the *Dark Age of Camelot* (DAOC) game Version 1.70i Release Notes, posted on July 1, 2004. *Dark Age of Camelot* is a Massive Multiplayer Online Role-Playing Game (MMORPG) that is continually modified by design to continue to expand and enhance the players' game experience. As a result, it is patched frequently with the dual purpose of fixing bugs and adding or modifying capabilities. This gives us the opportunity to examine it as it is being developed, as opposed to a game that has a single point of release to the public.

The defect description by itself doesn't tell us *how* the defect was introduced in the code—which is what the defect type classification describes. Since I don't have access to the development team's defect tracking system to know exactly how this bug occurred, let's take one specific bug and look at how it *could* have been caused by any of the defect types.

Here is a fix released in a patch for *Dark Age of Camelot* that will be referenced throughout the examples in this chapter:

"The Vanish realm ability now reports how many seconds of super-stealth you have when used."

If that's how it's supposed to work, then you can imagine the bug was logged with a description that went something like this:

"The Vanish realm ability fails to report how many seconds of super-stealth you have when it's used."

See the "Vanish" sidebar for additional details of this ability.

Functions

A *Function* error is one that affects a game capability or how the user experiences the game. The code providing this function is missing or incorrect in some or all instances where it is required.

VANISH

Description:

Provides the stealther with super stealth, which cannot be broken. Also will purge DoTs and Bleeds and provides immunity to crowd control. This ability lasts for 1 to 5 seconds depending on level of Vanish. The stealther also receives an increase in movement speed as listed. A stealther cannot attack for 30 seconds after using this ability.

Effect:

L1 - Normal Speed, 1 sec immunity

L2 - Speed 1, 2 sec immunity

L3 - Speed 5, 5 second immunity

Type: Active

Re-use: 10 min.

Level 1: 5

Level 2: 10

Level 3: 15

Classes for ability Vanish:

Infiltrator, Nightshade, Shadowblade

from Allakhazam's *Magical Realm* at http://camelot.allakhazam.com/ability.html?cabil=73

Here's an imaginary code snippet that illustrates code that could be used to set up and initiate the Vanish ability. The player's Vanish ability level is passed to a handler routine specific to the Vanish ability. This routine is required to make all of the function calls necessary to activate this ability. The `g_vanishSpeed` and `g_vanishTime` arrays store values for each of the three levels of this ability, plus a value of 0 for level 0. These arrays are named with the "`g_`" prefix to indicate they are global, since the same results apply for all characters that have this ability. Values appearing in all uppercase letters indicate these are constants.

Missing a call to a routine that displays the time of the effect is an example of a Function type defect for this code. Maybe this block of code was copied from some other ability and the "vanish" globals were added but without the accompanying display code. Alternatively, there could have been a miscommunication about how this ability works and the programmer didn't know that the timer should be displayed.

```
void HandleVanish(level)
{
        if (level == 0)
                return;         // player does not have this ability so leave
        PurgeEffects(damageOverTime);
        IncreaseSpeed(g_vanishSpeed[level]);
        SetAttack(SUSPEND, 30SECONDS);
        StartTimer(g_vanishTime[level]);
        return;
} // oops! Did not report seconds remaining to user - hope they don't notice
```

Alternatively, the function to show the duration to the user could have been included, but called with one or more incorrect values:

```
        ShowDuration(FALSE, g_vanishTime[level]);
```

Assignments

A defect is classified as an *Assignment* type when it is the result of incorrectly setting or initializing a value used by the program or when a required value assignment is missing. Many of the assignments take place at the start of a game, a new level, or a game mode. Here are some examples for various game genres:

Sports

   Team schedule

   Initialize score for each game

   Initial team lineups

   Court, field, rink, etc. where game is being played

   Weather conditions and time of day

RPG, Adventure

   Starting location on map

   Starting attributes, skills, items, and abilities

   Initialize data for current map

   Initialize journal

Racing

 Initialize track/circuit data

 Initial amount of fuel or energy at start of race

 Placement of powerups and obstacles

 Weather conditions and time of day

Casino Games, Collectible Card Games, Board Games

 Initial amount of points or money to start with

 Initial deal of cards or placement of pieces

 Initial ranking/seeding in tournaments

 Position at the game table and turn order

Fighting

 Initial health, energy

 Initial position in ring or arena

 Initial ranking/seeding in tournaments

 Ring, arena, etc. where fight is taking place

Strategy

 Initial allocation of units

 Initial allocation of resources

 Starting location and placement of units and resources

 Goals for current scenario

First Person Shooters (FPS)

 Initial health, energy

 Starting equipment and ammunition

 Starting location of players

 Number and strength of CPU opponents

Puzzle Games

 Starting configuration of puzzle

 Time allocated and criteria to complete puzzle

 Puzzle piece or goal point values

 Speed at which puzzle proceeds

You can see from these lists that any changes could tilt the outcome in favor of the player or the CPU. Game programmers pay a lot of attention to balancing all of the elements of the game. Initial value assignments are important to providing that game balance.

Even the Vanish defect could have been the result of an Assignment problem. In the imaginary implementation that follows, the Vanish ability is activated by setting up a data structure and passing it to a generic ability handling routine.

```
ABILITY_STRUCT          realmAbility;
realmAbility.ability = VANISH_ABILITY;
reamAbility.purge = DAMAGE_OVER_TIME_PURGE;
realmAbility.level = g_currentCharacterLevel[VANISH_ABILITY];
reamAbility.speed = g_vanishSpeed[realmAbility.level]
realmAbility.attackDelay = 30SECONDS;
realmAbility.duration = g_vanishTime[realmAbility.level];
realmAbility.displayDuration = FALSE;  // wrong flag value
HandleAbility(realmAbility);
```

Alternatively, the assignment of the `displayDuration` flag could be missing altogether. Again, cut and paste could be how the fault was introduced, or it could have been wrong or left out as a mistake on the part of the programmer, or a misunderstanding about the requirements.

Checking

A *Checking* defect type occurs when the code fails to properly validate data before it is used. This could be a missing check for a condition or the check is improperly defined. Some examples of improper checks in C code would be the following:

- "=" instead of "==" used for comparison of two values
- Incorrect assumptions about operator precedence when a series of comparisons are not parenthesized
- "Off by one" comparisons, such as using "<=" instead of "<"
- A value (`*pointer`) compared to NULL instead of an address (`pointer`)—either directly from a stored variable or as a returned value from a function call
- Ignored (not checked) values returned by C library function calls such as `strcpy`

Back to our friend the Vanish bug. The following shows a Checking defect scenario where the ability handler doesn't check the flag for displaying the effect duration or checks the wrong flag to determine the effect duration.

```
HandleAbility (ABILITY_STRUCT ability)
{
        PurgeEffect(ability.purge);
        if (ability.attackDelay > 0)
                StartAttackDelayTimer(ability.attackDelay);
        if (ability.immunityDuration == TRUE)
        // should be checking ability.displayImmunityDuration!
                DisplayAbilityDuration(ability.immunityDuration);
}
```

Timing

Timing defects have to do with the management of shared and real-time resources. Some processes may require time to start or finish, such as saving game information to a hard disk. Operations that depend on that data shouldn't be prevented until completion of the dependent process. A user-friendly way of handling this is to present a transition such as an animated cut scene or a "splash" screen with a progress bar that shows the player that the information is being saved. Once the save operation is complete, the game resumes.

Other timing-sensitive game operations include preloading audio and graphics so that they are immediately available when the game needs them. Many of these functions are now handled in the gaming hardware, but the software still may need to wait for some kind of notification, such as a flag that gets set, an event that gets sent to an event handler, or a routine that gets called once the data is ready for use.

Note

> As an example of an audio event notification scheme, Microsoft DirectMusic provides an AddNotificationType routine, which programmers can set up to notify their game when the music has started, stopped, been removed from the queue, looped, or ended. SetNotificationHandle is used to assign an event handle (created by the CreateEvent function), which is used when the game calls WaitForSingleObject with the notification handle, and then calls GetNotificationPMsg to retrieve the notification event.

User inputs can also require special timing considerations. Double-clicks or repeated presses of a button may cause special actions in the game. There could be mechanisms in the game platform operating system to handle this or the game team may put its own into the code.

In MMORPG and multiplayer mobile games, information is flying around between players and the game server(s). This information has to be reconciled and handled in the proper order or the game behavior will be incorrect. Sometimes the game software tries to predict and fill in what is going on while it is waiting for updated game information. When your character is running around, this can result in jittery movement or even a "rubber band" effect, where you see your avatar run a certain distance and, all of a sudden, you see your character being attacked way back from where you thought you were.

Getting back to the familiar Vanish bug, let's look at a Timing defect scenario. In this case, pretend that one function starts up an animation for casting the Vanish ability, and a global variable g_animationDone is set when the animation has finished playing. Once g_animationDone is TRUE, the duration should be displayed. A Timing defect can occur if the ShowDuration function is called without waiting for an indication that the Vanish animation has completed. The animation will overwrite anything that gets put on the screen. Here's what the defective portion of code might look like:

```
StartAnimation(VANISH_ABILITY);
ShowDuration(TRUE, g_vanishImmunityTime[level]);
```

And this would be the correct code:

```
StartAnimation(VANISH_ABILITY);
while(g_animationDone == FALSE)
        ; // wait for TRUE
ShowDuration(TRUE, g_vanishImmunityTime[level]);
```

Build/Package/Merge

Build/package/merge or, simply *Build* defects are the result of mistakes in using the game source code library system, managing changes to game files, or identifying and controlling which versions get built.

Building is the act of compiling and linking source code and game assets such as graphics, text, and sound files in order to create an executable game. Configuration management software is often used to help manage and control the use of the game files. Each file may contain more than one asset or code module. Each unique instance of a file is identified by a unique version identifier.

The specification of which versions of each file to build is done in a configuration specification—config spec for short. Trying to specify the individual version of each file to build can be time-consuming and error-prone, so many configuration management systems provide the ability to label each version. A group of specific file versions can be identified by a single label in the config spec.

Table 3.1 shows some typical uses for labels. Your team may not use the exact label names shown here, but they will likely have similarly named labels that perform the same functions.

Table 3.1 Typical Labels and Uses

Label	Usage
[DevBuild]	Identifies files that programmers are using to try out new ideas or bug fix attempts.
[PcOnly]	Developing games for multiple platforms may require a different version of the same file that is built for only one of the supported platforms.
[TestRelease]	Identifies a particular set of files to use for a release to the testers. Implies that the programmer is somewhat certain the changes will work. If testing is successful, the next step might be to change the label to an "official" release number.
[Release1.1]	After successful building and testing, a release label can be used to "remember" which files were used. This is especially helpful if something breaks badly later on and the team needs to backtrack either to debug the new problem or revert to previous functionality.

Each file has a special evolutionary path called the *mainline*. Any new versions of files that are derived from one already on the mainline are called *branches*. Files on branches can also have new branches that evolve separately from the first branch. The changes made on one or more branches can be combined with other changes made in parallel by a process called a *merge*. Merging can be done manually, automatically, or with some assistance from the configuration management system, such as highlighting which specific lines of code differ between the two versions being merged together. A *version tree* provides a graphical view of all versions of a file and their relationship to one another. See Figures 3.1 through 3.3 for examples of how a version tree evolves as a result of adding and updating files in various ways.

When a programmer wants to make a change to a file using a configuration management system, the file gets checked out. Then, once the programmer is satisfied with the changes and wants to return the new file as a new version of the original one, the filed is checked in. If at some point in time the programmer changes her mind, the file check out can be cancelled and no changes are made to the original version of the file.

With that background, let's explore some of the ways a mistake can be made.

Specifying a wrong version or label in the configuration specification may still result in successfully generating a game executable, but it will not work as intended. It may be that only one file is wrong, and it has a feature used by only one type of character in one particular scenario. Mistakes like this keep game testers in business.

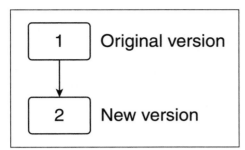

Figure 3.1 Mainline of a simple version tree.

It's also possible that the configuration specification is correct, but one or more programmers did not properly label to the version that needed to be built. The label can be left off, left behind on an earlier version, or typed in wrong so that it doesn't exactly match the label in the config spec.

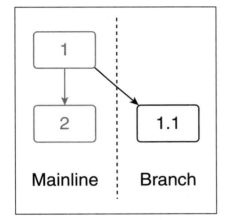

Figure 3.2 A version tree with a branch.

Another problem can occur as a result of merging. If a common portion of code is changed in each version being merged, it will take skill to merge the files and preserve the functionality in both changes. The complexity of the merge increases when one version of a file has deleted the portion of code that was updated by the version it is being merged with. If a real live person is doing the merges, these problems may be easier to spot than if the build computer is making these decisions and changes entirely on its own.

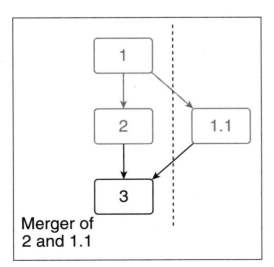

Figure 3.3 Merging back to the mainline.

Sometimes the code will give clues that something is wrong with the build. Comments in the code like `// TAKE THIS OUT BEFORE SHIPPING!` could be an indication that a programmer forgot to move a label or check a newer version of the file back into the system before the build process started.

Referring back to Figure 3.3, assume the following for the Vanish code:

1. Versions 1 and 2 do not display the Vanish duration.
2. Version 1.1 introduced the duration display code.
3. Merging versions 2 and 1.1 produces version 3, but deletes the part of the code in version 1.1 that displays the duration.

For the Vanish display bug, here are some possible Build defect type scenarios:

- The merge that produced version 3 deleted the part of the code in version 1.1 that displays the duration. Version 3 gets built but we get no duration display.

- Versions 1.1 and 2 were properly merged, so the code in version 3 will display the duration. However, the label used by build specification has not been moved up from version 2 to version 3, so version 2 gets built and we get no duration display.

- Versions 1.1 and 2 were properly merged, so the code in version 3 will display the duration. The build label was also moved up from version 2 to version 3. However, the build specification was hard-coded to build version 2 of this file instead of using the label, so we get no duration display.

Algorithms

Algorithm defects include efficiency or correctness problems that result from some calculation or decision process. Think of an algorithm as a process for arriving at a result (for example, the answer is 42) or an outcome (for example, the door opens). Each game is packed with algorithms that you may not even notice if they are working right. Improper algorithm design is often at the root of ways people find to gain an unexpected advantage in a game. Here are some places where you can find algorithms and Algorithm defects in games from various genres:

Sports

CPU opponent play, formation, and substitution choices

CPU trade decisions

Modeling the play calling and decision making of an actual coach or opponent

The individual AI behavior for all positions for both teams in the game

Determining camera angle changes as the action moves to various parts of the field/court/ice, etc.

Determining penalties and referee decisions

Determining player injuries

Player stat development during the course of the season

Enabling special powerups, awards, or modes (NBA Street Vol. 2, NCAA Football 2005)

RPG, Adventure

Opposing and friendly character dialog responses

Opposing and friendly character combat decisions and actions

Damage calculations based on skills, armor, weapon type and strength, etc.

Saving throw calculations

Determining the result of using a skill, for example stealth, crafting, persuading, etc.

Experience point calculations and bonuses

Ability costs, duration, and effects

Resources and conditions needed to acquire and use abilities and items

Weapon and ability targeting, area of effect, and damage over time

Racing

CPU driver characteristics, decisions and behaviors—when to pit stop, use powerups, etc.

Damage and wear calculations for cars, and damaged car behavior

Rendering car damage

Automatic shifting

Factoring effects of environment such as track surface, banking, weather

CPU driver taunts

Casino Games, Collectible Card Games, Board Games

Opposing player styles and degree of skill

Applying the rules of the game

House rules, such as when dealer must stay in Blackjack

Betting options and payouts/rewards

Fair distribution of results, for example no particular outcome (card, dice roll, roulette number, etc.) is favored

Fighting

CPU opponent strike (offensive) and block (defense) selection

CPU team selection and switching in and out during combat

Damage/point calculation, including environmental effects

Calculating and rendering combat effects on the environment

Calculating and factoring fatigue

      Enabling special moves, chains, etc.

   Strategy

      CPU opponent movement and combat decisions

      CPU unit creation and deployment decisions

      Resource and unit building rules (pre-conditions, resources needed, etc.)

      Damage and effect calculations

      Enabling the use of new units, weapons, technologies, devices, etc.

   First Person Shooters (FPS)

      CPU opponent and teammate AI

      Opposing and friendly character combat decisions and actions

      Damage calculations based on skills, armor, weapon type and strength, etc.

      Weapon targeting, area of effect, and damage over time

      Environmental effects on speed, damage to player, deflection or concentration of weapons (for example, *Unreal Tournament* Flak Cannon rounds will deflect off of walls)

   Puzzle Games

      Points, bonus activation, and calculations

      Determining criteria for completing a round or moving to the next level

      Determining success of puzzle goals, such as forming a special word, or matching a certain number of blocks

      Enabling special powerups, awards, or modes

To complicate matters further, some game titles incorporate more than one game "type" and its algorithms. For example, *Star Wars: Knights of the Old Republic* (KOTOR) is an RPG/Adventure game that also has points in the story line where you can play a card game against non-player characters in the game and engage in swoop bike racing—though not both at the same time! *Unreal Tournament 2004* is typically considered an FPS, but it also incorporates adventure and sports elements at various stages of the tournament.

Some other areas where Algorithm type defects can appear in the game code are graphics rendering engines and routines, mesh overlay code, z-buffer ordering, collision detection, and attempts to minimize the processing steps to render new screens.

For the Vanish bug, consider an Algorithm defect scenario where the duration value is calculated rather than taken from an array or a file. Also suppose that a duration of 0 or less will not get displayed on the screen. If the calculation (algorithm) fails by always producing a 0 or negative number result, or the calculation is missing altogether, then the duration will not get displayed.

The immunity duration granted by Vanish is one second at Level 1, two seconds at Level 2, and five seconds at Level 3. This relationship can be expressed by the equation

```
vanishDuration = (2 << level) - level;
```

So at Level 1, this becomes $2 - 1 = 1$. For Level 2, $4 - 2 = 2$, and Level 3, $8 - 3 = 5$. These are the results we want, according to the specification.

Now what if by accident the modulus (%) operator was used instead of the left shift (<<) operator? This would give a result of $0 - 1 = -1$ for Level 1, $0 - 2 = -2$ for Level 2, and $2 - 5 = -3$ for Level 3. The immunity duration would not get displayed, despite the good code that is in place to display this duration to the user. An Algorithm defect has struck!

Documentation

Documentation defects occur in the fixed data assets that go into the game. This includes text, audio, and graphics file content, as listed here:

Text
Dialogs
User interface elements (labels, warnings, prompts, etc.)
Help text
Instructions
Quest journals
Audio
Sound effects
Background music
Dialog (human, alien, animal)
Ambient sounds (running water, birds chirping, etc.)
Celebration songs
Video
Cinematic introductions
Cut scenes
Environment objects
Level definitions
Body part and clothing choices
Items (weapons, vehicles, etc.)

This special type of defect is not the result of improper code. The errors themselves are in the bytes of data retrieved from files or defined as constants. This data is subsequently used by statements or function calls that print or draw text on the screen, play audio, or write data to files. Defects of this type are detectable by reading the text, listening to the audio, checking the files, and paying careful attention to the graphics.

String constants in the source code that get displayed or written to a file are also potential sources of Documentation type errors. When the game has options for multiple languages, putting string constants directly in the code can cause a defect. Even though it might be the proper string to display in one language, there will be no way to provide a translated version if the user selects an alternate language.

The examples in this section take a brief detour from the Vanish bug and examine some other bugs fixed in the *Dark Age of Camelot* 1.70i release, which appear at the end of the "New Things and Bug Fixes" list:

- **If something damages you with a DoT and then dies, you see "A now dead enemy hits you for X damage" instead of garbage.**

This could be a Documentation type defect where a NULL string, or no string, was provided for this particular message, instead of the message text that is correctly displayed in the new release. However, there may be other causes in the code. Note that this problem has the condition "…and then dies" so maybe there is a Checking step that had to be added to retrieve the special text string. A point to remember here is that the description of the defect is usually not sufficient to determine the specific defect type, although it may help to narrow it down. Someone has to get into the bad code to determine how the defect occurred.

- **Grammatical fixes made to bug report submissions messages, autotrain messages, and grave error messages.**

This one is almost certainly a Documentation type defect. No mention is made of any particular condition under which these are incorrect. The error is grammatical, so text was provided and displayed, but the text itself was faulty.

- **Sabotage ML delve no longer incorrectly refers to siege equipment.**

This description refers to doing a /delve command in the game for the Sabotage Master Level ability. The quick conclusion is that this was a Documentation defect fixed by correcting the text. Another less likely possibility is that the delve text was retrieved for some other ability similar to Sabotage due to a faulty pointer array index—perhaps due to an Assignment or Function defect.

Interfaces

The last ODC defect type that needs to be discussed is the *Interface* type. An interface occurs at any point where information is being transferred or exchanged. Inside the game code, Interface defects occur when something is wrong in the way one module makes a call to another. If the parameters passed on somehow don't match what the calling routine intended, then undesired results occur. Interface defects can be introduced in a variety of ways. Fortunately, these too fall into logical categories:

1. Calling a function with the wrong value of one or more arguments
2. Calling a function with arguments passed in the wrong order
3. Calling a function with a missing argument
4. Calling a function with a negated parameter value
5. Calling a function with a bitwise inverted parameter value
6. Calling a function with an argument incremented from its intended value
7. Calling a function with an argument decremented from its intended value

Here is how each of these could be the cause of the Vanish problem. Let's use ShowDuration, which was introduced earlier in this chapter, and give it the following function prototype:

```
void ShowDuration(BOOLEAN_T bShow, int duration);
```

This routine does not return any value, and takes a project-defined Boolean type to determine whether or not to show the value, plus a duration value, which is to be displayed if it is greater than 0. So, here are the Interface type defect examples for each of the seven causes:

1. ShowDuration(TRUE, g_vanishSpeed[level]);

In this case, the wrong global array is used to get the duration (speed instead of duration). This could result in the display of the wrong value or no display at all if a 0 is passed.

2. ShowDuration(g_vanishDuration[level], TRUE);

Let's say the BOOLEAN_T data type is #defined as int, so inside ShowDuration the duration value (first parameter) will be compared to TRUE, and the TRUE value (second parameter) will be used as the number to display. If the duration value does not match the #define for TRUE, then no value will be displayed. Also, if TRUE is #defined as 0 or a negative number, then no value will be displayed because of our rule for ShowDuration that a duration less than or equal to zero does not get displayed.

3. `ShowDuration(TRUE);`

No duration value is provided. If it defaults to 0 as a result of a local variable being declared within the `ShowDuration` routine, then no value will be displayed.

4. `ShowDuration(TRUE, g_vanishDuration[level] | 0x8000);`

Here's a case where the code is unnecessarily fancy and gets into trouble. An assumption was made that the high-order bit in the duration value acts as a flag that must be set to cause the value to be displayed. This could be left over from an older implementation of this function or a mistake made by trying to reuse code from some other function. Instead of the intended result, this changes the sign bit of the duration value and negates it. Since the value used inside of `ShowDuration` will be less than zero, it will not be displayed.

5. `ShowDuration(TRUE, g_vanishDuration[level] ^ TRUE);`

More imaginary complexity here has led to an Exclusive OR operation performed on the duration value. Once again, this is a possible attempt to use some particular bit in the duration value as an indicator for whether or not to display the value. In the case where `TRUE` is `0xFFFF`, this will invert all of the bits in the duration, causing it to be passed in as a negative number, thus altering its value and preventing it from being displayed.

6. `ShowDuration(FALSE, g_vanishDuration[level+1]);`

This can happen when an incorrect assumption is made that the level value needs to be incremented to start with array element 1 for the first duration. When `level` is 3, this could result in a 0 duration, since `g_vanishDuration[4]` is not defined. That would prevent the value from being displayed.

7. `ShowDuration(FALSE, g_vanishDuration[level-1]);`

Here the wrong assumption is made that the level value needs to be decremented to start with array element 0 for the first duration. When `level` is 1, this could return a 0 value and prevent the value from being displayed.

Okay, some of these examples are way out there, but pay attention to the variety of ways every single parameter of every single function call can be a ticking time bomb. One wrong move can cause a subtle, undetected, or severe Interface defect.

Summary

Testing happens.

Anytime someone plays a game, it is being tested. When someone finds a problem with the game, it makes an impression. A beta release is published for the express purpose of being tested. Hasn't the game already been extensively tested prior to the beta release? Why are problems still found by the Beta testers? Even after the game is released to the general public, it's still being tested. Game companies scramble to get patches out to fix bugs in PC and online games, but unfortunate console game publishers have to live with the bugs that were burned onto the game cartridge or CD-ROM. Even patches can miss stuff or create new problems that have to be fixed in yet another patch. All those bugs escaped the game company's paid and volunteer testers.

Despite the best efforts of everyone on the game team, games get made wrong. When games go wrong it's because of defects described by the eight ODC defect types covered in this chapter: Function, Assignment, Checking, Timing, Build/Package/Merge, Algorithm, Documentation, and Interface.

In Memoirs of Constant, Volume III, Chapter IX, it is written "…there is much in common between smugglers and policemen, the great art of a smuggler being to know how to hide, and that of the detective to know how to find." (www.napoleonic-literature. com/Book_11/V3C9.html) This chapter has shown you the ways of the smuggler in the hope that it will make you a better game testing policeman.

Exercises

1. Is game testing important?
2. Which of the defect types do you think is the hardest for testers to find? Explain why.
3. List five situations where assignments are likely to occur in a simulation game, such as *The SIMS* or *Zoo Tycoon*.
4. List five types of algorithms that you might find in a simulation game.
5. From the following code example from the publicly available source code for *Castle Wolfenstein: Enemy Territory*, identify line numbers (added in parentheses) that might be a source of a defect for each of the ODC defect types.

```
/*
===============
RespawnItem
===============
*/
(0) void RespawnItem( gentity_t *ent ) {
(1)        // randomly select from teamed entities
(2)        if (ent->team) {
(3)                gentity_t          *master;
(4)                int        count;
(5)                int choice;

(6)                if ( !ent->teammaster ) {
(7)                        G_Error( "RespawnItem: bad teammaster");
(8)                }
(9)                master = ent->teammaster;

(10)               for ( count = 0, ent = master;
(11)                       ent;
(12)                       ent = ent->teamchain, count++)
(13)                        ;

(14)               choice = rand() % count;

(15)               for (        count = 0, ent = master;
(16)                       count < choice;
(17)                       ent = ent->teamchain, count++)
(18)                        ;
(19)        }

(20)        ent->r.contents = CONTENTS_TRIGGER;
(21)        //ent->s.eFlags &= ~EF_NODRAW;
(22)        ent->flags &= ~FL_NODRAW;
(23)        ent->r.svFlags &= ~SVF_NOCLIENT;
(24)        trap_LinkEntity (ent);

(25)        // play the normal respawn sound only to nearby clients
(26)        G_AddEvent( ent, EV_ITEM_RESPAWN, 0 );

(27)        ent->nextthink = 0;
}
```

6. That was fun! Let's do it again with another *Wolfenstein* example:

```
/*
============
G_SpawnItem

Sets the clipping size and plants the object on the floor.

Items can't be immediately dropped to floor, because they might
be on an entity that hasn't spawned yet.
============
*/
(0) void G_SpawnItem (gentity_t *ent, gitem_t *item) {
(1)     char      *noise;

(2)     G_SpawnFloat( "random", "0", &ent->random );
(3)     G_SpawnFloat( "wait", "0", &ent->wait );

(4)     ent->item = item;
(5)     // some movers spawn on the second frame, so delay item
(6)     // spawns until the third frame so they can ride trains
(7)     ent->nextthink = level.time + FRAMETIME * 2;
(8)     ent->think = FinishSpawningItem;

(9)     if(G_SpawnString("noise", 0, &noise))
(10)            ent->noise_index = G_SoundIndex(noise);

(11)    ent->physicsBounce = 0.50;            // items are bouncy

(12)    if(ent->model) {
(13)            ent->s.modelindex2 = G_ModelIndex(ent->model);
(14)    }

(15)    if ( item->giType == IT_TEAM ) {
(16)            G_SpawnInt( "count", "1", &ent->s.density );
(17)            G_SpawnInt( "speedscale", "100", &ent->splashDamage );
(18)            if( !ent->splashDamage ) {
(19)                    ent->splashDamage = 100;
(20)            }
(21)    }
}
```

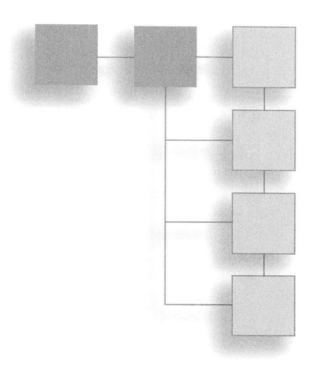

PART II

MAKING GAMES

CHAPTER 4

CHAPTER 5

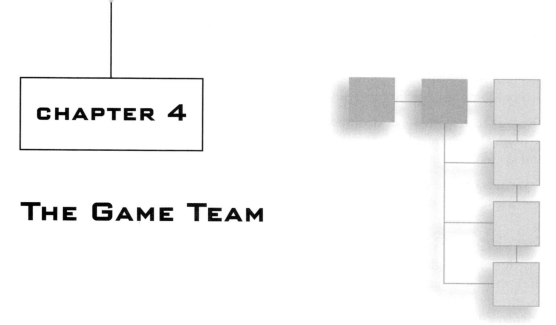

CHAPTER 4

THE GAME TEAM

Game teams come in different sizes, shapes, locations, and skill sets. They can vary by company, game title, or platform. The different disciplines that are required to produce a working game are often organized into distinct teams within the overall game team. The people on the game team must work together to complete the tasks that are needed to get the game done on time and without serious defects. This chapter explores typical team roles, different teams within the game team, and some typical ways people are organized into teams and game projects.

The Development Team

This is the team that is responsible for producing properly working game code. Their programming skills are used to bring the game design to life on the game hardware platform(s). Problem-solving skills are used to quickly and efficiently deal with problems or new situations as they arise. A mastery of the software development tools used for the project comes in handy when trying to do optimizations or fix particularly difficult defects.

Development Lead

The development lead defines the development activities that are needed for the project and allocates them to the individual programmers. Additional tasks may be identified, planned, and adjusted during the course of the project.

The development lead also establishes technical procedures and standards. He is usually responsible for selecting the right development tools and technologies to use both for the production of the game code and for use by the game. This responsibility includes the selection of compilers, engines, middleware, databases, servers, editors, drivers, common code libraries, and reuse of code from previously developed games.

During the project, the development lead provides technical direction and assistance to other programmers when needed, and represents the development team in planning and status meetings, including participation on the project's Change Control Board.

On smaller game development teams, the development lead is also responsible for developing some of the code.

Development Engineer

Development engineers are also referred to as programmers or developers. They produce the code that the testers test. Their job involves translating the concepts, elements, and story of the game into programming language code. This code is subsequently converted by the build process into information that gets stored and executed on the target game device.

Development engineers make or break the game. The code has to fit within a certain budget, use a limited amount of working memory while the game is running, and be able to have enough performance to make things such as user input responses and animations flow smoothly.

A programmer's code also has to fit within a certain environment or framework that the development team is using. The environment may include elements such as a game *engine*—which follows defined rules for automating the processing of certain game elements—and *middleware*—which provides a common interface to certain game functions so the same code can be moved from one platform to another without loss of function and/or performance. Programmers also have to deal with operating systems, device drivers, and communications protocols for multiplayer games. Those each have their own complexities and pitfalls.

Programmers may also be involved in the porting of game code from one platform to another. Certain portions of the code should remain the same, whereas others must be changed to accommodate differences in the new platform. Porting from Xbox to PC may not be so difficult because of the platform similarities in terms of operating system and underlying DirectX APIs. However, the PC version needs to account for a variety of screen resolutions, graphics cards, installed memory, audio devices, and input devices. Going from Xbox to PS2 would provide a different set of challenges, and porting a PC or console game such as *True Crime: Streets of LA* to a mobile or handheld device may turn into a brand new design and development effort.

Some teams or projects may identify their programmers by their specific area of responsibility or specialty. Openings for the following programmer specialties have been listed on the Internet. Each of these has its own distinct set of skills and responsibilities.

Next Generation Console Programmer

PS2 Engine Programmer

Xbox/GameCube Console Programmer

Max Tools Programmer

Wireless Developer

PS2 Online Programmer

Special Effects Programmer

Junior (Script) Programmer

Build Engineer

For relatively small projects such as mobile games or Web-based leisure games, this function might be performed by the same people who develop the code. For larger efforts, such as PC games or MMORPGs, these activities are performed by one or more people on the project who are subject matter experts and specialists.

Build engineer responsibilities may include the following:

1. Set up code and game asset libraries and file structures
2. Define and maintain build specifications for each release
3. Perform merges
4. Do builds
5. Do a "sanity test" after a build
6. Document and publish release notes to the team

The last item is of particular interest to the testers. Check the release notes for important clues as to where you should direct your test efforts. Some of the important information testers can find in the release notes includes:

☐ Which defects are supposed to be fixed in the new build.

☐ What new code was added since the previous build.

☐ What code changed since the previous build.

☐ What build errors or warnings were issued by the compiler or linker.

☐ How much memory (RAM and ROM) is being used by the game.

If your team's release notes don't include some of this information, ask your build engineer to add the missing parts. Even if you still have to run most or all of your tests, the ones you choose to run first should be based on the build information.

The Test Team

The test team can be very dynamic during the course of the game project. In many instances, there is little or no testing at the beginning of the project, and a massive army of testers plugging away at the very end.

"Test" is often used interchangeably with "Quality Assurance" (QA). This is especially true on the publishing side, where testing is the main tool publishers use to make certain their investment is being protected. To some people this gives the misleading notion that testing is responsible for the quality of the game. Testing can identify how good (or bad) the game is, but it's up to the programmers, artists, and sound engineers to make a quality product.

Test Lead

The test lead will sometimes be identified by other titles such as QA lead or lead game tester. Her functions are in many ways parallel to those of the development lead. The difference is that the test lead plans and orchestrates testing activities performed over the course of the game development project.

The test lead is responsible for the on-time delivery of test development and test execution results. Test activities and individual assignments are identified, planned, and adjusted as necessary during the course of the project.

The test lead also establishes test procedures and standards. This includes selecting the right test tools and technologies to use for testing the game code. In many cases, test tools need to be supported or otherwise compatible with certain details of the game code. The test lead defines these "testability" requirements for the game and works with the programmers to see that they get properly implemented.

During the project, the test lead provides technical direction and assistance to testers when needed, and represents the test team in planning and status meetings, including participation on the project's Change Control Board.

On smaller game development teams, the test lead is also responsible for doing some of the game testing.

Test Engineers

Many aspects of the tester's work have been described in earlier chapters of this book. However, within the context of the overall game team, there is a paradoxical relationship between programmers and testers that is based on the fact that they both want the same outcome—producing a superb game—but have opposing roles in making that happen.

Test engineers will sometimes be identified by other tiles such as game tester, QA game tester, or QA engineer. Their job is to break stuff while the programmers are trying to make them work. Testers focus on what is wrong with the game and programmers are looking to make things right. Both should approach their job with passion and fervor. However, both can also work with each other to be better at what they do. A tester can do her job better by gaining insight into how the code is designed and produced, and then exploiting that in the way the game tests are written and executed. The developer can continue to improve his code and write better code to begin with by learning from what kinds of problems the testers are finding.

One way to tell if this relationship is healthy—either at the individual or the team level—is to see how the two groups interact when the time comes to verify a bug. In a healthy relationship, testers will work closely with programmers and together they will experiment and collaborate to track down a particularly difficult bug. Unhealthy behavior includes finger-pointing, shouting, and bad-mouthing their counterparts.

Beta Testers

Beta testers are a very special component of the game team. They provide a "volunteer army" of testers made up of game players who sign up to donate their time to playing pre-release "Beta" versions of a game. The size of the Beta testing team can range from several dozen to several hundred or more. They can expect to endure severe game problems and frequent downloads of new game releases or patches. To get this privilege, Beta testers commit to documenting any problems they find so the game programmers can have the opportunity to fix those defects prior to the official release of the game. Beta bug reporting is typically done by emailing problem forms or posting to special Beta tester message forums set up by the game company.

For their efforts, Beta testers can be rewarded in various ways, such as:

- getting special items to use in the released game
- getting to keep their characters
- getting first dibs on particular character names

- bragging rights to being the first on their block to see and know all about the game before it's even been released

- getting real-world game-related items such as free t-shirts

- having their name listed in the game credits, in the game code, and/or in the printed game manual

Becoming a Beta tester is a good way for someone who does not have formal training or game industry experience to build a resume of accomplishments. One way to draw attention to your work is to find important defects and report them in a professional manner, as described earlier in this book. You can go to www.betawatcher.com as well as game company Web sites to check for the most recent Beta test news and opportunities.

The Art Team

Without the art team, we would only be playing text-based games like *Colossal Caverns* or *Pirate Adventure*. The public's expectation for the artistic experience of the game is higher than it's ever been. Titles based on movie franchises such as *Lord of the Rings*, *Spider-Man*, and *Star Wars* already come with a built-in expectation of a visual game experience that parallels what you would see in the movie theater. This expectation spans the realism of the art, character movements, and the camera angles used to render and present game scenes on the screen.

Art Director

The title and role of art director is sometimes designated as lead artist. This person provides visual themes and leadership for the game. This usually involves leading the art team in conceiving, modeling, and evaluating a variety of visual concepts and models before dishing out specific work to the rest of the art team. The art director provides direction and standards for which art tools and middleware will be used for the project.

Storyboards are a vehicle for capturing a progression of scenes that will occur during the progression of the game. They can be used to lay out the art direction and sequence for a game with a linear storyline, such as *StarWars: Knights of the Old Republic*, or used to plan scenes for other game types, as shown in the sports game examples that follow. The art director's vision provides consistency and familiarity when a game is a sequel to a previous story line, follows a movie plot, or is the newest version of an ongoing franchise. Game testing needs to cause each of the different scenes to appear in order to ensure they appear in the game and are rendered properly, according to the art director's intentions.

Football (for example, NFL) Game Scenes

    Coin flip

    Kickoff

    Player on offense

    Player on defense

    Referee calls penalty

    Coach argues with ref

    Player celebration after touchdown

    Injured player removed from field

    Kicking an extra point or field goal

Baseball Game Scenes

    Batter coming to plate

    Pitcher pitching

    Batter reacts to being hit by pitch

    Batter goes to first base on a walk

    Catcher throwing out runner trying to steal

    Catcher and runner collide at plate

    Manager argues with umpire

    Team in dugout celebrates

    Manager comes out to replace pitcher

Basketball Game Scenes

    Opening tip off

    Regular play on the court

    Referee calls a foul

    Player shoots from free-throw line

    Player dunks

    Bench players react to game events

    Player substituted in

    Attendant wipes sweat from court

    Cheerleaders perform at halftime

Hockey Game Scenes

    Face-offs

    Regular play up and down the ice

Players fight

Referee calls a penalty

Player reacts in penalty box

Player reacts to goalie save

Penalty shot

Players come on and off ice during stoppage of play

Injured player carried off ice

Player gets ejected from game

Soccer (the "real" Football) Game Scenes

Teams pose for photo prior to game

Opening possession at midfield to start each half

Player reacts to being fouled

Referee gives yellow or red card

Corner kick

Free kick

Goalie reacts to letting in a goal

Players celebrate a goal

Penalty shot

Winning team celebrates at end of game

The art director also provides leadership for how the user interface (UI) will be integrated into the game. Again, storyboards can be used to work out how each UI screen should look and function. The end result should be consistent with the look and feel of the game, and provide the user intuitive access to and control of in-game functions.

Additionally, the art director has responsibility for the overall memory and polygon budgets for the game art. Once the various game scenes and UI screens are worked out, art tasks are listed in detail and assigned to individual artists, along with specific memory and polygon budgets for each task.

The Power of Art

"What initially grabbed our attention were the stunning visuals of the urban settings. Colorful weapon effects, smoke-trails from rockets, shields offering a shimmering wall of protection, and bodies flying through the air, propelled by bold, powerful grenade explosions."

From a preview of *Snowblind* in Issue #34 of the *Official Xbox Magazine*.

Artists

Artists combine drawing skills with colors, textures, shapes, and lighting with drawing tools and technologies to bring realism to the games we play and test. The various art elements in the game are referred to as "art assets." They exist in separate files from the game code, and may be combined or compressed in some way to minimize the amount of memory they use. The art in a game may be provided on a very small scale, such as individual decals to apply to a race car, or on a bigger scale such as rendering a planetary landscape.

Art elements should also be minimized in terms of the number of polygons that will be drawn by the graphics hardware. This minimization must be done within the established memory and polygon budget, and in such a way as to not create too much overhead for the game code, which would adversely affect game loading times or in-game rendering performance.

A number of games intentionally expose the art, or at least provide access to it, so that players can create their own custom modifications to the look of the game. These custom versions are known as "mods." The act of creating mods is known as "modding." Some mods are designed to supplement the existing game with behavioral and textual changes such as changing unit names or defining a new type of gun that can shoot a mortar round horizontally. Another common type of mod is to create new maps, or change existing maps to reflect major cities such as New York or Chicago. Other mods are made for the purpose of giving a whole new look and feel to the game, such as replacing existing game characters and elements with those from the *Simpsons* or *DragonballZ*.

Here is a list of the game elements that can be changed or added by mods:

- Maps
- Character models
- Character skins
- Startup screens
- Weapons
- Vehicles

The most popular games for modding are those with combat, action, first-person shooter, or role playing themes, such as *StarWars: Knights of the Old Republic*, *Unreal Tournament*, and *Battlefield 1942*. Some moddable games that fall into other categories are *SimCity 3000*, *Midnight Club 2*, and *MVP Baseball 2004*.

If the ability to create mods is supported by a game and considered one of its features, then testers need to be able to define mods to verify this capability. It's also important to check that any tools provided with the game to support modding work properly and have a friendly enough interface for non-programmers and non-artists to use. Sometimes tester-created content can end up in the released version of the game. The test team that worked on the *Battle Realms* map editor saw some of their skirmish maps included alongside the maps created by the professional level editors.

Some companies or projects may establish specialized artist positions with titles such as:

2D Artist

3D Artist

Environment Artist

Texture Artist

Vehicle Artist

Character Modeler

Animators

Animators add realism and motion to the game. Animations need to be smooth and properly scaled in terms of time and space, taking gravity into account. An animation is made up of a series of frames. Each frame contains a specific pose and when frames are played together, your eyes fill in the blanks between poses.

The animation may also be done at a component level, where the subject of the animation is defined as a set of connected elements. A *skeleton* defines the ways in which these elements connect to one another. In this case, poses are defined for each element that gets calculated and drawn independently in the game, but remain connected according to the relationship defined by the animator. Figure 4.1 shows an example of a skeleton frame with its connected elements.

Characters and creatures are believable when they are properly animated. On a large scale, they are animated to walk, run, and jump. Their movement needs to be consistent with their weight, physiology, and the local force of gravity. At a smaller level, facial expressions and body language are animated to communicate emotion. Even when a character is not moving around in the game space, many games provide an in-place animation, such as small movements that accompany breathing, to maintain the sense that the character or creature has life. This standing pose, known as an "idle" animation, can also communicate the character's feelings or attitude.

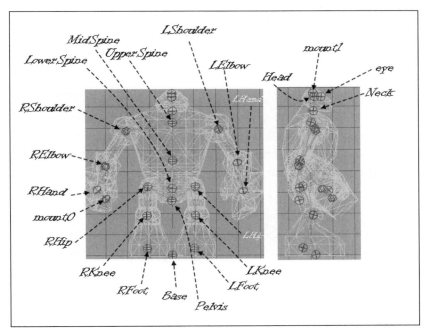

Figure 4.1 3D skeleton frame.

In games where audio accompanies the dialog text, facial movement is sometimes animated to provide the sense that a character or creature is speaking. Animals, monsters, and aliens are easier to believe because many of their sounds don't rely on the lip and jaw movements that accompany human speech.

Inanimate vehicles are expected to behave in a manner similar to organic life forms. For example, when a car turns a corner, you expect it to dip and pull according to the speed of the car and the traction of the road surface. When the car jumps, you expect it to bounce when it lands.

In sports games, character animations are very important because there are specific expectations about how a particular action should look, such as pitching a baseball, throwing a football, or making a putt. In order not to appear robotic, there may be a variety of animations broken into different categories for each activity. For example, a baseball game could provide both sidearm and overhand throwing animations for pitchers. During gameplay, the proper animation should be chosen based on the pitcher's actual style. Some games go further by providing animations for one or more individual players based on their specific style and equipment. Pieces of sports equipment should be animated as well. Balls rotate when thrown, kicked, or hit. Bats fly apart when they break. Helmets and mouthpieces fly off after big hits. Gloves flex and rebound when receiving a ball.

Explosive and destructive effects provide excitement and urgency to the game. The explosion could come from the end of a gun or from a remote detonation. There will be a central core effect, such as an expanding ball of light, followed by after-effects such as smoke or a concussion wave. The explosion itself can send rocks, vehicles, or your opponents flying. Rocks or walls can break when a player is sent smashing into them.

Animating effects of nature help give a sense that you are part of the game environment. Leaves should spin and float as they fall, rather than drop straight down as if in a vacuum. Environmental interactions may also occur as the result of movement, such as water rippling and splashing when a character steps in or moves around in it.

Level Designers

Level designers, also known as level artists, define what goes into the various "levels" or parts of the world you explore or inhabit when playing your game. You can usually tell when you are going from one level to another because there is a pause in the game, which might also be followed by a "Loading[…]" screen and progress bar. This is necessary because new graphic elements must be loaded into game memory so you can smoothly explore the new territory.

The level designer must make each level interesting and different, but it should also fit into the context and theme of the game or world it is a part of. This is accomplished by the following:

- Defining the shape of the level and the routes that you can take to travel around in the level.
- Choosing tiles, meshes, and textures to fit the theme of the level and the game.
- Placing objects in the world and defining which ones can be used or affected by player actions. This includes ammunition, doors, levers, traps, computer panels, and containers that themselves may hold useful items.
- Placing lighting sources and defining their attributes to create desired effects. For example, position bright sunlight to come through a window in a great hall so it highlights a statue that contains a valuable gem.
- Placing "pinch points," which slow down action and allow new game assets to be loaded.
- Placing and marking paths, doors, or gateways leading to a new level.
- Placing non-players characters (NPCs) who may provide information that advances the story line (these usually are given a unique name in the game), or who simply provide a sense of which factions are occupying the level.

A test strategy for each level should include the items listed in Table 4.1.

Table 4.1 Level Test Checklist

☐ Check the placement and behavior of objects in the level

☐ Check the placement and behavior of NPCs

☐ Check the fit and form of each unique tile, mesh, and texture used in the level

☐ Check the function and load times of transitions from one level to another

The Sound Team

The sound team provides us with our audible experience of the game. Just like in the movies, a well-done audible experience will make you feel part of the game. This team collaborates with designers and programmers to provide an experience consistent with the game genre, time period, and story.

Sound Engineer

One of the main functions of a sound engineer is to provide a lot of little sounds that provide the player with audible clues about what is happening in the game. A player can't see what's going on in the game beyond what is shown on the screen, but he can hear sounds coming from all directions. A basic list of contributions includes ambient sounds, character sounds, sounds that items make, and sounds to indicate the success or failure of an effect. You will find some more detailed types of sounds provided for various game genres in the lists that follow. These lists are meant to be representative but not exhaustive. As games continue to cross traditional category boundaries, and include "games within games," the sound engineer's job will become more complex, diverse, and interesting. As a game tester, each presents a new responsibility for something you need to check for.

Sports

    Crowd noises: cheering, booing, ambient, vendors

    Player movement sounds: running, skating, swimming, etc.

    One object striking another: ball and glove, ball and bat, ball and foot, etc.

    Player collisions

    Player taunts

    Announcers and coaches

    Weather effects: rain, thunder, wind

RPG, Adventure

    Spell casting and spell effects

    Weapon firing, clashing, and effects

    Creature sounds: walking, grunting, howling, etc.

    Vehicle sounds

    Player and NPC dialog

Racing

    Car engine sounds: starting, shifting, etc.

    Wheel sounds: braking, spinning, cornering, etc.

    Road effects: potholes, puddles, ramps, etc.

    Opening and closing sounds: doors, hood, trunk, seat belt, etc.

    Sirens: police, ambulance, fire truck, etc.

    Powerup sounds

    Dialog and taunts

Casino Games, Collectible Card Games, Board Games

    Ambient sounds: environment, crowd

    Indicate success or failure of a turn

    Movement and placement of pieces: cards, dice, blocks, board pieces, etc.

    Betting sounds: depositing a coin, stacking chips, etc.

Fighting

    Weapon sounds

    Striking and blocking sounds

    Environment sounds: weather, arena, etc.

    Crowd sounds: cheer, boo, ambient

    Announcers

    Player and NPC taunts

Strategy

    Combat sounds

    Accept or reject action

    Movement of units

    Creation of units and structures

    Indicate goal, command, or milestone completed

    Warning of enemy activities

First Person Shooters (FPS)

>   **Player running, walking**
>
>   **Ammo pickup, load, and reload**
>
>   **Weapon firing effects: gunshot, explosion, lightning, etc.**
>
>   **Player and NPC commands, acknowledgements, and taunts**
>
>   **Vehicle sounds**
>
>   **Creature sounds: walking, grunting, howling, etc.**

Puzzle Games

>   **Indicate goal, command, or milestone completed**
>
>   **Indicate success or failure of a move**
>
>   **Indicate point increase or decrease**
>
>   **Timer ticking and warnings**

The sound engineer's job is further complicated by continued advances in "immersive" sound technologies such as a growing variety of surround sound and positional sound formats. It is also important for the game to provide support for these systems without short-changing users who use basic two-channel speakers or headphones. These technologies complicate the game tester's job as well.

Music Director/Producer

The music director or music producer's job can involve composing new songs or acquiring existing ones. Someone in this role is expected to play at least one musical instrument and be able to read and write music. As a tester, your job isn't to comment on whether to use a major or minor chord at the start of the second movement of the soundtrack, but rather to verify the proper synchronization of the music with the game's events, verify the music is not unnecessarily cut off either by player or game actions, and whether the right piece of music is being played at the right time. Some games will let the user add and/or select songs to include in the game. Testing needs to verify that the songs start and stop properly and that the ones selected are the ones that get played.

Here are some examples of how songs by popular artists have been incorporated into video games:

- Jukebox selections in *The Crib* (*ESPN NFL 2K5*), which can also be selected for stadium music during home games
- Tuning into radio stations while driving a stolen car (*Grand Theft Auto: Vice City*)
- Music for dance competitions (*Britney's Dance Beat*, *Dance Dance Revolution Ultramix*)

Other Technical Roles

Some roles on the game team aren't specific to one particular discipline. They might be staffed by people who have broad skills experience. Unless you are part of a very small game team or game company, these are roles you grow into over time after gaining experience and showing aptitude, usually with some time previously spent being mentored by someone in that same position.

Project Manager

The project manager's job is to see that the game gets done on time and within budget. Both the game developer and the game publisher may each employ their own project manager, who is also referred to as the game's producer. To help accomplish this, a schedule is made with dates for particular "milestones," which define a set of tasks or goals that should be achieved. The milestone provides an indication that the game is making sufficient progress and builds confidence that the game will be ready on time.

In addition to the milestones, schedules may assign specific detailed tasks to specific people or job roles, along with a due date for each task. At any point in time on the schedule, the project manager can know how many people are needed, which tasks should have been completed, and which tasks should be in progress. Adding up all of the people at each point in time provides a staffing budget.

In addition to staffing, which translates into wages, the project manager may need to budget monetary expenses for equipment, supplies, and services. This includes new computers, hardware, and software tool licenses for programmers, artists, and testers.

The staffing, scheduling, and budgeting details may get written into a formal Software Project Management Plan. This plan makes the project plan visible to the team and the game company.

A Risk Management Plan may also be created and provided as a separate document or as part of the project management plan. This document lists risks that the project manager has identified as being possible for the current project. These risks may be based on the team's experience with previous games, or on new factors. Some examples of project risks are:

Two games will be tested at the same time; may not be enough testers for both.

Next-gen console hardware may not be ready in time to begin testing on schedule.

New graphics concept depends on rendering tool plug-in that is not yet available.

The project manager collects status reports from team members to evaluate game progress. When some aspect of the game seems to be falling behind, he may call for more resources, or figure out how to reduce the scope of work in order to keep things on track. Likewise, the project manager should participate in the Change Control Board to help make judgments about defect priorities and which approach to take to fix or work around a defect when there are alternatives.

Game Designer

The game designer is usually the person who is primarily responsible for conceiving and defining the game you are testing. He is a storyteller, entertainer, and inventor all rolled up into one. It is his concepts that give birth to game worlds, characters, and mythologies. Persistence is a useful trait for game designers who may have to make many proposals before getting game company approval to go ahead and make the game.

The game designer also tries to define game mechanics that are easy to learn, remember, and access during gameplay. Successful games lead to sequels and become a standard to which new games are compared. Some examples of successful long-lasting designs are the *Pokémon*, *Final Fantasy*, *Madden Football*, and *Ultima* titles. When testing any new game in a series, you implicitly accept the responsibility for testing the consistency and continuity with its predecessors.

Game design might develop from a top-down approach, where the designer starts with a high-level idea and then breaks it down into more and more detail until it's described sufficiently for artists, sound engineers, and programmers to develop the game. Alternatively, the game designer might have a bottom-up approach, starting with a few ideas for some detailed scenes or events he'd like to put into a game, and then working his way up to come up with the higher-level story and settings that tie together the low-level concepts.

Whichever way the game designer arrived at the design, he is responsible for producing the game design documents that are used by the other disciplines to guide how they do their parts of the work. This document can also be a useful resource for testers to ensure that the designer's ideas are incorporated into the game, and that the game maintains the proper relationship between design elements.

Figure 4.2 shows a game state flow diagram from the game design document for *Super Street Racer*, which was produced by students of a game programming course at the University of Calgary. Figure 4.3 shows the screen layout design for the Dealership screen, also from the game design document. Testers can use this information to get an early jump on planning and creating the tests for the game. The full document has been provided on the CD-ROM that accompanies this book.

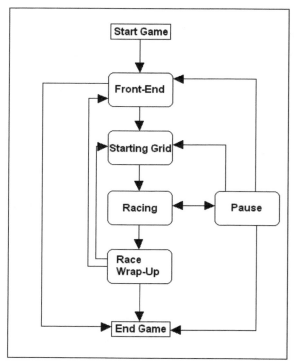

Figure 4.2 *Super Street Racer* game state flow.

Testers should use this design documentation as the basis for providing a complete range of tests. From the flow diagrams provided, write tests to cover all of the states and transitions. In addition to checking the flows that are designed to work, make sure you can't make any transitions that are intentionally left out of the design. For example, using the game state flow diagram in Figure 4.2, you want to test that you can Pause while Racing and also test that you cannot Pause during the Race Wrap-Up.

The same approach should be used with any screen layouts documented in the game design. You can use the screen layout test checklist in Table 4.2 as a guideline.

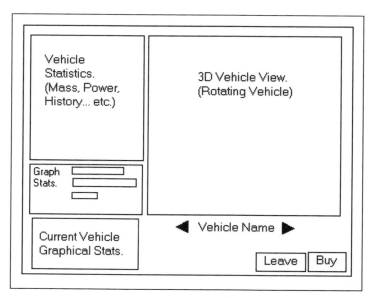

Figure 4.3 *Super Street Racer* Dealership screen layout.

Table 4.2 Screen Layout Test Checklist

☐ Check that each defined region appears on the screen

☐ Check that text within each region is correct

☐ Check that graphics within each region are correct

☐ Check that the full range of values within each region are used and displayed properly

☐ Check that you can navigate from each region to any other region

☐ Check that control buttons in each region work properly

☐ Check that values or graphics in each region do not change or disappear except when defined to do so

Organizing the Teams

It's not enough to have someone around to fill the various roles described in the previous sections. Each person knows their relationship to one another in their company. Likewise, they should know and understand their relationship to the other team members of the specific game they are working on.

One way to organize teams is to appoint a single person in charge of the game, which could be the project manager or the designer, for example, and let them form a team that will stay together from one project to another. This is a good way to maintain continuity and efficiency between multiple releases or patches in the same series. Although this may create problems for people who don't feel their role or contributions are sufficiently appreciated by their boss, it does make it easy to resolve conflicts and make decisions within the team since everyone is accountable to the same person.

Another way to create game teams is to have a *matrix* organization, where the team members have a person who they work for—usually one of the senior or lead people in their discipline, but when they are on a game project, they are also accountable to the person in charge of that game. Staffing each game is like choosing sides for a softball game. Once the team roster is filled, the remaining people go back to their current assignments or stand ready to be picked for the next team that gets formed. At any given time the choices may be limited by who is already committed to working on a different game, and any people who are designated as "off-limits" for one reason or another.

In this matrixed organization, the roles assigned to each contributor can be shown in a table or matrix, as in Figure 4.4. It is also possible to have people who are not assigned to any one specific project, but who act as "floaters" in order to assist any of the active projects on an as-needed basis.

PROJECT	DESIGN TEAM	ART TEAM	SOUND TEAM	DEV TEAM	TEST TEAM
Tiddlywinks 2K5	Billy, Bob	Vic, Sam	Louie	Lisa, Mac, Hal	Jim, Mike, Al, Janice, Sandy
Super Cart Racing 8	Jean	Nate	Herbie	Brad, AJ	Kevin, Bill, Lori
Wacky Pinball	Don	Ryan, Frank	Stanley	Bud, Margie, Norma	Steve, Mike. Elena
Floaters		Alice			Larry

Figure 4.4 Job role/project assignment matrix.

In small game companies, there may only be enough people for one game at a time, so the same person may have different roles. The team from Digital Eel that created the game *Dr. Blob's Organism* includes one person who contributed to code, design, and art, and another who worked on the design, art, and sound. A simple chart or email can let everyone know who is doing what.

Summary

Teams make games. Testers are part of the team. Everyone on the team wants to deliver a good game and has one or more roles to play in making that happen, and the people on the team should be aware of the contributions and responsibilities of the other members. Testers need to examine the individual products delivered by each role as well as their relationship to one another within the context of the game. Any game project documentation provided along the way, from the game design document to the release notes, can be used to accelerate test development and improve the effectiveness of the tests.

Exercises

1. Do game teams exist?

2. List all of the game state transitions for the game state diagram in Figure 4.2.

3. List all of the game state transitions that are not shown in Figure 4.2, and therefore should not be possible in the game.

4. The Vehicle View portion of the screen layout shown in Figure 4.3 will display the vehicle selected by clicking the left and right arrows below the Vehicle View window. Write at least three tests to verify these two functions work properly together.

5. 5. Pretend that your house, apartment, dormitory, or favorite store is the first level of a major role playing game your company is developing. Using the level test checklist in Table 4.1, write a set of tests for this level of your game. Start by listing the items that apply (for example, NPCs, textures, doors, etc.) to your level, and then write tests for each item, according to the checklist.

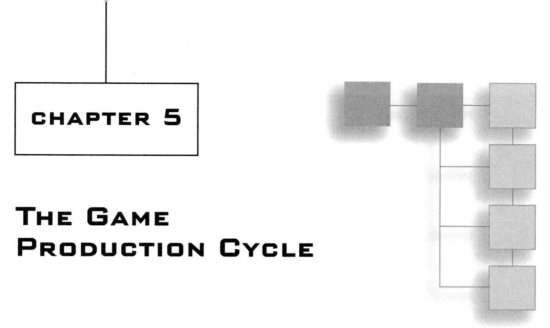

CHAPTER 5

THE GAME PRODUCTION CYCLE

Some games are developed in six months. Others take many years. No matter how long projects last, each one goes through well-defined phases that have become standard across the industry.

This chapter looks at nine development phases and describes the tasks that accompany them. Some game projects may not incorporate all of these phases. For example, console games typically do not get patched. It's also possible for the activities of one phase to continue while part of the team begins work on the next one.

1. Concept Development
2. Preproduction
3. Development
4. Alpha
5. Beta
6. Code Freeze
7. Release to Manufacture (RTM)
8. Patches
9. Upgrades

Concept Development

Concept development is the fuzzy front end of game design. It lasts from the moment someone first comes up with a game idea until the day the game goes into preproduction.

The team is very small during this period. It typically consists of the designer, the tech lead, a concept artist, and a producer (who may only spend part of his time on the project).

The main goal of concept development is to decide what your game is about and to write this down so clearly that anyone can understand it instantly. During this phase you decide on your major gameplay elements, create concept art to show what the game will look like on the screen, and flesh out the story (if there is one).

If you work for an independent developer, this phase will probably not be funded by another company. Unless your studio has an amazing track record, it's unlikely that you will find a publisher willing to pay you to sit around and think up new ideas.

The documents that come out of concept development are the high concept, the game proposal (or "pitch doc"), and the concept document.

The High Concept

The *high concept* is a one- or two-sentence description of what your game is about. It's the "hook" that makes your game exciting and sets it apart from the competition.

A strong high concept is also valuable during the development phase because it helps you decide which features to include and which to leave out. If game development is like trying to find your way through a jungle of possibilities, the high concept is a path that has already been cleared so that you don't get lost. Any feature that doesn't contribute to the game's main focus is a direction you don't need to explore.

The high concept should have some of the following elements, adapted from Bonnie Orr's list at screentalk.biz[1]:

1. The player must be dealing with a BIG PROBLEM. If your game has a story line, it should have both internal and external conflict.
2. Some of the visual scenes are huge. We don't see a couple of fighter planes in the sky. We see dozens or hundreds!
3. The player is an ordinary hero in an extraordinary world or an extraordinary hero in an ordinary world. The *Metal Gear Solid* series is about an extraordinary man. *Final Fantasy Tactics Advance* uses an ordinary boy.
4. The concept must be original. There may be several games about fighting off an alien invasion, but what if the story is from the alien's perspective (for example, *Alien Hominid*)?
5. The concept is a twist on a well-known successful game title.

1. Orr, Bonnie. (2002). "High Concept." SCREENTALK. <http://www.screentalk.biz/art043.htm> (19 January 2005).

The Game Proposal ("Pitch Doc")

The *game proposal* is a two-page handout you speak from during pitch meetings to seek funding for your game. In just a few pages, you must summarize what your game is about, why it will be successful, and how it will make money. This document covers the same territory as the concept document, but in abbreviated form.

The Concept Document

The *concept document* is the fleshed-out version of the pitch doc. It is a 10–20 page "leave-behind" that members of the publishing team will not have time to review during a pitch meeting, but will want to peruse afterward to gain a more detailed understanding of your game.

The concept doc should be presented in a professional binder, on good paper stock, with an eye-catching cover and excellent game art throughout. It should contain the following sections.

The High Concept

The concept document leads off with the high concept. Write it as a quick description you would give to an executive if you only had thirty seconds to pitch your game.

Genre

Explain which genre your game belongs to, along with crossover elements to other genres if applicable.

Gameplay

Describe what the player will do while he is playing the game. Emphasize any new twists to the genre that your game provides.

Features

This is the list of the features that will make your game exceptional. It can include anything from an unusual graphical style to advanced engine technology. Write this section as if you are writing copy for the back of the game box.

Setting

Describe the world in which your game is set. Include concept art if you have any. If it is a story game, highlight the most interesting features of the setting and explain how they affect the plot. Figure 5.1 shows a piece of concept art used for the game *James Bond 007: Everything or Nothing*.

Figure 5.1 Train chase concept art from *Everything or Nothing*.

Story

If your game has a story, take a page or so to summarize the plot. Introduce the main character, identify his problem, describe the villain, and explain how the hero will ultimately defeat him. This part may also include a story diagram. Figure 5.2 shows various patterns that might be used to tell your game's story.

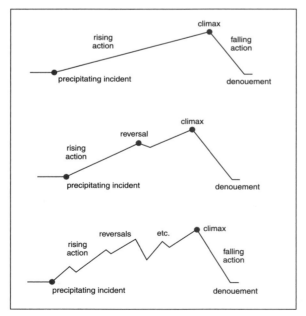

Figure 5.2 Story patterns of varying length and complexity.

Target Audience

Explain who you are developing the game for and why you think it will appeal to them. You can also specify which ESRB (Entertainment Software Rating Board) rating you are expecting to receive for the game: Early Childhood, Everyone, Teen, Mature, or Adults Only.

Hardware Platforms

List the devices the game will be played on: PC, consoles, handhelds, mobile phones, and so on.

Estimated Schedule, Budget, and P&L

Break out the major phases of development and the level of effort associated with each to show how you arrived at the estimates in the pitch doc.

If you work for a publisher, he or she is likely to require a P&L (Profit and Loss) estimate at this stage. This is an estimate of all the costs of bringing a game to market, along with estimates of all its anticipated income. Your business division will have templates for these calculations, usually in the form of plug-in spreadsheets that have cells for wholesale costs, sales estimates, license royalties, and so on.

If you are an independent developer making a proposal to a publisher, you won't know his or her cost structures and your royalties have yet to be negotiated. Instead of a P&L, simply include your development budget. Make sure to break out the amount you want to charge for the preproduction phase, however, because getting that funded is the whole point of this project proposal.

You can't come up with all the numbers on the P&L by yourself. Work with several divisions of the company to come up with reliable estimates:

- The development group supplies the direct costs of creating the game. This is derived by multiplying the man-month estimate by the group's salaries, then adding in equipment costs, overhead costs, and any external costs (technology license fees, voice recording, Full Motion Video (FMV) shoots, and so on).

- From the production group comes the Cost of Goods (COGS) estimate. These are the costs of the physical materials that go into the game box—the media, the jewel case, the manual, the box itself, and so on.

- From the marketing department comes the estimate of how much it will spend to promote the game in magazine ads, TV ads, point-of-purchase displays, sell-sheets, and so on.

- From the sales group come the Market Development Fund (MDF) costs that the publisher pays stores in the retail channel for prime shelf space, end caps, shelf talkers, and ads in their circulars.
- The sales group is also the source for income estimates. Most companies do not give credence to a P&L statement until the sales department indicates that it believes the unit sales estimates to be achievable.
- From the business group come allowances for returns, corporate overhead, and calculations for royalty payments if your game is based on an external license.

The bottom line of the P&L is the Return on Investment (ROI) number. This must show that the company can make more money investing in your game than in some less risky venture, such as putting the money in the bank and drawing interest for two years. Companies are in business to make money. If you can't convince them that your game will be profitable enough to justify the risk, it will never be approved.

Competitive Analysis

Make a list of the games that will be competing with yours for sales and explain the ways in which your game will be better. If you believe the game is similar to past successful games, explain the similarities to those hits and present their sales numbers.

Team

Summarize the credentials of your team and its key individuals, with an emphasis on how their experience shows they have the ability to deliver the game. Publishers frequently put as much weight on people and their track records as they do on the actual proposal in front of them. The goal of this section is to instill confidence that your group can get the job done.

Risk Analysis

Lay out all the things that can go wrong and how you plan to deal with problems that might arise. Some common risks that threaten projects are

- Difficulties recruiting personnel
- Late delivery of console dev-kits
- Reliance on external sources for key technology components
- Changes in the installed base of the target platform
- Competitive technology developments

This section should also include your comments on which parts of the project are relatively safe. If you have any of the traditional risks covered (for example, having a full team already in place or being able to re-use an existing game engine), then say so.

Summary

The goal of concept development is to produce a game proposal and a concept document. These should emphasize the high points of your game and the ability of your team to deliver a quality product, on time and on budget. As a tester or test lead, provide estimates for the schedule, estimate test equipment costs for the budget, and identify test risks for the risk analysis.

Preproduction (Proof of Concept)

Preproduction is gearing-up time. Your goal is to complete the game design, create the art bible, establish the production path, write up the project plan, and create a prototype. This phase is also used to do technical prototyping to demonstrate the feasibility of any new technology you hope to deliver. Preproduction basically proves that your team can make the game and that the game is worth making.

If you are an independent developer, your publisher can also use preproduction as a test-the-waters period for your relationship with them. If they learn that you are professional, reasonable, and able to deliver on time, they're likely to go ahead. Otherwise, they might write off their loss and move on.

The work products of this phase are the game design document (GDD), the art production plan, the technical design document (TDD), and the project plan, which itself is actually a suite of documents. Preproduction culminates in the delivery of the game prototype—a working piece of software that shows off how fun the game is to play.

The Game Design Document

By the end of preproduction, you should have a game design document that exhaustively details everything that will happen in the game. The features in this document become the requirements from which the art production plan and the technical plan are made.

During the development cycle, the game design document should always be the most current representation of everything there is to know about what the player experiences in the game. This should include complete information about the gameplay, user interface, story, characters, monsters, AI, and everything else, down to the finest detail.

Such a document, if committed to paper, would be the size of a telephone directory, impossible to maintain, read by no one, and almost instantly out of date. Instead, put it on your internal network as a set of Web pages. See www.openwiki.com for a methodology that makes this easy.

Maintaining your documents as Wiki pages not only has the advantage of keeping the design up to date, but also enables everyone on the team to have easy access to everything at all times. The savings to the group over the course of development are enormous.

The Art Production Plan

Preproduction is when you establish the "look" of your game and decide how the art will be created.

The Art Bible

During preproduction, the designer, art director, and concept artist collaborate on setting the artistic style of the game. The concept artist makes reference sheets for other artists to work from. Together, the team arrives at a unified "look." Establishing this art bible early on helps orient new artists coming on to the project and ensures the final product will have a consistent style throughout.

Most of this art can take the form of pencil sketches, but it's often useful in selling the game to develop a few glossy pieces that capture the high concept and pack a good visual punch.

In the early stages of the game it's also a good idea to assemble a visual reference library of images that reflect the direction you want the art to take. These images can come from anywhere—magazines, travel books, movie posters, and so on—as long as they are used only for guidance and do not find their way into the final product.

Production Path

The production path is the process by which you go from concept to reality, from an idea in someone's head to actual figures and gameplay on the screen. For example, to create a functioning character in an action game, you must find the most efficient way to go from a designer's spec to a concept sketch to a 3D model to a skin for the model to animation for the figure to applying AI to the character to dropping him in the game and seeing how he works. All the tools you select along the way must be compatible. They must be able to "talk" with each other so that the work you do at one step can be imported to the next step, manipulated, and passed up the line.

Assets, Budgets, Tasks, and Schedules

The production plan also includes the first draft of the asset list, team task lists, equipment budget, costs, and so on. Like the game design document, this plan must be updated and kept current throughout the life of the project.

The Technical Design Document

The technical design document sets out the way your tech lead plans to transform the game design from words on a page to software on a machine. It establishes the technical side of the art production path, lays out the tasks of everyone involved in development, and estimates the time to completion of those tasks. From these man-month estimates, you learn how many people you need on the project and how long they'll be with you. This, in turn, has a direct effect on your budget.

In addition, the TDD specifies

- What core tools will be used to build the game
- Which tools are already in-house
- Which tools have to be bought or created
- What hardware and software must be purchased
- What changes must be made to your organization's infrastructure—for example, storage capacity, backup capabilities, and network speed—in order to support development

The Project Plan

The project plan is the roadmap that tells you how you're going to build the game. It starts with the raw tasklists in the tech plan, establishes dependencies, adds overhead hours, and turns all that into a real-world schedule. The final project plan is broken down into several independently maintained documents.

Manpower Plan

The manpower plan is a spreadsheet that lists all the personnel on the project, when they will start, and how much of their salaries will be applied to the project.

Resource Plan

The resource plan calculates all the external costs of the project. It takes from the tech plan the timing of the hardware purchases to support internal personnel, and it estimates when the external costs (voice, music, video, and so on) will be incurred.

Project Tracking Doc

This is where you keep track of whether you're on schedule. Some producers use project management software for this, but many find the programs too inflexible to manage all aspects of the game's development. The producer usually enters tasklist data into the software to create a Gantt chart that reveals dependencies and the critical path, but he frequently also uses a hodgepodge of other homegrown techniques to keep track of the project.

Budget

After applying the overhead multipliers to the manpower plan, you combine these numbers with the resource plan to derive your month-by-month cash requirements and the overall budget for the game.

P&L

The original Profit and Loss estimate was made during the concept phase. As development progresses and costs become clearer, the P&L must be kept current.

Development Schedule

Many developers chafe against creating a firm schedule and committing to a specific release date, but you owe it to yourself and your company to do exactly that. After a release date has been set, a whole different machine goes into motion. The marketing team books advertisements that will appear in the months running up to the release date. The PR department negotiates with magazines for cover stories and well-timed previews and feature articles. The sales group commits to end caps in the software stores. Changing the release date of the software is likely to torpedo all the carefully planned efforts of these groups and result in your game selling far fewer units than it could have.

Milestone Definitions

Milestones are significant points in development marked by the completion of a certain amount of work (a *deliverable*). These deliverables should be concrete and very precisely defined, with language such as "Concept sketches for fifteen characters, front, side, and back" or "Weapon #1 modeled, skinned, and operational within the game with a placeholder sound effect, but without animations or visual effects."

Avoid fuzzy deliverables, such as "Design 25% complete." The best deliverables are binary: They're either complete or they're not, with no room for argument in between.

Game Prototype

The tangible result of preproduction is the game prototype. This is a working piece of software that captures on-screen the essence of what makes your game special, what sets it apart from the rest of the crowd, and what will turn it into a hit.

This "look and feel" demo can be the single greatest influencer of whether the project goes forward. Publishers like to be able to look at a screen and "get it" right away. If they can't see the vision within a minute or two, they're less likely to fund the rest of the project. This is a tough task to pull off, especially if the project requires a new engine or if one of your hooks is new technology that won't be built until much later in development. When this is the case, most developers simulate what the final product will look like. Most often that is done by pre-rendering material that will be rendered in real-time during the game.

Another approach is to prepare stand-alone demonstrations that prove that the various pieces of planned technology are feasible. These small tech demos might not be much to look at from the artistic point of view, but they show that your goals are reachable. Typical tech demos might show nothing more than a lighting scheme on a few spheres, the camera moving through a featureless "cube" environment, or a bunch of particles bouncing off one another as they stream from an invisible source. The point is to show that the building blocks of your technology are solid. The features you choose to prototype in this way should be the most difficult ones, the ones that present the greatest risk.

The finished prototype not only shows the vision, but also establishes that your production path is working and that you can go from ideas to reality in a reasonable and effective way. It also gives testers their first look at what's going into the game. If the prototype includes working code, this is a good time to try out some of your tests using your test environment, which itself may be a prototype at this point in the project.

Development

Development is the long haul.

Your development schedule is likely to last six months to two years. Some Flash and mobile games can be designed, coded, and tested in less than six months. At the other end of the spectrum, games that are longer than two years in development run the risk of going stale, suffering personnel turnover, having features trumped or stolen by other games, or seeing technology lapped by hardware advances. Any of these problems can cause redesign and rework which, in turn, lead to schedule delays.

The deceptive part of development is how long it seems at the start. You have a good plan, and it's easy to think that anything and everything can be accomplished. This phase of the project can be dangerously similar to summer vacation. At the beginning, all you see are weeks and months stretching out in front of you, with plenty of time to accomplish everything that's on your mind. Then, as the deadline draws near, you wonder where all the time went and suddenly start scrambling to fit everything in.

The trick to surviving this long stretch is to break large tasks into small, manageable tasks that are rigorously tracked. You can't know whether you're behind on a project if you don't track the tasks. This is something that you should do as often as once a week.

One successful task-management technique is to have each developer track his own tasklist, complete with time estimates. These individual lists roll up into a master list that shows at a glance the estimated time to completion for the entire project. This method is particularly useful for seeing whether one person's taskbar sticks out beyond the others. If this happens, that person is the de facto critical path for the project and you should take a close look at his list to see whether some tasks can be offloaded onto someone else.

This method also has the advantage of leaving the developer or artist in charge of his own estimates, instead of imposing them from above. This increases their buy-in to the schedule and makes them less likely to miss deadlines.

If you are an external developer working for a publisher, your progress is tracked for you in the form of contractual milestones. The incentive to stay on schedule is clear: if you don't meet the milestone, you don't get paid. Well-run internal groups use the same structure. Milestones are established at the start of development and there is usually a companywide, monthly project status meeting where all the producers get together and go over the status of their projects in detail. What senior managers look for during project reviews is not only whether the project is on schedule, but also how the producer is working to minimize any risks that could endanger the project in the future.

Here are some non-technical tips for surviving the development phase:

- Bring the test lead on at the beginning of development. If you are the test lead, get yourself involved early. Add testers at first to create the tests you will need and then transition them to test execution as development progresses toward Alpha.
- Maintain good communication across the team. Keep the project documents updated and accessible (especially the game design doc, tech design doc, and the art production plan). Establish internal mailing lists that allow groups to email their peers without clogging the inboxes of the entire group.

- Track your actual expenditures against your budget.

- Maintain the team's identity and spirit. You don't have to use some management guru's oddball exercise for this. Instead, find an activity that fits the personality of your group, whether it's going to an amusement park, playing laser tag or paintball, or just going out for a movie and popcorn every once in a while.

- Work with marketing and PR to keep them fed with the materials they need. The resulting previews and features will re-energize your team members when their spirits are low.

- When it's time for a tradeshow, remember that demo versions of the game are like miniature projects—they cannot be tossed off in a few overtime hours. Demos need their own tasklist and schedule and must be included in the technical plan from the start. Testing should be included in any demo plans. It's also a good idea to form a mini-team, including testers, that is dedicated to making the demo successful. Their work should include doing dry runs and testing of demo hardware setup, software installation, in-house execution of the demo, and, when the time comes, performing at the demo site. The dates of major tradeshows are known years in advance, so no one should be caught short when the next one rolls around.

- Be ready for a shock or two. We work in a volatile industry and any project that lasts more than a year is likely to experience at least one management upheaval, corporate buyout, or other calamitous experience. The trick to surviving these is to keep your head down and *do the work*. Things are rarely as bad as they seem. If you stay focused on the job at hand, the corporate storms that rage above your head are less likely to kill you.

- Lastly, have a few features ready to "throw off the back of the wagon" to help you manage scope.

Alpha

The definition of Alpha varies from company to company. Generally, it is the point at which the game is mostly playable from start to finish. There might still be a few workarounds or gaps and all the assets might not be final, but the engine, user interface, and all other major subsystems are complete.

As you enter Alpha, the focus starts to shift from building to finishing, from creating to polishing. Now is the time to take a hard look at game features and content to decide whether any must be dropped in order to make the schedule. Now is when more testers come on to start ferreting out bugs. Now is the first time the game is seen and evaluated by people outside the development team.

The good news about Alpha is that it is the beginning of the end. The bad news is that reaching the end is seldom easy.

Beta

At Beta, all assets are integrated, all development stops, and the only thing that happens thereafter is bug fixing. Stray bits of art can be upgraded, or bits of text rewritten, but the goal at this point is to stabilize the project and eliminate as many bugs as is necessary before shipping.

Compliance Testing

If yours is a console game that is subject to the approval of the console manufacturer, the final weeks of Beta will include submissions to that company so its testers can verify that the game meets their own quality standards.

A PC game can be sent to an outside testing firm for compatibility testing. This should uncover any pieces of hardware, or combinations of hardware, that keep the game from working properly.

A mobile game may need approval from handset manufacturers and/or the wireless carriers that will be hosting the game and making it available to their subscribers for downloading. The handset manufacturers are mostly concerned about interoperation with the phone's built-in features, while the carriers want to be confident that the game will not disrupt service on their network.

Crunch Time

The last portion of Beta testing has come to be called *crunch time*. During these weeks, people have been known to stay in the office for days at a time, sleep under their desks, eat nothing but carryout, ingest massive amounts of caffeine, and become strangers to their families. All in all, it's a weird twilight world where the only important thing is finishing the game.

When this goes well, you end up with a team of dedicated people who believe they're working on something special and are willing to make sacrifices in other areas of their lives to see this creation come out right. The people work hard because they *want* to, because it's important to them, and because it's fun. Their motivation comes from an internal desire rather than an external mandate. If you've ever worked hard with a group of people to achieve a cherished goal, you know how exhilarating and rewarding it can be.

On the other hand, when it goes poorly, you have people who feel pressured to put in long hours so that they won't lose their jobs, who don't care what's in the game as long as it gets done, and who feel bitter and exploited. If you've ever had to grind away at a pointless task that was doomed to failure anyway, you know how mind numbing and soul deadening *that* can be.

When it goes *really* poorly, crunch time turns into a *death march*, which is any period of extraordinary effort that lasts more than one month. Avoid this at all costs. The benefits of overtime are lost in mistakes caused by exhaustion. Apathy sets in. The team breaks down. You are very likely to deliver the game later than if you just kept plugging along in the first place. If you ever find yourself saying, "We can make the deadline if everyone works two months of mandatory overtime," take a deep breath, step back, and re-evaluate.

Crunch time does come to every project. When it arrives, be prepared to walk on eggshells. As time runs out, emotions run high and tempers can flare. One of the hardest parts of making a game is the last-minute agonizing over how important any given bug is. Such decisions are likely to be made in the supercharged atmosphere of too little time and not enough sleep. In these final days, try to keep your sense of proportion, understand that there is rarely a "right" decision, and remember that even if you disagree with what is happening, you still need to work for the good of the game.

Finally, when putting together the release-candidate disks, always work from a punchlist and have two people check off each task as it is performed. Trusting a single exhaustion-addled engineer to remember all the ins and outs of creating the final disk is a recipe for disaster.

Beta Test

The Beta test phase not only gives developers valuable gameplay and balance feedback, but it's also a great way for the game team to check for defects they may have missed because there simply weren't enough testers to execute massive multiplayer test scenarios.

Some games have a "Closed Beta" testing period where testers are either randomly chosen or hand-picked based on information they send in when they request to participate. Depending on the project plan or the results from the Closed Beta, there may be a subsequent "Open Beta" period. During this time applicants who were not selected for Closed Beta can participate, as well as any new players who apply during this time. Other rounds of Beta testing may be defined with their own specific objectives, such as testing how well an MMORPG performs with a fully loaded world server.

Code Freeze

This is not a phase where you take your master disk outside in Seattle in the middle of January. Rather, at the end of Beta you are likely to be in a *code freeze*, when all the work is done and the preparation of candidate master disks begins. Each of these disks is sent to testing. The only changes allowed to the code base are those that specifically address showstopper bugs that turn up.

Release to Manufacture

The game is released to manufacture when a candidate release has been thoroughly tested and found to be acceptable. You can finally celebrate.

Patches

On the PC side of the house, it has become almost inevitable that a game gets patched after its release. Contrary to opinions expressed on Internet message boards, this is not necessarily because the developer has rushed a poorly tested product out the door. In a world where literally thousands of hardware combinations exist, it is just as literally impossible to test all of them. When a customer finds that his particular combination of BIOS, graphics card, sound card, monitor, CPU, operating system, keyboard, mouse, and joystick causes problems in the game, most developers will work with him to figure out the source of the problem. If the problem is pervasive enough, the developer issues a patch.

Patches can also be applied to games running on consoles that have hard disk drives and Internet connections, such as the Xbox. At the present time, these patches focus on repairs to online/multiplayer-specific issues and updating content such as maps and levels.

Upgrades

An upgrade is different from a patch. It represents additional content created to enhance the original game. Companies create upgrades for a number of reasons. In some cases, it is simply to extend the life of the original game. If add-ons appear, retailers are more likely to keep the original on the shelves. In other cases, it's an effective strategy to keep part of the team gainfully employed while a smaller group goes on to the early stages of their next project.

Fresh content is an important issue for multiplayer online gamers who are paying monthly subscription fees. They expect that as they level-up and explore their online world there will always be new places to go and interesting things to experience.

Many of the multiplayer game companies conduct seasonal or holiday events for their subscribers, which could include special limited-time missions, crafting options, and/or item drops.

In any case, an upgrade is a mini-project and needs to be handled like one, with testing, milestones, and all the other paraphernalia associated with good software management.

Summary

The project life cycle provides a logical structure for successfully conceiving, pitching, funding, and executing a game project. A specific series of documents allows the game to unfold in increasing detail so that the right game is developed and tested. Even people outside of the game company have defined roles and responsibilities that contribute to the success of the game. The game team's project responsibilities may continue after the game is shipped, handling quality issues and keeping the game content fresh.

Exercises

1. Draw a line to connect each of the game titles on the left to with its "high concept" on the right.

Star Wars: Knights of the Old Republic	Rapid-fire games without rules
Halo	Can one man save the universe?
Unreal Tournament	*SimCity* set in a zoo
Zoo Tycoon	*Mortal Kombat* with guns
True Crime: Streets of LA	Ordinary guy finds out he's extraordinary
Wario Ware, Inc.	*Grand Theft Auto* in reverse

---

2. In which project phase is each of the following deliverables or activities produced?

   Art bible

   Competitive analysis

   Game prototype

   New maps

Risk analysis

Game design document

Test lead on-board

Technical design document

Code submitted for compliance testing

Celebrate

Concept document

Volunteer testers participate

3. For each of the following game project deliverables, indicate whether they are relatively High or Low detailed:

High concept

Estimated budget

Story in concept document

Game design document

Development schedule in project plan

Game prototype

Beta release

Manpower plan in project plan

Asset list in preproduction plan

4. Which of the following must be kept current throughout the life of the project?

Game design document

Prototype

Project plan

Art production plan

Patches

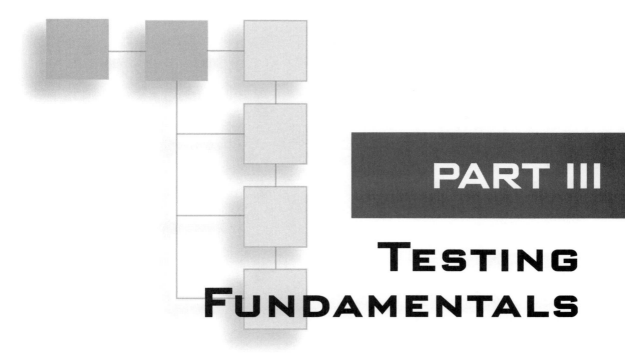

PART III

TESTING FUNDAMENTALS

CHAPTER 6

SOFTWARE QUALITY

Software quality can be determined by how well the product performs the functions for which it was intended. For game software, this includes the quality of the player's experience plus how well the game features are implemented. Various activities can be performed to evaluate, measure, and improve game quality.

In his book, *Quality is Free*, Philip Crosby states that, well, "Quality is free." This should be the high concept (remember that from Chapter 5?) of your quality program. If the cost of performing some quality function is not expected to produce an eventual saving, find a way to do it cheaper or better. If you can't, then stop doing it.

Game Quality Factors

Different gamers may have different criteria for what makes a game "good" for them. Some qualities are likely to be important to many game customers:

Quality of the story

Quality of the game mechanics

Quality (for example, style, realism) of in-game audio and visual effects

Beauty of the visual style

Use of humor and exaggeration

"Human-like" non-player character Artificial Intelligence (AI)

Additionally, games should have an interface that is easy to use and clear to understand. This includes both the graphical user interface elements presented on the screen during gameplay and the game control(s) provided for the player to operate and affect the game. The user interface can consist of multiple elements such as on-screen displays and menus. The game control includes the way players control and operate their characters (or teams, cars, armies, and so on) during the game, as well as the way they can control their experience through point-of-view and lighting settings. The game should also support a variety of controllers, such as joysticks for air combat and steering wheels for driving, that are especially suited for the game's genre.

Another factor in providing a quality experience for the user is to ensure game code and assets are compatible with the memory constraints of the target platform. This includes the available working memory required for the game to run properly and both the size and number of target media such as cartridges, CD-ROMs, or DVDs used for distribution of the game.

Higher memory requirements may affect game performance while time is spent switching game assets in and out of memory during play. Each additional disk or higher-capacity memory card affects the cost of manufacturing and distributing the game. A price increase to compensate for the additional media cost could affect sales. Adding a disk without increasing the price will reduce profits. The vast majority of console games are expected to fit on only one disk, but complex PC games can take up anywhere from 2–6 disks. Handheld device memory is not upgradeable like PCs are. Games have to fit within the memory constraints of the onboard memory chips and removable memory devices that are supported. Mobile games tend to be the most constrained in terms of available fixed and removable memory.

Any efforts at "code crunching" get more and more expensive the later they happen in the game development cycle. The cost isn't just in the labor to do the reduction work. Shrinking game code or reformatting assets to fit on the target media or memory footprint can introduce new hard-to-find bugs late in the project. This creates an extra burden on development, project management, defect tracking, version control, and testing.

Game Quality Appraisal

The actual quality of the game is established by its design and subsequent implementation in code. However, appraisal activities are necessary to identify the difference between what was produced and what should have been produced. Once identified, these differences can be repaired before—and sometimes after—releasing the game.

Testing is considered an appraisal activity. It establishes whether the game code performs the functions for which it was intended. But testing is not the most economical way to find game defects; it's best to catch problems at the point they are introduced.

Having peers review game deliverables as they are being produced provides immediate feedback and the opportunity to repair problems before they are introduced and commingled with the rest of the game. It will be much harder and more expensive to find and repair these problems at later phases of the project.

Peer reviews come in different "flavors." In each case, there are times when you, the tester, will be required to participate. If you don't put in the necessary time and effort to contribute to the review, you and your team will be less likely to be asked to participate in the future. Make sure you take this responsibility seriously when your number gets called.

Walkthroughs

Walkthroughs are one form of peer review. A general outline of a walkthrough is as follows:

1. Leader (for example, the designer) secures a room and schedules the walkthrough
2. Leader begins the meeting with an overview of work including scope, purpose, and special considerations
3. Leader displays and presents document text and diagrams
4. Participants ask questions and raise issues
5. New issues raised during the walkthrough are recorded during the meeting

The room should comfortably fit the number of people attending and have a projector for presentations. A whiteboard or paper easel pad can be used by the leader or participants to elaborate on questions or answers. Limit attendance to 6–8 people at most. This should not turn into a team meeting. Only include a representative from each project role that is potentially affected by the work you are walking through. For example, someone from the art team does not have to be in most code design walkthroughs, but there should be an experienced game artist there when graphics subsystem designs are being presented. Don't invite the test lead to every single walkthrough that affects the test team. If you do, then game knowledge and walkthrough experience won't get passed on to other testers. This also keeps the test lead from spending too much time on walkthroughs and not enough time on test leading. Work with the test lead to find other capable representatives on her team. If you are the test lead, send someone capable from your team in your place when you can.

Be sure to invite one or more developers to your test walkthroughs. It's a great way to find out if what you intend to test is really what the game is going to do once it's developed.

Conversely, get yourself invited to design and code walkthroughs. Brush up on the design techniques and programming language your team is using. Even if you don't have any comments to improve the author's work, you can use what you learn there to make your tests better.

It's also not a bad idea to use some walkthroughs as mentoring or growth opportunities for people on your team. The "guests" should limit their own questions and comments during the meeting to the material being presented and have a follow-up time with their "host" to go over any other questions about procedures, the design methodology being used, and so on. This probably should not be done for every walkthrough, but in situations where someone already has a background in the topic and/or is expected to grow into a lead role for some portion of the project.

Here's a list of representatives to consider inviting to walkthroughs of various project artifacts:

- **TDD**—tech lead, art director, producer, project manager
- **Story board**—producer, dev lead, artists
- **SQAP**—project manager, producer, development lead, test lead, QA lead, and engineer(s)
- **Code designs, graphics**—key developers, art representative, test representative
- **Code designs, other**—key developers, test representative
- **Code**—key developers, key testers
- **Test plan**—project manager, producer, development lead, key testers
- **Tests**—feature developer, key testers

Relevant topics to cover in walkthroughs include:
- Possible implementations
- Interactions
- Appropriate scope
- Traceability to earlier work products
- Completeness

Issues raised during the walkthrough are also recorded during the meeting. Sometimes the presenter will realize a mistake simply by talking about his work. The walkthrough provides an outlet for that. One participant acts as a recorder, recording issues and presentation points that are essential to understand the material. Other participants may end up using the information for downstream activities, such as coding or testing. The leader is responsible for promptly closing each issue and distributing the meeting notes to the team within one week of the walkthrough. QA is expected to follow up by checking that the issues were indeed closed before any work was done based on the material that was walked through and that the notes were distributed to the participants.

Reviews

Reviews are a little more intimate than walkthroughs. Fewer people are involved—typically 4 to 6—and the bulk of time is spent on the reviewers' comments.

Reviewers are expected to prepare their comments prior to the review meeting and submit them to the review leader so that they can be consolidated prior to the actual meeting. Comments sent electronically are easier to compile and understand. Be sure to let the review leader know when you are going to submit a pen-and-paper markup instead of an electronic file. The review leader may or may not be the author of the material being reviewed.

The review itself can be an in-person meeting between the author and reviewers or simply a review of the comments by the author alone who contacts individual reviewers if he has any questions about their issues. An in-between approach is for the author to look over the reviewer comments prior to the review meeting and limit the meeting time to discussions over the few issues that the author disagrees with or has questions about. This meeting can also take place virtually using network meeting software and phone headsets. That is especially useful for projects distributed across studios that are separated in space and time.

During the meeting, someone—usually the review leader—must take notes and publish the resolution of each item to the team. If the opinions of a reviewer differ from what the author believes should be done, decisions on technical matters are left to the author whereas procedural matters can be resolved by QA.

Checklist-based Reviews

Another form of review takes place between only two people: the author and a reviewer. In this case, the reviewer follows a checklist to look for mistakes or omissions in the author's work. The checklist should be thorough and based on specific mistakes that are common for the type of work being reviewed. Requirements, code, and test reviews of this type would each use different checklists. At times it would even be appropriate to have checklists specific to a game project. These checklists should constantly evolve to include new types of mistakes that start to show up. Mistakes found during the checklist review that were not on the checklist should be recorded and considered for use in the next version. Technology, personnel, and methodology changes could all lead to new items being added to the checklist.

Inspections

Inspections are more structured than reviews. Fagan Inspections are one particular inspection methodology from which many others have been derived. They were defined by Michael Fagan in the 1970s based on his work at IBM, and are now part of the Fagan Defect-Free Process. You can find out more about his process at www.mfagan.com.

A Fagan Inspection follows these steps:

1. Planning
2. Overview
3. Preparation
4. Meeting
5. Rework
6. Follow-Up
7. Causal Analysis

The inspection meeting is limited to four people, with each session taking no more than two hours. Larger work should be broken up into multiple sessions. These guidelines are based on data that shows a decline in the effectiveness of the inspection if these limits are exceeded. If you don't know your inspection rates, such as pages per hour or lines of code per hour, measure them for the first 10 or so inspections you do. Then use those results to calculate how many sessions are needed for any future inspections.

In the Fagan Inspection method, each participant plays a specific role in the inspection of the material. The Moderator, who is not the Author, organizes the inspection and checks that the materials to be inspected satisfy predefined criteria. As with the checklist reviews, you will need to establish these criteria for different items that you will be inspecting. Once the criteria are met, the Moderator schedules the review meeting, plus an "overview" session that takes place prior to the review. This is to discuss the scope and intent of the inspection with the participants. Participants may also have questions that can be answered here or soon after the meeting. Typically there should be two working days between the overview and the inspection meeting. This is to give reviewers adequate preparation time.

Each of the inspectors is assigned a role to play in the inspection meeting. The Reader is expected to paraphrase the material being inspected. The idea is to communicate any implied information or behavior that the Reader interprets to see if it matches the Author's intended function. For example, here is a line of code to read:

```
LoadLevel(level[17], highRes, 0);
```

You could just say "Call LoadLevel with level seventeen, high res and zero." A better reading for inspection purposes would be to say "Call LoadLevel without checking the return value. Pass the level information using a constant index of seventeen, the stored value of highRes and a hard-coded zero." This second reading raises the following potential issues:

1. The return value of LoadLevel is not checked. Should it return a value to indicate success, or a level number to verify the level you intended to load did in fact get loaded?

2. Using a constant index for the level number may not be a good practice. Should the level number come from a value passed to the routine that this code belongs to or should the number 17 be referenced by a more descriptive defined constant such as HAIKUDUNGEON in case something in the future causes the level numbering to be re-ordered?

3. The value of 0 provides no explanation about its function or the parameter it is being assigned to.

You can get similar results from reading test cases. Having another person try to literally understand your test steps word for word may not turn out as you intended.

The Tester does not have to be the person from the test team. This is a role where the person questions things like whether the material being inspected is internally consistent or consistent with any project documents it is based on. It is also good if the Tester can foresee how this material will fit in with the rest of the project and how it would potentially be tested.

A Recorder takes detailed notes about the issues raised in the inspection. The Recorder is a second role that can be taken on by any of the four people involved. The Reader is probably not the best choice for Recorder and you may find that it works best if the Moderator accepts the Recorder role. The Moderator also helps keep the meeting on track by limiting discussions to the material at hand.

Throughout the meeting the participants should not feel confined by their roles. They need to become engaged in discussions of potential issues or how to interpret the material. A successful inspection is one that invites the "Phantom Inspector." This is neither an actual person nor a supernatural manifestation. Rather, it is a term to explain the source of extra issues that are raised by the inspection team coming together and feeding off of each other's roles.

Once the meeting has concluded, the Moderator determines whether any rework is required before the material can be accepted. He continues to work with the Author to follow up on issues until they are closed. An additional inspection may be necessary, based on the volume or complexity of the changes.

The final step of this process involves causal analysis of the product (inspected item) faults and any inspection process (overview, preparation, meeting, and so on) problems. Issues can be discussed, such as how the overview could have been more helpful, or requiring stricter compiler flags to be set that could flag certain code defects prior to submitting the code for inspection.

Game Standards

Among its many responsibilities, the QA team should establish that the project work products follow the right formats. This includes assuring that the game complies with any standards that apply. User interface standards and coding standards are two kinds of standards applicable to game software.

User Interface Standards

User interface (UI) standards help players identify with your game title.

Following are some examples of user interface standards, which are derived from Rob Caminos' 2004 GDC presentation "Cross-Platform User Interface Development." As part of your Quality Assurance function you would examine relevant screens to confirm they had the properties and characteristics called for in the standards.

1. Text should be large and thick, even at the expense of creating an extra page of text.
2. Make all letter characters the same size.
3. Avoid using lowercase letters. Instead, user smaller versions of uppercase letters.
4. Use an outline for the font where possible.
5. On-screen keyboards should resemble the look of an actual keyboard.
6. On-screen keyboards should have the letters arranged alphabetically. Do not use the QWERTY arrangement.
7. Split alphabet, symbol, and accent characters into three separate on-screen keyboards.
8. Common functions such as Done, Space, Backspace, Caps Lock, and switching between character sets should be mapped to available buttons on the game controller.
9. Assign Space and Backspace keyboard functions to the left and right shoulder buttons.
10. Each menu should fit on one screen.

11. The cursor should blatantly draw attention to the currently selected menu item.

12. Avoid horizontal menus.

13. Vertical menus should consist of no more than 6–8 items, each with its own button.

14. Menus should by cyclic, allowing the player to loop through the menu choices.

15. Leave breathing room for text localization. (Some languages, such as German, may require more letters per word than your game's native language.)

16. Place button icons next to their functions instead of using lines to connect the functions to the buttons.

17. Point button icons to their location on the controller.

18. Separate thumb-stick movement functions from button functions.

Additional standards could apply to consistent keyboard assignments ("F1 should always be the Help button") or the flexibility of game controller options ("There shall always be an option to enable or disable vibration").

Your list of standards can be used as a checklist that gets filled out for each screen. The checklist should include other information such as the QA person's name, the date of the appraisal, the name of the software build and/or identifier being checked, and the name of the screen. Don't wait until the UI is coded and put into a release before you check it. Work with developers to verify that the standard is being followed in their UI design. Some checking should also take place after code is released to verify that the implementation matches the intent. This may include a suite of tests that specifically check that each UI standard is met.

You may find that some of these items above make perfect sense for your game, while some don't. Use what's right for you and your customers. The important thing is to have some standards, have a reason for including each item in the standard, and have a way to periodically check that the team uses the standard.

Coding Standards

Coding standards can prevent the introduction of defects when the game code is written. Some of the topics typically addressed by coding standards include

- File naming conventions
- Header files
- Comment and indentation styles
- Use of macros and constants
- Use of global variables

To many critics, coding standards pay too much attention to the format of the code rather than its substance. On the other hand, there must be some reason why development tool companies continue to provide more and more coding assistance using visual means such as colors and graphs. Both have the same goal in mind: to help the developer get the code right the first time.

Even so, coding standards aren't just about formatting. Many of the rules are designed to address important issues such as portability, clarity, modularity, and reusability. The importance of these standards is magnified in a project that is distributed across different teams, sites, and countries. There are few things less fun than tracking down a defect caused by one team defining SUCCESS as 0 and another team defining SUCCESS as 1.

Here are some excerpts from the C Coding Standards for the Computer Associates Ingres® project:

> **Do not use constants to check for machine dependent ranges or values. Use the symbolics instead (For example: UINT_MAX not 4294967295).**
>
> **Constants must be properly typed to match their usage. For example, a constant 1 that will be passed to a procedure expecting a long must be defined as ((long)1).**
>
> **Do not use the literal zero as a NULL pointer value.**
>
> **Use TYPEDEF, not #define, to declare new types.**

As a tester, you should be aware that these standards also give clues as to how code will fail under certain situations. For example, if machine-dependent ranges are hard-coded, you will see the resulting failure on one type of machine but not on another. So, features that depend on values that could be machine dependent should be tested on different machines.

In a QA role, your responsibility is to check that the programmers have coding standards which they apply to their code. This is typically done by sampling files from the game code and doing a manual or automated check against the appropriate standards. If you are doing QA on behalf of a publisher or third-party QA group, you can still do this by gaining access to the programmer's standards, tools, and files. Alternatively, you could require the programming team to submit evidence, such as printouts, that they did this checking themselves.

Game Quality Measurements

How good is "good" game software? Certainly the amount of defects in the code has something to do with goodness. The team's ability to find defects in its product is another factor to consider. A "sigma level" establishes the defectiveness of game code relative to its size, while "phase containment" provides an indicator of how successful the team is at finding defects at their source, leaving fewer to escape to your customers.

Six Sigma Software

A "sigma level" is one way to establish a goal for the outgoing quality of your game. For software this measure is based on defects per million lines of code, excluding comments (also referred to as "non-commented source lines" or "NCSL"). The "lines of code" measure is often normalized to Assembly-equivalent lines of code (AELOC) in order to balance the different level of abstraction across the variety of languages in use such as C, C++, Java, Visual Basic, and so on. The level of abstraction of each language is reflected in its multiplier. For example, each line of C code is typically regarded as the equivalent of three to four AELOC, whereas each line of Perl code is treated as about 15 AELOC. It's best to measure this factor based on your specific development environment and use that factor for any estimates or projections you need to make in the future. If you are using different languages for different parts of your game, multiply the lines of code for each portion by the corresponding language factor.

Figure 6.1 shows the defect rates required to achieve a software quality measure anywhere between three and six sigma. Six sigma (only 3.6 defects per million lines of code) is typically regarded as an outstanding result, and getting in the 5.5 sigma range is very good.

Released Defects per (AELOC)				Sigma
20,000	100,000	250,000	1,000,000	Value
124	621	1552	6,210	4
93	466	1165	4,660	4.1
69	347	867	3,470	4.2
51	256	640	2,560	4.3
37	187	467	1,870	4.4
27	135	337	1,350	4.5
19	96	242	968	4.6
13	68	171	687	4.7
9	48	120	483	4.8
6	33	84	337	4.9
4	23	58	233	5
3	15	39	159	5.1
2	10	27	108	5.2
1	7	18	72	5.3
0	4	12	48	5.4
0	3	8	32	5.5
0	2	5	21	5.6
0	1	3	13	5.7
0	0	2	9	5.8
0	0	1	5	5.9
0	0	0	3.4	6

Figure 6.1 Sigma table excerpt for various sizes of delivered software.

Don't fool yourself by measuring your sigma on the sole basis of the open defects you know about in the product. This might reward poor testing which did not find many defects that still remain in the game, but wouldn't reflect the experience your customers will have. The defects being counted must include both the game defects you know about that have not been fixed, whatever defects your customers have already found, and your projection of defects that remain in the software which haven't been discovered yet. It's best to wait anywhere from 6 to 18 months after shipping to calculate your sigma. If you still have a good result after that, continue to operate your projects in a similar manner by repeating what went "right" but also fix what went "wrong." If you have poor results, take a good hard look at what changes you can make to avoid a repeat performance. You can start by going through the list of non-conformances that QA found during the project.

Phase Containment

Phase containment is the ability to detect faults in the project phase in which they were introduced. Phase Containment Effectiveness (PCE) is a measure of how well that is being done.

Faults that are found in the phase in which they are introduced are known as in-phase faults or "errors." Faults that don't get caught in the same phase in which they are introduced are said to escape and become "defects." The principle is that if any subsequent work is derived from the faulty item, then a defect has occurred. Think of the 18" Stonehenge descending from the ceiling in the movie *Spinal Tap*. That could have been avoided (but not as funny…) if someone noticed the size was given in inches instead of feet on the drawing given to the artist.

Errors are typically found by reviews, walkthroughs, or inspections. Defects are most noticeably found by testing and unhappy customers, but they can also be found in reviews of downstream work products. For example, a code inspection issue might actually be the result of incorrect design or requirements. Because other work has already been done based on the fault, this is a defect.

PCE is typically tracked and reported by showing the faults found in each development phase. The faults are organized into columns for each phase in which they might be found. A coding fault can't be detected in the requirements phase because the code does not exist at that point. Calculate PCE by dividing the number of in-phase faults by the sum of faults found in all phases to come up with the PCE for that phase. From the data in Figure 6.2, the design phase PCE is calculated by dividing the number of faults found in the coding phase, 93, by the sum of all faults introduced by coding, which is $93 + 6 + 24 = 123$. The result is $93/123 = 0.76$. Figure 6.3 shows a graph summarizing the code PCEs for each phase.

Phase created	Phase where faults are found				PCE
	REQMTS	DESIGN	CODING	TEST	
REQMTS	114	27	4	15	0.71
DESIGN		93	6	24	0.76
CODING			213	105	0.67
Totals	114	120	223	144	

Figure 6.2 Game code phase containment data.

Alternatively, test results could be broken out into separate categories, as shown in Figure 6.4. These extra categories do not affect the PCE numbers or graphs, but this could be more convenient for data collection if different systems or categories are used for different release types. This data also helps the team understand whether there will be additional testing activities that could further reduce the PCE numbers as more defects are found. In Figure 6.4, no Beta testing results are available to add to the table. So, the PCE numbers for requirements, design, and coding only represent the maximum possible value. New defects found in Beta testing will be sourced to these phases and reduce the corresponding PCEs.

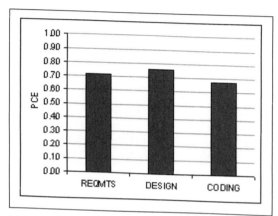

Figure 6.3 Game code phase containment graph.

Phase created	Phase where faults are found								PCE
	REQMTS	DESIGN	CODING	TESTING					
				DEV TEST	DEMOS	ALPHA	BETA		
REQMTS	114	27	4	11	3	1			0.71
DESIGN		93	6	19	5	0			0.76
CODING			213	90	10	5			0.67
Totals	114	120	223	120	18	6	0		

Figure 6.4 Game code phase containment data with expanded test categories.

If this practice is useful for understanding how well the team is capturing defects in the game code, it should also be applied to the work produced by the testers. Figure 6.5 shows example PCE data for testing deliverables and Figure 6.6 shows the corresponding graph.

As the test PCE data shows, some faults in the tests don't get noticed until the test is executed on the game code. The problem might have been recognized as a test defect by the tester running the test, or it may have started out as a code defect before analysis and retesting uncovered the fact that the test was wrong, not the code. You can imagine how much more time consuming that is versus finding the defect before releasing the test.

Phase created	Phase where faults are found				PCE
	DESIGN	SCRIPTING	CODING	EXECUTION	
DESIGN	211	56	23	7	0.71
SCRIPTING		403	37	16	0.88
CODING			123	24	0.84
Totals	211	459	183	47	

Figure 6.5 Game test phase containment data.

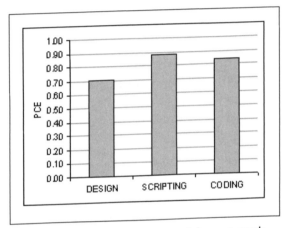

Figure 6.6 Game test phase containment graph.

Remember, this is not a measure of how well the executed tests perform. This is a measure of how well faults were captured in the test designs, scripts, and/or code. Any mistakes made in one of these activities will need to be repaired when they are eventually discovered. Test mistakes that don't get discovered could impact the quality of the game itself. A missing test, or a test that checks for the wrong result and passes, can send game bugs on their merry way to the paying public.

As with the sigma value, look for ways to improve your PCE. If you had 100% containment in all of your phases, you would only have to run each test once and they would all pass. Your customers wouldn't find any problems and you'd never have to issue a patch. Think of the time and money that would save! Since the PCE is a function of the faults produced and the faults, you can attack a low PCE at both ends. Programmers can improve their ability to prevent the introduction of faults. Testers and QA can improve their ability to detect faults.

In both cases, some basic strategies to address low PCE areas are:

- Improve knowledge of the subject matter and provide relevant training.
- Have successful team members provide mentoring to less-successful members.
- Document methods used by successful individuals and deploy them throughout the team.
- Increase compliance with existing methods and standards.
- Add standards which, by design, help prevent faults.
- Add checking tools that run during the creation process, such as color-coded and syntax-aware editors.
- Add checking tools that run after the creation process, such as stronger compilers and memory leak checkers.

Quality Plans

Each game project should establish its own plan for how quality will be monitored and tracked during the project. This is typically documented in the Software Quality Assurance Plan (SQAP). The SQAP contains *no* information about testing the game. That is covered in the game's Software Test Plan. An SQAP is strictly concerned with the independent monitoring and correction of product and process quality issues. It should address the following topics, most of which are covered in more detail here:

- QA personnel
- Standards to be used in the product
- Reviews and audits that will be conducted
- QA records and reports that will be generated
- QA problem reporting and corrective actions
- QA tools, techniques, and methods
- QA metrics
- Supplier control
- QA records collection, maintenance, and retention
- QA training required
- QA risks

The book's CD provides a link to an SQAP template document from Teraquest (www.teraquest.com) that follows this outline.

QA Personnel

Begin this section by describing the organizational structure of the QA team. Show who the front-line QA engineers work for and who the head of QA reports to. Identify at which level the QA reporting chain is independent from the person in charge of the game development staff. This helps establish a path for escalating QA issues and identifies which key relationships should be nurtured and maintained during the project. A good rapport between the QA manager and the development director will have a positive effect on both the QA staff and the development staff.

Describe the primary role of each person on the QA team for this project. List what kinds of activities each of them will be involved in. Be as specific as possible. If a person is going to be responsible for auditing the user interface screens against the company's UI standards, then say that. If another person is going to take samples of code and check them with a static code analysis tool, then say that. Use a list or a table to record this information.

Strictly speaking, QA and testing are separate, distinct functions. QA is more concerned with auditing, tracking, and reporting, whereas testing is about the development and execution of tests in the relentless pursuit of finding operational defects in the game. However, depending on the size and skills of your game project team, you may not have separate QA and test teams. It's still best to keep those two plans separate even if some or all of the same people are involved in both kinds of work.

Standards

Two types of standards should be addressed in this section: product standards and process standards. Product standards apply to the function of things that are produced as part of the game project. This includes code, graphics, printed materials, and so on. Process standards apply to the way things are produced. This includes file naming standards, code formatting standards, and maintenance of evolving project documents such as the technical design document. Document all of the standards that apply as well as which items they apply to. Then describe how the QA staff will monitor them and follow up on any discrepancies.

Reviews and Audits

The kinds of reviews performed by QA are not the same as developers or testers would do for code or test designs. A QA review is usually done by a single QA engineer who evaluates a work product or ongoing process against some kind of reference such as a checklist or standard. QA reviews and audits span all phases and groups within the game project.

Project documents, project plans, code, tests, test results, designs, and user documentation are all candidates for QA review. QA should also audit work procedures used by the team. These can include the code inspection process, file backup procedures, and the use of tools to measure game performance over a network.

Reviews and audits can be performed on the results of the process, such as checking that all required fields in a form are filled in with the right type of data and that required signatures have been obtained. Another way to audit is to observe the process in action. This is a good way to audit peer reviews, testing procedures, and weekly backups. Procedures that occur very infrequently, such as restoring project files from backup, can be initiated by QA to make sure that the capability is available when it is needed.

QA itself should be subject to independent review (Rule 2). If you have multiple game projects going on, each project's QA team can review the work of the other in order to provide feedback and suggestions to ensure that they are doing what they documented in the SQAP. If no other QA team exists, you could have someone from another function such as testing, art, or development use a checklist to review your QA work.

The QA activities identified in this section of the SQAP should be placed on a schedule to ensure that the QA people will have the time to do all of the activities they are signed up for. These activities should also be coordinated with the overall project schedule and milestones so you can count on the work products or activities that are being audited to be available at the time you are planning to audit them.

As part of being a good citizen, planned QA activities that will disrupt other people's work, such as restoring backups or sitting down with someone to review a month's worth of TDD updates, should be incorporated into the overall project schedule so the people affected will be able to set aside the appropriate amount of time for preparing and participating in the audit or review. This is not necessary for activities such as sitting in on a code review because the code review was going to take place whether or not you were there.

Feedback and Reports

The SQAP should document what kinds of reports will be generated by SQA activities and how they will be communicated. Reporting should also include the progress and status of SQA activities against the plan. These get recorded in the SQAP along with how frequently the QA team's results will be reported and in what fashion. Items that require frequent attention should be reported on regularly. Infrequent audits and reviews can be summarized at longer intervals. For example, the QA team might produce weekly reports on test result audits, but produce quarterly reports on backup and restoration procedure audits. Test result audits would begin shortly after testing starts and continue through the remainder of the project. Backup and restoration audits could start earlier, once development begins.

SQA reporting can be formal or informal. Some reports can be sent to the team via email, while others may aggregate into quarterly results for presentation to company management at a quarterly project quality review meeting.

Problem Reporting and Corrective Action

SQA is not simply done for the satisfaction of the QA engineers. The point of SQA is to provide a feedback loop to the project team so that they are more conscientious about the importance of doing things the right way. This includes keeping important records and documents complete and up to date. It's up to QA to guide the team or the game company in determining which procedures and work products benefit the most from this compliance. Once an SQA activity finds something to be non-compliant, a problem report is generated.

Problem reports can be very similar to the bug reports you write when testing finds a defect in the software. They should identify which organization or individual will be responsible and describe a timeframe for resolving the issue. The SQAP should define what data and statistics on non-compliant issues should be reported, as well as how and when they are to be reviewed with the project team.

History has shown, unfortunately, that some project members might be more reluctant to spend time closing SQA problems because they have their "real job" to do—development, testing, artwork, and so on. As a consequence, it's a good idea to define the criteria and process for escalating unresolved issues. Similarly, there should be a defined way for resolving issues with products that can't be fixed within the game team, such as software tools or user manuals.

In addition to addressing compliance issues one at a time, SQA should also look for the causes of negative trends or patterns and suggest ways to reverse them. This includes process issues such as schedule slippages and product issues such as game asset memory requirements going over budget. The SQAP should document how the QA team will detect and treat the causes of such problems.

Tools, Techniques, and Methods

Just like development and testing, the QA team can benefit from tools. Since QA project planning and tracking needs to be coordinated with the rest of the project, it's best if they use the same project management tools as the rest of the game team. Likewise, tracking issues found in QA audits and reviews should be done under the same system used for code and test defects. Different templates or schemas might be needed for QA issue entry and processing, but this will keep the team software licensing and operation costs down and make it easy for the rest of the team to access and update QA issues.

Some statistical methods might be useful for QA analysis of project and process results. Many of these methods are supported by tools. Such tools and methods should be identified in the SQAP. For example, Pareto Charts graph a list of results in descending order. The bars furthest on the left are the most frequently occurring items. These are the issues you should spend your time on first. If you are successful at fixing them, the numbers will go down and other issues will replace them on the left of the chart. You can go on forever addressing the issue at the left of the chart because there will always be one. This is kind of like trying to clean out your garage. At some point in time, you can decide the results are "good enough" and move on to some entirely different result to improve.

Figure 6.7 shows an example Pareto Chart of the number of defects found per thousand lines of code (KLOC) in each major game subsystem. The purpose of such a chart could be to identify which portion of the code would benefit the most from using a new automated checking tool. Because there are costs associated with new technologies—purchasing, training, extra effort to use the tool, and so on—it should be introduced where it would have the greatest impact. In this case, start with the rendering code.

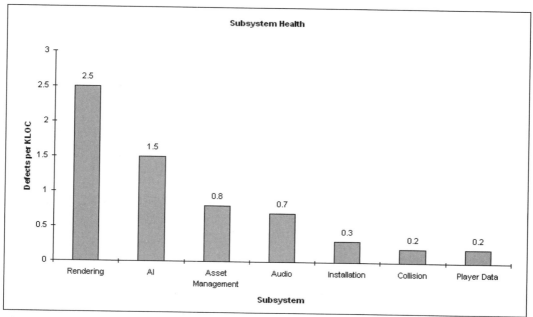

Figure 6.7 Pareto Chart of defects per KLOC for each game subsystem.

Another useful software QA method is to plot control charts of product or process results. The control chart shows the average result to expect and "control limit" boundary lines for the set of data provided. Any items outside of the control limits fall beyond the range of values that would indicate they came from the same process as the rest of the data. This is like having a machine that stamps metal squares a certain way, but every once in a while, one comes out very different from the others. If you have the right amount of curiosity to be a QA person, you would want to know why the square comes out wrong some of the time. The same is true for software results that come out "funny." The control chart reveals results that should be investigated to understand their cause. It might simply be a result of someone entering the wrong data (date, time, size, defects, and so on). Figure 6.8 shows an example control chart for new lines of delta (added or deleted) code changes in the game each week. The numbers are in KLOC.

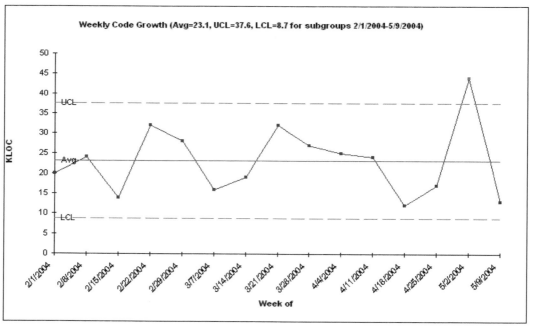

Figure 6.8 Control chart of weekly code change in KLOC.

The solid line running across the middle of the chart is the average value for the data set. The two dashed lines labeled UCL and LCL represent the Upper Control Limit and the Lower Control Limit, respectively. These values are calculated from the data set as well. The data point for the week of 5/2/2004 lies above the UCL. This is a point that should be investigated.

Note

The Pareto Chart and control chart in Figures 6.7 and 6.8, respectively, were created using SPC for Excel (www.spcforexcel.com). A link to a demo version is provided on the book's CD-ROM.

I remember one project where there was a noticeable dip in the number of defects submitted one week. This was a good result for the developers but bad for the testers. A quick investigation revealed that "Bud"—a particularly productive tester—had been on vacation that week. The test data for the rest of the team was within the normal range. Legitimately bad results should be understood and subsequently prevented from happening in the future. Especially good results are just as important to understand so they can be imitated. Additional tools and techniques can be identified in the SQAP for those purposes. This result also suggests that the data could be reported in a different way, such as defects per tester, to account for inevitable fluctuations in staffing. This could replace the original chart or be used in addition to it.

Supplier Control

Your game is not just software. It's a customer experience. The advertisements in the store, the game packaging, the user's manual, and the game media are all part of that experience. In many cases these items come from sources outside the game team. These are some of your "suppliers." Their work is subject to the same kinds of mistakes you are capable of producing on your own. You may also have software or game assets supplied to you that you use within the game, such as game engines, middleware, art, and audio files.

In both of these cases, QA should play a role in determining that the supplied items are "fit for use." This can be done in the same way internal deliverables are evaluated. Additionally, the QA team can evaluate the supplier's capability to deliver a quality product by conducting on-site visits to evaluate the supplier's processes. When you go to the deli, it's nice to see that the food is laid out nicely in the display case. You also appreciate the fact that a food inspector has checked out the plant from which the food originates to see that it is uncontaminated, and that the produced in a clean and healthy environment. The same should be true for game-related software and materials that are supplied to you from other companies.

Training

If new tools, techniques, and/or equipment are going to be used in the development of the project, it may be necessary for one or more QA personnel to become acquainted so they can properly audit the affected deliverables and activities. The impact of the new technologies may affect QA preparation as well, such as requiring new audit checklists to be created or new record types to be defined in the audit entry and reporting system.

The QA training should be planned and delivered in time for QA to conduct any activities related to work products or processes using the new technology. If the team is already having an in-house course delivered, then add some seats for QA. If the team is inventing something internally, try to get a briefing from one of the inventors. Some tools and development environments come with their own tutorials, so get some QA licenses and allocate time to go through the tutorial.

New tools or techniques identified for QA-specific functions should be accompanied with appropriate training. Identify these, document them in the SQAP, and get your training funded.

Risk Management

Risk management is a science all unto itself. In addition to all of the risks involved with developing a game, there are also risks that could hamper your team's QA efforts. Some typical SQA risks are

- Project deliverables go out of sync with planned audits
- QA personnel diverted to other activities such as testing
- Lack of independent QA reporting structure
- Lack of organization commitment to take corrective actions and/or close out issues raised by QA
- Insufficient funding for new QA technologies
- Insufficient funding for training in new development and/or QA technologies

It's not enough to list your risks in the SQAP. You also need to identify the potential impact of each risk and any action plans you can conceive to describe how you would proceed if the risk occurs and/or persists.

Summary

Software quality is certainly affected by testing, but there are other activities that can impact quality sooner and less expensively. Various forms of peer reviews can find faults before they escape to other phases of the project. Standards can be defined and enforced as a way to prevent defects from being introduced into the game, many of which are difficult to detect by testing. Measures such as sigma value and phase containment provide stakes in the ground from which you can set improvement goals.

The Software Quality Assurance organization carries out activities according to a plan that monitor and promote the use of these techniques and measures. Their cost must be weighed against the consequences and costs of releasing a poor quality game.

Note

For more information and resources on software quality, check out the American Society for Quality Web site at www.asq.org.

Exercises

1. Your game code size is 200,000 AELOC. It had 35 defects you knew about when you released it. The people who bought it have reported 17 more. What sigma level is your code at?

2. Describe the differences between the leader role in a walkthrough and the Moderator role in a Fagan Inspection.

3. Add the following defects found in Beta testing to the data in Figure 6.4: Requirements—5, Design—4, Coding—3. What are the updated code PCEs for the requirements, design, and coding phases?

4. Using the SPC Tool demo, create a control chart of the following test case review rates, measured in pages per hour:

   - Review 1: 8.5
   - Review 2: 6.1
   - Review 3: 7.3
   - Review 4: 4.5
   - Review 5: 13.2
   - Review 6: 9.1

   Which reviews, if any, fall above or below the control limits? Describe which are "good" and which are "bad." How might a high or low review rate impact the number of faults found in those reviews?

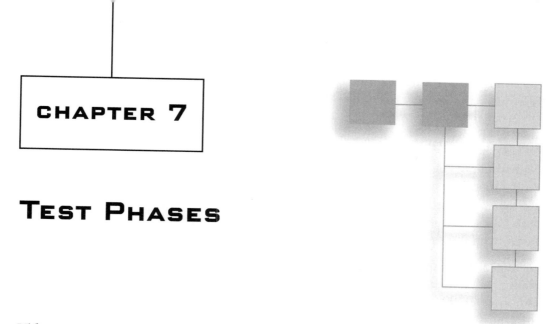

CHAPTER 7

TEST PHASES

Videogames can range in size from tiny downloadable mobile phone games that take a few weeks to produce to epic, massively multiplayer online role-playing games developed over several years. No matter what size the game and how long the production schedule, the testing of the game should always follow the same basic structure:

1. Pre-production
2. Kickoff
3. Alpha
4. Beta
5. Gold
6. Release
7. Post-release

Like the plot of a suspense thriller, each sequence occurs more rapidly, and with much more heightened excitement (and stress), than the next. Figure 7.1 illustrates a very rough timeline for a hypothetical mid-budget console racing game.

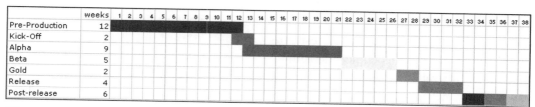

Figure 7.1 Console racing game timeline.

The following sections examine each phase in order to understand why it is vital to the project and distinct from the other phases.

Pre-Production

Depending on your role on the team and when you were brought into the project, you may think that testing begins sometime after a good portion of the game is developed. In reality, testing begins when the project begins. There may not be people called "testers" involved at the beginning, but project scope, design, and assets are being produced from the start that need to be evaluated, critiqued, and corrected.

Much of what happens at the early stages of the project will set the tone for how well testing will go later on. This means both how good the software stands up to testing, and how well the tests themselves are organized and executed. The bottom line is that both the development and test teams can go home earlier at night if more effort and skill is applied to testing activities at the beginning of the project rather than trying to fix things later on by throwing more testers (and more overtime work) at it.

You can't test quality into a game. The quality of the game is established by the code, graphics, and sounds that are produced and compiled into the game code. All testing can do is tell the development team what is wrong with the code. Testing better earlier can get problems fixed sooner and cheaper.

If you received a coupon in the mail at the beginning of your project that said "send in this coupon to save 20% or more on your project," would you send it in? When you save testing for the end of the project it's like having that coupon but not sending it in because you didn't want to pay for the postage to mail it.

Planning Tasks

Almost as soon as a project is conceived, planning for test begins. Test planning includes the tasks outlined in the following sections.

Determine the Scope of Testing the Project Will Require

The design document, TDD, and project schedule are reviewed by the test manager in order to formulate a "scope of test" document that outlines how much testing resources—that is, time, people, and money—he or she will need to get the game tested thoroughly for release (see the following sidebar, "Expansion Plans").

Expansion Plans

The following is brief scope-of-test memo written at a small publisher planning to develop an expansion pack to an RTS released earlier that same year.

MEMORANDUM

To: Executive Producer

From: Manager of Quality Assurance

RE: RTS EXPANSION TEST PLAN SUMMARY

Summary

It will take 1,760 hours to test this expansion pack, based on the following assumptions:

·   50-day production schedule,

·   Four-person test team,

·   10% allowance for overtime, and

·   No post-release patch testing.

Single Player (900 hours)

A significant amount of QA time will be spent testing the new campaign. Because the story mode of these missions will be highly script-dependent, testers will be tasked with breaking those scripts to ensure the user will have a seamless, immersive gameplay experience.

Because the developer has not designed cheats in the game, and because our experience with the original game was such that saved games could not reliably be brought forward from prior builds, campaign mode will take up the majority of test time.

Multiplayer (650 hours)

The thrust of multiplayer testing will be to:

1.   Ensure correct implementation of new units and the new tile set,

2.   Debug new maps,

3.   Debug "interface streamlining" (new functionality described in design doc),

4.   Stress test game size,

5.   Stress test army size,

6.   Stress test game length, and (as time permits)

7.   Balance testing.

Because the expansion pack introduces 12 new units, we will be concerned only with high-level balance testing—if one of the new units gives its clan an overwhelming advantage (or disadvantage), we would bug it out. We do not have the resources available to re-evaluate each of the more than 50 existing units against the new units. We will count on the developer's design team (and user feedback compiled since the release of the original game) to fine-tune the balance of the expansion pack.

Test Matrices (210 hours)

Because this a product for the PC and not a console, there will not be first-party TRC component to the testing. However, we will provide a similar standards-based level of final release testing based on a number of PC standards developed from our own experience as well as standards used at other PC game publishers.

We will run the following standard matrices on the game:

1. Install/Uninstall matrix (with an emphasis on interoperability with the previous product)

2. Windows "gotchas" matrix

3. Publisher Standards matrix

4. Multiplayer connectivity matrix

We will also produce and run the unit matrix developed while testing the original game on each new unit in the expansion pack.

Compatibility (0 hours)

Because the minimum system requirements will not change from the original game, we do not anticipate needing the services of a third-party hardware compatibility lab for compatibility testing. If any machine-specific bugs on the varied hardware in our internal lab crop up during the normal course of testing, we will evaluate at that point whether a full compatibility sweep is warranted.

Overtime (tbd)

Because this product has only modest upside for the company, QA will work with Production to make best efforts to contain overtime costs. At this point we anticipate working overtime only on such occasions that failure to do so will make the product late.

Assign a Lead Tester

This is no trivial matter. The lead tester's experience, temperament, and skill set will have a tremendous influence over the conduct of the testing cycle. This may be the single most important decision the test manager makes on the project. A lead tester must be

- A leader—able to motivate the test team and keep them focused and productive
- A team player—able to recognize the role test plays as part of the larger project team
- A communicator—able to gather and to present information clearly and concisely
- A diplomat—able to manage conflicts as they arise (and they will arise)

The test manager, or the lead tester, should then appoint a "vice lead tester," often called a *primary tester*. On very large teams (for example, more than 30 testers), it's not uncommon to have more than one primary tester, each leading specific sub-teams (for example, multiplayer, career mode, and so on).

Determine Phase Acceptance Criteria

In an ideal world, you will be working from a contract, design spec, or product plan that defines very specific criteria for each phase of testing. But it's seldom an ideal world.

The lead tester should take whatever materials are available and write a specification for the Alpha, Beta, and Gold (release) versions of the game. By establishing clear and unambiguous entry acceptance criteria for each phase of testing, you can avoid conflicts later in the project when you may feel pressure from various parts of the organization to begin, say, Beta testing on a build that isn't truly Beta. Once the test manager has approved these criteria, they should be disseminated to all senior members of the project team.

Three elements are required in the certification planning for each test phase:

- Entry criteria: The set of tests that a build must pass before entering a given test phase. The game won't be considered "at Alpha" until the code passes the Alpha Entry test, for example.
- Exit criteria: The set of tests that a build must pass before completing a test phase.
- Target date: The date both the development and test teams are working toward for a specific phase to launch.

Participate in Game Design Reviews

As mentioned in earlier chapters, all stakeholders benefit from test playing an active role from the beginning of a project. The lead tester or primary tester should participate regularly in design reviews. Their role is not to design the game, but rather to stay abreast of the latest design changes, as well as to advise the project manager of any technical challenges or testing complications that may arise from any anticipated feature revision. Changes in the scope and design of the game will dictate changes in the scope and flow of the testing; forewarned is forearmed.

Set Up the Defect Tracking Database

This is a critical step, in that a poorly designed database can waste precious seconds every time someone uses it, and those seconds add up quickly to man-hours toward the end a project—man-hours you will wish you had back! Figure 7.2 shows a typical entry in a bug database—note that the bug type "Unexpected Result" is too general. Aren't all bugs unexpected?

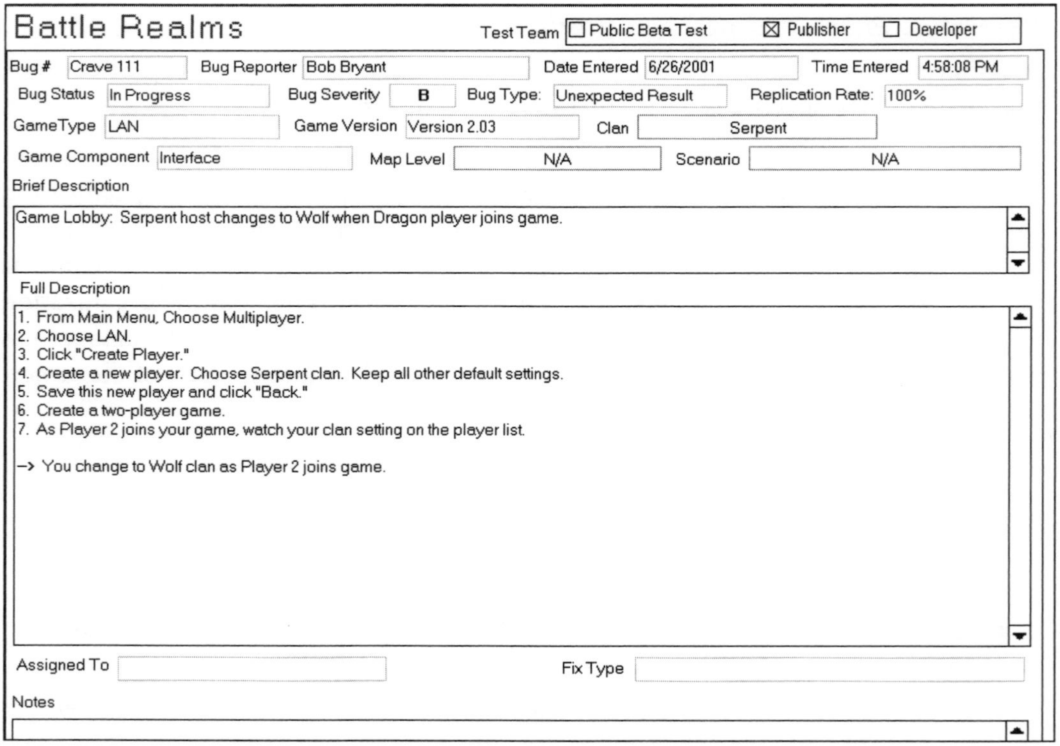
Battle Realms

Test Team ☐ Public Beta Test ☒ Publisher ☐ Developer

Bug # Crave 111 Bug Reporter Bob Bryant Date Entered 6/26/2001 Time Entered 4:58:08 PM

Bug Status In Progress Bug Severity B Bug Type: Unexpected Result Replication Rate: 100%

GameType LAN Game Version Version 2.03 Clan Serpent

Game Component Interface Map Level N/A Scenario N/A

Brief Description

Game Lobby: Serpent host changes to Wolf when Dragon player joins game.

Full Description

1. From Main Menu, Choose Multiplayer.
2. Choose LAN.
3. Click "Create Player."
4. Create a new player. Choose Serpent clan. Keep all other default settings.
5. Save this new player and click "Back."
6. Create a two-player game.
7. As Player 2 joins your game, watch your clan setting on the player list.

--> You change to Wolf clan as Player 2 joins game.

Assigned To Fix Type

Notes

Figure 7.2 Typical entry in a bug database.

The lead tester and project manager should mutually agree on appropriate permissions—that is, which team members have edit rights to which fields. The lead tester should also ask the project manager for a list of development team members to whom bugs will be assigned. The "assigned to" field allows the lead tester, project manager, or anyone else so entrusted to review new bugs and assign them to the right member of the development team to be investigated and fixed. Programmers and artists then search the database for bugs assigned to them. Once they've resolved the bug, they can assign the bug back to the lead tester so that the fix can be verified on the next build.

Whether the bug database is going to sit on an internal server or be accessible over the Internet, it's a good idea at this point to populate the bug database with a few dummy records and double-check all passwords and permissions, both locally and remotely. Every person who will have access to the bug base should be assigned an individual password, and the lead tester can allow or block edit rights to individual fields based on the role that person will play on the project team (see the following sidebar, "Too Many Cooks?").

Draft Test Plan and Design Tests

Having current and detailed knowledge of the game design is critical as the lead tester begins to draft the test documents. Begin drafting an overall test plan that defines what types of tests will be done and what the individual suites and matrices will look like (see Chapter 8, "The Test Process"). This is the point in the project where you can put the methods described in Part IV of this book to good use. Remember: *Prior planning prevents poor performance.*

Test Plan

A *test plan* acts as the playbook for the test team. It identifies the test team's goals along with the resources (staff, time, tools, and equipment) and methods that are necessary to achieve them. Test goals are typically defined in terms of time and scope. They may also be tied to dependencies on other groups. The testing timeline often includes intermediate goals for one or more milestones that occur prior to the final release of the game. Any risks that could affect the ability to meet the test goals are identified in the test plan along with information about how to manage those risks if they occur. The scope of a test plan can be limited to a single subsystem of the game or it can span many game features and releases. If the game is being developed at multiple sites, the test plan helps define what test responsibilities are allocated to each team. Appendix C contains a basic test plan outline and the book's CD provides a link to a test plan template document you can fill in for your own projects.

Too Many Cooks?

A defect tracking database (or bug database or "bug base") that is editable by only the lead tester is not very useful—these tend to be very static and incapable of conveying up-to-the minute information about the state of the project. Neither is a bug base in which every member of the team can edit every field—these are chaotic and ultimately useless.

In designing the bug base, the lead tester must balance the need for members of the project team to communicate with each other about a particular defect with the equally important need to control the flow of information to all members of the project team. Programmers need to be able to comment on or ask questions about a defect in the Developer Comments or Notes field, but they can't be allowed to close the defect arbitrarily by changing the Status field to "closed." Testers need to be able to describe the bug in the Brief Description and Full Description fields, but they may not be qualified to judge who should own the bug in the Assigned To field.

Here are some recommendations:

- **Status** should be editable by the lead tester only. The default value for this field should be "New," so that as testers enter bugs, they can be reviewed and refined by the lead tester before the status is changed to "Open" and is assigned to a member of the development team.

- **Severity** should be editable by the lead tester or primary testers. Remember that the severity of a defect is not the same as its "fix priority." Testers tend, rightly, to be passionate about the defects they find. It is the job of the test team leaders to check against this and assign a severity in an objective manner.

- **Category Fields** should be input by the testers and editable by the lead or primary tester. These fields include such specifics as Game Type, Level, Bug Type, Reproduction Rate, and any other field that includes specific information about the bug.

- **Brief/Full Description** should be input by the testers and editable by the lead or primary tester.

- **Assigned To** is a field that should be editable by the lead tester and any member of the development team. The lead tester will typically assign new bugs to the project manager, who will then review the bug and assign it to a specific programmer or artist to be fixed. Once the bug is fixed, that person can either assign it back to the project manager for further review, or back to the lead tester so that the fix can be verified in the next build and the bug can be closed.

- **Developer Comments** should be editable by the project manager and any member of the development team.

- **Priority** should be editable by the project manager and senior members of the development team. This field is primarily a tool to help the project manager prioritize the flow of work to members of the development team.

Test Case

A *test case* describes an individual test that is to be performed by a tester or testers. Each test case has a distinct objective, which is part of the test case description. A test case also describes what operations to perform in order to meet its objective. Each individual operation within a test case is a *test step*. The level of detail in the test case can vary based on the standards of a particular test organization. Test cases are conceived and documented by each tester who is assigned a set of responsibilities in the test plan. The total set of test cases produced by a tester should fully cover his or her assigned responsibilities.

Test Suite

A *test suite* is a collection of related test cases that are described in further detail. The test suite gives step-by-step instructions about what operations to perform on the game and what details to check for as a result of each step. These instructions should be sufficient for manual execution of the test or for writing code to automate the test. Depending on how the detailed tests are written, they may or may not depend on the steps that were taken in a previous test. Ideally, each test in the suite can be individually identified and executed independently of the other tests in the suite. Think of the test cases as individual chapters in a table of contents, while the test suite is a book that puts the test cases together into a detailed, cohesive story.

Testing Before Testing Begins

You may soon begin to get proto-builds in bits and pieces, with requests from the development team to do very directed testing of certain narrow features in order to help them build the code. This sub-phase is sometimes called *modular testing*, because you're testing individual "modules" of code, not a complete build.

At this stage of development, it is entirely likely that as code becomes functional and modules are tested, the design of the game may be revised significantly "on the fly." Patience is required as you make several iterative revisions to your test documents.

During modular testing, it is premature to begin writing bugs beyond the narrow scope of the module's test case. True defect testing won't begin until the game is accepted for Alpha testing.

Finally, the lead tester should begin to recruit or hire additional team members as necessary according to his or her resource plan. Once the team is in place, test kickoffs can begin.

Test Kickoffs

Kickoffs are known to have a positive impact on software development, leading to better process definition, better problem solving, and cycle time reduction. On a team in which testers have various levels of testing and game project experience, individual needs are not likely to be addressed at the project kickoff. It benefits the team to have kickoffs at the next lowest level: a test kickoff for each "test" that is being created or executed by individual testers. The test kickoff illustrates the principle that increasing an organization's speed results from an iterative process of identifying obstacles, designing a new process that eliminates them, and ensuring that the new way is implemented.

Test kickoff activities are broken into two parts: tester preparation and the kickoff meeting, which is conducted according to the kickoff agenda. The tester's preparation steps and the kickoff agenda are documented on a test kickoff checklist, as shown in Figure 7.3.

TEST KICKOFF CHECKLIST
version 01.00

Game/Feature ______________________________

Tester ____________________ **Date** __________

Tester Preparation

- ☐ Read the requirements for the feature being tested
- ☐ Gather equipment needed per the test equipment list
  - game platform(s) hardware
  - monitor
  - cables
  - controllers
  - save files
  - updates/patches/mods
  - test instruments
- ☐ Read the test script/report

Kickoff Agenda

Kickoff Leader

- Gives feature overview
- Addresses feature questions
- Brings up special instructions
- Brings up and solicits relevant improvement suggestions
- Addresses test execution questions/issues

Figure 7.3 Test kickoff checklist.

From the test kickoff checklist, the tester prepares in the following ways:

1. Reads the requirements and/or documentation for the game feature being tested
2. Gathers equipment, files, and programs needed for the test
3. Reads through the tests

The tester should consult with a "test expert" if there are any roadblocks or questions regarding the completion of any preparation activities. The test expert can be the original author of the test, a tester who already has much experience with the game feature, or the test lead. The expert should also be familiar with the recent defect history of the game and feature(s) to be tested. Experienced testers should not be exempt from this preparation process, and this process should be completed fully before conducting the kickoff meeting.

Once the tester has completed the preparation activities, a kickoff meeting is held. The test expert leads the kickoff meeting by doing the following:

1. Giving a feature overview
2. Addressing feature questions
3. Bringing up any special test instructions
4. Bringing up and soliciting any relevant test improvement suggestions
5. Addressing any test execution questions or issues
6. Recording important issues on the kickoff form and providing a copy to the tester after the meeting is completed

Following the preparation steps listed on the checklist and participating in the interactive meeting per the kickoff agenda benefits testing in the following ways:

- Prepares and equips the tester to run through the entire test without stopping for equipment or questions
- Familiarizes the tester with the expected behavior of the game or module during testing to increase tester awareness of right from wrong
- Resolves any test instruction conflicts prior to executing the test in order to eliminate retesting because of test ambiguities or errors
- Provides a forum for test improvement at the grassroots level, improving tester involvement and ownership

Each test kickoff is an opportunity to improve test understanding, test quality, and test execution. These opportunities would have been missed or identified much later in the test phase if the kickoff process was not used. The net result is that the test kickoff acts as a "pre-mortem" identifying important issues prior to performing the test, rather than waiting to identify them in a post-mortem after testing has already been done. As kick-off records are collected, systemic issues can be identified and addressed in the *current* test phase. Checklists, group meetings, and email are ways to communicate the lessons learned from the kickoffs and suggest remedies to implement on the current project.

By collecting and evaluating the results of kickoffs for each project, actions can be taken to prevent these problems in future test efforts. The preventative analysis of test kickoff results and the cycle time impacts achieved by the initial deployment point out the potential for improving the way hundreds of other tests will be conducted as you use this process going forward. The across-the-board use of test kickoffs will translate into further test execution cycle time improvements and uncover more defects, leading to better game quality.

The following behaviors, which are driven by the use of test kickoffs, can reduce the size of the testing critical path:

- **Make fewer mistakes (reduce wasted effort)**
  The test kickoff steps are designed to ensure that testing does not begin until the tester is equipped to test and understands the details and goals of the testing. Among other things, this results in quicker and more accurate measurement of results.

- **Reduce cyclical efforts (shortest distance between two points is a line)**
  As part of preparation, the tester reviews the test and requirements in their entirety. This reduces misunderstood and improperly performed steps, resulting in much less test effort spent on backing up and redoing test sections.

- **All effort results in something that will be used**
  The metrics show that the use of test kickoffs reduces the testing cycle time, even when accounting for the time it takes to hold the kickoffs.

- **Truth telling is encouraged**
  The one-on-one forum of a test kickoff is less intimidating than the group setting of a phase or release kickoff. The kickoff leader should make the tester comfortable and remind the tester of the kickoff goals. When testers see that their feedback results in improvements, they are more open about voicing their opinions and ideas.

- **Have constructive discussions rather than unnecessary effort and debate**
  The test kickoff meeting gets every tester involved in process improvement. It also gives the tester and kickoff leader shared responsibility to address the issues raised and recorded in the meeting. Sticking to the kickoff meeting agenda will keep the meeting focused on test-related issues.

I realize it's a foreign concept that having a meeting will actually save time. I needed to know this for myself when test kickoffs were just an "idea." In the project I was working on at the time, I held test kickoffs for a portion of tests while the rest were executed without a kickoff. The "kicked-off" tests were executed at 1.4 times the rate of the "non-kickoff" testing. Putting it another way, testers who had a kickoff completed 40% more tests that those who did not have a kickoff.

Test kickoffs can provide the same benefits for test creation as they can for test execution. All it takes is a slightly different agenda and checklist, as shown in Figure 7.4.

Both test kickoff checklists shown in this chapter are available on the book's CD-ROM.

GAME TEST CREATION KICKOFF CHECKLIST
version 01.00

Game/Feature   _____

Tester   _____   Date   _____

Test Creator Preparation

☐   Read the requirements for the feature being tested

☐   Read existing test scripts from similar features and/or games

Kickoff Agenda

Kickoff Leader

• Gives feature Overview

• Addresses feature Questions

• Brings up special instructions

• Brings up and solicits relevant improvement suggestions

• Addresses test case questions/issues

Figure 7.4 Test creation kickoff checklist.

Alpha

It's time to get busy. The project manager delivers you an Alpha candidate. You certify it against the Alpha criteria you established in the planning phase. Now full-bore testing can begin.

Over the course of Alpha testing, the game design is fine-tuned. Features are play tested and revised (or scrapped). Missing assets are integrated. Systems developed by different programmers are linked together. It's an exciting time.

As each member of the code and art team checks new work into the build, they're also checking for new defects. This means that the game at this phase is a "target-rich environment" for a tester. It can also seem very overwhelming (remember Rule #1: Don't Panic). It is critical at this stage that the test suites are strictly adhered to. They will provide a structure for bringing order to what may seem like chaos.

Over the course of Alpha testing, all modules of the game should be tested at least once, and performance baselines should be established (frame rate, load times, and so on). These baselines will help the development team determine how far they have to go to get each performance standard up to the target for release. For example, a frame rate of 30 (or even 15) frames of video per second (fps) may be acceptable in the early stages of developing a 3D action game, but the release target should be a solid 60 fps with no prolonged dips during scenes when there are greater-than-usual numbers of characters and special effects on-screen.

Alpha Phase Entry Criteria

The following are Alpha entry criteria typical for a console game:

1. **All major game features exist and can be tested.** Some may still be in separate modules for testing purposes.

2. **A tester can navigate the game along some path from start to finish.** This assumes the game is linear, or has some linear component (for example, career mode in a racing game). Because many games are non-linear, the lead tester and project manager must agree ahead of time on a content completion target for such games (for example, three of 12 mini-games).

3. **The code passes at least 50% of platform TRC.** Each console game has a set of standards published and tested against by the manufacturer of that platform. When you produce a PlayStation game, the Format QA team at Sony Computer Entertainment America (SCEA) will test it against the PlayStation Technical Requirements Checklist (TRC) to make certain that the game complies with platform conventions. These requirements are very exacting, such as specifying the precise wording of error messages a game must display if a player pulls his memory card out during a game save.

4. **Basic interface is complete and preliminary documentation is available to QA.** The main menu, most submenus, and the in-game interface (sometimes

called the Heads-Up Display, or HUD) should be functional, if not yet finalized and visually polished. *Preliminary documentation* in this context means any explanation of new functionality, changed controller maps, and cheat codes (if any).

5. **The game is compatible with most specified hardware and software configurations.** For a cross-platform console game, this means that the game will run on every targeted platform (PlayStation 2 and Xbox, for example). For a PC game, this criterion dictates that the game must run on a variety of systems with varying specifications (a range of CPU speeds, a range of RAM caches, and so on).

6. **Level scripting is implemented.** This pertains primarily to single-player story mode. An Alpha candidate that required the tester to load each level manually would fail this criterion.

7. **First-party controllers and memory cards work.** Each platform manufacturer (SCEA, Microsoft, Nintendo, and so on) either manufactures or licenses for manufacture its own line of peripherals. Since support of these first-party peripherals is required by the platform TRCs, and because the majority of testing will be done using first-party peripherals, they need to be supported by Alpha.

8. **Final or placeholder art is in for all areas of the game.** All the levels and characters must be textured and animated, though these textures, animations, and even the level geometry, may be subject to refinement as the game approaches Beta.

9. **Online multiplayer can be tested.** Enough network code must be implemented so that at least two consoles can connect over a LAN and play a game.

10. **Placeholder audio is implemented.** It is entirely possible that the voice recording sessions with the final talent have not yet taken place at Alpha. In this case, members of the development team should record "stub" audio and integrate it where needed.

Over the course of Alpha testing, all modules of the game should be tested at least once, and performance baselines should be established (for example, frame rate, load times, and so on). These baselines will help the development team determine how far they have to go to get each performance standard up to the target for release. For example, a frame rate of 30 (or even 15) frames of video per second (fps) may be acceptable in the early stages of developing a 3D action game, but the release target should be a solid 60 fps with no prolonged dips during scenes when there are greater-than-usual numbers of characters and special effects on-screen.

Beta

By the end of Alpha, the development team should have very clear idea of the game they're creating. The development team has, for the most part, stopped creating new code and new artwork, and will now shift their focus to perfecting what they've already created. It's time to identify and fix the remaining bugs.

Although the term "Beta testing" frequently refers to any outside testing, it is only at the early stages of the Beta phase that final gameplay testing should take place with people outside the design team. The majority of testing done by outside Beta testers during true Beta is bug reporting and load testing. Gameplay feedback and suggestions should continue to be recorded for possible post-release implementation in a patch or sequel.

Beta Phase Entry Criteria

The following Beta phase criteria are typical for a console game:

1. **All features and options are implemented.** The game is "feature complete."
2. **The code passes at least 100% of platform TRC.** Toward the end of Beta, the game should be ready for a "pre-certification" submission to the platform manufacturer. This process allows the platform manufacturer's QA team to test the game against the latest TRC and warn of any potential compliance issues.
3. **The game can be navigated on all paths.** Any bugs that may have closed off portions of the game are eliminated.
4. **The entire user interface is final.**
5. **The game is compatible with all specified hardware and software configurations.**
6. **The game logic and AI is final.** Programming is complete on the "gameplay" of the game. The game knows its own rules. All AI profiles are complete.
7. **All controllers work.** Those third-party peripherals that have been chosen by the development team (and the publisher) to be supported function with the game.
8. **Final artwork is implemented.** There should be no placeholder artwork left. Beta is the phase when most screenshots, trailers, and running footage will be taken to use in the packaging and to market the game.
9. **Final audio is implemented.** All placeholder audio is has been replaced with final assets of the voice talent. (There may be a few do-over, or "pick-up" lines that have yet to be integrated, but these should not have an impact on in-game event timing or level scripting.)

10. **All online modes are complete and testable.**

11. **All language version text is implemented and ready for simultaneous release.** The game script (both written and spoken) is locked and can be sent forward for translation and integration into the foreign-language versions of the game.

Design Lock

At some point during Beta testing, the project manager should declare the game to be in a state of *design lock* (sometimes called *feature lock*). The play testing has concluded. Questions of balance have been resolved as best they can. The focus of the test team at this point should be to continue to run the test cases against the builds in an iterative manner, because each defect fixed at this point may have introduced another defect elsewhere in the game.

Toward the end of Beta, many tough decisions must be made. The teams are tired, tempers are on edge, and time is running out. In this charged atmosphere, with very little sleep themselves, the project team leaders have to make such critical choices as the following:

- **Whether or not to implement that last-minute feature enhancement.** The designers may have had a great idea at the eleventh hour and are eager to introduce a new feature, character, or level. The project team leaders must weigh the risks of implementing the new feature (and possibly implementing new bugs and schedule slippage) against shipping a perhaps less compelling game on time.

- **Whether to cut that level that just doesn't seem to be much fun.** Occasionally it becomes clear during the course of testing that a level or other content component is a "problem child," and requires too much work relative to the time left in the schedule to redesign. Cutting it out entirely may be problematic, however, in that the game will require new tests to ensure that the remaining levels run seamlessly around the deleted features. Critical story information may have been presented in the problem level, and other levels will have to be rewritten (and retested) to accommodate this.

- **Which bugs to ship with.** In many ways, this is the toughest decision of all—which bugs to let go.

Letting Bugs Go

As a gamer, you may have encountered a defect in a game you bought. Your reaction may likely have been, "I wonder how the testers missed this one?" Chances are they didn't miss it.

There will be times, especially later in the project, when the development team determines that they can't (or won't) fix a bug. This can happen for a variety of reasons. Perhaps the technical risks involved in the fix outweigh the negative impact of the defect. Perhaps there is a workaround in place that the technical support team can supply to players who encounter the defect. Perhaps there simply isn't time.

Whatever the reason, each project must have a quick and orderly process in place to determine which defects will be *waived,* that is, which will not be fixed by the development team. This designation has many different names. Waived bugs can be known as "as is," ISV (In Shipped Version), DWNF (Developer Will Not Fix), or CBP (Closed by Producer). The worst name I've ever encountered for the waived status is "featured," which institutionalized the cynical joke, "That's not a bug, it's a feature." (Not surprisingly, that studio is now defunct, having released too many buggy games.)

Cynicism, defeatism, and defensiveness have no place in the bug waiving process. On the one hand, testers work very hard and want to feel as though their effort matters to the project. On the other hand, developers work just as long (if not longer) and have a duty to ship their game on time. It is crucial that all parties involved maintain an understanding and respect for the role each plays in the overall project team.

Ideally, the senior members of the project team will meet regularly and often to discuss those bugs that the development team have requested to be waived. These can be flagged as "waive requested" or "request as is" in the Status or Developer Status fields of the bug database. The senior members of the project team (the producer, executive producer, lead tester, and QA manager) can meet to evaluate each bug and discuss the positives and negatives of fixing it versus leaving it in the game. Other team members such as programmers or testers should be available for these meetings as needed. This decision-making body is sometimes called the CCB (Change Control Board) or the Bug Committee.

In some cases, where a post-release software update, or *patch,* is anticipated, a number of bugs will be designated for fixing after the game has been shipped (see "Post-release Testing," later in the chapter). In the case of most console games, however, this is not yet an option.

Once a bug has been waived, it's important to remind both the bug author and the test team as a whole that merely because the bug was waived doesn't mean that it wasn't a legitimate bug. Nor does it mean that they shouldn't continue to find defects with the same level of diligence. It is the role of the test team to write up every bug, every time, no matter when in the cycle they find it. They supply the lead tester, project manager, and the business unit heads with the best information possible about the state of the game so that the best business decisions can be made.

Gold Testing

Once the Beta test phase winds down, the game should be at a state that resembles the following set of typical release guidelines:

1. All known Severity 1 bugs (crashes, hangs, major function failures) are fixed.
2. Greater than 90% of all known Severity 2 bugs are fixed.
3. Greater than 85% of all known Severity 3 bugs are fixed.
4. Any known open issues have a workaround that has been communicated to Technical Support (or documented in the README.TXT file, in the case of PC games).
5. Release-level performance has been achieved (60-fps frame rate).

Upon meeting your release criteria, the game is declared to be at "code lock." A brief, intense period of testing is performed on what everyone on the team hopes will be (but which will probably not be) the final build. Since the version of the game that is sent to be manufactured is known as the *gold master*, the final few versions tested are known as *gold master candidates (GMCs)* or *release candidates*.

At this point the game look and feels like any other retail game. It's up to the testers to serve as the last line of protection for both the player and the project team by sniffing out any remaining hidden defects that would have a significant impact on player satisfaction. This should be done by rerunning one final time all of the test suites, or as many as time permits. In addition, a number of testers should be tasked with "breaking" the game one final time. Any remaining bug found during this final effort deemed too severe to be waived is called a *showstopper*, because it causes the gold master candidate to be rejected. A new GMC must be prepared with a fix for the new defect, and release testing must start over again from the beginning.

Last-Minute Defects

Because the final stages of the project are so intense and pressure-laden, people will react negatively to showstoppers: "Why are we [or you] just finding this now? Test has been going on for months!" This refrain is frequently heard from stressed-out executives. It is best for the test team to take such emotional comments in stride and remember several inviolable truths of game development:

1. There is seldom enough time in any project to find every bug.
2. Every time a programmer touches the code, bugs may be introduced.
3. Code changes accumulate over time, so that several iterative changes to different parts of the game may result in a bug showing up downstream from those changes.

4. Programmers are much more tired and prone to mistakes toward the end of the project.

5. Testers are much more tired and prone to miss things toward the end of the project.

6. Bugs happen.

In the case of a PC game, a Web game, or any other game in which the publisher or financing entity is the sole arbiter of whether to release the product, once the Gold testing phase has been concluded, the game is ready for manufacture. In the case of a console game, however, there is one final gatekeeper who must certify the code. This final certification process is known as *release testing*.

Release Certification

A clean GMC is sent to the platform manufacturer for final certification once the project team has finished Gold testing. The platform manufacturer (for example, Nintendo, SCEA, or Microsoft) then conducts its own intensive testing on the GMC. Their testing consists of two phases, which can happen concurrently or consecutively. The standards phase tests the code against the Technical Requirements Checklist. The functionality phase tests the code for functionality and stability. The release testers always play the game through at least once per submission. They often find showstopper bugs of their own.

At the end of certification testing, the platform manufacturer's QA team will issue a report of all the bugs they found in the GMC. Representatives of the publisher will discuss this bug list with the account representatives at the platform manager, and will mutually agree upon which bugs on the list must be fixed.

The development team is well advised to fix only those bugs on the "must fix" list, and to avoid fixing each and every minor bug on the list in an effort to please the platform manufacturer. Fixing more bugs than is absolutely necessary to win final certification only puts the code at risk for more defects.

Once the game has been re-submitted and certified by the platform manufacturer, it is "Gold." The champagne should flow. But the project is not over yet.

Post-Release Testing

Software updates, or *patches*, are a fact of life. Users don't like them, but want them if they're available. Publishers don't like them, because they potentially add to the overall cost of the project. Developers don't like them, because they can be perceived as a tacit admission of failure. However, if the game was shipped with even one or two bad defects, either intentionally or inadvertently, it's time for a patch.

The upside of developing and testing a patch is that it allows the development team to revisit the entire list of waived bugs and last-minute design tweaks and incorporate some additional polish into the game. Each additional bug fix or feature polish means more testing, however, and should be planned for accordingly.

Sometimes the development team will release more than one patch. In that case, the testing becomes more complicated, because *interoperability* must be tested. Each new patch must be tested to see whether it functions with both the base retail game and earlier patched versions.

Summary

Structured game testing breaks the test activities into distinct phases, each of which has its own inputs, deliverables, and success criteria. The phases correspond with the progressive completion and improvement of the game code until it is finally fit to be sold to your customers. Once test planning and preparation are completed, different types of testing are utilized in the remaining phases. Like pieces of a mosaic, they each reveal something different about the game code—in the right place and at the right time.

Exercises

1. What are the main responsibilities of a lead tester?
2. Which fields in the bug database should the primary tester be allowed to modify?
3. The Beta build is the version that will be sent to manufacturing. True or false?
4. Describe whether each of the following is an appropriate topic to discuss during a test execution kickoff, and why:
   a) Possible contradictions in the feature requirements
   b) Ideas for new tests
   c) Company stock prices
   d) Identical tests already being run in other test suites
   e) How "buggy" this feature was in the previous release
   f) Recent changes to the game data file formats
   g) Lack of detail in the test case documentation
5. Feature lock should happen in Alpha. True or false?
6. Online multiplayer features can be tested in Alpha. True or false?

7. Being a team player is not an important criterion for a lead tester. True or false?

8. All bugs MUST be fixed before a game can be certified as GMC. True or false?

9. Explain the difference between a test plan and a test case.

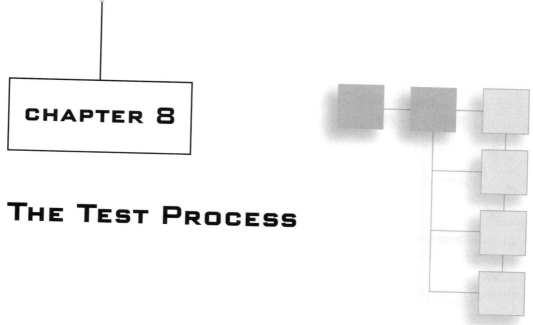

CHAPTER 8

THE TEST PROCESS

Programmers don't fully test their own games. They don't have time to, and even if they did, it's not a good idea. Back at the dawn of the videogame era, the programmer of a game was often also its artist, designer, and tester. Even though games were very small—the size of email—the programmer spent most of his time designing and programming. Little of his time was spent testing. The programmer of *Astrosmash*, a space shooter for the Intellivision system, made an assumption when he designed the game that no player would ever score 10 million points. As a result, he didn't write a check for score overflowing. He read over his own code and—based on his own assumptions—it seemed to work fine. It was a fun game—its graphics were breathtaking (at the time) and the game went on to become one of the best-selling games on the Intellivision platform.

Weeks after the game was released, however, a handful of customers began to call with complaints. When they scored more than 9,999,999 points, the score displayed negative numbers, letters, and other non-numeric symbols. This was after the catalog described the game as having "unlimited scoring potential." The problem was exacerbated by the fact that the Intellivision console had a feature that allowed players to play the game in slow motion, making it much easier to rack up high scores. John Sohl, the programmer, learned a hard lesson: *The user will always surprise you.*

"Black Box" Testing

Almost all game testing is *black box* testing; testing done from outside the application. No knowledge of, or access to, the source code is granted to the tester. Game testers typically don't find defects by reading the game code. Rather, game testers try to find defects using the same input devices available to the normal player. Black box testing is the most cost-effective way to test the extremely complex network of systems and modules that even the simplest videogame represents.

Figure 8.1 illustrates some of the various inputs you can provide to a videogame and the outputs you can receive back. The most basic of inputs are positional and control data in the form of button presses and cursor movements. These can come from a variety of input devices: joysticks, keyboards, mice, and such esoteric devices as dance pads, bass fishing controllers, maraca controllers, and drum controllers. Audio input can come from microphones in headsets or attached to a game controller. Video input can come from USB cameras. Input from other users can come from a second controller, a local network, or the Internet. Finally, stored data such as saved games and options settings can be called up as input from memory cards or a hard drive.

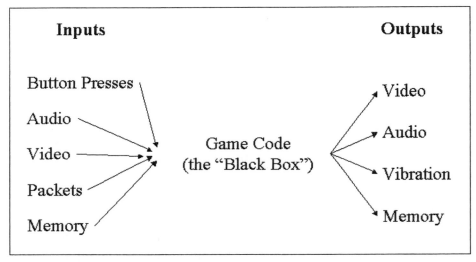

Figure 8.1 Black box testing: planning inputs and examining outputs.

Once some or all of these types of input are received by the game, it reacts in interesting ways and produces such output as video, audio, vibration (via force feedback devices), and data saved to memory cards or hard drives.

The input path of a videogame is not one-way, however. It's a feedback loop, where the player and the game are constantly reacting to each other. Players don't receive output from a game and stop playing. They constantly alter and adjust their input on the fly based on what they see, feel, and hear in the game. The game, in turn, makes similar adjustments in its outputs based on the inputs it receives from the user. Figure 8.2 illustrates this loop.

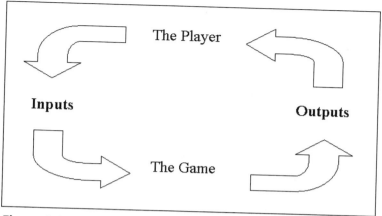

Figure 8.2 The player's feedback loop adjusts to the game's input and vice versa.

If the feedback received by the user was entirely predictable all the time, the game would be no fun. Nor would the game be fun if the feedback received by the player was entirely random all the time. Instead, feedback from games should be just random enough to be unpredictable. It is the unpredictability of the feedback loop that makes games fun. Because the code is designed to surprise the player and the player will always surprise the programmer, black box testing gets testers to think and behave like players.

"White Box" Testing

In contrast to black box testing, *white box* testing gives the tester an opportunity to exercise the source code directly in ways no end user ever could. It can be a daunting challenge for a white box tester to read a piece of game code and predict every single manner in which it will interact with every other bit of code, and whether the code has accounted for every combination and order of inputs possible. Testing a game using only white box methods is also extremely difficult because it is nearly impossible to account for the complexity of the player feedback loop. There are, however, situations in which white box testing is more practical and necessary than black box testing. These include the following:

- Tests performed by developers prior to submitting new code for integration with the rest of the game
- Testing code modules that will become part of a reusable library across multiple games and/or platforms

- Testing code methods or functions that are essential parts of a game engine or middleware product

- Testing code modules within your game that might be used by third-party developers or "modders" who, by design, could expand or modify the behavior of your game to their own liking

- Testing low-level routines that your game uses to support specific functions in the newest hardware devices such as graphic cards or audio processors

In performing white box testing, you execute specific modules and the various paths that the code can follow when you use the module in various ways. Test inputs are determined by the types and values of data that can be passed to the code. Results are checked by examining values returned by the module, global variables that are affected by the module, and local variables as they are processed within the module. To get a taste of white box testing, consider the TeamName routine from *Castle Wolfenstein: Enemy Territory*:

```
const char *TeamName(int team)  {
    if (team==TEAM_AXIS)
        return "RED";
    else if (team==TEAM_ALLIES)
        return "BLUE";
    else if (team==TEAM_SPECTATOR)
        return "SPECTATOR";
    return "FREE";
}
```

Four white box tests are required for this module to test the proper behavior of each line of code within the module. The first test would be to call the TeamName function with the parameter TEAM_AXIS and then check that the string "RED" is returned. Second, pass the value of TEAM_ALLIES and check that "BLUE" is returned. Third, pass TEAM_SPECTATOR and check that "SPECTATOR" is returned. Finally, pass some other value such as TEAM_NONE, which makes sure that "FREE" is returned. Together these tests not only exercise each line of code at least once, they also test the behavior of both the "true" and "false" branches of each if statement.

This short exercise illustrates some of the key differences between a white box testing approach and a black box testing approach:

- Black box testing should test all of the different ways you could choose a test value from within the game, such as different menus and buttons. White box testing requires you to pass that value to the routine in one form—its actual symbolic value within the code.

- By looking into the module, white box testing reveals all of the possible values that can be provided to and processed by the module being tested. This information may not be obvious from the product requirements and features descriptions that drive black box testing.

- Black box testing relies on a consistent configuration of the game and its operating environment in order to produce repeatable results. White box testing relies only on the interface to the module being tested and is concerned only about external files when processing streams, file systems, or global variables.

The Life Cycle of a Build

A basic game testing process consists of the following steps:

1. **Plan and design the test.** Although much of this is done early on during the planning phase, planning and design should be revisited with every build. What has changed in the design spec since the last build? What additional test cases have been added? What new configurations will the game support? What features have been cut? The scope of testing should ensure that no new issues were introduced in the process of fixing bugs prior to this release.

2. **Prepare for testing.** Code, tests, documents, and the test environment are updated by their respective owners and aligned with one another. By this time the development team should have marked the bugs fixed for this build in the defect database so the QA or test team can subsequently verify those fixes and close the bugs.

3. **Perform the test.** Run the test suites against the new build. If you find a defect, test "around" the bug to make certain you have all the details necessary to write as specific and concise a bug report as possible. The more research you do in this step, the easier and more useful the bug report will be.

4. **Report the results.** Log the completed test suite and report any defects you found.

5. **Repair the bug.** The test team participates in this step by being available to discuss the bug with the development team and to provide any directed testing they may require to track it down.

6. **Return to step 1 and re-test.** With new bugs and new test results comes a new build.

These steps not only apply to black box testing, but they also describe white box testing, configuration testing, compatibility testing, and any other type of QA. These steps are identical no matter what their scale. If you substitute the word "game" or "project" for the word "build" in the preceding steps, you will see that they can also apply to the entire game, a phase of development (Alpha, Beta, and so on), or an individual module or feature within a build. In this manner, the software testing process can be considered fractal—the smaller system is structurally identical to the larger system, and vice versa.

As illustrated in Figure 8.3, the testing process itself is a feedback loop between the tester and the developer. The tester plans and executes tests on the code, then reports the bugs to the developer, who fixes them and compiles a new build, which the tester plans and executes tests on, and so on.

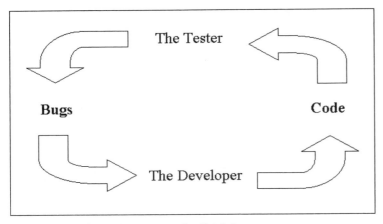

Figure 8.3 The testing process feedback loop.

A comfortable scale from which to examine this process is at the level of testing an individual build. Even a relatively small game project may consist of dozens of builds over its development cycle.

Test Cases and Test Suites

As discussed in the previous chapter, a single test performed to answer a single question is a test case; a collection of test cases is a test suite. The lead tester, primary tester, or any other tester tasked with test creation should draft these documents prior to the distribution of the build. Each tester will take his or her assigned test suites and perform them on the build. Any anomalies should be noted and checked against the defect database. Any anomalies not already present in the database should be written up as new bugs.

In its simplest form, a test suite is a series of incremental steps that the tester can perform sequentially. Subsequent chapters in this book discuss in depth the skillful design of test cases and suites through such methods as combinatorial tables and test flow diagrams. For the purposes of this discussion, consider a short test suite you would execute on *Minesweeper*, a simple game available with most versions of Microsoft Windows. A portion of this suite is shown in Figure 8.4. You will find a sample test suite in Appendix E.

Step

Step	Pass	Fail	Comments
1. Launch Minesweeper.			
2. Menu options are "Game" and "Help"?			
3. Left number (bombs left) displayed is 10?			
4. Right number (time elapsed) displayed is 0?			
5. Middle button shows a smiley face?			
6. Click the "Game" option on the menu and choose "Exit."			
7. Game closes?			
8. Re-launch Minesweeper.			
9. Click the "Game" option on the menu.			
10. "Beginner" is checked?			
11. Click "Custom..."			
12. In the "Custom Field" submenu, enter 0 in the height box.			
13. 0 accepted as input?			
14. Click "OK."			
15. Playing grid 9 rows high?			
16. Playing grid 9 rows wide (unchanged)?			
17. Click "Game," "Custom..."			
18. In the "Custom Field" submenu, enter 999 in the height box.			
19. 999 accepted as input?			
20. Click "OK."			
21. Playing grid 24 rows high?			
22. Playing grid 9 rows wide (unchanged)?			

Figure 8.4 Portion of a test suite for *Minesweeper*.

This is a very small portion of a very simple test suite for a very small and simple game. The first section (steps one through seven) tests launching the game, ensuring that the default display is correct, and exiting. Each step either gives the tester an incremental instruction or asks the tester a simple question. Ideally, these questions are binary and unambiguous. The tester performs each test case and records the result.

Because the testers will inevitably observe results that the test designer hadn't planned for, the Notes field allows the tester to elaborate on a Yes/No answer, if necessary. The lead or primary who receives the completed test suite can then scan the Notes field and make adjustments to the test suite as needed for the next build.

Where possible, the questions in the test suite should be written in such a way that a "yes" answer indicates a "pass" condition—the software is working as designed and no defect is observed. "No" answers, in turn, indicate that there is a problem and a defect should be reported. There are several reasons for this: it's more intuitive, since we tend to group "yes" and "pass" (both positives) together in our minds in the same way we group "no" and "fail." Further, by grouping all passes in the same column, the completed test suite can be easily scanned by both the tester and test managers to determine quickly whether there were any fails. A clean test suite will have all the checks in the Pass column.

For example, consider a test case covering the display of a *tool tip*, a small window with instructional text incorporated into many interfaces. A fundamental test case would be to determine whether the tool tip text contains any typographical errors. The most intuitive question to ask in that test case is

```
Does the text contain typographical errors?
```

The problem with this question is that a pass (no typos) would be recorded as a "no." It would be very easy for a hurried (or tired) tester to mistakenly mark the Fail column. It is far better to express the question so that a "yes" answer indicates a "pass" condition:

```
Is the text free of typographical errors?
```

As you can see, directed testing is very structured and methodical. After the directed testing has concluded, or concurrently with directed testing, a less structured, more intuitive form of testing, known as *ad hoc* testing, takes place.

Entry Criteria

It's advisable to require that any code release meets some criteria for being fit to test before you do any testing on it. This is similar to the checklists that astronauts and pilots take to evaluate the fitness of their vehicle systems before attempting flight. Builds submitted to testing that don't meet the basic entry criteria are likely to waste the time of both testers and programmers. The countdown to testing should stop until the test "launch" criteria are sufficiently met.

The following is a list of suggestions for entry criteria to use. Don't keep these a secret from the rest of the development team. Make the team aware of the purpose—to prevent waste—and work with them to produce a set of criteria that the whole team can commit to.

- The game code should be built without compiler errors. Any new compiler warnings that occur are analyzed and discussed with the test team.
- The code release notes should be complete and provide the detail that testers need to plan which tests to run or re-run for this build.

- Defect records for any bugs closed in the new release should be updated so they can be used by testers to make decisions about how much to test in the new build.

- Tests and builds should be properly version controlled, as described in the following sidebar.

- When you are sufficiently close to the end of the project, you also want to receive the game on the media that it will ship on. Check that the media provided contains all of the files that would be provided to your customer.

Version Control: Not Just for Developers

A fundamental principle of software development is that every build of an application should be treated as a separate and discrete version. Inadvertent blending of old code with new is one of the most common (and most preventable) causes of software defects. The process of tracking builds and ensuring that all members of a development team are checking current code and assets into the current version is known as *version control*.

Test teams must practice their own version control. There's nothing more time-wasting than for a test team to report a lot of bugs on an old build. This is not only a waste of time, but it can cause panic on the part of the programmers and the project manager.

Proper version control for the test team includes the following steps:

1. Collect all prior versions from the test team before distributing the new build. The prior versions should be stacked together and archived until the project is complete.

2. Archive all paperwork. This includes not only any build notes you received from the development team, but also any completed test suites, old test plans, screen shots, saved games, notes, .AVIs, and any other material generated during the course of testing a build. It is sometimes important to retrace steps along the paper trail, whether to assist in isolating a new defect or determining in what version an old bug was introduced.

3. Verify the build number with the developer prior to duplicating it.

4. In cases where builds are transmitted electronically, verify the byte count, file dates, and directory structure before building it. It's vital in situations where builds are sent via FTP or email that the test team makes certain they are testing a version identical to the version the developers uploaded. Confirm the integrity of the transmitted build before giving it to the testers.

5. Renumber all test suites and any other build-specific paperwork with the current version number.

6. Distribute the new build for smoke testing.

Configuration Preparation

Before the test team can work with the new build, some housekeeping is in order. The test equipment must be readied for a new round of testing. The test lead must communicate the appropriate hardware configuration to each tester for this build. Configurations typically change little over the course of testing. To test a single-player-only console game, you need the game console, a controller, and a memory card. That hardware configuration typically will not change for the life of the project. If, however, the new build is the first in which network play is enabled, or a new input device or PC video card has been supported, you may need to augment their hardware configurations to perform the tests on that new code.

Perhaps the most important step in this preparation is eliminating any trace of the prior build from the hardware. "Wiping" the old build on a Nintendo GameCube is simple because the only recordable media for that system is a memory card. All you have to do is remove and archive the saved game you created with the old build. More careful test leads will ask their testers to go the extra step of reformatting the memory card, which completely erases the card, to ensure that not a trace of the old build's data will carry forward during the testing of the new build.

Tip

> Save your saves! Always archive your old user-created data, including game saves, options files, custom characters, and custom levels.

Not surprisingly, configuration preparation can be much more complicated for PC games. The cleanest possible testing configuration for a PC game is

- A fresh installation of the latest version of the operating system, including any patches or security updates.
- The latest drivers for all components of the computer. This not only includes the obvious video card and sound card drivers, but also chipset drivers, motherboard drivers, ethernet card drivers, and so on.
- The latest versions of any "helper apps" or middleware the game requires to run. These can range from Microsoft's DirectX multimedia libraries to multiplayer matchmaking software such as GameSpy Arcade.

The only other software on the computer should be the new build.

"Bob" once walked into a QA lab that was testing a very cutting-edge 3D PC game. Testing of the game had fallen behind, and he was sent from the company's corporate headquarters to investigate. Bob arrived late in the morning, and at noon he was appalled to see the testers exit the game they were testing and fire up email, IRC, Web browsers, and file sharing programs—a host of applications that were installed on their test computers. Some even jumped into a game of *Unreal Tournament*. Bob asked the assistant test manager why he thought it was a good idea for all the testers to have these extraneous programs on their test configurations. "It simulates real-world conditions," he shrugged, annoyed by Bob's question.

As you may have already guessed, this lab's failure to wipe their test computers clean before each build led to a lot of wasted time chasing false defects—symptoms testers thought were defects in the game, but which were in fact problems brought about by, for example, email or file sharing programs running in the background, taxing the system's resources and network bandwidth. This wasted tester time also meant a lot of wasted programmer time, as the development team tried to figure out what in the game code might be causing such (false) defects.

The problem was solved by reformatting each test PC, freshly installing the operating system and latest drivers, and then using a drive image program to create a system restore file. From that point forward, testers merely had to reformat their hard drive and copy the system restore file over from a CD.

Whatever protocol is established, *config prep* is crucial prior to the distribution of a new build.

Smoke Testing

The next step after accepting a new build and preparing to test it is to certify that the build is worthwhile to formally test. This process is sometimes called performing a *smoke test* on the build, because it's used to determine whether a build "smokes" (malfunctions) when run. At a minimum, it should consist of a "load & launch," that is, the lead or primary tester should launch the game, enter each module from the main menu, and spend a minute or two playing each module. If the game launches with no obvious performance problems and each module implemented so far loads with no obvious problems, it is safe to certify the build, log it, and duplicate it for the test team.

So the build is distributed. Time to test for new bugs, right? Not just yet. Before testing can take a step forward, you must take a step backward and verify that the bugs the development team claims to have fixed in this build are indeed fixed. This process is known as *regression testing*.

Regression Testing

Fix verification can be at once very satisfying and very frustrating. It gives the test team a good sense of accomplishment to see the defects they report disappear one by one. It can be very frustrating, however, when a fix of one defect creates another defect elsewhere in the game, as can often happen.

The test suite for regression testing is the list of bugs claimed to be fixed by the development team. This list, sometimes called the *knockdown list*, is ideally communicated through the bug database. When the programmer or artist fixes the defect, all they have to do is change the value of the Developer Status field to "Fixed." This allows the project manager to track the progress on a minute-to-minute basis. It also allows the lead tester to sort the regression set (by bug author or by level, for example). At a minimum, the knockdown list can take the form of a list of bug numbers sent from the development team to the lead tester.

Tip

Don't accept a build into test unless it is accompanied by a knockdown list. It is a waste of the test team's time to regress every open bug in the database every time a new build enters test.

Each tester will take the bugs they've been assigned and perform the steps in the bug write-up to verify that defect is indeed fixed. The fixes to many defects are easily verified (typos, missing features, and so on). Some defects, such as hard-to-reproduce crashes, may *seem* fixed, but the lead tester may want to err on the side of caution before he closes the bug. By flagging the defect as *verify fix*, the bug can remain in the regression set for the next build (or two), but out of the open set that the development team is still working on. Once the bug has been verified as fixed in two or three builds, the lead tester can then close the bug with more confidence.

At the end of regression testing, the lead tester and project manager can get a very good sense of how the project is progressing. A high fix rate (number of bugs closed divided by the number of bugs claimed to have been fixed) means the developers are working efficiently. A low fix rate is cause for concern. Are the programmers arbitrarily marking bugs as fixed if they think they've implemented new code that may address the defect, rather than troubleshooting the defect itself? Are the testers not writing clear bugs? Is there a version control problem? Are the test systems configured properly? While the lead tester and project manager mull over these questions, it's time for you to move on to the next step in the testing process: performing structured tests and reporting the test results.

Test "Around" the Bug

The old saying in carpentry is "measure twice, cut once." Good testers thoroughly investigate a defect before they write it up, anticipating any questions the development team may have.

Before you begin to write a defect report, ask yourself questions such as the following:

1. Is this the only location or level where the bug occurs?
2. Does the bug occur while using other characters?
3. Does the bug occur in other game modes (for example, multiplayer as well as single player, skirmish as well as campaign)?
4. Can I eliminate any steps along the path to reproducing the bug?
5. Does the bug occur across all platforms (for example, PlayStation2 and Xbox)?
6. Is the bug machine-specific (for example, does it occur only on PCs with a certain hardware configuration)?

These are the types of questions you will be asked by the lead tester, project manager, or developer. Try to develop the habit of second-guessing such questions by performing some quick additional testing before you write the bug. Test to see if the defect occurs in other areas. Test to determine whether the bug happens when you choose a different character. Test to check which other game modes contain the issue. This practice is known as testing "around" the bug.

Once you are satisfied that you have anticipated any questions the development team may ask, and you have your facts ready, you are ready to write the bug report.

Report the Results

Good bug writing is one of the most important skills a tester must learn. A defect can only be fixed if it is communicated clearly and effectively. One of the oldest jokes in software development goes something like this:

Q: How many programmers does it take to screw in a light bulb?

A: None—it's not dark where they're sitting.

Good bug report writing gets programmers to "see the light" of the bug. But programmers are by no means the only people who will read your bug. The audience may include

- The lead tester or primary tester, who may wish to review the bug before they give it an "open" status in the bug database.
- The project manager, who will read the bug and assign it to the appropriate member of the project team.
- Marketing and other business executives, who may be asked to weigh in on the possible commercial impact of fixing (or not fixing) the bug.

- Third parties, such as middleware vendors, who may be asked to review a bug that may be related to a product they supply to the project team.
- Customer service representatives, who may be asked to devise workarounds for the bug.
- Other testers, who will reproduce the steps if they are asked to verify a fix during regression testing.

Because you never know exactly who will be reading your bug report, you must always write in as clear, objective, and dispassionate a manner as possible. You can't assume that everyone reading your bug report will be as familiar with the game as you are. Testers spend more time in the game—exploring every hidden path, closely examining each asset—than almost anyone else on the entire project team. A well-written bug will give a reader who is not familiar with the game a good sense of the type and severity of defect it describes.

Just the Facts, Ma'am

The truth is that defects stress out development teams, especially during "crunch time." Each new bug added to the database means more work still has to be done. An average-sized project can have hundreds or thousands of defects reported before it is completed. Developers can feel very overwhelmed and will, in turn, get very hostile if they feel their time is being wasted by frivolous or arbitrary bugs. That's why good bug writing is fact-based and unbiased.

```
The guard's hat should be blue.
```

This is neither a defect nor a fact; it's an unsolicited and arbitrary opinion about design. There are forums for such opinions—discussions with the lead tester, team meetings, play testing feedback—but the bug database isn't one of them.

A common complaint in many games is that the AI (artificial intelligence) is somehow lacking. (AI is a catch-all term used to mean any opponents or NPCs controlled by the game code.)

```
The AI is weak.
```

This may indeed be a fact, but it is written in such a vague and general way that it is likely to be considered an opinion. A much better way to convey the same information is to isolate and describe a specific example of AI behavior and write up that specific defect. By boiling issues down to specific facts, you can turn them into defects that have a good chance of being fixed.

But before you begin to write a bug report, you have to be certain that you have all your facts.

Brief Description

Larger databases may contain two description fields: Brief Description and Full Description. The Brief Description field is used as a quick reference to identify the bug. This should not be a cute nickname, but a one-sentence description that allows team members to identify and discuss defects without having to read the longer full description each time. Think of the brief description as the headline of the defect report.

```
Crash to desktop.
```

This not a complete sentence, nor is it specific enough for a brief description. It could apply to one of dozens of defects in a database. The brief description must be brief enough to be read easily and quickly, but long enough to describe the bug.

```
The saving system is broken.
```

This is a complete sentence, but is it not specific enough. What did the tester experience? Did the game not save? Did a saved game not load? Does saving cause a crash?

```
Crash to desktop when choosing "Options" from Main Menu.
```

This is a complete sentence, and it is specific enough so that anyone reading it will have some idea of the location and severity of the defect.

```
Game crashed after I killed all the guards and doubled back through the level to get
all the pick-ups and killed the first re-spawned guard.
```

This is a run-on sentence that contains far too much detail. A good way to boil it down might be

```
Game crashed after guards respawned.
```

The TV listings in your newspaper can provide excellent examples of a brief description—they boil down an entire half-hour sitcom or two-hour movie into one or two sentences.

Tip

> Write the full description first, and then write the brief description. Spending some time polishing the full description will help you understand the most important details to include in the brief description.

Full Description

If the brief description is the headline of a bug report, the Full Description field provides the gory details. Rather than a prose discussion of the defect, the full description should be written as a series of brief instructions so that anyone can follow the steps and reproduce the bug. The steps should be written in second person imperative, as though you were telling someone what to do. The last step is a sentence (or two) describing the bad result.

```
1.  Launch the game.
2.  Watch the animated logos.  Do not press ESC to skip through them.
->  Notice the bad strobing effect at the end of the Developer logo.
```

The fewer steps, the better, and the fewer words, the better. Remember Brad Pitt's warning to Matt Damon in *Ocean's Eleven*: "Don't use seven words when four will do." Likewise, don't use seven steps when four will do. Time is a precious resource when developing a game. The less time it takes a programmer to read and understand the bug, the more time he has left over to fix it.

```
1.  Launch game.
2.  Choose Multiplayer.
3.  Choose Skirmish.
4.  Choose "Sorrowful Shoals" map.
5.  Choose two players.
6.  Start game.
```

These are very clear steps, but for the sake of brevity they should be boiled down to

```
1.  Start a two-player skirmish game on "Sorrowful Shoals."
```

Sometimes, however, you need several steps. The following bug describes a problem with a power-up called "mugging," which steals any other power-up from any other unit.

```
1.  Create a game against one human player.  Choose Serpent tribe.
2.  Send a Swordsman into a Thieves Guild to get the Mugging power-up.
3.  Have your opponent create any unit and give that unit any power-up.
4.  Have your Swordsman meet his unit somewhere neutral on the map.
5.  Activate the Mugging battle gear.
6.  Attack your opponent's unit.
->  Crash to desktop as Swordsman strikes.
```

This may seem like a lot of steps, but it is the quickest way to reproduce the bug. Every step is important to isolate the behavior of the mugging code. Even small details, like meeting in a neutral place, are important, since meeting in occupied territory might bring allied units from one side or another into the fight, and the test might then be impossible to perform.

Great Expectations

Oftentimes, the defect itself may not be obvious from the steps in the full description. Because the steps produce a result that deviates from user expectation, but does not produce a crash or other severe symptom, it is sometimes necessary to add two additional lines to your full description: Expected Result and Actual Result.

Expected Result describes the behavior that a normal player would reasonably expect from the game if the steps in the bug were followed. This expectation is based on the tester's knowledge of the design specification, the target audience, and precedents set (or broken) in other games, especially games in the same genre.

Actual Result describes the defective behavior. Here's an example:

```
1.  Create a multiplayer game.
2.  Click Game Settings.
3.  Using your mouse, click any map on the map list.  Remember the map you clicked on.
4.  Press up or down directional keys on your keyboard.
5.  Notice the highlight changes.  Highlight any other map.
6.  Click Back.
7.  Click Start Game.
Expected Result:  Game loads map you chose with the keyboard.
Actual Result:  Game loads map you chose with the mouse.
```

Although the game loaded a map, it wasn't the map the tester chose. That's a bug, albeit a subtle one.

Use the Expected/Actual Result steps sparingly. Most of the time, the defect is obvious.

```
4.  Click "Next" to continue.
Expected Result:  You continue.
Actual Result:  Game locks up.  You must reboot the console.
```

It is understood by all members of the project team that the game shouldn't crash. Don't waste time pointing out the obvious.

Things to Avoid

For the sake of clarity, effective communication, and harmony among members of the project team, try to avoid a couple of common bug-writing pitfalls: humor and jargon.

Although humor is welcome in high-stress situations, it is not welcome in the bug database. Ever. There are too many chances for misinterpretation and confusion. During crunch time tempers are short and nerves are frayed. The defect database may already be a point of contention. Don't make the problem worse with attempts at humor (even if you think your joke is hilarious).

It may seem counterintuitive to want to avoid jargon in such a specialized form of technical writing, but it is wise to do so. Although some jargon is unavoidable, and each development team quickly develops its own slang specific to the project they're working on, testers should avoid using (or misusing) too many obscure technical terms. Remember that your audience ranges from programmers to financial executives, so use plain language as much as possible.

Summary

Although testing build after build may seem repetitive, each new build provides exciting new challenges with its own successes (fixed bugs and passed tests) and shortfalls (new bugs and failed tests). The purpose of going about the testing of each build in a structured manner is to reduce waste and get the most out of the game team. Each time around, you get new build data that is used to re-plan test execution strategies and update or improve your test suites. From there, you prepare the test environment and perform a smoke test to ensure the build is functioning well enough to deploy to the entire test team. Once the test team is set loose, your top priority is typically regression testing to verify recent bug fixes. After that, you perform many other types of testing in order to find new bugs and check that old ones have not re-emerged. New defects should be reported in a clear, concise, and professional manner after an appropriate amount of investigation. Once you complete this journey, you are rewarded with the opportunity to do it all over again.

Exercises

1. Briefly describe the difference between the Expected Result and the Actual Result in a bug write up.
2. What's the purpose of regression testing?
3. Briefly describe the steps in configuration preparation.
4. What is a "knockdown list?"
5. True or False: Black box testing refers to examining the actual game code.
6. True or False: The Brief Description field of a defect report should include as much information as possible.
7. True or False: White box testing describes testing gameplay.
8. True or False: Version control should be applied only to the developers' code.
9. True or False: A "Verify Fix" status on a bug means it will remain in at least one more test cycle.

10. True or False: A tester should write as many steps as possible when reporting a bug to ensure the bug can be reliably re-created.

11. On a table next to a bed is a touch-tone telephone. Write step-by-step instructions for using that phone to dial the following number: 555-1234. Assume the person reading the instructions has never seen or used a telephone before.

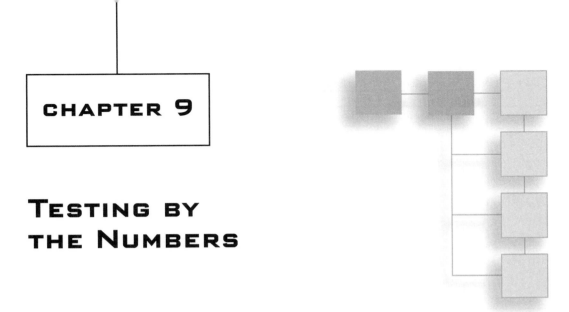

CHAPTER 9

TESTING BY THE NUMBERS

Product metrics, such as the number of defects found per line of code, tell you how fit the game code is for release. Test metrics can tell you about the effectiveness and efficiency of your testing activities and results. A few pieces of basic test data can be combined in ways that reveal important information you can use to keep testing on track while getting the most out of your tests and testers.

Testing Progress

Collecting data is important to understanding where the test team is and where they are headed in terms of meeting the needs and expectations of the overall game project. Data and charts can be collected by the test lead or the individual testers. Take responsibility for knowing how well you're doing. For example, in order to estimate the duration of the test execution for any portion of the game project, estimate the total number of tests to be performed. This number is combined with data on how many tests can be completed per staff-day of effort, how much of a tester's calendar time is actually spent on testing activities, and how many tests you expect to be redone.

Figure 9.1 provides a set of data for a test team starting to run tests against a new code release. The project manager worked with the test lead to use an estimate of 12 tests per day as the basis for projecting how long it would take to complete the testing for this release. Thirteen days into the testing, the progress lagged what had been projected, as shown in Figure 9.2. It looks like progress started to slip on the fifth day, but the team was optimistic that they could catch up. By the tenth day they seemed to have managed to steer back toward the goal, but during the last three days the team lost ground again, despite the re-assignment of some people on to and off of the team.

Date	Daily Execution		Total Execution	
	Planned	Actual	Planned	Actual
22-Dec	12	13	12	13
23-Dec	12	11	24	24
28-Dec	12	11	36	35
29-Dec	12	12	48	47
30-Dec	12	8	60	55
4-Jan	12	11	72	66
5-Jan	12	10	84	76
6-Jan	12	11	96	87
7-Jan	12	11	108	98
8-Jan	12	16	120	114
10-Jan	12	10	132	124
11-Jan	12	3	144	127
12-Jan	12	7	156	134

Figure 9.1 Planned and actual test execution progress data.

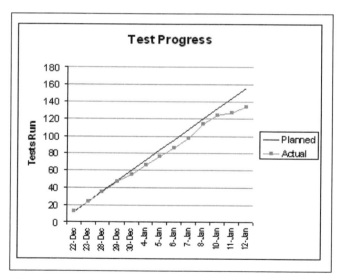

Figure 9.2 Planned and actual test execution progress graph.

To understand what is happening here, collect data for each day that a tester was available to do testing and the number of tests he or she completed each day. This information can be put into a chart, as shown in Figure 9.3. The totals show that an individual tester completes an average of about four tests a day.

DATE	TESTER					TESTER DAYS	COMPLETED TESTS
	B	C	D	K	Z		
22-Dec	*				*	2	13
23-Dec	*				*	2	11
28-Dec	*				*	2	11
29-Dec	*				*	2	12
30-Dec	*				*	2	8
4-Jan	*		*		*	3	11
5-Jan	*		*		*	3	10
6-Jan	*		*		*	3	11
7-Jan	*		*		*	3	11
8-Jan		*	*	*	*	4	16
10-Jan	*	*	*			3	10
11-Jan	*	*	*			3	3
12-Jan			*			1	7
					TOTALS	33	134
					TESTS/TESTER DAY		4.06

Figure 9.3 Test completion rate per tester per day.

Once you have the test effort data for each person and each day, you must compare the test effort people have contributed to the number of work days they were assigned to participate in system testing. Ideally, this ratio would come out to 1.00. The numbers you actually collect will give you a measurement of something you may have felt was true, but couldn't prove before: Most testers are unable to spend 100% of their time on testing. This being the case, don't plan on testers spending 100% of their time on a single task! Measurements will show you how much to expect from system testers based on various levels of participation. Some testers will be dedicated to testing as their only assignment. Others may perform a dual role, such as developer/tester or QA engineer/tester. Collect effort data for your team members that fall into each category as shown in Figure 9.4.

This data leads to a number of important points. One is that, given tester "overhead" tasks such as training, meetings, preparing for demos, and so on, a full-time tester may only be able to contribute about 75% of his or her time at best, and 50%–60% on average over the course of a long project. If you are counting on people with other responsibilities—for example, artists, developers, or QA—to help with testing, then expect only half as much participation as the full-time testers. Using the numbers in Figure 9.4, that would be about 30% of their total available time. You will need to make these measures for your own particular project.

FULL-TIME TESTERS

WEEK	1	2	3	4	5	6	7	TOTAL
TESTER DAYS	15.5	21.5	35.5	31.5	36.5	22	23.5	186
ASSIGNED DAYS	44	50	51	53	50	41	41	330

FULL-TIME TESTER AVAILABILITY 56%

PART-TIME TESTERS

WEEK	1	2	3	4	5	6	7	TOTAL
TESTER DAYS	0	0	0	18.5	18.5	6	15	58
ASSIGNED DAYS	0	0	0	49	54	53	46	202

PART-TIME TESTER AVAILABILITY 29%

CUMULATIVE

TESTER DAYS	244
ASSIGNED DAYS	532
AVAILABILITY	46%

Figure 9.4 Tester participation rate calculations.

Also, by combining the individual productivity numbers to get a team productivity number, you can see that this team performs only half as many tests as they could if they had 100% of their time to perform testing. This number can be combined with your effort estimate to give an accurate count of calendar work days remaining before testing will be finished. Using the number of 125 tests remaining, and a staff size of 11 testers, you would approximate 11 staff-days of testing remaining. However, now that you know what the team's productivity is, you divide 11 by 46% to get 24 calendar work days remaining, or nearly five "normal" work weeks. If you committed to the original, optimistic number of 11 days, there would be much gnashing of teeth when the tests weren't actually completed until three weeks after they were promised!

You need this kind of information to answer questions such as "How many people do you need to get testing done by Friday?" or "If I can get you two more testers, when can you be done?" Also burn into your mind that it's easier to stay on track by getting a little extra done day to day than trying to make up a big chunk in a panic situation (remember Rule 1…). Going back to Figure 9.1 you can see that on 8-Jan the team was only six tests behind the goal. Completing one extra test on each of the previous six work days would have had the team on goal. If you can keep short-term commitments to stay on track, you will be able to keep the long-term ones.

Testing Effectiveness

Measure your Test Effectiveness (TE) by adding up defects and dividing by the number of tests completed. This measurement not only tells you how "good" the current release is compared to previous ones, but it can also be used to predict how many defects will be found by the remaining tests for that release. For example, with 30 tests remaining and a TE of 0.06, testers should find approximately two more defects. This may be a sign to developers to delay a new code release until the two expected defects are identified, classified, and removed. An example table of TE measurements is shown in Figure 9.5. Measure TE for each release as well as for the overall project. Figure 9.6 shows a graphical view of this TE data.

Code Release	Defects		Tests Run		Defects/Test	
	New	Total	Release	Total	Release	Total
DEV1	34	34	570	570	0.060	0.060
DEV2	47	81	1230	1800	0.038	0.045
DEV3	39	120	890	2690	0.044	0.045
DEMO1	18	138	490	3180	0.037	0.043
ALPHA1	6	144	220	3400	0.027	0.042

Figure 9.5 Test Effectiveness measurements.

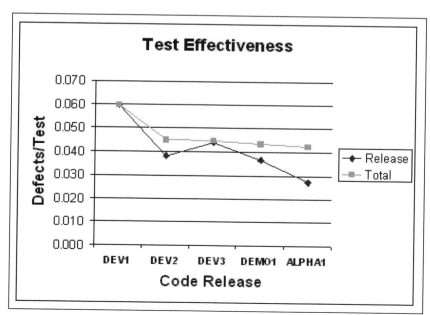

Figure 9.6 Test Effectiveness graph.

Notice how the cumulative TE reduced with each release and settled at .042. You can take this measurement one step further by using test completion and defect detection data for each tester to calculate individual TEs. Figure 9.7 shows a snapshot of tester TEs for the overall project. You can also calculate each tester's TE per release.

TESTER	B	C	D	K	Z	TOTAL
TESTS RUN	151	71	79	100	169	570
DEFECTS FOUND	9	7	6	3	9	34
DEFECTS/TEST	0.060	0.099	0.076	0.030	0.053	0.060

Figure 9.7 TE measured for individual testers.

Note that for this project, the effectiveness of each tester ranges from 0.030 to 0.099, with an average of 0.060. The effectiveness may be as much a function of the particular tests each tester was asked to perform as it is a measure of the skill of each tester. However, like the overall TE measurement, this number can be used to predict how many additional defects a particular tester may find when performing a known number of tests. For example, if tester C has 40 more tests to perform, expect her to find about four more defects.

In addition to measuring how many defects you detect (quantitative), it is important to understand the severity of defects introduced with each release (qualitative). Using a defect severity scale of 1 to 4, where 1 is the highest severity, detection of new severity 1 and 2 defects should be reduced to 0 prior to shipping the game. Severity 3 and 4 defect detection should be on a downward trend approaching 0. Figures 9.8 and 9.9 provide examples of severity data and a graph of these trends, respectively.

Take a moment to examine the graph. What do you see? Notice how the severity 3 defects dominate. They are also the only category to significantly increase after Dev1 testing, except for some extra 4s popping up in the Demo1 release. When you set a goal that does not allow any severity 2 defects to be in the shipping game, there will be a tendency to push any borderline severity 2 issues into the severity 3 category. Another explanation could be that the developers focus their efforts on the 1s and 2s so they leave the 3s alone early in the project with the intention of dealing with them later. This approach bears itself out in Figures 9.8 and 9.9, where the severity 3 defects are brought way down for the Demo1 release and continue to drop in the Alpha1 release. Once you see "what" is happening, try to understand "why" it is happening that way.

Release	Defects by Severity				
	1	2	3	4	All
Dev1	7	13	13	1	34
Dev2	4	11	30	2	47
Dev3	2	3	34	0	39
Demo1	1	2	12	3	18
Alpha1	0	0	6	0	6

Figure 9.8 Defect severity trend data.

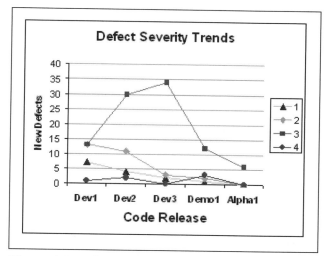

Figure 9.9 Defect severity trend graph.

Tester Performance

You can implement some other measurements to encourage testers to find defects and give them a sense of pride in their skills. One of them is the "Star Chart." This chart is posted in the testing area and shows the accomplishments of each tester according to how many defects they find of each severity. Tester names are listed down one side of the chart and each defect is indicated by a stick-on star. The star's color indicates the defect's severity. For example, you can use blue for 1, red for 2, yellow for 3, and silver for 4. Points can also be assigned to each severity (for example, A=10, B=5, C=3, D=1), and a "Testing Star" can be declared at the end of the project based on who has the most points. In my experience, this chart has led to a friendly sense of competition between testers, increased their determination to find defects, promoted tester ownership of defects, and has caused testers to pay more attention to the severity assigned to the defects they find. This approach turns testing into a game for the testers to play while they're testing games. Did you follow that? Figure 9.10 shows what a Star Chart looks like prior to adding the testers' stars.

STAR CHART FOR XYZZY	
TESTERS	STARS (Sev. 1 = BLUE, 2 = RED, 3 = YELLOW, 4 = SILVER)
B	
C	
D	
K	
Z	

Figure 9.10 Empty Star Chart.

If you're worried about testers getting into battles over defects and not finishing their assigned tests fast enough, you can create a composite measure of each tester's contribution to test execution and defects found. Add up the total number of test defects found and calculate a percentage for each tester based on how many they found divided by the project total. Then do the same for tests run. You can add these two numbers for each tester. Whoever has the highest total is the "Best Tester" for the project. This may or may not turn out to be the same person who becomes the Testing Star.

Here's how this works for testers B, C, D, K, and Z for the Dev1 release:

Tester B executed 151 of the team's 570 Dev1 tests. This comes out to 26.5%. B has also found 9 of the 34 Dev1 defects, which is also 26.5%. B's composite rating is 53.

Tester C ran 71 of the 570 tests, which is 12.5%. C found 7 out of the 34 total defects in Dev1, which is 20.5%. C's rating is 33.

Tester D ran 79 tests, which is approximately 14% of the total. D also found 6 defects, which is about 17.5% of the total. D gets a rating of 31.5.

Tester K ran 100 tests and found 3 defects. These represent 17.5% of the test total and about 9% of the defect total. K has a 26.5 rating.

Tester Z ran 169 tests, which is about 29.5% of the 570 total. Z found 9 defects, which is 26.5% of that total. Z's total rating is 56.

Tester Z has earned the title of "Best Tester."

Note

When you have someone on your team who keeps winning these awards, take her to lunch and find out what she is doing so you can win some too!

Be careful to use this system for good and not for evil. Running more tests or claiming credit for new defects should not come at the expense of other people or the good of the overall project. You could add in factors to give more weight to higher-severity defects to discourage testers from spending all their time chasing and reporting low-severity defects that won't contribute as much to the game as a few very important high-severity defects.

Use this system to encourage and exhibit positive test behaviors. Remind your team (and yourself!) that some time spent automating tests could have a lot of payback in terms of test execution. Likewise, spending a little time up front to design your tests before you run off and start banging on the game controller will probably lead you to more defects. You will learn more about these strategies and techniques as you proceed to Parts IV and V of this book.

Summary

This chapter introduced you to a number of metrics you can collect to track and improve testing results. Each metric from this chapter is listed here, along with the raw data you need to collect for each in parentheses:

- Test Progress Chart (# of tests completed by team each day, # of tests required each day)
- Test Completed/Days of Effort (# of tests completed, # days of test effort for each tester)
- Test Participation (# of days of effort for each tester, # of days each tester assigned to test)
- Test Effectiveness (# of defects, # of tests: for each release and/or tester)
- Defect Severity Profile (# of defects of each severity for each release)

- Star Chart (# of defects of each severity for each tester)
- Testing Star (# of defects of each severity for each tester, point value of each severity)
- Best Tester (# of tests per tester, # of total tests, # of defects per tester, # of total defects)

Testers or test leads can use these metrics to aid in planning, predicting, and performing game testing activities. Then you will be *testing by the numbers*.

Exercises

1. How does the data in Figure 9.3 explain what is happening on the graph in Figure 9.2?

2. How many testers do you need to add to the project represented in Figures 9.1 and 9.2 in order to bring the test execution back on plan in the next 10 working days? The testers will begin work the very next day that is plotted on the graph.

3. Tester C has the best TE as shown in Figure 9.7, but did not turn out to be the "Best Tester." Explain how this happened.

4. You are tester X working on the project represented in Figure 9.7. If you have run 130 tests, how many defects did you need to find in order to become the "Best Tester?"

5. Describe three positive and three negative aspects of measuring the participation and effectiveness of individual testers. Do not include any aspects already discussed in this chapter.

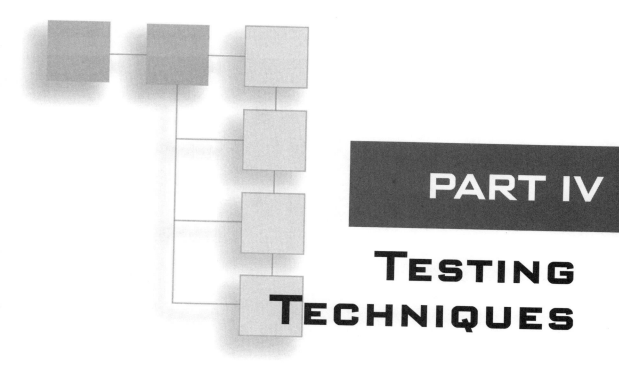

PART IV

TESTING TECHNIQUES

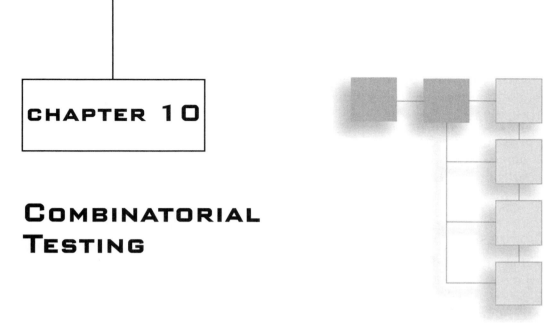

CHAPTER 10

COMBINATORIAL TESTING

Like Goldilocks, testers and project managers are continually struggling with the issue of how much testing is too little, too much, or just right. Game quality has to be good enough for consumers but testing can't go on forever if the game is going to hit its release date. Trying to test every possible combination of game event, configuration, function, and options is neither practical nor economical under these circumstances. Taking shortcuts or skipping some testing is risky business.

Pairwise combinatorial testing is a way to find defects and gain confidence in the game software while keeping the test sets small relative to the amount of functionality they cover. "Pairwise" combination means that each value you use for testing needs to be combined at least once with each other value of the remaining parameters.

Parameters

Parameters are the individual elements of the game that you want to include in your combinatorial tests. You can find test parameters by looking at various types of game elements, functions, and choices such as:

- Game events
- Game settings
- Gameplay options
- Hardware configurations
- Character attributes
- Customization choices

The test you create can be *homogenous*—designed to test combinations of parameters of the same type, or *heterogeneous*—designed to test more than one type of parameter in the same table.

For example, testing choices from a Game Options screen for their effect on gameplay is done with a homogenous combinatorial table. If you go through various menus to select different characters, equipment, and options to use for a particular mission, then that results in a heterogeneous table.

Values

Values are the individual choices that are possible for each parameter. Values could be entered as a number, entered as text, or chosen from a list. There are many choices for a gamer to make, but do they all need to be considered in your testing? That is, does every single value or choice have the same weight or probability of revealing a defect, or can you reduce the number of values you test without impacting your test's ability to reveal the defects in the game?

Defaults

Consider whether or not default values should be used in your tests. These are the settings and values that you get if you don't select anything special and just start playing the game as installed. You might also want to consider the first item in any list—say, a choice of hairstyle for your character—to be a kind of default value, since if you want to start playing as quickly as possible and bang on the Select key to get through all of the mandatory choices, these are the values you will be using.

If the combinatorial testing is the only testing that will be using these parameters, then the defaults should be included. They are the values that will be most often used, so you don't want to let bugs escape that will affect nearly everyone who plays the game.

On the other hand, if combinatorial testing is going to be a complement to other types of testing, then you can reduce your test burden by leaving the default values out of your tables. This strategy relies on the fact that the defaults will be used so often that you can expect them to show up in the other testing being done for the game. If you consider leaving these values out, get in touch with the other groups or people who are testing to make sure they do plan on using default values. If you have a test plan for your game, use it to document which sets of tests will incorporate default values and which ones will not.

Enumerations

Many choices in a game are made from a set of distinct values or options that do not have any particular numerical or sequential relationship to one another. Choosing which car to drive, or which baseball team to play, or which fighter to use are examples of this kind of choice.

Regardless of the number of unique choices (team, car, fighter, weapon, song, hairstyle, and so on), each one should be represented somewhere in your tests. It's easy to find bugs that happen independent of which particular choice is made. The ones that do escape tend to only happen for a very few of the choices.

Ranges

Many of the game options and choices require the player to pick a number from a range or list. This could be done by directly entering a number or scrolling through a list to make a selection. For each range of numbers, three particular values tend to have special defect-revealing properties: Zero, Minimum, and Maximum.

Anytime a zero (0) is a presented as a possible choice or entry, it should be included in testing. This is partly due to the unique or ambiguous way that the value 0 might affect the game source code. Here is a partial list of possible unintended zero-induced effects:

- A loop may prematurely exit or may always do something once before checking for zero
- Confusion between starting loop counts at 0 or 1
- Confusion with arrays or lists starting at index 0 or 1
- 0 is often used to represent special meaning, such as to indicate an infinite timer or that an error has occurred
- 0 is the same value as the string termination (NULL) character in C
- 0 is the same value as the logical (Boolean) False value in C

Minimum values are also a good source of defects. They can be applied to numerical parameters or list choices. Look for the opportunity to use minimum values with parameters related to the following:

- Time
- Distance
- Speed
- Quantity
- Size
- Bet amount

For example, using a minimum time may not allow certain effects to be completed once they are started, or may make certain goals unachievable.

Maximum values can also cause undesirable side effects. They are especially important to use where they place an extra burden of time or skill for the tester to reach the maximum value. Both developers and testers will tend to pass over these values in favor of "easier" testing.

Use maximum values for the same minimum value parameter categories in the preceding list. In addition to testing in-game elements, be sure to also include tests for the maximum number of players, maximum number of saved files, and maximum storage (disk, cartridge, and so on) space.

Boundaries

When a child (or even an adult) colors in a page of a coloring book, we judge how they do based on how well they stay within the lines. Likewise, it is the responsibility of the game tester to check the game software around its boundaries. Game behavior that does not "stay within the lines" leads to defects.

Some of the boundaries to test may be physically rendered in the game space, such as the following:

- Town, realm, or city borders
- Goal lines, sidelines, foul lines, and end lines on a sports field or court
- Mission or race waypoints
- Start and finish lines
- Portal entrances and exits

Other boundaries are not physical. These can include:

- Mission, game, or match timers
- The speed that a character or vehicle can achieve
- The distance a projectile can travel
- The distance at which graphic elements become visible, transparent, or invisible

Dig deep into the rules of the game to identify hidden or implied boundaries.

For example, in football there are rules and activities tied in with the timing of the game. The timing of a football game is broken into four quarters of equal length, with a halftime pause in the game that occurs after the end of the second quarter. The game ends if one team has more points than another at the end of the fourth quarter. With two minutes left in each half, the referee stops the clock for the Two Minute Warning.

To test a football game, two-minute quarters are a good boundary value to see if the 2nd and 4th quarters of the game each start normally or with the special Two Minute Warning. A three-minute duration may also be interesting because it is the smallest duration that would have a period of play prior to the Two Minute Warning.

Another example is related to The CRIB feature in *ESPN NFL 2K5*, which awards players points for accomplishments during a single game, during the course of a season, and over the course of their career. Some of these accomplishments will not be rewarded if the game duration is less than five minutes and greater than eight minutes. This creates two more quarter-length boundary values of interest.

Constructing Tables

To see how a combinatorial table is constructed, start with a simple table using parameters that have only two possible values. Games are full of these kinds of parameters, providing choices such as On or Off, Male or Female, Mario or Luigi, or Night or Day. This test combines character attributes for a Jedi character in a *Star Wars* game to test their effects on combat animations and damage calculations. The three test parameters are character Gender (Male or Female), whether the character uses a one-handed (1H) or two-handed (2H) Light Saber, and whether the character follows the Light side or the Dark side of the Force.

The table starts with the first two parameters arranged in the first two columns so that they cover all four possible combinations, as shown in Figure 10.1.

To construct a full combinatorial table, repeat each of the Gender and Light Saber pairs, and then combine each with the two possible Force values. When the Light and Dark "Force" choices are added in this way, the size of the table—determined by the number of rows—doubles, as shown in Figure 10.2.

Gender	Light Saber
Male	1H
Male	2H
Female	1H
Female	2H

Figure 10.1 First two columns of Jedi combat test.

Gender	Light Saber	Force
Male	1H	Light
Male	1H	Dark
Male	2H	Light
Male	2H	Dark
Female	1H	Light
Female	1H	Dark
Female	2H	Light
Female	2H	Dark

Figure 10.2 Complete three-way combinatorial table for Jedi combat test.

For a pairwise combinatorial table, it's only necessary to combine each value of every parameter with each value of every other parameter at least once somewhere in the table. A pair that is represented in the table is said to be "satisfied," while a pair not represented in the table is "unsatisfied." The following twelve pairings must be satisfied for the Jedi combat table:

Male Gender paired with each Light Saber choice (1H, 2H)

Female Gender paired with each Light Saber choice (1H, 2H)

Male Gender paired with each Force choice (Light, Dark)

Female Gender paired with each Force choice (Light, Dark)

One-Handed (1H) Light Saber paired with each Force choice (Light, Dark)

Two-Handed (2H) Light Saber paired with each Force choice (Light, Dark)

To make the pairwise version, rebuild from the table in Figure 10.1 by adding a column for the Force values. Next, enter the Light and Dark choices for the Male character, as shown in Figure 10.3.

Adding the "Dark" value to the first Female row will complete the pairwise criteria for the "1H" Light Saber value, as illustrated in Figure 10.4.

Gender	Light Saber	Force
Male	1H	**Light**
Male	2H	**Dark**
Female	1H	
Female	2H	

Figure 10.3 Adding Force choices for the Male rows.

Gender	Light Saber	Force
Male	**1H**	**Light**
Male	2H	Dark
Female	**1H**	**Dark**
Female	2H	

Figure 10.4 Adding the first Force choice for the Female character tests.

Finally, fill in the Light value in the second Female row to get the table in Figure 10.5 that satisfies the pairwise criteria for all parameters. In this case, it ends up being the same size as the two-parameter table. Including the Force parameter in these tests is free in terms of the resulting number of test cases. In many cases, pairwise combinatorial tables let you add complexity and coverage without increasing the number of tests you will need to run. This will not always be true; sometimes you will need a few more tests as you continue to add parameters to the table. However, the growth of the pairwise table will be much slower than full combinatorial tables for the same set of parameters and their values.

In this simple example, the pairwise technique has cut the number of required tests in half as compared to creating every mathematically possible combination of all of the parameters of interest. This technique and its benefits are not limited to tables with two-value parameters. Parameters with three or more choices can be efficiently combined with other parameters of any dimension. When it makes sense, incorporate more parameters to make your tables more efficient.

Gender	Light Saber	Force
Male	1H	Light
Male	2H	Dark
Female	1H	Dark
Female	2H	Light

Figure 10.5 Completed pairwise combinatorial table for three Jedi combat parameters.

The number of choices (values) tested for a given parameter is referred to as its *dimension*. Tables are characterized by the dimensions of each parameter. They can be written in descending order, with a superscript to indicate the number of parameters of each dimension. In this way, the Jedi combat table completed in Figure 10.5 is described as a 2^3 table. A table with one parameter of three values, two parameters of four values, and three parameters of two values is described as a $4^2 3^1 2^3$. Another way to describe the characteristics of the table is to list the parameter dimensions individually in descending order with a dash in between each value. Using this notation, the Jedi combat table is a 2-2-2 table, and the second example mentioned above is described as 4-4-3-2-2-2. You can see how the second notation takes up a lot of space when there are a lot of parameters. Use whichever one works best for you.

Create pairwise tables of any size for your game tests using the following short and simple process. These steps may not always produce the optimum (smallest possible) size table, but you will still get an efficient table.

1. Choose the parameter with the highest dimension.
2. Create the first column by listing each test value for the first parameter N times, where N is the dimension of the next-highest dimension parameter.
3. Start populating the next column by listing the test values for the next parameter.
4. For each remaining row in the table, enter the parameter value in the new column that provides the greatest number of new pairs with respect to all of the preceding parameters entered in the table. If no such value can be found, alter one of the values previously entered for this column and resume this step.

5. If there are unsatisfied pairs in the table, create new rows and fill in the values necessary to create one of the required pairs. If all pairs are satisfied, then go back to step 3.

6. Add more unsatisfied pairs using empty spots in the table to create the most new pairs. Go back to step 5.

7. Fill in empty cells with any one of the values for the corresponding column (parameter).

The next example is a little more complicated than the previous one. Use the preceding process to complete a pairwise combinatorial table for some of the *NFL 2K5* Game Options, as shown in Figure 10.6.

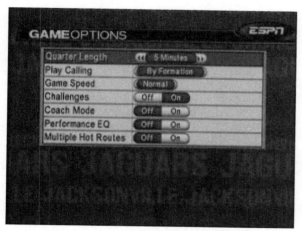

Figure 10.6 *ESPN NFL 2K5* Game Options screen.

Quarter Length is selectable from 1 to 15 minutes, with 5 as the default. You will use 1, 5, and 15 in your table. Play Calling choices are By Package, By Formation, and Let Coach Pick. Game Speed choices are Slow, Normal, and Fast. Three other options—Challenges, Coach Mode, and Multiple Hot Routes—all have the choice of being either On or Off. The Performance EQ option is not included in this example. As a result, you will create a $3^3 2^3$ table consisting of three parameters with three choices: Quarter Length, Play Calling, Game Speed, and three parameters with two choices: Challenges, Coach Mode, and Multiple Hot Routes.

If you aren't familiar with the game or the detailed rules of football, that doesn't matter right now. You just need to be able to understand and follow the seven steps previously listed.

Begin the process with steps 1 and 2 and list the Quarter Length values three times in the first column of the table. This is because Quarter Length is one of the parameters with the highest dimension (3). One of the parameters with the next highest dimension is Play Calling, which also has a dimension of three.

Next, apply step 3 and put each of the three Play Calling values in the first three rows of column 2. Figure 10.7 shows what the table looks like at this point.

Apply step 4 to continue filling in the next column. Starting with the fourth row, enter a Play Calling parameter that creates the most number of new pairs. Because this is only the second column, you can only create one new pair. "Package" Play Calling has already been paired with "1 min" Quarter Length, so you can put "Formation" in row 4 to create a new pair. Likewise, "Coach" and "Package" can go in rows 5 and 6 to create new pairs with "5 min" and "15 min," respectively. Figure 10.8 shows the resulting table at this point in the process.

Continue with step 4 to complete the Play Calling column. At the seventh row, enter a Play Calling parameter that creates a new pair with the "1 min" Quarter Length value. "Package" (row 1) and "Formation" (row 4) have already been paired, so "Coach" is the correct value for this row. By the same process, "Package" goes in row 8 and "Formation" in row 9. Figure 10.9 shows the first two columns completed in this manner.

Quarter Length	Play Calling
1 min	Package
5 min	Formation
15 min	Coach
1 min	
5 min	
15 min	
1 min	
5 min	
15 min	

Figure 10.7 Starting the *NFL 2K5* Game Options test table.

Quarter Length	Play Calling
1 min	Package
5 min	Formation
15 min	Coach
1 min	Formation
5 min	Coach
15 min	Package
1 min	
5 min	
15 min	

Figure 10.8 Adding the second set of Play Calling values.

Quarter Length	Play Calling
1 min	Package
5 min	Formation
15 min	Coach
1 min	Formation
5 min	Coach
15 min	Package
1 min	Coach
5 min	Package
15 min	Formation

Figure 10.9 Completing the Play Calling column.

Applying step 5, check that all of the pairs required for the first three columns are satisfied:

Quarter Length = "1 min" is paired with "Package" (row 1), "Formation" (row 4), and "Coach" (row 7).

Quarter Length = "5 min" is paired with "Package" (row 8), "Formation" (row 2), and "Coach" (row 5).

Quarter Length = "15 min" is paired with "Package" (row 6), "Formation" (row 9), and "Coach" (row 3).

Since all of the pairs required for the first two columns are represented in the table, step 5 sends us back to step 3 to continue the process with the Game Speed option and its three test values. Applying step 3, list the "Slow," "Normal," and "Fast" Game Speed values at the top of the third column, as shown in Figure 10.10.

Quarter Length	Play Calling	Game Speed
1 min	Package	Slow
5 min	Formation	Normal
15 min	Coach	Fast
1 min	Formation	
5 min	Coach	
15 min	Package	
1 min	Coach	
5 min	Package	
15 min	Formation	

Figure 10.10 Starting the Game Speed column.

Proceed with step 4 to add the Game Speed value that creates the most pairs for row 4 ("1 min" and "Formation"). "Slow" is already paired with "1 min" in row 1 and "Normal" is already paired with "Formation" in row 2, so "Fast" is the correct entry for this row. In the same manner, "Slow" creates two new pairs in row 5, and "Normal" creates two new pairs in row 6. Figure 10.11 shows what the test table looks like at this point.

Again, continue with step 4 to complete the Game Speed column. "Normal" produces two new pairs in row 7, "Fast" in row 8, and "Slow in row 9. Figure 10.12 shows the completed Game Speed column.

Quarter Length	Play Calling	Game Speed
1 min	Package	Slow
5 min	Formation	Normal
15 min	Coach	Fast
1 min	**Formation**	**Fast**
5 min	**Coach**	**Slow**
15 min	**Package**	**Normal**
1 min	Coach	
5 min	Package	
15 min	Formation	

Figure 10.11 Adding the second set of Game Speed values.

Quarter Length	Play Calling	Game Speed
1 min	Package	Slow
5 min	Formation	Normal
15 min	Coach	Fast
1 min	Formation	Fast
5 min	Coach	Slow
15 min	Package	Normal
1 min	**Coach**	**Normal**
5 min	**Package**	**Fast**
15 min	**Formation**	**Slow**

Figure 10.12 Completing the Game Speed column.

It's time again to check that all the required pairs are satisfied. Because the first two columns have been previously verified, there's no need to check them again. Check the new Game Speed column against all of its predecessors, as follows:

Quarter Length = "1 min" is paired with "Slow" (row 1), "Normal" (row 7), and "Fast" (row 4).

Quarter Length = "5 min" is paired with "Slow" (row 5), "Normal" (row 2), and "Fast" (row 8).

Quarter Length = "15 min" is paired with "Slow" (row 9), "Normal" (row 6), and "Fast" (row 3).

Play Calling = "Package" is paired with "Slow" (row 1), "Normal" (row 6), and "Fast" (row 8).

Play Calling = "Formation" is paired with "Slow" (row 9), "Normal" (row 2), and "Fast" (row 4).

Play Calling = "Coach" is paired with "Slow" (row 5), "Normal" (row 7), and "Fast" (row 3).

With all of the required pairs satisfied at this point, step 5 sends you back to step 3 to add the Challenges parameter. Figure 10.13 shows the two Challenges test values added to the top of the fourth column.

Apply step 4 and add the Challenges value in row 3 ("15 min", "Coach," and "Fast") that creates the most pairs with column 4. Either "Yes" or "No" will create a new pair with all three of the other values in this row. For this exercise, choose "Yes" for row 3. Continue from there and add the right values for rows 4 through 6. A "Yes" in row 4 would only create one new pair with "Formation" so "No" is the right value to put here, creating pairs with "1 min" and "Fast." Rows 5 and 6 are populated with "No" to create two new pairs in each of these rows as well. Figure 10.14 shows the table with "Yes" chosen for row 3, and the subsequent values for rows 4, 5, and 6.

Quarter Length	Play Calling	Game Speed	Challenges
1 min	Package	Slow	Yes
5 min	Formation	Normal	No
15 min	Coach	Fast	
1 min	Formation	Fast	
5 min	Coach	Slow	
15 min	Package	Normal	
1 min	Coach	Normal	
5 min	Package	Fast	
15 min	Formation	Slow	

Figure 10.13 Starting the Challenges column.

Quarter Length	Play Calling	Game Speed	Challenges
1 min	Package	Slow	Yes
5 min	Formation	Normal	No
15 min	**Coach**	**Fast**	**Yes**
1 min	Formation	**Fast**	**No**
5 min	**Coach**	**Slow**	**No**
15 min	**Package**	Normal	**No**
1 min	Coach	Normal	
5 min	Package	Fast	
15 min	Formation	Slow	

Figure 10.14 Adding the second set of Challenges values.

Now choose the right values for the remaining rows. A "No" in row 7 does not create any new pairs, since "1 min" is already paired with "No" in row 4 and "Coach" is already paired with "No" in row 6. "Yes" in this row does create a new pair with "Normal," so it is the only correct choice. Rows 8 and 9 must also be populated with "Yes" to create new pairs with "5 min" and "Formation," respectively. Figure 10.15 shows the completed Challenges column.

Quarter Length	Play Calling	Game Speed	Chal-lenges
1 min	Package	Slow	Yes
5 min	Formation	Normal	No
15 min	Coach	Fast	Yes
1 min	Formation	Fast	No
5 min	Coach	Slow	No
15 min	Package	Normal	No
1 min	Coach	**Normal**	**Yes**
5 min	Package	Fast	**Yes**
15 min	**Formation**	Slow	**Yes**

Figure 10.15 Completing the Challenges column.

Now check that all the required pairs for the Challenges column are satisfied:

Quarter Length = "1 min" is paired with "Yes" (rows 1, 7) and "No" (row 4).

Quarter Length = "5 min" is paired with "Yes" (row 8) and "No" (rows 2, 5).

Quarter Length = "15 min" is paired with "Yes" (rows 3, 9) and "No" (row 6).

Play Calling = "Package" is paired with "Yes" (rows 1, 8) and "No" (row 6).

Play Calling = "Formation" is paired with "Yes" (row 9) and "No" (rows 2, 4).

Play Calling = "Coach" is paired with "Yes" (rows 3, 7) and "No" (row 5).

Game Speed = "Slow" is paired with "Yes" (rows 1, 9) and "No" (row 5).

Game Speed = "Normal" is paired with "Yes" (row 7) and "No" (rows 2, 6).

Game Speed = "Fast" is paired with "Yes" (rows 3, 8) and "No" (row 4).

So far, so good! Having satisfied all of the pairs required by the Challenges column, go back again to step 3 to continue with the Coach Mode option. Add the "Yes" and "No" Coach Mode values to the top of the fifth column, as shown in Figure 10.16.

Step 4 requires the value in column 5 that creates the most for row 3. Only "No" creates a new pair with the four other values in this row ("15 min," "Coach," "Fast," and "Yes"). Repeat for row 4 and choose "Yes," which creates three new pairs ("Formation," "Fast," and "No"), while "No" only

Quarter Length	Play Calling	Game Speed	Chal-lenges	Coach Mode
1 min	Package	Slow	Yes	Yes
5 min	Formation	Normal	No	No
15 min	Coach	Fast	Yes	
1 min	Formation	Fast	No	
5 min	Coach	Slow	No	
15 min	Package	Normal	No	
1 min	Coach	Normal	Yes	
5 min	Package	Fast	Yes	
15 min	Formation	Slow	Yes	

Figure 10.16 Starting the Coach Mode column.

provides one new pair with "1 min." Populating rows 5 and 6 with "Yes" creates two new pairs in each of these rows, while "No" would only add one new pair in each case. Figure 10.17 shows the table with "No" chosen for Coach Mode in row 3, and "Yes" for rows 4, 5, and 6.

A "No" in the remaining rows produces a new pair for each: "1 min," "Package," and "Slow." Figure 10.18 shows the completed Coach Mode column.

It's time again to check that all the required pairs for the new column are satisfied:

Quarter Length = "1 min" is paired with "Yes" (rows 1, 4) and "No" (row 7).
Quarter Length = "5 min" is paired with "Yes" (row 5) and "No" (rows 2, 8).
Quarter Length = "15 min" is paired with "Yes" (row 6) and "No" (rows 3, 9).
Play Calling = "Package" is paired with "Yes" (rows 1, 6) and "No" (row 8).
Play Calling = "Formation" is paired with "Yes" (row 4) and "No" (rows 2, 9).
Play Calling = "Coach" is paired with "Yes" (row 5) and "No" (rows 3, 7).
Game Speed = "Slow" is paired with "Yes" (rows 1, 5) and "No" (row 9).
Game Speed = "Normal" is paired with "Yes" (row 6) and "No" (rows 2, 7).
Game Speed = "Fast" is paired with "Yes" (row 4) and "No" (rows 3, 8).
Challenges = "Yes" is paired with "Yes" (row 1) and "No" (rows 3, 7, 8, 9).
Challenges = "No" is paired with "Yes" (rows 4, 5, 6) and "No" (row 2).

Quarter Length	Play Calling	Game Speed	Chal- lenges	Coach Mode
1 min	Package	Slow	Yes	Yes
5 min	Formation	Normal	No	No
15 min	**Coach**	**Fast**	**Yes**	**No**
1 min	**Formation**	**Fast**	**No**	**Yes**
5 min	**Coach**	Slow	No	**Yes**
15 min	Package	**Normal**	No	**Yes**
1 min	Coach	Normal	Yes	
5 min	Package	Fast	Yes	
15 min	Formation	Slow	Yes	

Figure 10.17 Adding to the Coach Mode column.

Quarter Length	Play Calling	Game Speed	Chal- lenges	Coach Mode
1 min	Package	Slow	Yes	Yes
5 min	Formation	Normal	No	No
15 min	Coach	Fast	Yes	No
1 min	Formation	Fast	No	Yes
5 min	Coach	Slow	No	Yes
15 min	Package	Normal	No	Yes
1 min	Coach	Normal	Yes	**No**
5 min	**Package**	Fast	Yes	**No**
15 min	Formation	**Slow**	Yes	**No**

Figure 10.18 Completing the Coach Mode column.

This confirms that the pairs required for the Coach Mode column are all satisfied. The process sends you back to step 3 to pair the Multiple Hot Routes values, which will be placed in the table's "Multiple Routes" column. Add the "Yes" and "No" values to the top of the this column, as shown in Figure 10.19.

Quarter Length	Play Calling	Game Speed	Chal- lenges	Coach Mode	Multiple Routes
1 min	Package	Slow	Yes	Yes	Yes
5 min	Formation	Normal	No	No	No
15 min	Coach	Fast	Yes	No	
1 min	Formation	Fast	No	Yes	
5 min	Coach	Slow	No	Yes	
15 min	Package	Normal	No	Yes	
1 min	Coach	Normal	Yes	No	
5 min	Package	Fast	Yes	No	
15 min	Formation	Slow	Yes	No	

Figure 10.19 Starting the Multiple Routes column.

As you proceed from here, something new happens. Either of the Multiple Routes values added to row 3 creates four new pairs, so neither value can be selected. A "Yes" creates new pairs with "15 min," "Coach," "Fast," and "No" (Coach Mode), while a "No" creates new pairs with "15 min," "Coach," "Fast," and "Yes" (Challenges). As you go through the table, you will find that no preferred value can be found for any of the remaining rows. Don't trust me on this (remember Rule 2?)—check for yourself! According to step 4, one of the Multiple Routes values in the first two rows should be changed. Figure 10.20 shows the updated table with the second Multiple Routes value changed to "Yes."

Quarter Length	Play Calling	Game Speed	Chal- lenges	Coach Mode	Multiple Routes
1 min	Package	Slow	Yes	Yes	Yes
5 min	Formation	Normal	No	No	Yes
15 min	Coach	Fast	Yes	No	
1 min	Formation	Fast	No	Yes	
5 min	Coach	Slow	No	Yes	
15 min	Package	Normal	No	Yes	
1 min	Coach	Normal	Yes	No	
5 min	Package	Fast	Yes	No	
15 min	Formation	Slow	Yes	No	

Figure 10.20 Restarting the Multiple Routes column.

Continue to step 4 from this point and see that there are now clear choices for the remaining rows. A "No" in row 3 provides new pairs with all of the first five columns, versus only four new pairs that would be provided by a "Yes." Another "No" in row 4 provides four new pairs versus three from using "No," and rows 5 and 6 get two new pairs from a "No" versus only one from a "Yes." Figure 10.21 shows how the table looks with these values filled in.

Quarter Length	Play Calling	Game Speed	Chal-lenges	Coach Mode	Multiple Routes
1 min	Package	Slow	Yes	Yes	Yes
5 min	Formation	Normal	No	No	Yes
15 min	**Coach**	**Fast**	**Yes**	**No**	**No**
1 min	**Formation**	Fast	**No**	**Yes**	**No**
5 min	Coach	**Slow**	No	Yes	**No**
15 min	**Package**	**Normal**	No	Yes	**No**
1 min	Coach	Normal	Yes	No	
5 min	Package	Fast	Yes	No	
15 min	Formation	Slow	Yes	No	

Figure 10.21 Adding to the Multiple Routes column.

Complete the final three values for the table in the same manner. "Yes" is the only value that produces a new pair in each of these rows. The completed table is shown in Figure 10.22.

Quarter Length	Play Calling	Game Speed	Chal-lenges	Coach Mode	Multiple Routes
1 min	Package	Slow	Yes	Yes	Yes
5 min	Formation	Normal	No	No	Yes
15 min	Coach	Fast	Yes	No	No
1 min	Formation	Fast	No	Yes	No
5 min	Coach	Slow	No	Yes	No
15 min	Package	Normal	No	Yes	No
1 min	**Coach**	Normal	Yes	No	**Yes**
5 min	Package	**Fast**	Yes	No	**Yes**
15 min	Formation	Slow	Yes	No	**Yes**

Figure 10.22 The completed Game Options test table.

Now, for perhaps the last time, check that all the required pairs for the Multiple Routes column are satisfied:

Quarter Length = "1 min" is paired with "Yes" (rows 1, 7) and "No" (row 4).

Quarter Length = "5 min" is paired with "Yes" (row 2) and "No" (rows 5, 8).

Quarter Length = "15 min" is paired with "Yes" (row 9) and "No" (rows 3, 6).

Play Calling = "Package" is paired with "Yes" (rows 1, 8) and "No" (row 6).

Play Calling = "Formation" is paired with "Yes" (rows 2, 9) and "No" (row 4).

Play Calling = "Coach" is paired with "Yes" (row 7) and "No" (rows 3, 5).

Game Speed = "Slow" is paired with "Yes" (rows 1, 9) and "No" (row 5).

Game Speed = "Normal" is paired with "Yes" (rows 2, 7) and "No" (row 6).

Game Speed = "Fast" is paired with "Yes" (row 8) and "No" (rows 3, 4).

Challenges = "Yes" is paired with "Yes" (rows 1, 7, 8, 9) and "No" (row 3).

Challenges = "No" is paired with "Yes" (row 2) and "No" (rows 4, 5, 6).

Coach Mode = "Yes" is paired with "Yes" (row 1) and "No" (rows 4, 5, 6).

Coach Mode = "No" is paired with "Yes" (rows 2, 7, 8, 9) and "No" (row 3).

Well done! By creating a pairwise combinatorial table, you developed nine tests that can test this set of parameters and values comprising 216 possible mathematical combinations (3*3*3*2*2*2). It was certainly worth the effort to create the table in order to save 207 test cases! Also note that for this table you didn't have to resort to steps 6 and 7. That won't be true in every case, so don't rule it out for the future.

Now you are ready to test the game using the combinations in the table and check for any irregularities or discrepancies with what you expect to happen. Create test tables as early as possible, for example by using information provided in the design document way before any working code is produced. Check any available documentation to see if there is a clear definition of what should happen for each of your combinations. That will equip you to raise questions about the game that may not have been considered. This is an easy way to prevent bugs and improve gameplay.

A second approach is to ask people involved with code or requirements "What happens if…" and read your combinations. You may be surprised how many times you will get an answer like "I don't know" or "I'll have to check and get back with you." This is a much more economic alternative to finding surprises late in the project. It is also much more likely that your issues will be fixed, or at least considered, by the time the code is written.

Don't just check for immediate or near-term effects of your combinatorial tests. It's important to make sure that a menu selection is available or a button performs its function when pressed, but mid-term and far-term effects can lock up or spoil the game down the road. Here are some of these effects to consider:

- ☐ Does my game or session end properly?
- ☐ Do achievements get recorded properly?
- ☐ Can I progress to appropriate parts of the game or story?
- ☐ Did actions taken in the game get properly counted toward season/career accomplishments and records?
- ☐ Can I properly start and play a new session?
- ☐ Can I store and retrieve sessions or files?

Here are some of the observations you might make from running the *NFL 2K5* Game Options tests you completed in Figure 10.22:

- ▪ Playing in Coach Mode prevents the user from selecting or controlling any of the players during the game. With that mode on, what is the function of the Multiple Hot Routes choice, since the player is prevented from assigning any Hot Routes? Maybe this relationship could be made clear to the user by "graying out" the Multiple Hot Routes choices if Coach Mode is set to "Yes."
- ▪ Normally, the A button (on Xbox) is used to change player selection and skip over in-game events such as timeouts. In Coach Mode, some of the A button actions, like active player selection, are blocked. As a side effect, Coach Mode prevents the user from interrupting timeouts. You end up waiting approximately 90 seconds for the timeout to expire before gameplay resumes.
- ▪ According to NFL rules and the game's own documentation, coaches should not be allowed to challenge plays in the last two minutes of the half. If this is literally applied, then no coaches' challenges should be possible at all in a game where each quarter is only one minute long. However, *NFL 2K5* does permit coaches to challenge plays during the 1st and 3rd quarters of the game when Quarter Length = 1 minute.
- ▪ One of the features of *NFL 2K5* is to provide Crib Points for various accomplishments during the game and one of the rewards is 10 points for every hour of gameplay. When playing with Quarter Length = 15 minutes, the actual gameplay time (four quarters) takes more than 1 hour. During the game you will get pop-up notifications of a 10-point crib reward. This can happen two or three times depending on the pace you play. Once the game ends, the summary of Crib Points earned during that game shows that the 10-point game time award was only counted once.

Combinatorial Templates

Some pre-constructed tables are included in Appendix C and on the CD-ROM you got with this book. You can use them by substituting the names and values of the parameters you want to test for the entries in the template. This will be a fast way to produce tables of fewer than 10 tests without having to develop them from scratch and then verify that all of the necessary pairs are covered. Wherever an "*" appears after a letter in the template, such as B*, that means you can substitute any of the test values for that parameter and the table will still be correct.

To see how this works, create a test table based on the *HALO* Advanced Controls settings. Start by determining how many parameters and values you want to test. Figure 10.23 shows the five Advanced Controls parameters and their default values. The Look Sensitivity parameter can be a value from 1 to 10 and the remaining parameters are Yes/No parameters. A good set of values for Look Sensitivity would be the default, minimum, and maximum values, which are 3, 1, and 10, respectively. This test requires a combinatorial table of five parameters, where one parameter has three values and the remaining parameters have two test values. Scan through Appendix C to find that Figure C.18 corresponds to this configuration.

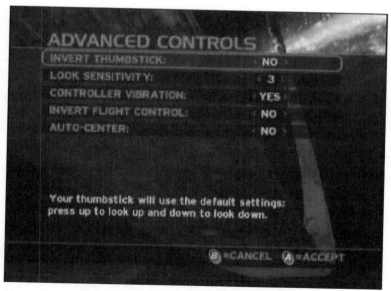

Figure 10.23 *HALO* Advanced Controls option selection screen.

For each parameter, assign one of the test values to the alphanumeric placeholders in the table template. Since Look Sensitivity is the only parameter with three values, it goes in the first column. The default value (3) will be assigned to A1, the minimum value (1) to A2, and the maximum (10) to A3. Replace each instance of A1, A2, and A3 in the table with their assigned values. The table at this point should look like Figure 10.24.

Test	Look Sensitivity	ParamB	ParamC	ParamD	ParamE
1	3	B1	C1	D1	E1
2	1	B2	C2	D1	E1
3	10	B1	C2	D2	E1
4	3	B2	C2	D2	E2
5	1	B1	C1	D2	E2
6	10	B2	C1	D1	E2

Figure 10.24 Look Sensitivity values placed into table template.

Next, choose one of the two-value parameters, and substitute its name and values in the template's ParamB column. Choose the Invert Thumbstick parameter, assigning the default value (NO) to each instance of B1 in the table and the YES value to each B2. The table now looks like Figure 10.25.

Test	Look Sensitivity	Invert Thumbstick	ParamC	ParamD	ParamE
1	3	No	C1	D1	E1
2	1	Yes	C2	D1	E1
3	10	No	C2	D2	E1
4	3	Yes	C2	D2	E2
5	1	No	C1	D2	E2
6	10	Yes	C1	D1	E2

Figure 10.25 Invert Thumbstick values added to the table.

Continue this process for the remaining columns using the default values for the first entry and the remaining value for the other choice. The completed table is shown in Figure 10.26.

Test	Look Sensitivity	Invert Thumbstick	Controller Vibration	Invert Flight Control	Auto-Center
1	3	NO	YES	NO	NO
2	1	YES	NO	NO	NO
3	10	NO	NO	YES	NO
4	3	YES	NO	YES	YES
5	1	NO	YES	YES	YES
6	10	YES	YES	NO	YES

Figure 10.26 Completed Advanced Controls table.

To use one of the template files included in the book's CD-ROM, start by selecting the right file based on your table dimensions. If all of your test parameters have only two values, then use the file CombTemplates2Values.xls. If one or more of your parameters has three values, use the file CombTemplates3Values.xls. If you have any parameters with four or more values, then you need to construct your table by hand or see the "Combinatorial Tools" section that follows.

Once you have identified the right template file to use, click the tab at the bottom of the worksheet that corresponds to the number of test parameters you are using. Then find the template on that sheet that matches your parameter configuration.

For the *HALO* Advanced Controls test you just completed, you would open the CombTemplates3Values.xls file and click the "5 params" tab at the bottom of the worksheet. Scroll down until you find the table labeled "1 parameter with 3 values, 4 parameters with 2 values." You will see that this table is identical to the one in Appendix D that produced the test table in Figure 10.26. Cut this table out and paste it into your own test file. Lastly, do a textual substitution for each of the test values to arrive at the same result.

Combinatorial Tools

At some point, you will find it difficult to construct and verify large parameter and value counts. Fortunately, James Bach has made a tool available to the public at www.satisfice.com/tools.shtml that handles this for you. It is also provided on the CD-ROM that comes with this book. The Allpairs tool uses a tab-delimited text file as input and produces an output file that includes a pairwise combinatorial table as well as a report on how many times each pair was satisfied in the table.

To use Allpairs, start by creating a file that contains tab-delimited columns of parameter names with the test values in the following table. Here is an example based on match settings from the fighting game *Dead or Alive 3* (DOA3):

Difficulty	MatchPoint	LifeGauge	RoundTime
Normal	1	Smallest	NoLimit
Easy	2	Small	30
Hard	3	Normal	40
VeryHard	4	Large	50
	5	Largest	60
			99

Remember, this is not an attempt at a combinatorial table—the tool will provide that. This is a description of the parameters you want to test: Difficulty level, Match Points needed to win a match, Life Gauge size displayed on the screen, and Round Time in seconds. Even though there are only four parameters, the fact that they have 4, 5, 5, and 6 values to each to test would make this difficult to construct and validate by hand. That also means there are 600 (4*5*5*6) values if you try to test all four-wise combinations. You should expect a much smaller test set from a pairwise combinatorial test of these options—somewhere in the 30–40 range—based on the dimensions of the two largest parameters (6*5).

Now open a DOS (yes—DOS!) window and enter `allpairs input.txt > output.txt` where *input.txt* is the name of your tab-delimited parameter list file, and *output.txt* is the name of the file where you want to store the generated combinatorial table. Make sure you are in the directory where the files are located, or provide the full path.

For this *DOA3* table, the command might be `allpairs doaparams.txt > doapairs.txt`. Here's what the test case portion of the output looks like:

TEST CASES

Case	Difficulty	MatchPoint	LifeGauge	RoundTime	Pairings
1	Normal	1	Smallest	NoLimit	6
2	Easy	2	Small	NoLimit	6
3	Hard	3	Normal	NoLimit	6
4	VeryHard	4	Large	NoLimit	6
5	Hard	1	Small	30	6
6	VeryHard	2	Smallest	30	6
7	Normal	3	Large	30	6
8	Easy	4	Normal	30	6
9	VeryHard	1	Normal	40	6
10	Hard	2	Large	40	6
11	Easy	3	Smallest	40	6
12	Normal	4	Small	40	6
13	Easy	1	Large	50	6
14	Normal	2	Normal	50	6
15	VeryHard	3	Small	50	6
16	Hard	4	Smallest	50	6
17	Normal	5	Largest	60	6
18	Easy	1	Largest	60	4
19	Hard	2	Largest	60	4
20	VeryHard	3	Largest	60	4
21	Easy	5	Smallest	99	5
22	Normal	4	Largest	99	4
23	Hard	5	Small	99	4
24	VeryHard	5	Normal	99	4
25	~Normal	5	Large	NoLimit	2
26	~Easy	5	Largest	30	2
27	~Hard	5	Largest	40	2
28	~VeryHard	5	Largest	50	2
29	~Hard	4	Smallest	60	2
30	~Hard	1	Large	99	2
31	~VeryHard	~1	Largest	NoLimit	1
32	~Normal	~1	Small	60	1
33	~Easy	~2	Normal	60	1
34	~Easy	~3	Large	60	1
35	~Normal	2	~Smallest	99	1
36	~Easy	3	~Small	99	1

Aren't you glad you didn't have to do that by hand! The "case" and "pairings" columns are added to the output by the Allpairs tool. "Case" is a sequential number uniquely identifying each test case. The "pairings" number indicates how many necessary parameter pairs are represented by the set of values in each row. For example, the "pairings" value in row 18 is 4. You can check for yourself that row 18 produces four new pairs: Easy-Largest, Easy-60, 1-Largest, and 1-60. The Largest-60 pair was satisfied earlier in the table at row 17, and the Easy-1 pair first appears in row 13.

Values that begin with the "~" symbol are wildcards. That is, any value of that parameter could be placed there without removing one of the necessary pairings to complete the table. The tool arbitrarily chooses but you, the knowledgeable tester, can replace those with more common or notorious values, such as defaults or values that have caused defects in the past.

The output from Allpairs also produces a Pairing Details list, which is an exhaustive list of each necessary pair and all of the rows that include that pair. One of the pairings listed for the DOA3 table is

| MatchPoint | Difficulty | 1 | Easy | 2 | 13, 18 |

which means that the pair Match Point = 1 and Difficulty = Easy occurs 2 times—in rows 13 and 18 of the table.

In the same list, the entry

| RoundTime | LifeGauge | 60 | Largest | 4 | 17, 18, 19, 20 |

traces the RoundTime = 60 and LifeGauge = Largest pair to rows 17–20 of the combinatorial table. This kind of information is especially useful if you want to limit your testing to all the instances of a particular pair. One reason for doing that would be to limit verification testing of a release that fixed a bug caused by one specific pair.

Another use for the Pairing Details information is to quickly narrow down the possible cause of a new defect by immediately testing the other entries in the table that had the same pairs as the test that just failed. For example, if the test in row 13 fails, search the Pairing Details list for other pairs that were included in row 13. Then run the tests on any rows listed in addition to row 13. Here are the pairs that are satisfied by row 13:

RoundTime	MatchPoint	50	1	1	13
RoundTime	LifeGauge	50	Large	1	13
RoundTime	Difficulty	50	Easy	1	13
MatchPoint	LifeGauge	1	Large	2	13, 30
MatchPoint	Difficulty	1	Easy	2	13, 18
LifeGauge	Difficulty	Large	Easy	2	13, 34

From this information, tests 18, 30, and 34 could be run next to help identify the pair that causes the defect. If none of those tests fail, then the cause is narrowed down to the first three pairs, which are only found in row 13: 50-1, 50-Large, or 50-Easy. If test 18 fails, then look for the 1-Easy pair to be the cause of the problem. Likewise, if test 30 fails then suspect the 1-Large combination. If test 34 fails you can suggest Large-Easy as the cause of the problem in your defect report.

The Allpairs output file is tab delimited so you can paste it right into Microsoft Excel or any other program supporting that format. The Allpairs tool files and the examples from this chapter, including the complete output file, are provided on the book's CD-ROM.

Combinatorial Economics

The examples used in this chapter have produced tables with significant efficiency, covering hundreds of potential combinations in no more than a few dozen tests. As it turns out, these are very modest examples. Some configurations can yield reductions of more than 100:1, 1000:1, and even beyond 1,000,000:1. It all depends on how many parameters you use and how many test values you specify for each parameter. But do you always want to do *less* testing?

Some game features are so important that they deserve more thorough testing than others. One way to use pairwise combinatorial tests for your game is to do full combinatorial testing for critical features, and pairwise for the rest. Suppose you identify 10% of your game features as "critical" and that each of these features has an average of 100 tests associated with them (approximately a 4x4x3x2 matrix). It is reasonable to expect that the remaining 90% of the features could be tested using pairwise combinatorial tables, and only cost 20 tests per feature. The cost of full combinatorial testing of all features is 100*N, where N is the total number of features to be tested. The cost of pairwise combinatorial testing 90% of those features is $100*0.1*N + 20*0.9*N = 10*N+18*N = 28*N$. This provides a 72% savings by using pairwise for the non-critical 90%.

Another way to use combinatorial tests in your overall strategy is to create some tables to use as "sanity" tests. The number of tests you run early in the project will stay low, and then you can rely on other ways of doing "traditional" or "full" testing once the game can pass the sanity tests. Knowing which combinations work properly can also help you select which scenarios to feature in pre-release videos, walkthroughs, or public demos.

Summary

In each of these situations, the cheapest way for your team to find and remove the defects is to create pairwise combinatorial tables as early as possible in the game life cycle and investigate the potential results of each test case. Once the design document or storyboards become available, create combinatorial tables based on the information available to you at the time and question the designers about the scenarios you generate.

If you know your testing budget in terms of staff, effort, or dollars early in the project, you have to make choices about how to distribute your resources to test the game the best you can. Pairwise combinatorial tests provide a good balance of breadth and depth of coverage, which allows you to test more areas of the game than if you concentrate resources on just a few areas.

Exercises

1. Explain the difference between a pairwise combinatorial table and a full combinatorial table.

2. Explain the difference between a parameter and a value.

3. Use the appropriate template to add the Performance EQ parameter to the *NFL 2K5* Game Options test table in Figure 10.22.

4. Since some of the issues found with the NFL 2K5 table are related to the Two Minute Warning, add three new rows to the Game Options test table that pair the "2 min" Quarter Length with the other five parameters.

5. Use the Allpairs tool to create a combinatorial table for the Player Appearance options under the Create Player feature in *NFL 2K5*. The first parameter is Body Type with a default value of Skinny, plus additional values of Normal, Large, and Extra Large. The second parameter is Skin Tone with a default value of Lightest and additional values of Light, Light Medium, Dark Medium, Dark, and Darkest. The third parameter is Face with a default value of Type 2 and other values of Type 1 and Type 3 through 7. The Height parameter has a default of 6'0", and ranges from 5'6" to 7'0". Weight is the final parameter, with a default of 220 and a range from 150 to 405.

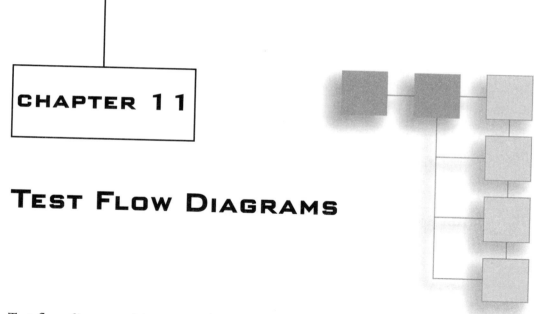

CHAPTER 11

TEST FLOW DIAGRAMS

Test flow diagrams (TFDs) are graphical models representing game behaviors from the player's perspective. Testing takes place by traveling through the diagram to exercise the game in both familiar and unexpected ways.

TFDs provide a formal approach to test design that promotes modularity and completeness. Testers can enjoy a high degree of TFD reuse if the same behaviors are consistent across multiple game titles or features. This benefit extends to sequels and ports to other platforms. The graphical nature of the TFD gives testers, developers, and producers the ability to easily review, analyze, and provide feedback on test designs.

TFD Elements

A TFD is created by assembling various drawing components called *elements*. These elements are drawn, labeled, and interconnected according to certain rules. Following the rules makes it possible for your tests to be understood throughout your test organization and makes them easier to reuse in future game projects. The rules will become even more important if your team develops software tools to process or analyze the TFD contents.

Flows

Flows are drawn as a line connecting one game state to another, with an arrowhead indicating the direction of flow. Each flow also has a unique identification number, one *event*, and one *action*. A colon (":") separates the event name from the flow ID number and a slash ("/") separates the action from the event. During testing, you *do* what is specified by the event and then *check* for the behavior specified by both the action and the flow's destination *state*. An example flow and each of its components are shown in Figure 11.1.

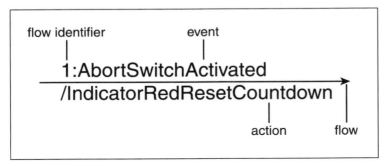

Figure 11.1 Flow components.

Events

Events are operations initiated by the user, peripherals, multiplayer network, or internal game mechanisms. Think of an event as something that is explicitly done during the game. Picking up an item, selecting a spell to cast, sending a chat message to another player, and an expiring game timer are all examples of events. The TFD does not have to represent all possible events for the portion of the game being tested. It is left up to each tester, who is now in the role of a test designer, to use his knowledge and judgment in selecting the right events that will achieve the purpose of a single TFD or a set of related TFDs. Three factors should be considered for including a new event

1. Possible interactions with other events.
2. Unique or important behaviors associated with the event.
3. Unique or important game states that are a consequence of the event.

Only one event can be specified on a flow, but multiple operations can be represented by a single event. An event name can appear multiple times on a TFD when each instance carries the exact same meaning. Events may or may not cause a transition to a new game state.

Actions

An *action* exhibits temporary or transitional behavior in response to an event. It is something for the tester to check as a result of causing or performing an event. Actions can be perceived through human senses and gaming platform facilities, including sounds, visual effects, game controller feedback, and information sent over a multiplayer game network. Actions do not persist over time. They can be perceived, detected, or measured when they occur but can no longer be perceived, detected, or measured some time later.

Only one action can be specified on a flow, but multiple operations can be represented by a single action. An action name can appear multiple times on a TFD when each instance carries the exact same meaning.

States

States represent persistent game behavior and are re-entrant. As long as you don't exit the state you will continue to observe the same behavior, and each time you return to the state you should detect the exact same behavior.

A state is drawn as a "bubble" with a unique name inside. If the same behavior applies to more than one state on your diagram, consider whether they could be the same state. If so, remove the duplicates and reconnect the flows accordingly. Each state must have at least one flow entering and one flow exiting.

Primitives

Events, actions, and states are also referred to as *primitives*.

Primitive definitions provide details of the behavior represented on the TFD without cluttering the diagram. Primitive definitions form a "data dictionary" for the TFD. These definitions could be in text (for example, English), a software language (for example, C), or an executable simulation or test language (for example, TTCN). See the "Data Dictionary" section later in the chapter for details and examples.

Terminators

These are not machines from the future programmed for war. *Terminators* are special boxes placed on the TFD that indicate where testing starts and where it ends. Exactly two terminators should appear on each TFD. One is the IN box, which normally has a single flow that goes to a state. The other is the OUT box, which has one or more flows entering from one or more states.

TFD Design Activities

Creating a TFD is not just a matter of mechanically typing or drawing some information you already have in another form. It is a design activity that requires the tester to become a *designer*. A sound approach to getting your TFDs off and running is to go through three stages of activities: preparation, allocation, and construction.

Preparation

Collect sources of game feature requirements.

Identify the requirements that fall within the scope of the planned testing, based on your individual project assignment or the game's test plan. This would include any storyboards, design documents, demo screens, or formal software requirements, as well as legacy titles that the new game is based on such as a sequel or a spin-off.

Allocation

Estimate the number of TFDs required and map game elements to each.

Separate large sets of requirements into smaller chunks and try to cover related requirements in the same design. One way to approach this is to test various *abilities* provided in the game, such as picking up a weapon, firing a weapon, healing, and so on. Plan on having one or more TFDs for each ability depending on how many variations exist, such as distinct weapon types or different ways to regain health. Another approach is to map situations or scenarios to individual TFDs with a focus on specific *achievements*. These could be individual missions, quests, matches, or challenges, depending on the type of game you are testing. In this case, you are establishing that particular goals or outcomes are achievable according to which path you take in the game. Basing the TFD design on achievements could be used either instead of or in addition to the abilities approach. Don't try to squeeze too much into a single design. It's easier to complete and manage a few simple TFDs than one complex one.

Construction

Model game elements on their assigned TFDs using a "player's perspective."

A TFD should not be based on any actual software design structures within the game. The TFD is meant to represent the tester's interpretation of what she expects to happen as the game flows to and from the game states represented on the diagram. Creating a TFD is not as mechanical as constructing a combinatorial table. There is an element of art to it. TFDs for the same game feature may turn out quite different depending on which tester developed them.

Begin the TFD with a blank sheet or a template. You can start on paper and then transfer your work to an electronic form or do the whole thing in one shot on your computer. The use of templates is discussed later in this chapter. Use the following the steps to begin constructing your TFD from scratch. An example appears later in this chapter that illustrates the application of these steps.

1. Open a file and give it a unique name that describes the scope of the TFD.

2. Draw a box near the top of the page and add the text "IN" inside of it.

3. Draw a circle and put the name of your first state inside of it.

4. Draw a flow going from the IN box to your first state. Add the event name "Enter" to the flow. Note: Do not number any of the flows at this time. This will be done at the end to avoid recordkeeping and editing the numbers if you change the diagram during the rest of the design process.

   Unlike the steps given for developing a pairwise combinatorial table in Chapter 10, the middle steps for creating a test flow diagram do not have to be followed in any particular order. Construct your diagram as your mind flows through the game scenario you are testing. The creation of the diagram should be iterative and dynamic, as the diagram itself raises questions about possible events and their outcomes. Refer to the following steps when you get stuck or when you think you are done to make sure you don't leave out any parts of the process.

5. From your first state, continue to add flows and states. Flows can be connected back to the originating state in order to test required behavior that is transient (action) or missing (ignored, resulting in no action).

6. Record the traceability of each flow to one or more requirements, options, settings, or functions. This could be as simple as ticking it off from a list, highlighting portions of the game design document or done formally by documenting this information in a Requirements Traceability Matrix (RTMX).

7. For each flow going from one state (A) to another state (B), check the requirements for possible ways to go from B to A, and add flows as appropriate. If the requirements neither prohibit nor allow the possibility, review this with the game, feature, or level designer to determine if a requirement is missing (most likely), wrong, or ambiguous.

8. Once all requirements are traced to at least one flow, check the diagram for alternative or additional ways to exercise each requirement. If a flow seems appropriate, necessary, or obvious but can't be traced to any game documentation, determine if there might be a missing or ambiguous requirement. Otherwise, consider whether the flow is outside of the defined scope of the TFD currently being constructed.

Go through these final steps in the order they appear here:

9. Add the OUT box.

10. Select which state or states should be connected to the OUT box. Your criteria should include choosing places in the test that are appropriate for stopping one test and starting the next one or states that naturally occur at the end of the ability or achievement modeled by the TFD. For each of these states, provide a connecting flow to the OUT box with an "Exit" event. There should be no more than one such flow coming from any state.

11. Update your IN and OUT box names to IN_xxx and OUT_xxx where xxx is a brief descriptive name for the TFD. This is done at the end in case your scope or focus has changed during the process of creating the TFD.

12. Number all of the flows.

Using SmartDraw

The TFD examples in this chapter were drawn using SmartDraw 6. A demo version of this software is included on the book's CD-ROM. After you install SmartDraw 6, launch it and you will be prompted for which version you want to try. Select the Standard version and click the Try It Free button. Click Try It Free again when you get the SmartDraw Free Trial window. You will now be at the Welcome to SmartDraw! window shown in Figure 11.2. Click the "Create a new drawing" icon and then click OK. Later on, when you launch SmartDraw again to work on an existing TFD, click on "Open a recently used Drawing," select it from the pull down list, and then click OK.

Now select Software Design from the Create New Drawing window as shown in Figure 11.3. This has drawing elements that you can use for your TFD, or you can just stick with the basic geometric figures that will also appear in the drawing window. Click Create Blank Drawing and you get the SmartDraw Hint window. You can view the tutorial or click OK to proceed. There are a number of drawing icons across the top of the blank drawing window. You only need to use a few of these for your TFD, namely the Draw a Rectangle, Draw a Connector Symbol (Circle), and any or all of the four line types: Straight Line, Arc, Segmented Line, or Curved Line.

Drag from the figure icon to place one in your diagram, or click the figure's icon and draw the figure to whatever size you desire. To draw flows, click one of the line types, click the starting point of the line, drag the cursor to the end point, and unclick. The first time you do this the line will not have an arrowhead. To add one, click the line and go up to the Line menu at the top of the SmartDraw window. Pull down the Line menu and click Arrowheads… to get the window shown in Figure 11.4. Select one of the Right arrowheads. One example is highlighted in the figure.

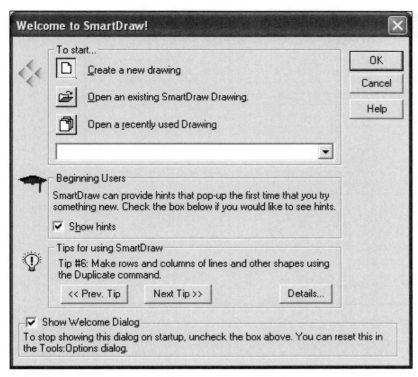

Figure 11.2 Welcome to SmartDraw! window.

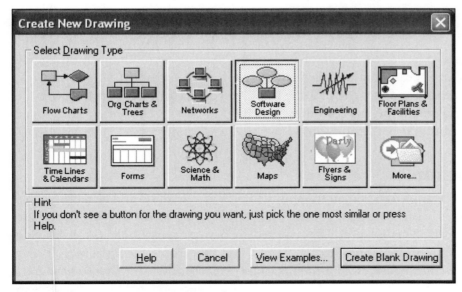

Figure 11.3 Create New Drawing window.

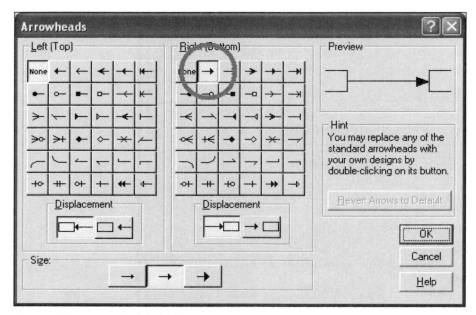

Figure 11.4 Arrowheads window.

To delete an unwanted element, click it and press the Delete key. To add text to any element, click it and type the text you want. To copy an element, click it and choose Duplicate from the Edit menu or just type Ctrl+D. To move an element, click it and drag it to the desired position. Select a set of elements by dragging a rectangle around them. Once selected, they can be moved, duplicated, or deleted in a single operation.

Elements can also be edited. Resize or reshape an element by grabbing and dragging the handles that appear. Rotate an element by holding the cursor over the small circle that appears nearby and move the mouse in the direction you want to rotate with the left button held down. You can customize your TFD further by changing colors, fonts, and other attributes using various pull-down menu selections.

A TFD Example

The first TFD example is based on the ability to pick up a weapon and its ammo while the game properly keeps track of your ammo count and performs the correct audible and visual effects. This is an ability required in first-person shooters, role playing games, action/adventure games, arcade games, and even some racing games. It may seem like a trivial thing to test, but the first four patches for *Unreal Tournament 2004* fixed five ammo-related defects and fourteen other weapon-related bugs that were in the original release.

Note

I recommend that you use SmartDraw or your favorite drawing tool to create your own diagram file as you follow the example. Do your own editing first and then compare what you have to the example diagrams each step along the way. Refer to the "Using SmartDraw" section to get started with SmartDraw.

All TFDs start with an IN box, followed by a flow to the first state of the game that you want to observe or that you need to reach in order to begin testing. Don't begin every test with the startup screen unless that's what you are trying to test with the TFD. Jump right to the point in the game where you want to start doing things (events) with the game that you want the tester to check (actions, states).

In this TFD, the first state represents the situation where the player has no weapon and no ammo. Draw a flow to connect the IN box to the NoGunNoAmmo state. Per the process described earlier in this chapter, provide the event name "Enter" on the flow but don't provide an ID number yet. Figure 11.5 shows how the TFD looks at this point.

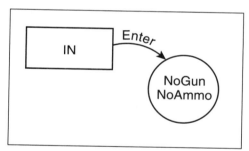

Figure 11.5 Starting the Ammo TFD.

The next step is to model what happens when the player does something in this situation. One likely response is to find a gun and pick it up. Having a gun creates observable differences from not having a gun. A gun appears in your inventory, your character is shown holding the gun, and a crosshair now appears at the center of the screen. These are reasons to create a separate state for this situation. Keep the naming simple and call the new state HaveGun. Also, in the process of getting the gun, the game may produce some temporary effects such as playing the sound of a weapon being picked up and identifying the weapon the display. The temporary effects are represented by an action on the flow. Name the flow's event GetGun and name the action GunEffects. The TFD with the gun flow and new state is shown in Figure 11.6.

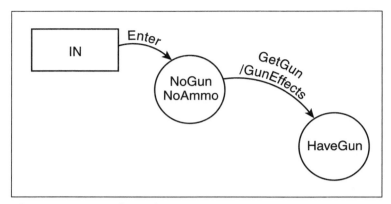

Figure 11.6 TFD after picking up a weapon.

Because it's possible that the player could find and pick up ammo before getting the weapon, add another flow from NoGunNoAmmo to get ammo and check for the ammo sound and visual effects. A new destination state should also be added. Call it HaveAmmo to be consistent with the HaveGun state name format. Your TFD should look like Figure 11.7 at this point.

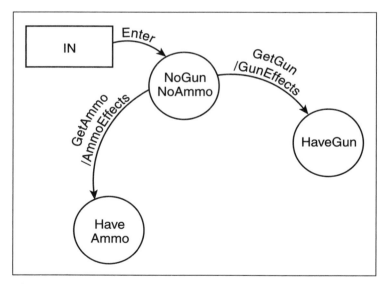

Figure 11.7 TFD with HaveGun and HaveAmmo states.

Now that there are a few states on the diagram, check if there are any flows you can add that go back from each state to a previous one. You got to the HaveGun state by picking up a weapon. It may also be possible to go back to the NoGunNoAmmo state by dropping the weapon. Likewise, there should be a flow from HaveAmmo going back to NoGunNoAmmo when the player somehow drops his ammo. If there are multiple ways to do this, each should appear on your TFD. One way might be to remove the ammo from your inventory and another might be to perform a reload function. For this example, just add the generic DropAmmo event and its companion DropSound action. To illustrate how actions might be reused within a TFD, the diagram reflects that the same sound is played for dropping either a weapon or ammo. That means the DropGun event will also cause the DropSound action. The return flows from HaveGun and HaveAmmo are shown in Figure 11.8.

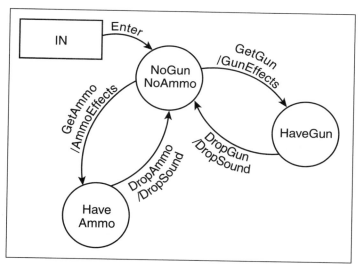

Figure 11.8 Return flows added from HaveGun and HaveAmmo.

Now that the test represents gun-only and ammo-only states, tie the two concepts together by grabbing ammo once you have the gun. Call the resulting state HaveGunHaveAmmo. You should recognize that picking up the gun once you have the ammo will also take you to this very same state. Figure 11.9 shows the new flows and the HaveGunHaveAmmo state added to the TFD.

You may have noticed that when new states are added it's good to leave some room on the diagram for flows or states that you might decide to add when you get further into the design process. Use up some of that empty space now by doing the same thing for HaveGunHaveAmmo that you did with the HaveAmmo and HaveGun states: create return flows to represent what happens when the gun or the ammo is dropped. One question that

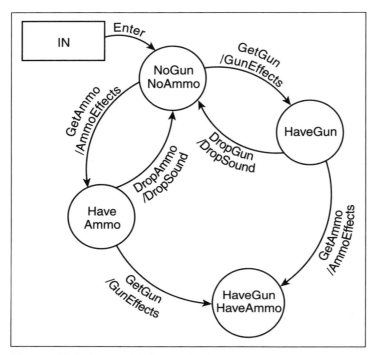

Figure 11.9 Flows added to get both gun and ammo.

arises is whether the ammo stays in your inventory or is lost when the gun is dropped. This test is based on the ammo automatically loading when you have the matching weapon, so the DropGun event will take you all the way from HaveGunHaveAmmo to NoGunNoAmmo. Be careful not to get caught up in the symmetry that sometimes arises from the diagram. Flows coming out of states don't always return to the previous state. The TFD with these additional flows is shown in Figure 11.10.

At this point, evaluate whether there's anything else that could be added that remains consistent with the purpose of this test. That is, are there any ways to manipulate the ammo or the gun that would require new flows and/or states on the TFD? Start from the furthest downstream state and work your way up. If you have the gun and ammo, is there any other way to end up with the gun and no ammo besides dropping the ammo? Well, shooting the gun uses ammo, so you could keep shooting until all of the ammo is used up and then end up back at HaveGun. Since both of the states involved in this transition are already on the diagram, you only need to add a new flow from HaveGunHaveAmmo to HaveGun. Likewise, besides picking up an empty gun, you might get lucky and get one with some ammo in it. This creates a new flow from NoGunNoAmmo to HaveGunHaveAmmo. Figure 11.11 shows the diagram with these new interesting flows added.

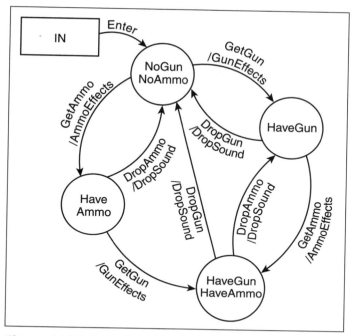

Figure 11.10 Return flows added from HaveGunHaveAmmo.

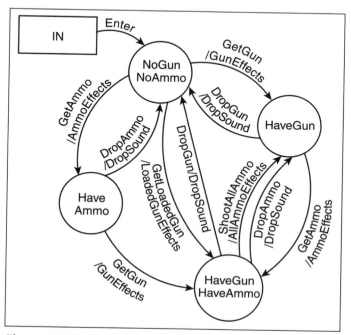

Figure 11.11 Loaded gun and shooting flows added.

Note that some of the existing flows were moved around slightly to make room for the new flows and their text. ShootAllAmmo will cause sounds, graphic effects, and damage to another player or the environment. Doing GetLoadedGun will cause effects similar to the combined effects of separately picking up an unloaded gun and its ammo. The actions for these new events were named AllAmmoEffects and LoadedGunEffects to reflect the fact that these multiple effects are supposed to happen and need to be checked by the tester. The ShootAllAmmo event illustrates that your test events do not have to be atomic. You do not need a separate event and flow for firing each individual round of ammo, unless that is exactly what your test is focusing on.

Do the same for HaveGun and HaveAmmo that you just did for HaveGunHaveAmmo. Question whether there are other things that could happen in those states to cause a transition or a new kind of action. You should recognize that you can attempt to fire the weapon at any time whether or not you have ammo, so a flow should come out from HaveGun to represent the game behavior when you try to shoot with no ammo. But where does this flow go to? It ends up right back at HaveGun. This is drawn as a loop as shown in Figure 11.12.

At this point, only two things remain to do according to the procedures given earlier in this chapter: add the OUT box and number the flows. Keep in mind that the numbering is totally arbitrary. The only requirement is that each flow has a unique number.

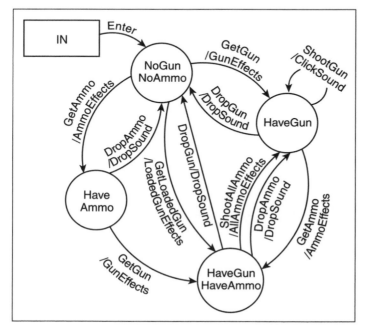

Figure 11.12 Flow added to shoot gun with no ammo.

Another thing that has been done is to name the IN and OUT boxes to identify this specific TFD, which might be part of a collection of multiple TFDs created for various features of a game. This also makes it possible to uniquely specify the test setup and tear-down procedures in the data dictionary definition for these boxes. This is described in further detail later in this chapter.

Once you complete your diagram, be sure to save your file and give it an appropriate descriptive name. Figure 11.13 shows the completed Ammo TFD.

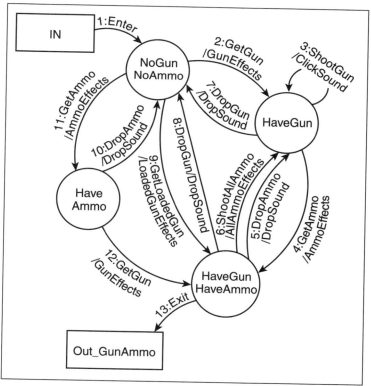

Figure 11.13 The completed Ammo TFD.

Data Dictionary

The *data dictionary* provides detailed descriptions for each of the uniquely named primitive elements in your TFD collection. This also implies that any primitive name you reuse within a TFD and across multiple TFDs will carry the same meaning during testing. Think of the primitive names on the TFD as a hyperlink to pages that contain their definitions. When you mentally "click" on one of those names, you get the same definition regardless of which instance of the name you click on.

Data Dictionary Application

If you are using SmartDraw to create and maintain your TFDs, you can do this literally by highlighting the text for an event, action, or state and selecting Insert Hyperlink from the Tools pull-down menu. Then manually browse for a text or HTML file that contains the description of the primitive. If you use HTML files for the description, you can also export your diagram to make your test accessible as a Web page. Do this by selecting Publish to the Web from the File menu.

It is up to you to decide how formal your definitions should be. In small teams intimate with the product, the TFD by itself may be sufficient if you can trust the person running the test (Rule 2…) to remember and consistently apply all of the details of each primitive. For large teams, especially when new people are moving in and out of the test team during the course of the project, the data dictionary will provide more consistent and thorough checking, as well as better adherence to the intent of the test. You may also want to keep TFD use informal in early development stages until the development team better understands how they really want the game to behave. Once the game stabilizes, capture that information in the data dictionary.

Data Dictionary Reuse

The data dictionary can also be an important tool for reusing your TFDs for different games or game elements. For example, the Ammo TFD in Figure 11.13 refers abstractly to "Gun" and "Ammo." Most games involving weapons provide multiple types of weapons and ammo that is specific for each. You could cover this by making copies of the TFD for each of the different weapon types, changing the event, action, and state names to match. An alternative is to keep a generic TFD and then apply different data dictionaries to interpret the TFD specifically for each weapon and ammo type.

An example for *Unreal Tournament* would be to use a single TFD but have different data dictionaries for the various weapon/ammo pairs such as Flak Cannon/Flak Shells, Rocket Launcher/Rocket Pack, Shock Rifle/Shock Core, and so on. Each data dictionary could elaborate on the different audio, visual, and damage effects associated with each pair.

Data Dictionary Example

Build the data dictionary by defining each of the elements in the diagram. The "do" items (events) are written normally. The "check" items (actions and states) should be written in list form with a leading dash to visually separate them from the "do" items. You can also use an empty box character (□) that can be checked off as the test is run. This is good for providing a physical record of what the tester saw.

Some of the primitives for the Ammo TFD in Figure 11.13 are defined below for the Bio-Rifle weapon in *Unreal Tournament 2004*. They are arranged in alphabetical order for easy searching. Individual definition files are also provided on the book's CD-ROM. The "do" items (events) are written normally. The "check" items (actions and states) are written in list form with a leading dash to visually separate them from the "do" items. As an alternative to the leading dash character, you could use an empty box character (□) that can be ticked as each check is made by the tester. This is good for providing a physical record of what the tester experienced.

AmmoEffects

□ Check that the Bio-Rifle ammo sound is made

□ Check that the game temporarily displays "You picked up some Bio-Rifle ammo" in white text above the gun icons at the bottom of the screen

□ Check that the temporary text on the display fades out slowly

DropGun

Hit the "\" key to drop your selected weapon.

DropSound

□ Check that the item drop sound is made

Enter

Select a match and click the FIRE button to start the match.

Exit

Hit the ESC key and exit the match.

GetAmmo

Find a Bio-Rifle ammo pack on the floor in the arena and walk over it.

GetGun

Find an unloaded Bio-Rifle hovering above the floor of the arena and walk into it.

GetLoadedGun

Find a Bio-Rifle loaded with ammo hovering above the floor of the arena and walk into it.

GunEffects

□ Check that the Bio-Rifle sound is made

□ Check that the game temporarily displays "You got the Bio-Rifle" in white text above the gun icons at the bottom of the screen

- ☐ Check that the game simultaneously displays "Bio-Rifle" temporarily in blue text above the "You got the Bio-Rifle" message

- ☐ Check that all temporary text on the display fades out slowly

HaveAmmo

- ☐ Check that the Bio-Rifle icon is empty in the graphical weapon inventory at the bottom of the screen

- ☐ Check that the Bio-Rifle barrel is not rendered in front of your character

- ☐ Check that you cannot select the Bio-Rifle weapon using the mouse wheel

- ☐ Check that the aiming reticle in the center of the screen has not changed

HaveGun

- ☐ Check that the Bio-Rifle icon is present in the graphical weapon inventory at the bottom of the screen

- ☐ Check that the Bio-Rifle barrel is rendered in front of your character

- ☐ Check that you can select the Bio-Rifle weapon using the mouse wheel

- ☐ Check that the Bio-Rifle aiming reticle appears as a small blue broken triangle in the center of the screen

- ☐ Check that the ammunition count in the right-hand corner of the screen is 0

HaveGunHaveAmmo

- ☐ Check that the Bio-Rifle icon is present in the graphical weapon inventory at the bottom of the screen

- ☐ Check that the Bio-Rifle barrel is rendered in front of your character

- ☐ Check that you can select the Bio-Rifle weapon using the mouse wheel

- ☐ Check that the Bio-Rifle aiming reticle appears as a small blue broken triangle in the center of the screen

- ☐ Check that the ammunition count in the right-hand corner of the screen is 40

IN_GunAmmo

Launch Unreal Tournament 2004 *on the test PC.*

LoadedGunEffects

- ☐ Check that the Bio-Rifle sound is made

- [ ] Check that the game temporarily displays "You got the Bio-Rifle" in white text above the gun icons at the bottom of the screen

- [ ] Check that the game simultaneously displays "Bio-Rifle" temporarily in blue text above the "You got the Bio-Rifle" message

- [ ] Check that all temporary text on the display fades out slowly

NoGunNoAmmo

- [ ] Check that the Bio-Rifle icon is empty in the graphical weapon inventory at the bottom of the screen

- [ ] Check that the Bio-Rifle barrel is not rendered in front of your character

- [ ] Check that you cannot select the Bio-Rifle weapon using the mouse wheel

OUT_GunAmmo

At the main menu, click "EXIT UT2004" to exit the game.

You can even include screen shots, art from design documents, or art from storyboards to provide a visual reference for the tester. This works well with the hyperlink and Web publishing approach. The reference graphics can be updated to reflect changes and maturing of the screen layout and art as the game gets closer to completion. For testing the Bio-Rifle, the AmmoEffects definition could include the screen shot in Figure 11.14. Likewise, Figure 11.15 would be useful for showing the Bio-Rifle GunEffects action.

Figure 11.14 *Unreal Tournament 2004* Bio-Rifle AmmoEffects.

Figure 11.15 *Unreal Tournament 2004* Bio-Rifle GunEffects.

TFD Paths

A test path is a series of flows, specified by the flow numbers in the sequence in which they are to be traversed. Paths begin at the IN state and end at the OUT state. A set of paths provides behavior scenarios appropriate for prototyping, simulation, or testing.

A path defines an individual test case that can be "executed" to explore the game's behavior. Path execution follows the events, actions, and states on the TFD. A textual script can be constructed by cutting and pasting primitives in the order they occur along the path. Testers then follow the script to execute each test, referring to the data dictionary for details of each primitive. Automated scripts are created in the same manner, except lines of code are being pasted together rather than textual instructions for a human tester.

Many paths are possible for a single TFD. Tests can be executed according to a single strategy for the duration of the project or path sets can vary according to the maturity of the game code as it progresses through different milestones. The TFD remains constant as long as the correct game requirements and behaviors do not change. Some useful strategies for selecting test paths are described in the following sections.

Minimum Path Generation

This strategy is designed to produce the smallest number of paths that will end up covering all of the flows in the diagram. In this context, "covering" means that a flow is used at least once somewhere in the test.

The benefits of using a minimum path set are that you have a low test count and the knowledge that you exercised all parts of the diagram at least once. The drawbacks are that you tend to get long paths that may keep you from testing some parts of the diagram until later in the project when something goes wrong early in the test path.

Here's how to come up with a minimum path for the TFD in Figure 11.13. Start at the IN and take flow 1 to NoGunNoAmmo. Then go to HaveGun via flow 2. Since flow 3 loops back to HaveGun, take that next and then exit HaveGun via flow 4. The minimum path so far is 1, 2, 3, 4.

Now from HaveGunHaveAmmo, go back to HaveGun via flow 5. Since flow 6 also goes from HaveGunHaveAmmo to HaveGun, take flow 4 again and this time use flow 6 to return to HaveGun. At this stage, the minimum path is 1, 2, 3, 4, 5, 4, 6, but there are still more flows to cover.

Take flow 7 out from HaveGun to go back to NoGunNoAmmo. From here you can take flow 9 to HaveGunHaveAmmo and return back using flow 8. Now the path is 1, 2, 3, 4, 5, 4, 6, 7, 9, 8. All that remains now is to use the flows on the left side of the TFD.

You are at NoGunNoAmmo again so take flow 11 to HaveAmmo and then return to NoGunNoAmmo via flow 10. Only flow 12 and 13 are left now, so take 11 back to HaveAmmo where you can take 12 to HaveGunHaveAmmo and finally exit via flow 13 to the OUT box. The completed minimum path is 1, 2, 3, 4, 5, 4, 6, 7, 9, 8, 11, 10, 11, 12, 13. All thirteen flows on the TFD are covered in fifteen test steps.

There is usually more than one "correct" minimum path for any given TFD. For example, 1, 11, 10, 11, 12, 8, 9, 5, 7, 2, 3, 4, 6, 4, 13 is also a minimum path for the TFD in Figure 11.13. Diagrams that have more than one flow going to the OUT box will require more than one path. Even if you don't come up with the smallest length path(s) mathematically possible, the purpose is to cover all of the flows in the smallest number of paths, which is one for the Ammo TFD.

Baseline Path Generation

Baseline path generation begins by establishing as direct a path as possible from the IN Terminator to the OUT Terminator that travels through as many states without repeating or looping back. This is designated as the *baseline path*. Then, additional paths are derived from the baseline by varying where possible, returning to the baseline path and following it to reach the OUT Terminator. The process continues until all flows in the diagram are used at least once.

Baseline paths are more comprehensive than minimum paths, but still more economical than trying to cover every possible path through the diagram. They also introduce small changes from one path to another, so a game defect can be traced back to the operations that were different between the paths that passed and the one(s) that failed. One drawback of baseline paths is the extra effort to generate and execute the paths versus using the minimum path approach.

Still using the TFD in Figure 11.13, create a baseline path starting at the IN box and then traveling across the most number of states you can in order to get to the OUT box. Once you get to the NoGunNoAmmo state from flow 1, the farthest distance to the OUT box is either through HaveGun and HaveGunHaveAmmo or through HaveAmmo and HaveGunHaveAmmo. Take the HaveGun route by taking flow 2, followed by flow 4, and exiting through flow 13. This results in the baseline path of 1, 2, 4, 13.

The next thing to do is branch wherever possible from the first flow on the baseline. These are called "derived" paths from flow 1. Flow 2 is already used in the baseline, so take flow 9 to HaveGunHaveAmmo. From there flow 8 puts you back on the baseline path. Follow the rest of the baseline along flows 2, 4, and 13. The first derived path from flow 1 is 1, 9, 8, 2, 4, 13.

Continue to check for other possible branches after flow 1. Flow 11 comes out from NoGunNoAmmo and has not been used yet so follow it to HaveAmmo. Then use flow 10 to return to the baseline. Finish this path by following the remainder of the baseline to the OUT box. This second path derived from flow 1 is 1, 11, 10, 2, 4, 13.

At this point there are no more new flows to cover from NoGunNoAmmo, so move along the next flow on the baseline, which is flow 2. Stop here and look for unused flows to follow. You need to create a path using flow 3. Since it comes right back to the HaveGun state, continue along the remainder of the baseline to get the path 1, 2, 3, 4, 13. The only other flow coming out of HaveGun is flow 7, which puts you right back on the baseline at flow 2. The final path derived from flow 2 is 1, 2, 7, 2, 4, 13.

Now on to flow 4! Flow 4 takes you to HaveGunHaveAmmo, which has three flows coming out from it that aren't on the baseline: 5, 6, and 8. We already used flow 8 in an earlier path, so there is no obligation to use it here. Flows 5 and 6 get incorporated into your baseline the same way since they both go back to the HaveGun state. The derived path using flow 5 is 1, 2, 4, 5, 4, 13 and the derived path for flow 6 is 1, 2, 4, 6, 4, 13.

It may seem like you are done now since the next flow along the baseline goes to the OUT box and you have derived paths from each other flow along the baseline. However, upon further inspection, there is still a flow on the diagram that is not included in any of your paths: flow 12 coming from the HaveAmmo state. It's not connected to a state that's along the baseline so it's easy to lose track of, but don't fall into that trap. Pick up this flow by taking flows 1 and 11 to HaveAmmo and then use flow 12. You're now at HaveGunHaveAmmo and you must get back to the baseline to complete this path. Take flow 8, which is the shortest route and puts you back at NoGunNoAmmo. Finish the path by following the rest of the baseline. This final path is 1, 11, 12, 8, 2, 4, 13.

As you can see, the baseline technique produces many more paths and results in much more testing time than a minimum path. Refer to the sidebar in this section for a summary of this baseline path set.

Summary of Baseline Path Set for Ammo TFD

Baseline:
1, 2, 4, 13

Derived from flow 1:
1, 9, 8, 2, 4, 13

1, 11, 10, 2, 4, 13

Derived from flow 2:
1, 2, 3, 4, 13

1, 2, 7, 2, 4, 13

Derived from flow 4:
1, 2, 4, 5, 4, 13

1, 2, 4, 6, 4, 13

Derived from flow 11:
1, 11, 12, 8, 2, 4, 13

Expert Constructed Paths

Expert constructed paths are simply paths that a test or feature "expert" traces based on her knowledge of how the feature is likely to fail or where she needs to establish confidence in a particular set of behaviors. They can be used by themselves or in combination with the minimum or baseline strategies. Expert constructed paths do not have to cover all of the flows in the diagram, nor do they have to be any minimum or maximum length. The only constraint is that like all other paths they start at the IN and end at the OUT.

Expert paths can be effective at finding problems when there is organizational memory of what has failed in the past or what new game functions are the most sensitive. These paths may not have showed up at all in a path list generated by the minimum or baseline criteria. The drawback of relying on this approach are the risks associated with not covering every flow and the possibility of tester bias producing paths that do not perform "unanticipated" sequences of events.

Some expert constructed path strategies are

- Repeat a certain flow or sequence of flows in combination with other path variations
- Create paths that emphasize unusual or infrequent events
- Create paths that emphasize critical or complex states
- Create extremely long paths, repeating flows if necessary
- Model paths after the most common ways the feature will be used

For example, the "emphasize critical or complex states" strategy can be used for the Ammo TFD in Figure 11.13. In this case, the HaveGun state will be emphasized. This means that each path will pass through HaveGun at least once. It is also a goal to cover all of the flows with this path set. To keep the paths short, head for the Exit flow once the HaveGun state has been used.

One path that works is to go to HaveGun, try to shoot, and then leave. This path would be 1, 2, 3, 4, 13. Another would incorporate the DropGun event in flow 7. The shortest way out from there is via flow 9 followed by 13, resulting in the path 1, 2, 7, 9, 13. You also need to include the two flows going into HaveGun from HaveGunHaveAmmo. This produces the paths 1, 2, 4, 5, 4, 13 and 1, 2, 4, 6, 4, 13. Finish covering all of the flows, leaving HaveGunHaveAmmo by using flow 8 in the path 1, 2, 4, 8, 9, 13.

All that remains are some slightly longer paths that cover the left side of the TFD. Flows 1, 11, and 12 get you to HaveGunHaveAmmo. The quickest way from there to HaveGun is either with flow 5 or 6. Choose flow 5, which results in the path 1, 11, 12, 5, 4, 13.

You can eliminate or keep the earlier path that was made for the sole purpose of covering flow 5 (1, 2, 4, 5, 4, 13). It is no longer essential since is has now also been covered by the path you needed for flow 12.

The last flow to cover is flow 10. Go to HaveAmmo, take flow 10, go back through HaveGun, and go out via flow 2. This gives you your final path of 1, 11, 10, 2, 4, 13. The following sidebar lists all of the paths that were just constructed for this set.

Expert Paths Emphasizing the *HaveGun* State

Expert path set:

1, 2, 3, 4, 13

1, 2, 7, 9, 13

1, 2, 4, 6, 4, 13

1, 2, 4, 8, 9, 13

1, 11, 12, 5, 4, 13

1, 11, 10, 2, 4, 13

Originally constructed but later eliminated:

1, 2, 4, 5, 4, 13

Combining Path Strategies

Testing uses time and resources that get more critical as the game project wears on. Here is one way to utilize multiple strategies that might make the best use of these resources for different stages of the project:

1. Use expert constructed paths early on when the game may not be code complete and everything might not be working. Limit yourself to paths that only include the parts that the developers are most interested in or paths that target the only parts of the game that are available for testing.

2. Use baseline paths to establish some confidence in the feature(s) being tested. This can begin once the subject of the TFD is feature complete. You may even want to begin by seeing if the game can pass the baseline path before trying to use the other paths in the set. Anything that fails during this testing can be narrowed down to a few test steps that vary between the failed path(s) and the successful ones.

3. Once the baseline paths all pass, use the minimum paths on an ongoing basis to keep an eye on your feature to see that it hasn't broken.

4. As any kind of delivery point nears, such as going to an investor demo, a trade show, or getting ready to go gold, revert back to baseline and/or expert paths.

This puts a greater burden on the construction of the test paths, but over the course of a long project it could be the most efficient use of the testers' and developers' time.

Creating Test Cases from Paths

Here's how to create a test case from a single TFD path. The subject of this example is again the Ammo TFD in Figure 11.13. The test case will test getting ammo, then getting the gun, and then exiting. This is path 1, 11, 12, 13. To describe this test case, use data dictionary definitions provided earlier in this chapter for the *Unreal Tournament* Bio-Rifle weapon.

Start constructing the test case with the data dictionary text for the IN box followed by the text for flow 1, which is the Enter flow:

Launch Unreal Tournament 2004 *on the test PC.*

Select a match and click the FIRE button to start the match.

Now add the text from the data dictionary for the NoGunNoAmmo state:

☐ *Check that the Bio-Rifle icon is empty in the graphical weapon inventory at the bottom of the screen*

☐ *Check that the Bio-Rifle barrel is not rendered in front of your character*

☐ *Check that you cannot select the Bio-Rifle weapon using the mouse wheel*

Now take flow11 to get the Bio-Rifle ammo. Use the data dictionary entries for both the GetAmmo event and the AmmoEffects action:

Find a Bio-Rifle ammo pack on the floor in the arena and walk over it.

☐ *Check that the Bio-Rifle ammo sound is made*

Flow 11 goes to the HaveAmmo state, so paste the HaveAmmo data dictionary text into the test case right after the text for flow 11:

☐ *Check that the Bio-Rifle icon is empty in the graphical weapon inventory at the bottom of the screen*

☐ *Check that the Bio-Rifle barrel is not rendered in front of your character*

☐ *Check that you cannot select the Bio-Rifle weapon using the mouse wheel*

☐ *Check that the aiming reticle in the center of the screen has not changed*

Next add the text for the `GetGun` event and `GunEffects` action along flow 12:

Find an unloaded Bio-Rifle hovering above the floor of the arena and walk into it.

☐ *Check that the Bio-Rifle sound is made*

☐ *Check that the game temporarily displays "You got the Bio-Rifle" in white text above the gun icons at the bottom of the screen*

☐ *Check that the game simultaneously displays "Bio-Rifle" temporarily in blue text above the "You got the Bio-Rifle" message*

☐ *Check that all temporary text on the display fades out slowly*

Then paste the definition of the `HaveGunHaveAmmo` state:

☐ *Check that the Bio-Rifle icon is present in the graphical weapon inventory at the bottom of the screen*

☐ *Check that the Bio-Rifle barrel is rendered in front of your character*

☐ *Check that you can select the Bio-Rifle weapon using the mouse wheel*

☐ *Check that the Bio-Rifle aiming reticle appears as a small blue broken triangle in the center of the screen*

☐ *Check that the ammunition count in the right-hand corner of the screen is 40*

Flow 13 is the last flow on the path. It is the Exit flow, which goes to `OUT_GunAmmo`. Complete the test case by adding the text for these two elements:

Hit the ESC key and exit the match.

At the main menu, click "EXIT UT2004" to exit the game.

That's it! Here's how all of the steps look when they're put together:

Launch Unreal Tournament 2004 *on the test PC.*

Select a match and click the FIRE button to start the match.

☐ *Check that the Bio-Rifle icon is empty in the graphical weapon inventory at the bottom of the screen*

☐ *Check that the Bio-Rifle barrel is not rendered in front of your character*

☐ *Check that you cannot select the Bio-Rifle weapon using the mouse wheel*

Find a Bio-Rifle ammo pack on the floor in the arena and walk over it.

☐ *Check that the Bio-Rifle ammo sound is made*

☐ *Check that the Bio-Rifle icon is empty in the graphical weapon inventory at the bottom of the screen*

☐ *Check that the Bio-Rifle barrel is not rendered in front of your character*

☐ *Check that you cannot select the Bio-Rifle weapon using the mouse wheel*

☐ *Check that the aiming reticle in the center of the screen has not changed*

Find an unloaded Bio-Rifle hovering above the floor of the arena and walk into it.

☐ *Check that the Bio-Rifle sound is made*

☐ *Check that the game temporarily displays "You got the Bio-Rifle" in white text above the gun icons at the bottom of the screen*

☐ *Check that the game simultaneously displays "Bio-Rifle" temporarily in blue text above the "You got the Bio-Rifle" message*

☐ *Check that all temporary text on the display fades out slowly*

☐ *Check that the Bio-Rifle icon is present in the graphical weapon inventory at the bottom of the screen*

☐ *Check that the Bio-Rifle barrel is rendered in front of your character*

☐ *Check that you can select the Bio-Rifle weapon using the mouse wheel*

☐ *Check that the Bio-Rifle aiming reticle appears as a small blue broken triangle in the center of the screen*

☐ *Check that the ammunition count in the right-hand corner of the screen is 40*

Hit the ESC key and exit the match.

At the main menu, click "EXIT UT2004" to exit the game.

You can see how indenting the action and state definitions makes it easy to distinguish tester operations from things you want the tester to check for. When something goes wrong during this test you will be able to document the steps that led up to the problem and what specifically was different from what you expected.

There are two techniques you can use to reuse this test case for another type of weapon. One is to copy the Bio-Rifle version and substitute the name of another weapon and its ammo type for "Bio-Rifle" and "Bio-Rifle ammo." This only works if all of the other details in the events, flows, and states are the same except for the gun and ammo names.

In this case, Bio-Rifle-specific details were put into some of the definitions in order to give a precise description of what the tester should check.

`GunEffects` contains the following check, which references text color that varies by weapon. It is blue for the Bio-Rifle but different for other weapons, such as red for the Rocket Launcher and white for the Minigun.

☐ *Check that the game simultaneously displays "Bio-Rifle" temporarily in blue text above the "You got the Bio-Rifle" message*

Likewise, the `HaveGunHaveAmmo` state describes a specific color and shape for the Bio-Rifle aiming reticle as well as an ammunition count. Both vary by weapon type.

☐ *Check that the Bio-Rifle aiming reticle appears as a small blue broken triangle in the center of the screen*

☐ *Check that the ammunition count in the right-hand corner of the screen is 40*

This leaves you with the option to copy the Bio-Rifle data dictionary files into a separate directory for the new weapon. These files should then be edited to reflect the details for the new weapon type you want to test. Use those files to construct your test cases for the new weapon in the same you did for the Bio-Rifle.

Remember that using text in the data dictionary is not your only option. You can also use screen shots or automated code. When executable code for each TFD element along a test path is pasted together, you should end up with an executable test case. Use the IN definition to provide introductory code elements such as including header files, declaring data types, and providing main routine opening braces. Use the OUT definition to perform cleanup actions such as freeing up memory, erasing temporary files, and providing closing braces.

Storing data dictionary information in separate files is also not your only option. You could keep them in a database and use a query to assemble the "records" for each TFD element into a report. The report could then be used for manual execution of the game test.

TFD Templates

Appendix D provides eight TFD templates you can apply to various situations for a wide variety of games. You can re-create the diagrams in your own favorite drawing tool or use the files provided on the book's CD-ROM in SmartDraw (.sdf) format. In the drawing files, suggested baseline paths are indicated by blue flows.

Flows in the template files are not numbered. There will be times when you will need to edit or otherwise customize the TFD to match the specific behaviors for your game. If you need an action and none is there, put in what you need. If there's an action on the TFD but you don't have one in your game, take the action out. Change the names of events, actions, or states to suit your game. Also feel free to add any states you want to test that aren't already provided. Once you've done all that, *then* add the flow numbers and define your paths.

To TFD or Not to TFD?

Table 11.1 provides some guidelines for making a choice between using a combinatorial table or TFD for your test. If a feature or scenario has attributes that fall into both categories, consider doing separate designs of each type. Also, for anything critical to the success of your game, create tests using both methods when possible.

Table 11.1 Test Design Methodology Selection

Attribute/Dependency	Combinatorial	Test Flow Diagram
Game Settings	X	
Game Options	X	
Hardware Configurations	X	
Game State Transitions		X
Repeatable Functions		X
Concurrent States	X	
Operational Flow		X
Parallel Choices	X	X
Game Paths/Routes		X

Summary

TFDs are used to create models of how the game should work from the player's perspective. By exploring this model the tester can create unanticipated connections and discover unexpected game states. TFDs also incorporate invalid and repetitive inputs to test the game's behavior. TFD tests will demonstrate if expected behavior happens and unexpected behavior doesn't. Complex features can be represented by complex TFDs, but a series of smaller TFDs is preferred. Good TFDs are the result of insight, experience, and creativity.

Exercises

1. Describe how you would apply the Ammo TFD in Figure 11.13 to an archer in an online role-playing game. Include any modifications you would make to the TFD structure as well as individual states, events, or actions.

2. Update the diagram in Figure 11.13 to account for what happens when the player picks up ammo that doesn't match the type of gun he has.

3. Create a set of baseline and minimum paths for the updated TFD you created in Exercise 2. Create data dictionary entries and write out the test case for your minimum path. Reuse the data dictionary entries already provided in this chapter and create any new data dictionary entries you need.

4. Construct a TFD for a mobile game that is suspended when the user receives a call or closes the phone's flip cover. Try to keep the number of states low. The game should be resumed once the call ends or the cover is lifted. Hint: Only one criterion must be satisfied to suspend the game, but both criteria to resume the game must be met before it actually resumes.

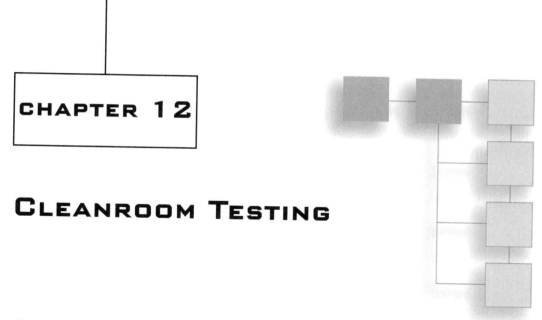

CLEANROOM TESTING

Cleanroom testing is a technique extracted from a software development practice known as Cleanroom Software Engineering. The original purpose of Cleanroom testing was to exercise software in order to make mean time to failure (MTTF) measurements over the course of the project. In this chapter, Cleanroom testing is applied to the problem of why customers find problems in games after they have been through thousands of hours of testing before being released. If one measure of a game's success is that the users (players) will not find any bugs, then the game team's test strategy should include a way to detect and remove the defects that are most likely to be found by users.

So how do users find defects? Users find defects in software by using it the way users use it. That's a little bit of a tongue twister, but it points to a testing approach that exercises the game according to the way the players are going to use it. That's what Cleanroom test development does; it produces tests that play the game the way players will play it.

Usage Probabilities

Usage probabilities, also referred to as usage frequencies, tell testers how often game functions should be used in order to realistically mimic the way customers will use the game. They can be based on actual data you might have from studies of game players or based on your own expectations about how the game will be played. Also take into account the possible evolution of a user's play during the life of the game. A player's patterns would be different just after running the tutorial than they would be by the time the player reaches the boss on the final level. Initially, the player would utilize fundamental operations and have few if any special items unlocked. Clicking dashboard icons would occur more frequently than key commands and user-defined macros. Matches or races might take longer at the end of the game due to the higher difficulty and closer matching of the player's skill to the in-game opponent(s). Usage information can be defined and utilized in three different ways:

- Mode-based usage
- Player-type usage
- Real-life usage

Mode-Based Usage

Game usage can change based on which mode the player is using such as single player, campaign, multiplayer, or online.

Single-player mode may involve one or only a few confrontations or missions. The action usually starts right away so the player is less likely to perform "build-up" operations such as building advanced units and spending money or points on expensive skill-boosting items. Some features may not be available at all to the single player, such as certain characters, weapons, or vehicles. The single player's character may also have limited race, clan, and mission options.

Campaigns tend to start the player with basic equipment and opponents and then introduce more and more complex elements as the campaign progresses. For sports games, Franchise or Season modes provide unique options and experiences that aren't available when playing a single game, such as draft picks, training camp, trading players, and negotiating salaries. RPG games will provide more powerful spells, armor, weapons, and opponents as your characters level up. Racing games may provide more powerful vehicles, add-ons, and powerups, as well as more challenging tracks.

Multiplayer gaming can take place on the same machine—usually for 2–4 players, across two interconnected consoles or over the Internet for more massive multiplayer experiences. Headset accessories are used for team confrontations, but aren't something you're likely to use by yourself unless the game has voice commands. Text chatting also is used in multiplayer games, giving the text keyboard a workout. Game controls can also be assigned to smack talk phrases and gestures, which you will also use to taunt your inferior opponents. The time spent on a multiplayer session can be much greater than what a single player will spend, sometimes extending into the wee hours of the morning. This also brings up the fact that multiplayer games may involve players from different time zones and geographical regions, bringing together a variety of game clocks and language settings.

Player-Type Usage

Another factor that influences game usage is the classification of four multi-user player categories described by Richard A. Bartle in "Hearts, Clubs, Diamonds, Spades: Players Who Suit MUDs." He describes players by their tendencies to emphasize either Achievement, Exploration, Socializing, or Killing when they participate in multiplayer games.

The Achiever wants to complete game goals, missions, and quests. He will gain satisfaction in advancing his character's level, point, and money totals in the most efficient way possible. Achievers may replay the game at a higher level of difficulty or under difficult circumstances such as using a last-place team or going into combat armed only with a knife. They will also be interested in reaching bonus goals and completing bonus missions.

Explorers are interested in finding out what the game has to offer. They will travel around to find obscure places and the edges of the map; unmapped territory will draw their attention. The Explorer will look around and appreciate the art and special beauty in the game such as a particularly nice moonrise or light shining through a stained glass cathedral window. She is also likely to attempt interesting features, animations, combos, and physics effects. Expect the Explorer to try to open every door and check the inventory at all of the stores. The Explorer wants to figure out how things work. Think of the phrase "I wonder what would happen if…?"

The goal of the Socializer is to use the game as a means to role play and get to know other players. Chat and messaging facilities are important to him, as well as joining social groups within the game such as clans, guilds, and so on. He may host meetings or tournaments, or bring many players together in one place for announcements, trading, or even an occasional wedding. Socializers will use special game features once they find out about them from other players.

Killers enjoy getting the best of other players. They engage in player versus player and real versus realm battles. Killers know where the taunt keys are and how to customize and activate an end zone celebration. Headsets, chats, and private messages are also tools that the Killer uses to bait and humiliate his opponents.

Finally, here are some other gamer "types" to consider when you go to test your game the same way players play the game:

Casual gamer: Sticks mostly to functions described in the tutorial, user manual, and on-screen user interface.

Hard-core gamer: Uses function keys, macros, turbo buttons, and special input devices such as joysticks and steering wheels. Checks the Internet for tricks and tips. May also have game hardware juiced up to run the highest graphics resolution and frame rate.

Button Masher: Values speed and repetition over caution and defense. Wears out the A button on the controller to run faster, jump higher, or strike first. Will run out of ammo. The advent of the Nintendo DS™ may also breed the Button Masher's cousin; the **Stylus Scratcher**.

Customizer: Uses all of the game's customization features and plays the game with custom elements. Will also incorporate unlocked items, decals, jerseys, teams, and so on.

Exploiter: Always looking for a shortcut. Will use cheat codes, look for cracks in zone walls, and pick off opponents from a secret or unreachable spot. Creates bots to craft items, earn points, and level up. Uses infinite card combos against AI and human Collectable Card Game (CCG) opponents.

Real-Life Usage

Some games now have a built-in mechanism for capturing your preferences and making the information visible to you. This mechanism can also be used for capturing or downloading your friends' tendencies when they play on your console, allowing you to practice against a "virtual" friend when they are away. Likewise, the tendencies of coaches and celebrity game players can be stored and delivered with the game so you can try out your own strategies against their unique styles of play. *ESPN NFL 2K5* has such a feature known as the VIP Profile. Figures 12.1 and 12.2 show graphics compiled from the game that chart two players' tendencies. You can compare Haiken's tendencies on the left to coach Danny's play patterns on the right.

Figure 12.1 *NFL 2K5* offensive tendencies for players Haiken and Danny.

In Figure 12.1 you see Haiken's preference for using the ball carrier's shoulder maneuver (Y button) versus Danny's preference for juking (L or R trigger). Haiken taps the A button almost exclusively to gain speed, while Danny holds down A to charge about 5% of the time.

Figure 12.2 *NFL 2K5* defensive tendencies for players Haiken and Danny.

On defense there are also differences between the two players, as shown in Figure 12.2. Haiken will tap the A button to speed up the active defender about 95% of the time while Danny taps A about 67% (two thirds) of the time on defense and holds down A to charge about 33% of the time (one third). Danny also shows about an 80% preference for Wrapping the ball carrier when tackling, where Haiken favors Wrapping only 60% of the time.

Why is it important to account for these tendencies? Testing based entirely on balanced use of the game features would not reveal defects such as a memory overflow caused by tapping the A button repeatedly on every play over the course of a maximum length game.

Even the VIP feature itself is not immune to usage bugs. In the VIP Viewer, Haiken's Passing Chart shows 999/999 for Middle Medium pass completions/attempts. The actual numbers of 1383 completions and 2278 attempts *are* properly shown in the Statbook view. It seems the Passing Chart doesn't account for pass-happy players running up large numbers by playing five seasons of Franchise mode with some 60-minute games thrown in.

Cleanroom Test Generation

It's possible to generate Cleanroom tests using any of the methods covered in this book. You can also create your own Cleanroom tests on-the-fly. A usage probability must be assigned to each step in the test. This can be done in writing or you can keep track in your head. Use the usage probability to select test steps, values, or branches and put them in sequence to produce tests that reflect your usages. For example, if you expect a simulation game player to develop residential property 50% of the time, commercial property 30% of the time, and industrial property 20% of the time, then your Cleanroom tests will reflect those same frequencies.

Cleanroom Combinatorial Tables

Cleanroom combinatorial tables will not necessarily be "pairwise" combinatorial tables. The number of tests to be created is determined by the test designer and the values for each test will be chosen on the basis of their frequency of use rather than whether or not they satisfy one or more necessary value pairs.

To produce Cleanroom combinatorial tables, assign usage probabilities to the test values of each parameter. The probabilities of the set of values associated with a single parameter must add up to 100%.

To illustrate how this is done, revisit the parameter and value choices for the *HALO* Advanced Controls table you completed in Figure 10.26. The test values for each parameter are listed below with the default values identified.

> *Look Sensitivity*: 1, 3 (default), 10
>
> *Invert Thumbstick*: Yes, No (default)
>
> *Controller Vibration*: Yes (default), No
>
> *Invert Flight Control*: Yes, No (default)
>
> *Auto Center*: Yes, No (default)

Next, usage percentages need to be determined for each of the table's parameters. If you are considering testing against more than one player profile, you can make a separate usage table for each parameter with a column of usage percentages for each of the profiles you intend to test. Figures 12.3 through 12.7 show multiple profile usage tables for each of the five *HALO* Advanced Controls parameters you will incorporate in your Cleanroom combinatorial table.

Note

Please, don't send emails to explain why any of these percentages are wrong. We have only presented a variety of numbers to illustrate differences between user types based on personal experience. If you have better data gathered through scientific means, then that is what you should be using. If these numbers don't make sense to you, then consider them "for entertainment purposes only" as you continue through the examples in this chapter.

Look Sensitivity	Casual	Achiever	Explorer	Multiplayer
1	10	0	10	5
3	85	75	70	75
10	5	25	20	20
TOTAL	100	100	100	100

Figure 12.3 Look Sensitivity values with usage percentages.

Invert Thumbstick	Casual	Achiever	Explorer	Multiplayer
Yes	10	40	30	50
No	90	60	70	50
TOTAL	100	100	100	100

Figure 12.4 Invert Thumbstick values with usage percentages.

Controller Vibration	Casual	Achiever	Explorer	Multiplayer
Yes	80	75	50	90
No	20	25	50	10
TOTAL	100	100	100	100

Figure 12.5 Controller Vibration values with usage percentages.

Invert Flight Control	Casual	Achiever	Explorer	Multiplayer
Yes	25	60	50	90
No	75	40	50	10
TOTAL	100	100	100	100

Figure 12.6 Invert Flight Control values with usage percentages.

Auto-Center	Casual	Achiever	Explorer	Multiplayer
Yes	30	0	20	10
No	70	100	80	90
TOTAL	100	100	100	100

Figure 12.7 Auto-Center values with usage percentages.

Cleanroom Combinatorial Example

A Cleanroom combinatorial table can be constructed for any of the player usage profiles you define. For this example, you will create one such table for the "Casual" player. To decide which value to choose for each parameter, you need a random number source. You could think of a number in your head, write a program to generate a list of numbers, or roll electronic dice on your PDA. Microsoft Excel can generate random numbers for you with the RAND( ) function or the RANDBETWEEN( ) function if you install the Analysis ToolPak add-in. There is no wrong way as long as the number selection is not biased toward any range of numbers.

Start building the table with an empty table that has column headings for each of the parameters. Decide how many tests you want and leave room for them in the table. A Cleanroom combinatorial table "shell" for the *HALO* Advanced Controls is shown in Figure 12.8. It has room for six tests.

Test	Look Sensitivity	Invert Thumbstick	Controller Vibration	Invert Flight Control	Auto-Center
1					
2					
3					
4					
5					
6					

Figure 12.8 *HALO* Advanced Controls Cleanroom combinatorial table shell.

Since there are five parameters, get five random numbers in the range of 1–100. These will be used one at a time to determine the values for each parameter in the first test. Construct the first test from the five numbers 30, 89, 77, 25, and 13.

Referring back to Figure 12.3, the Casual player is expected to set the Look Sensitivity to "1" 10% of the time, to "3" 85% of the time, and to "10" 5 percent of the time. Assigning successive number ranges to each choice results in a mapping of 1–10 for Look Sensitivity = 1, 11–95 for Look Sensitivity = 3, and 96–100 for Look Sensitivity = 10. The first random number, 30, falls into the 11–95 range, so enter "3" in the first column of the test table.

Likewise, Figure 12.4 provides a range of 1–10 for Invert Thumbstick = Yes and 11–100 for Invert Thumbstick = No. The second random number is 89, which is within the 11–100 range. Enter "NO" in the Invert Thumbstick column for Test 1.

In Figure 12.5, the Controller Vibration usage ranges for the Casual player are 1–80 for Yes and 81–100 for No. The third random number is 77, so enter "YES" in Test 1's Controller Vibration column.

Figure 12.6 defines a 25% usage for Invert Flight Control = Yes and a 75% usage for No. The fourth random number is 25, which is within the 1–25 range for the Yes setting. Enter "YES" in the Invert Flight Control column for Test 1.

Lastly, Figure 12.8 defines the Auto-Center Casual player usage as 30% for Yes and 70% for No. The last random number for this test is 13, placing it within the 1–30 range for the Yes setting. Complete the definition of Test 1 by putting "YES" in the Auto-Center column.

Figure 12.9 shows the first test constructed from the random numbers 30, 89, 77, 25, and 13.

Test	Look Sensitivity	Invert Thumbstick	Controller Vibration	Invert Flight Control	Auto-Center
1	3	NO	YES	YES	YES

Figure 12.9 The first Advanced Controls Cleanroom combinatorial test.

A new set of five random numbers is required to produce the second test case. Use 79, 82, 27, 8, and 57.

The first number is 79, which is within the 11–95 range for Look Sensitivity = 3. Put a "3" again in the first column for Test 2. The second usage number is 82. It falls within the 11–100 range for Invert Thumbstick = No, so put a "NO" in the Invert Thumbstick column for Test 2. Your third number is 27. This is within the 1–80 range for Controller Vibration = Yes. Add the "YES" to the third column of values for Test 2. The fourth random number is 8. This usage value corresponds to the Yes value range of 1–25 for the Invert Flight Control parameter. Enter "YES" into that column for Test 2. For the last parameter of the second test, the random number is 57. This number is in the 31–100 No range for Auto-Center. Complete Test 2 by entering "NO" in the last column. Figure 12.10 shows the first two completed rows for this Cleanroom combinatorial table.

Test	Look Sensitivity	Invert Thumbstick	Controller Vibration	Invert Flight Control	Auto-Center
1	3	NO	YES	YES	YES
2	3	NO	YES	YES	NO

Figure 12.10 Two Advanced Controls Cleanroom combinatorial tests.

The third test in this table is constructed from the random number sequence 32, 6, 64, 66, and 11. Once again, the first value corresponds to the default Look Sensitivity value of "3." The second usage number is 6, which results in the first Yes entry for the Invert Thumbstick parameter by virtue of being inside the 1–10 range for that value. The number to use for determining the Controller Vibration test value is 64, which maps to the 1–80 range for the Yes choice. The fifth number also provides another first—the first No value for Invert Flight Control, because it falls within the 26—100 range. The last random number for Test 3 is 11, which gives you a Yes value for the Auto-Center parameter. Figure 12.11 shows the first three tests entered in the table.

Test	Look Sensitivity	Invert Thumbstick	Controller Vibration	Invert Flight Control	Auto-Center
1	3	NO	YES	YES	YES
2	3	NO	YES	YES	NO
3	3	YES	YES	NO	YES

Figure 12.11 Three Advanced Controls Cleanroom combinatorial tests.

Continue by using the random numbers 86, 64, 95, 50, and 22 for Test 4. The 86 is within the 11–95 range for Look Sensitivity =3, so put a "3" again in column one. A 64 is next in the usage number list. It maps to the No range for Invert Thumbstick. The next number, 95, provides the first No value for Controller Vibration in this set of tests. The 50 for Invert Flight Control puts a No in the table and the last usage number, 22, corresponds to a Yes for Auto-Center. Figure 12.12 shows the table with four of the six tests defined.

Test	Look Sensitivity	Invert Thumbstick	Controller Vibration	Invert Flight Control	Auto-Center
1	3	NO	YES	YES	YES
2	3	NO	YES	YES	NO
3	3	YES	YES	NO	YES
4	3	NO	NO	NO	YES

Figure 12.12 Four Advanced Controls Cleanroom combinatorial tests.

Your fifth set of random numbers is 33, 21, 63, 85, and 76. The 33 puts a "3" in the Look Sensitivity column. The 21 is in the No range for Invert Thumbstick. The 63 corresponds to a Yes value for Controller Vibration. An 85 is within the No range for Invert Flight Control and the 76 causes a No to be put in the last column for the Auto-Center parameter. Figure 12.13 shows the Cleanroom combinatorial table with five tests defined.

Test	Look Sensitivity	Invert Thumbstick	Controller Vibration	Invert Flight Control	Auto-Center
1	3	NO	YES	YES	YES
2	3	NO	YES	YES	NO
3	3	YES	YES	NO	YES
4	3	NO	NO	NO	YES
5	3	NO	YES	NO	NO

Figure 12.13 Five Advanced Controls Cleanroom combinatorial tests.

One more number set is needed to complete the table. Use 96, 36, 18, 48, and 12. The first usage number of 96 is high enough to be in the 96–100 range for the "10" Look Sensitivity value. This marks the first time that value appears in the table. Moving through the rest of the numbers, the 36 puts a No in the Invert Thumbstick column, 18 corresponds to Controller Vibration = Yes, 48 is in the range for Invert Flight Control = No, and 12 completes the final test row with a Yes for Auto-Center. Figure 12.14 shows all six Cleanroom combinatorial test cases.

Test	Look Sensitivity	Invert Thumbstick	Controller Vibration	Invert Flight Control	Auto-Center
1	3	NO	YES	YES	YES
2	3	NO	YES	YES	NO
3	3	YES	YES	NO	YES
4	3	NO	NO	NO	YES
5	3	NO	YES	NO	NO
6	10	NO	YES	NO	YES

Figure 12.14 Completed Advanced Controls Cleanroom combinatorial table.

Your keen testing eye should have noticed that Look Sensitivity = 1 was never generated for this set of tests. That is a function of its relatively low probability (10%), the low number of test cases that you produced, and the particular random number set that was the basis for selecting the values for table. In fact, if you stopped generating tests after five test cases instead of six, the default value of "3" would have been the only value for Look Sensitivity that appeared in the table. This should not be considered a problem for a table of this size. If a value has a 5% or higher usage probability and you don't see it at all in a test set of 100 or more tests, then you may suspect that something is wrong with either your value selection process or your random number generation.

Also notice that some values appear more frequently or less frequently than their usage probability would suggest. Auto-Center = Yes only has a 30% usage for the Casual profile, but it appears in 67% (4/6) of the tests generated. This is mainly due to the low number of tests created for this table. With a test set of 50 or more you should see a better match between a value's usage probability and its frequency in the test set.

Just to reinforce the fact that the Cleanroom combinatorial table method doesn't guarantee it will provide all test value pairs that are required for a pairwise combinatorial table, confirm that the pair Controller Vibration = No and Auto-Center = No is absent from Figure 12.14. Now take a moment to see which other missing pairs you can find.

Note

If you use any of the random number sequences in this chapter for your lottery ticket and you win, please remember to share with the authors of this book.

You will recall that pairwise combinatorial tables are constructed vertically, one column at a time. Until you complete the process for building the table you don't know what the test cases will be or how many tests you will end up with. Because Cleanroom combinatorial tables are constructed horizontally—one line at a time, you get a completely defined test on the very first row, and every row after that for as many Cleanroom combinatorial tests as you choose to produce.

TFD Cleanroom Paths

Cleanroom TFD tests come from the same diagram you use for creating minimum, baseline, and expert constructed paths. Cleanroom test paths travel from state to state by choosing each subsequent flow based on its usage probability.

A usage probability must be added to each flow if the TFD is going to be used for Cleanroom testing. The probabilities of the set of flows exiting each state must add up to 100%. Figure 12.15 shows a flow with the usage probability after the action. If there is no action on the flow, then the usage probability gets added after the event.

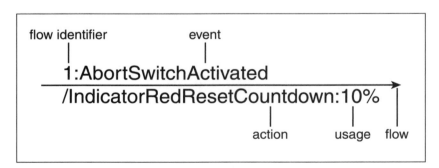

Figure 12.15 Example flow with usage probability.

Figure 12.16 shows an entire TFD with flow numbers and usage percentage amounts. Remember, the probabilities of flows exiting each state must add up to 100%. You may recognize this TFD from the templates provided in Appendix C. The flow numbers and usage percentages make this TFD ready for Cleanroom testing.

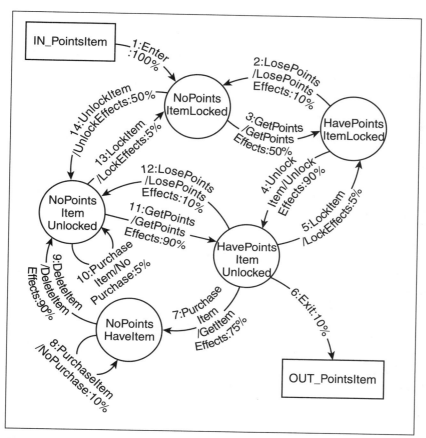

Figure 12.16 Unlock Item TFD with usage probabilities added.

TFD Cleanroom Path Example

With the usage information added to the TFD, generate random numbers to guide you around the diagram from flow to flow until you reach the OUT terminator. The resulting path defines a single test. Continue generating as many paths as you like, using new random number sets each time. Experience has shown that it is a good practice to always assign a 10% value to the Exit flow. A larger value will result in paths that exit too soon and a smaller value will cause too many paths that seem to go on forever before finally exiting. The 10% value provides a nice mix of long, medium, and short paths in your Cleanroom test set.

Each Cleanroom test case is described by the sequence of flow numbers along the Cleanroom path. Since the path length can vary from one test to another, you will not know ahead of time how many random numbers you need to generate for all of your paths. You may end up exiting some tests after only a few flows or you could travel around the diagram quite a bit before reaching the OUT box. Normally you would generate the random numbers as you need them, but for your convenience the random number set for the example in this section is 30, 27, 35, 36, 82, 59, 92, 88, 80, 74, 42, and 13.

Generating a test case for the TFD in Figure 12.16 starts at the IN box. The only flow from there has a 100% usage so there is no need to produce a random number—you must begin your test with this flow. Next, there are two possible ways out from the `NoPointsItemLocked` state: flow 3 and flow 14. Each of those flows has the usage probability of 50%. Assign them each a random number range according to their numerical order. Use flow 3 if the random number is 1–50 and use flow 14 if it is 51–100. Get the random number 30 from the list above and take flow 3 to `HavePointsItemLocked`. The test path so far is 1, 3.

There are two flows exiting state `HavePointsItemLocked`. Flow 2 has a 10% usage and flow 4 has a 90% usage. The range for flow 2 is 1–10 and for flow 4 it's 11–100. Use 27 as the random number for this flow. That sends the test along flow 4 to `HavePointsItemUnlocked`. The test path at this point is 1, 3, 4.

`HavePointsItemUnlocked` is the most interesting state so far, with four flows to choose from for the next step in your test. Flow 5 has a 5% usage, flow 6 has 10%, flow 7 has 75%, and flow 12 has 10%. The corresponding number ranges are 1–5 for flow 5, 6–15 for flow 6, 16–90 for flow 7, and 91–100 for flow 12. You anxiously await the next random number…and it's…35. Your test path now takes flow 7 to `NoPointsHaveItem`. The path is now 1, 3, 4, 7.

From `NoPointsHaveItem` there are two flow choices: flow 8 with a 10% usage and flow 9 with a 90% usage. You will take flow 8 if the random number is in the range 1–10 and flow 9 if it's within 11–100. Your new random number is 36, so take flow 9 to `NoPointsItemUnlocked`. The test path is currently 1, 3, 4, 7, 9.

Flows 10, 11, and 13 all leave `NoPointsItemUnlocked`. Flow 10's usage is 5% (1–5), flow 11 has a 90% usage (6–95), and flow 13 has a 5% (96–100) usage. Another random number is generated and it's 82. That's within the range for flow 11, so take that flow to `HavePointsItemUnlocked`. The path has grown to 1, 3, 4, 7, 9, 11, but you're not done yet.

You're back at `HavePointsItemUnlocked` and the next random number is 59. That fits in the 16–90 range for flow 7, taking you on another trip to `NoPointsHaveItem`. A usage of 92 here matches up with flow 9, going to `NoPointsItemUnlocked`. The test path is now 1, 3, 4, 7, 9, 11, 7, 9.

The next random number is 88. This takes you from `NoPointsItemUnlocked` to `HavePointsItemUnlocked` via flow 11. The 80 takes you along flow 7 for the third time in this path and the next number, 74, sends you to NoPointsItemUnlocked via flow 9. A 42 in the random number list chooses flow 11, which brings you once again to HavePointsItemUnlocked. These flows extend the path to 1, 3, 4, 7, 9, 11, 7, 9, 11, 7, 9, 11.

The next number to use is 13. This falls within the 6–15 range, which corresponds to flow 6. That's the Exit flow, which goes to the OUT terminator. This marks the end of this test path. The completed path is 1, 3, 4, 7, 9, 11, 7, 9, 11, 7, 9, 11, 6.

Once a path is defined, create the test cases using the data dictionary techniques described in Chapter 11. To create an overview of this test, list the flows, actions, and states in the order they appear along the path. List the flow number for each step in parentheses at the beginning of each line, as follows:

IN_PointsItem

(1) Enter, NoPointsItemLocked

(3) GetPoints, GetPointsEffects, HavePointsItemLocked

(4) UnlockItem, UnlockEffects, HavePointsItemUnlocked

(7) PurchaseItem, GetItemEffects, NoPointsHaveItem

(9) DeleteItem, DeleteItemEffects, NoPointsItemUnlocked

(11) GetPoints, GetPointsEffects, HavePointsItemUnlocked

(7) PurchaseItem, GetItemEffects, NoPointsHaveItem

(9) DeleteItem, DeleteItemEffects, NoPointsItemUnlocked

(11) GetPoints, GetPointsEffects, HavePointsItemUnlocked

(7) PurchaseItem, GetItemEffects, NoPointsHaveItem

(9) DeleteItem, DeleteItemEffects, NoPointsItemUnlocked

(11) GetPoints, GetPointsEffects, HavePointsItemUnlocked

(6) Exit, OUT_PointsItem

Generating this path provided some expected results. The path starts with the IN and ends with the OUT, which is mandatory. Flows with large percentages were selected often, such as flows 9 and 11, which each have a 90% usage probability.

Did anything surprise you? Some flows and states didn't appear in this path at all. That's okay for a single path. When you create a set of paths you should expect to explore a wider variety of flows and states.

Was the flow longer than you expected? Flows 7, 9, and 11 appeared multiple times in this path. This is not what you would expect from minimum or baseline path sets. It's also interesting to note that those three flows form a loop. They were used three times in a row before finally exiting and ending the path.

Was the path longer than you wanted it to be? Is this a path you would have chosen on your own? Since this technique is based on a process rather than the ideas or preconceptions of a particular tester, the paths are free of bias or limitations. Cleanroom paths also highlight the fact that the game is not played one operation at a time and then turned off. These paths will test realistic game-use scenarios if your percentages are reasonably correct. As a result, your Cleanroom tests will have the ability to reveal defects that are likely to occur during extended or repeated game use.

Flow Usage Maintenance

There will come a time when you will need to move one or more flows around on your TFD. This may or may not affect your usage values. When a flow's destination (arrowhead end) changes, you are not required to change its usage. Conversely, if you change a flow to originate from a new state, you must re-evaluate the usage values for all flows coming from both the new state and the original one.

Figure 12.17 shows an updated version of the Unlock Item TFD. Flow 9 on the left side of the diagram now goes all the way back to NoPointsItemLocked instead of NoPointsItemUnlocked. The usage percentage for flow 9 does not have to change. The percentages for all the flows coming from NoPointsHaveItem still add up to 100: 10% for flow 8 and 90% for flow 9.

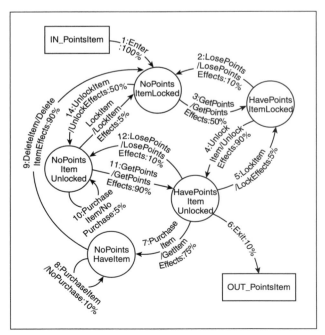

Figure 12.17 Unlock Item TFD with altered flow 9.

Figure 12.18 includes a second update to the Unlock Item TFD. Flow 6 originally started at `HavePointsItemUnlocked` but now it goes from `NoPointsHaveItem` to the OUT box. For this case, all flows coming from both `HavePointsItemUnlocked` and `NoPointsHaveItem` were re-evaluated to add up to 100% from each originating state.

For `HavePointsItemUnlocked`, one or more percentages need to increase since that state lost a flow. You can give flow 12 the 10% that used to be allocated to flow 6. That would not overly inflate the usage for flow 7 and it keeps flow 5's usage small. As Figure 12.18 shows, flow 12 now has a 20% usage instead of its original 10% value.

Additionally, one or more flows coming from `NoPointsHaveItem` must now be reduced to make room for the new flow. Since flow 6 is an Exit flow, it must have a 10% usage. Two other flows come from `NoPointsHaveItem`: flow 8 with a 10% usage and flow 9 with a 90% usage. Reducing flow 8 by 10% will put it at 0%, meaning it will never be selected for any Cleanroom paths for this TFD. Instead, take away 5% from flow 8 and 5% from flow 9. The new percentages for these flows are reflected in Figure 12.18. Alternatively, you could have taken 10% away from flow 9 and left flow 8 at 10%. Your choice depends on what distribution you think best reflects the expected relative usage of these flows according to the game player, mode, or data you are trying to model.

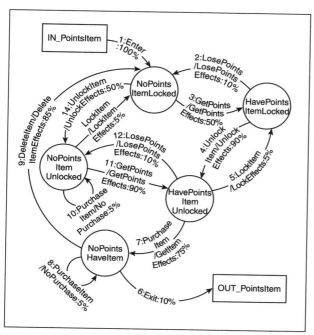

Figure 12.18 Unlock Item TFD with altered flows 6 and 9.

Flow Usage Profiles

You may want to have multiple usage profiles to choose from when you create TFD Cleanroom paths. One way to accomplish this is to create copies of the TFD and change the usage numbers to match each profile. Another solution is to do what you did for combinatorial profiles: produce a mapping between each test element and its usage probability for one or more game users, types, or modes. In this case, usage numbers should not appear on the TFD. Figure 12.19 shows the Unlock Item TFD without usage percentages on the flows.

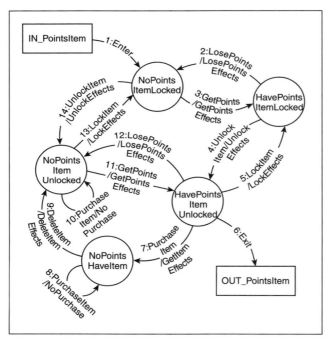

Figure 12.19 Unlock Item TFD without usage probabilities.

Figure 12.20 shows a table of how one profile's probabilities map to the flows on the TFD. Document the random number range that corresponds to each flow's usage. For example, since flows 3 and 14 go out from `NoPointsItemLocked`, flow 3 gets the range 1–50 and flow 14 gets the range 51–100. When you edit the TFD to add, remove, or move flows, you must revisit this table and update the usage and range data.

The total at the bottom of the flow probability table is a good way to check that your percentages add up right. The total should be equal to 100 (for the Enter flow) plus 100 times the number of states on the diagram (flows exiting each state must add up to 100%). The TFD in Figure 12.19 has five states, so 600 is the correct total.

Flow	Casual
1	100
2	10
3	50
4	90
5	5
6	10
7	75
8	10
9	90
10	5
11	90
12	10
13	5
14	50
TOTAL	600

Figure 12.20 Casual player usage table for Unlocked Item TFD flows.

Generate your Cleanroom tests from the flow usage table similar to the way you do when the flow usage is on the diagram. The only difference is the extra step to look up the flow's range in the table. If you are creating an automated process or tool to construct TFD Cleanroom paths, this table could be stored in a database or exported to a text file.

Admittedly, keeping track of flow usage in a table presents some problems. Because the flow numbering does not have to be related to the way flows appear on the diagram, it takes a little more work to identify the flows coming from each individual state. For example, the flows coming out from NoPointsItemLocked—13 and 14—are at opposite ends of the flow list. This wrinkle can become more of a problem when many flows are added, moved, or removed to adapt to changes in the game software. Just be careful and check your numbers when you are faced with this situation.

Inverted Usage

Inverted usage can be applied when you want to emphasize the less frequently used functions and behaviors in the game. This creates a usage model that might reflect how the game would be used by people trying to find ways to exploit or intentionally crash the game for their own benefit. It also helps draw out defects that escaped earlier detection because of the very fact that the game is rarely, if ever, expected to be used in this way.

Calculating Inverted Usage

Inverted usage is calculated using a three-step process.

1. Calculate the reciprocal of each usage probability for a test parameter (combinatorial) or for all paths exiting a state (TFDs).

2. Sum the reciprocals.

3. Divide each reciprocal from step 1 by the sum of the reciprocals calculated in step 2. The result is the inverted probability for each individual usage value.

For example, say there are three values A, B, and C with the usage 10%, 50%, and 40%, respectively. Apply step 1 of the inversion process to get reciprocal values of 10.0 for A (1/0.10), 2.00 for B (1/0.5), and 2.50 (1/0.40) for C. Add these reciprocals to get a sum of 14.5. The reciprocals are divided by this sum to get the inverted values of 69.0% (10/14.5) for A, 13.8% (2/14.5) for B, and 17.2% (2.5/14.5) for C. The can be rounded to 69%, 14%, and 17% for test generation purposes.

One characteristic of this process is that it inverts the proportions between each probability as compared to its companions for a given set of usage values. In the preceding example, B is used five times more frequently than A (50/10) and 1.25 times more frequently than C (50/40). The relationship between inverted A and inverted B is 69%/13.8%, which is 5.00. Likewise, the relationship between inverted C and inverted B is 1.25 (17.2%/13.8%).

For any case where there are only two usage values to invert, you can skip the math and simply reverse the usage of the two values in question. You will get the same result if you apply the full process, but why bother when you could use that time to do more testing?

Note

If an item has a 0% usage, then the first step in the inversion process will cause a divide by zero situation. Keep that from happening by adding 0.01% to each value before doing the three-step inversion calculation. This will keep the results accurate to one decimal place of precision in the results and maintain the relative proportions of usages in the same set.

Combinatorial Table Usage Inversion

Figure 12.3 showed a set of usage probabilities for the *HALO* Look Sensitivity test values of 1, 3, and 10. Construct a table of inverted values starting with the Casual player profile. The three usage probabilities in that column are 10, 85, and 5. These are percentages, so the numerical values of these probabilities are 0.10, 0.85, and 0.05. Apply step 1 and calculate 1/0.10 = 10. Do the same for 1/0.85, which is 1.18, and 1/0.05, which equals 20.

Add these numbers according to step 2. 10 + 1.176 + 20 = 31.176. Finish with step 3. Dividing 10, which is the reciprocal of the usage probability for Look Sensitivity = 1, by 31.18, which is the sum of all three reciprocals, gives an inverted probability of 0.321. Since the numbers in the table are percentages, this gets entered as 32.1. Likewise, divide 1.18 by 31.18 to get the second inverted usage result 0.038, or 3.8%. Complete this column by dividing 20 by 31.18 to get 0.641 and enter 64.1 as the inverted usage for Look Sensitivity = 10.

Comparing the inverted usage values to the original ones confirms that the relative proportions of each usage value have also been inverted. Originally, the usage for Look Sensitivity = 1 was 10% versus 5% for Look Sensitivity = 10: a 2 to 1 ratio. In the inverted table, the Look Sensitivity = 10 value is 64.2—twice that of the 32.1% usage for Look Sensitivity = 1. You can examine the values for each parameter to confirm that this holds true for the other values within each column.

The complete inverted Look Sensitivity usage table for all player profiles is provided in Figure 12.21.

Look Sensitivity	Casual	Achiever	Explorer	Multiplayer
1	32.1	99.9	60.9	75.9
3	3.8	0.0	8.7	5.1
10	64.1	0.0	30.4	19.0
TOTAL	100	100	100	100

Figure 12.21 Inverted usage percentages for the Look Sensitivity parameter.

Note

The "normal" and inverted usage tables for all of the *HALO* Advanced Controls parameters are provided in an Excel spreadsheet file on the book's CD-ROM. There are separate worksheets for the Normal and Inverted usages. You can change the values on the Normal Usage sheet and the values on the Inverted Usage sheet will be calculated for you.

TFD Flow Usage Inversion

The TFD Enter and Exit flows present special cases you must deal with when inverting usages. Since these are really "test" operations versus "user" operations, the usage percentage for these flows should be preserved. They will keep the same value in the inverted usage set that you assigned to them originally. Figure 12.22 shows the Unlock Item TFD's inverted Casual player usage table initialized with these fixed values.

Complete the table by performing the inversion calculation process for the flows leaving each state on the TFD. Go from state to state and fill in the table as you go along. Start at the top of the diagram with the NoPointsItemLocked state. Do inversion calculation for flows 3 and 14. Since these flows have the identical value of 50%, there's no need to do any math. The inverted result in this case is the same as the original. Put 50's in the table for these flows, as shown in Figure 12.23.

Flow	Casual
1	100
2	
3	
4	
5	
6	10
7	
8	
9	
10	
11	
12	
13	
14	

Figure 12.22 Inverted flow usage table initialized with Enter and Exit flow data.

Flow	Casual
1	100
2	
3	50
4	
5	
6	10
7	
8	
9	
10	
11	
12	
13	
14	50

Figure 12.23 Fixed usage added for flows leaving NoPointsItemLocked.

Moving clockwise around the diagram, do the inversion for flows 2 and 4 coming from HavePointsItemUnlocked. There are only two values, so you can swap values without having to do a calculation. Figure 12.24 shows the 90% inverted usage for flow 2 and the 10% inverted usage for flow 4 added to the table.

The next state on your trip around the TFD is HavePointsItemUnlocked. This is the state that has the Exit flow, which is already recorded as 10% in the inverted table. The trick here is to invert the other flows from this state while preserving the total usage of 100% when they are all added up, including the Exit flow. Have you figured out how to do this? For step 1, only calculate the reciprocals of flows 5 (5%), 7 (75%), and 12 (10%). These would be 20, 1.33, and 10, respectively. The sum of the reciprocals (step 2) is 31.33. Divide each reciprocal with the sum (step 3) to get 0.638, 0.042, and 0.319. Since it has already been established that flow 6 (Exit) accounts for 10% of the usage probability total for HavePointsItemUnlocked, then these other three flows must account for the remaining 90%. Multiply the inverted usages for flows 5, 7, and 12 by 0.9 (90%) to account for that. The final result for flow 5 is 0.574 (57.4%), for flow 7 is 0.038 (3.8%), and for flow 12 is 0.287 (28.7%). Figure 12.25 shows these numbers included with the results for the other flows usages calculated so far.

Flow	Casual
1	100
2	**90**
3	50
4	**10**
5	
6	10
7	
8	
9	
10	
11	
12	
13	
14	50

Figure 12.24 Inverted usage added for flows leaving `HavePointsItemLocked`.

Flow	Casual
1	100
2	90
3	50
4	10
5	57.4
6	10
7	3.8
8	
9	
10	
11	
12	28.7
13	
14	50

Figure 12.25 Inverted usage added for flows leaving `HavePointsItemUnlocked`.

Go to the next state, which is `NoPointsHaveItem`. This is another situation with only two flows to invert. Swap the usage values for flow 8 and flow 9. Figure 12.26 shows flow 8 added to the table with a 90% inverted usage and flow 9 with a 10% inverted usage.

`NoPointsItemUnlocked` is the last state to account for on the diagram. Three flows leave this state, so you have to do some calculations. Flow 10 has a 5% usage, so its reciprocal is 20. Flow 11 has a 90% usage. Its reciprocal is 1.11. Flow 13 has the same usage as flow 10 and, therefore, the same reciprocal of 20. Now do step 2 and add up the reciprocals. 20 +1.11 +20 = 41.11. Find the inverted usage of each flow by dividing their reciprocals by this total. For flows 10 and 13, calculate 20/41.11, which results in 0.486, or 48.6%. Calculate flow 11's inverted usage as 1.11/41.11, which is 0.027, or 2.7%. Enter these values to the table to get the completed version shown in Figure 12.27.

With these inverted percentages you can produce TFD Cleanroom paths and test cases in the same way you did earlier from the normal usage probabilities.

Flow	Casual
1	100
2	90
3	50
4	10
5	57.4
6	10
7	3.8
8	**90**
9	**10**
10	
11	
12	28.7
13	
14	50

Figure 12.26 Inverted usage added for flows leaving `NoPointsHaveItem`.

Flow	Casual
1	100
2	90
3	50
4	10
5	57.4
6	10
7	3.8
8	90
9	10
10	**48.6**
11	**2.7**
12	28.7
13	**48.6**
14	50

Figure 12.27 Completed table with inverted usage for `NoPointsItemUnlocked`.

One technique that makes it a little easier to keep track of the number ranges associated with each percentage is to add a Range column to the usage table. Figure 12.28 shows how this looks for the Unlock Item TFD inverted usages. This column can be especially helpful when the flows from a state are scattered around, like flows 3 and 12 coming from `NoPointsItemLocked`.

Flow	Casual	
	Usage	Range
1	100	1-100
2	90	1-90
3	50	1-50
4	10	91-100
5	57.4	1-57
6	10	58-67
7	3.8	68-71
8	90	1-90
9	10	91-100
10	48.6	1-49
11	2.7	50-52
12	28.7	72-100
13	48.6	53-100
14	50	51-100

Figure 12.28 Inverted Casual player usage and ranges for Unlock Item TFD.

Summary

Game players have tendencies and patterns of use that can be incorporated into game tests for the purpose of testing the game the way players play the game. The point of doing that is to find and remove the bugs that would show up when the game is played in those ways. If you are successful, those players will not find any bugs in your game. That's good for them and good for you.

When you sell millions of copies of your game, "rare" situations can happen a number of times over the life of a title. Tests based on inverted usage profiles can emphasize and expose those rare defects in your game.

Exercises

1. What type of player are you? If you do not match any of the types listed in this chapter, give your type a name and describe it. Now think of someone else you know and find their player type. Describe a scenario where you would expect you and your friend to play the game differently. How are the game functions, features, and elements used differently by your two styles?

2. Identify and list each pair of values that is missing from the Cleanroom combinatorial table in Figure 12.14. Explain why they are not necessary and why they may not even be desirable in this application.

3. Is it possible to have the same exact test case appear more than once in a Cleanroom test set? Explain.

4. Create a set of tables with the inverted Casual profile usage probabilities for each of the *HALO* Advanced Settings parameters.

5. Generate six Cleanroom combinatorial tests from the inverted usage tables you produced in Exercise 4. Use the same random number set that was used to generate the combinatorial tests shown in Figure 12.14. Compare the new tests to the original ones.

6. Modify the TFD from Figure 12.16 to incorporate the inverted usages in Figure 12.28. Round the usage values to the nearest whole percentage. Make sure the total probabilities of the flows exiting each state add up to 100. If not, adjust your rounded values accordingly.

7. Generate a path for the TFD you produced in Exercise 6. List the flows, actions, and states along your path using the same format shown earlier in this chapter. Compare the new path to the original one.

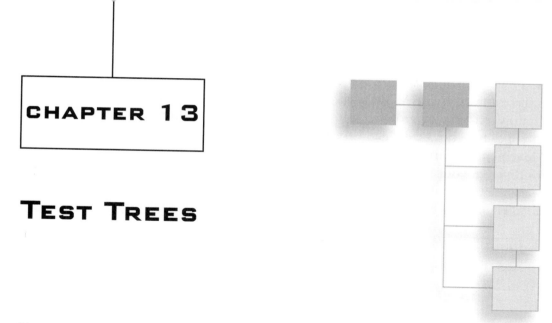

CHAPTER 13

TEST TREES

Test trees can be used for three different purposes in game testing:

1. *Test case trees* document the hierarchical relationship between test cases and game features, elements, and functions.
2. *Tree feature tests* reflect the tree structures of features or functions designed into the game.
3. *Test tree designs* are used to develop tests that systematically cover specific game features, elements, or functions.

Test Case Trees

In this application of test trees, the tests have already been developed and documented. The tree is used each time the game team sends a new release to the testers. The test lead can determine which tests to execute based on which defect fixes or new abilities were introduced in the release. Such an organization could also reflect the way the game itself is structured.

Take, for example, a tree of tests for *Warhammer 40,000: Dawn of War*, which is a real-time simulation (RTS) game for the PC. In this game up to eight players can compete against one another and/or computer AI opponents. Players control and develop their own race of warriors, each of which has its own distinct military units, weapons, structures, and vehicles. Games are won according to various victory conditions such as taking control of a location, defending a location for a given amount of time, or completely eliminating enemy forces.

At a high level, the *Dawn of War* tests can be organized into game Option tests, User Interface tests, Game Mode tests, Race-specific tests, and Chat capability tests. The Option tests can be grouped into Graphics, Sound, or Controls options. The User Interface tests can be divided between the Game Screen UI and the in-game Camera Movement. There are three major Game Modes: Campaign, Skirmish, and Multiplayer. Four player-selectable Races are available: Chaos, Eldar, Orks, and Space Marines. The Chat capability is available when connected via LAN, Online, or Direct Link. Figure 13.1 shows these top two levels of organization organized as a tree.

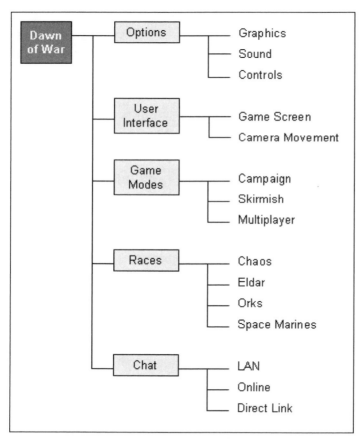

Figure 13.1 *Dawn of War* two-level test case tree.

Note

It's okay to draw your trees in either top-down or left-to-right fashion. They are drawn from left to right in this chapter simply to fit the orientation of the pages in this book.

During game development, each bug fix can affect one or more areas of the game. With the test case tree you can easily target which tests to run by finding them under the tree nodes related to the parts of the game affected by the new code. Some fixes may have to be rechecked at a high level, such as a change in the Chat editor font that applies to all uses of chat. Other fixes may be more specific, such as a change in the way Chat text is passed to the Online server.

It is also possible to go into finer detail to make a more precise selection of tests. For example, the Skirmish Game Mode tests could be further organized by which Map is used, how many Players are active in the match, which Race is chosen by the player, what Game Options are selected, and which Win Conditions are applied. Figure 13.2 shows the further breakdown of the Skirmish branch.

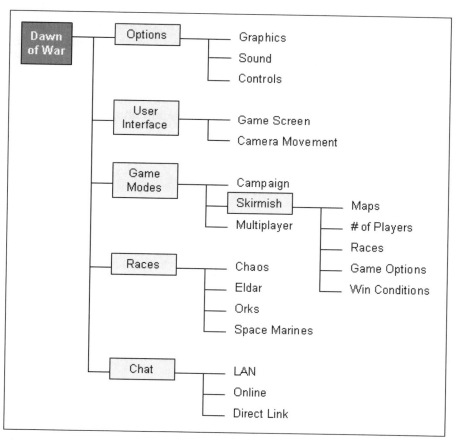

Figure 13.2 Skirmish Game Mode test case sub-tree added.

Revealing the additional details of the Skirmish mode is important because it exposes another set of tests that should be run if changes are made to any game assets or functionality that is specific to the Races. Whether your tests are stored in a regular directory system or a formal configuration management system you can organize them to match the hierarchy of game functions. That will make it easy to find the tests you want to run once you map them to the code changes in each release that is to be tested.

Tree Feature Tests

A second application of test trees is used to reflect actual tree structures of features that are implemented by the game. *Dawn of War* has such structures for the tech trees of each race. These trees define the dependency rules for which units, vehicles, structures, and abilities can be generated. For example, before the Eldars can produce Howling Banshee units, they must first construct an Aspect Portal and upgrade the structure with the Howling Banshee Aspect Stone. Other units can be produced immediately, such as the Rangers. These trees can be quite complex, with dependencies between multiple structures, upgrades, and research items. Test these trees by following the various possible paths to successfully construct each item. Figure 13.3 shows the Aspect Portal tech tree for the Eldar race.

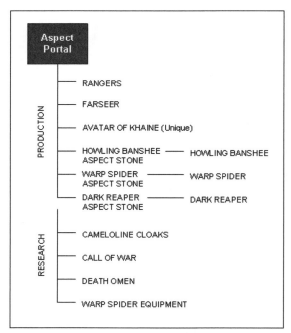

Figure 13.3 *Dawn of War* technology tree for Eldar Aspect Portal.

Another example of this type of tree is the job trees defined for each of the character races in *Final Fantasy Tactics Advance* (FFTA). Characters must develop a certain number of skills at one or more jobs before new job choices and their corresponding skills become available. For these kinds of trees think of the string of lights on a Christmas tree—the ones that won't light up if any of the individual lights is faulty. In this case, the job won't become available if any of the preconditions is not met. You find the faulty light by replacing each one until the string lights up again. Likewise, there should be a set of tests for this tree that leaves out each precondition one at a time, plus a test where they are all satisfied.

The new settings and behaviors should be checked each step along the way. In addition to checking that the job is available at the end of the tree, also check that it does not become available prematurely before all of the necessary conditions have been met.

Most of the FFTA job paths are straightforward. The Blue Mage and Illusionist jobs are not available until you require your character to learn abilities from two other jobs—White Mage and Black Mage. These job trees for Human characters are shown in Figure 13.4.

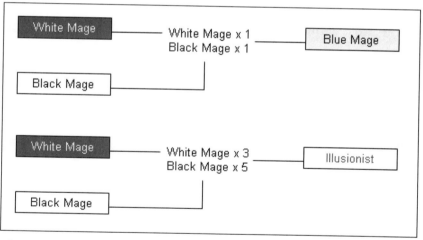

Figure 13.4 Blue Mage and Illusionist job trees for Humans in FFTA.

Define the tree feature tests for a particular job by providing the test values for each of the nodes along the tree branches. Tables 13.1 and 13.2 show the test case you should end up with for the trees in Figure 13.4.

Table 13.1 Tree Feature Tests for Human Blue Mage

White Mage Abilities	Black Mage Abilities	Blue Mage Available
0	1	NO
1	0	NO
1	1	YES

Table 13.2 Tree Feature Tests for Human Illusionist

White Mage Abilities	Black Mage Abilities	Illusionist Available
2	5	NO
3	4	NO
3	5	YES

Many other feature trees exist within games. Here is a list of other places you might find them:

- Technology trees
- Advancing jobs, careers, or skills
- Progressing through tournaments
- Game option menu structures
- Adding or upgrading spells, abilities, or superpowers
- Increasing complexity and types of skills needed to craft or cook items
- Earning new ranks, titles, trophies, or medals
- Unlocking codes, upgrades, or powerups
- Unlocking new maps, environments, or race courses
- Unlocking better cars, outfits, or opponents

One situation that is especially interesting to test is when different menu trees or tree paths can affect the same value, ability, or game element. Such values should be set and checked by all of the possible means (paths) provided by the game. For example, the *Dawn of War* Game Options that are set in Skirmish mode also become the values used in Multiplayer, LAN, Online, or Direct Host mode.

Test Tree Designs

On the other end of the spectrum, some features can seem downright chaotic. Take, for example, card battle games. In these games players take turns playing cards from a deck they have assembled. Winning the game usually involves eliminating the opponent, his creatures, or both. A card may have a special behavior as defined by the text on the card. Some cards can affect other players or cards. There are cards for offensive and defensive purposes. Hundreds of different cards can potentially interact and affect each other in unexpected or undesirable ways. Remember Rule #1—don't panic! Create a test tree design to derive a set of tests for special card capabilities.

For example, a test tree design could be created for the Black Pendant *Yu-Gi-Oh!* card in the *Eternal Duelist Soul* game for the GameBoy Advance. This card is shown in Figure 13.5 and the card text reads as follows:

"A monster equipped with this card increases its ATK by 500 points. When this card is sent from the field to the Graveyard, inflict 500 points of Direct Damage to your opponent's Life Points."

There is other information you need to know about the game to understand this card. Players ("duelists") battle each other by summoning monsters and casting spells from among the cards they hold in their hands. A new card is drawn at the beginning of each player's turn unless there is a spell or effect in play that prevents that from happening. A player can put cards into play from his hand. Some cards require a "Cost" to be put into play, such as loss of life points or sending a card to the graveyard. Cards that are in play are said to be in the "field." Field cards can be face up, or in a special face-down "Set" position. Cards that have somehow been destroyed are put face up into a "graveyard" pile. These cards can still play a role in the outcome of the game, because there are spells and effects that can bring cards in either player's graveyard back onto the field. There are also ways to remove cards from the game. This prevents their return via graveyard effects. Such cards are set aside away from the area of play.

Figure 13.5 Black Pendant card.

Specific types of cards can be put into play. Monster cards can be used to attack the opponent or defend against her attacks. Some monsters have special abilities that can affect other monsters or cards.

There are two types of spell cards: Magic Cards and Trap Cards. Spells can be beneficial or destructive and can affect creatures, players, or other spells. In addition to affecting cards already in play, they can also affect cards in a player's hand, deck, or graveyard. Some spells affect multiple cards and some can only target a single card.

Create a design to test the rule described in the second sentence of the Black Pendant card text. Two criteria must be met for the card to inflict 500 points of direct damage to your opponent:

1. The card is sent *from* the "field" and
2. The card is sent *to* the "graveyard"

From the brief description of the game just provided, you know that the card can either be in a player's hand, field, or graveyard, or removed from the game. Likewise, a card can be sent to a hand, field, or graveyard.

Establish the top level of the tree using the "from" criteria. This should include all of the "zones" that the card can originate from. Use rounded symbols for this design tree to distinguish it from the test case and game function trees shown earlier in this chapter. Also place some text at the top of the column to help remember what function these nodes represent. Your result should look like Figure 13.6.

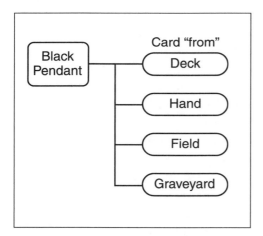

Figure 13.6 Top level of Black Pendant test tree.

Now add the "to" criteria possibilities. Since a card does not get sent to the same place it came from, exclude those branches from the tree. For example, there should not be a Hand branch below the top-level Hand node. Further constrain the tree by only including branches that contain at least one of the success criteria ("from hand" or "to graveyard"). This set of constraints eliminates the Graveyard-Graveyard branch, so remove the Graveyard node from the Card "from" level. At this stage of development the tree should look like Figure 13.7.

The next level of the tree should cover the possible causes of the removal of the Black Pendant card. From the preceding game description, this could be caused by a Magic, Spell, or Monster card. Figure 13.8 includes the addition of the cause nodes.

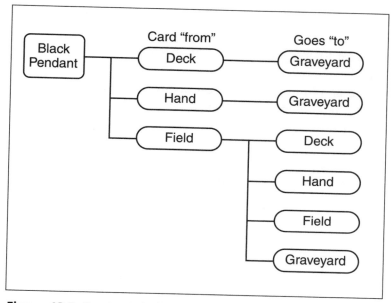

Figure 13.7 Two-level Black Pendant test tree design.

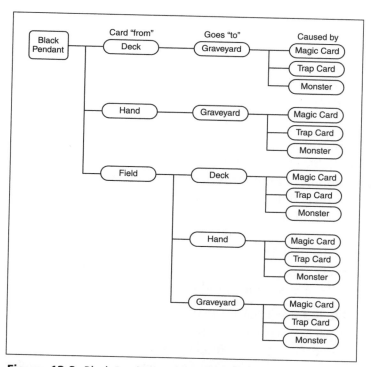

Figure 13.8 Black Pendant test tree design with causes added.

Finally, proceed through each Caused by node and add the possible categories of affected cards: One, Multiple, and All. Additionally, cards can be sent to a deck, hand, or graveyard as part of the cost to activate the effect of another card. This limits the Cost cause to branches that have Graveyard as the Goes "to" choice. The distinction between Multiple and All is that a Multiple card effect involves a selection process to determine which cards are affected, whereas the All effect does not involve this process. Figure 13.9 reflects the expanded tree structure for the Deck-Graveyard branch.

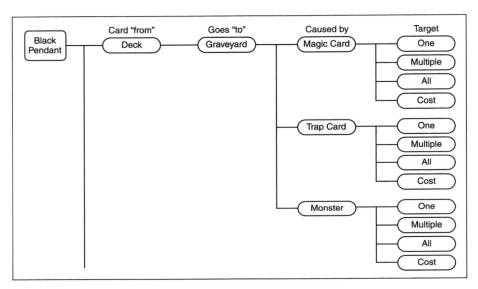

Figure 13.9 Expanded Deck-Graveyard branch.

In the last step of the design process, identify at least one card that meets the criteria for each end node of the tree. Reduce the tree along the way by identifying branches that are not possible given the abilities of the cards that are available in the game. For example, there is no Magic card that could send All players' Black Pendant cards from their deck to the graveyard, so the All node is eliminated from the Deck-Graveyard-Magic Card branch. In the case of the Trap Card, none of the ones provided in this game title send any cards from the deck to the graveyard, so Trap Card and its child nodes can be eliminated entirely from the Deck-Graveyard branch. Figure 13.10 shows the trimmed and completed Deck-Graveyard branch.

This simplifies things quite a bit, but don't rely on that happening every time you use this technique. The important part is that you identify the possible effects and then seek out examples within the game. Sometimes a missing example might be the result of missing functionality in the game. You might even find some defects without even having to run a test!

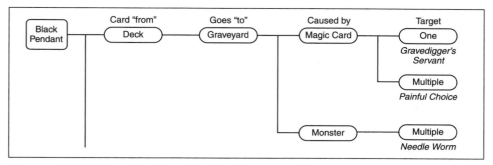

Figure 13.10 Trimmed and completed Deck-Graveyard branch.

Complete the structure for the Hand-Graveyard branch. It should look like Figure 13.11.

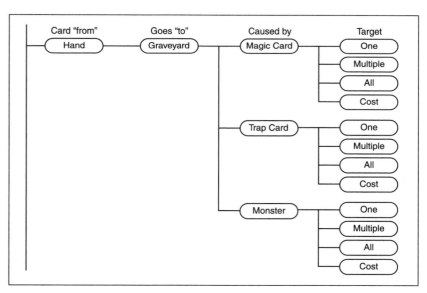

Figure 13.11 Expanded Hand-Graveyard branch.

Once again, carry out the identification and reduction process. Some of the card effects on this branch are not provided by any of the cards in this game, so more nodes will get trimmed, resulting in Figure 13.12.

N o t e

If you want to look up the details yourself for any of the cards used in this game, see Prima's *Official Strategy Guide for Yu-Gi-Oh! The Eternal Duelist Soul.*

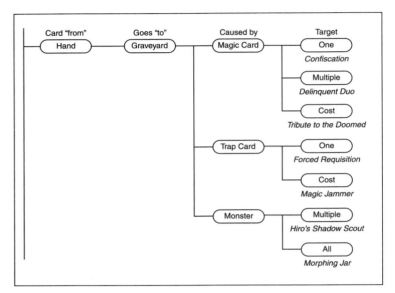

Figure 13.12 Trimmed and completed Hand-Graveyard branch.

Next, start processing the Card "from" Field-to-Deck branch. It just so happens that in this game there are no Magic, Trap, or Monster cards that send a card from the Field back to a player's deck, so this entire branch is eliminated from testing.

Next, expand the Field-Hand branch. There is one Magic card—Giant Trunade—that performs this function and affects All magic cards on the field. No Trap or Monster cards have this effect.

A variety of cards can send Black Pendant from the Field to the Graveyard. In the Magic card category, Mystical Space Typhoon can affect one card, Harpie's Feather Duster can affect multiple cards, and Heavy Storm will affect All magic cards on the field. Trap cards Driving Snow and Magical Hats can affect One or Multiple cards, respectively. Armed Ninja is a Monster capable of sending one Black Pendant card from the Field to the Graveyard. Figure 13.13 shows the test tree design branches for Black Pendant leaving the Field.

At this point you have finished defining the test cases from the original scope of the test tree design structure in Figure 13.8. The tests you have defined so far concern themselves with how the Black Pendant card itself is affected during the battle, but there is another design consideration to take into account. Since Black Pendant is used to "equip" a monster in play, the Black Pendant card is sent to the graveyard whenever the "host" monster leaves the field. This last-minute addition illustrates the iterative discovery process that can take place when using this design approach. Attempting to

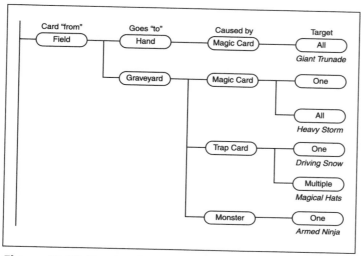

Figure 13.13 Test tree design portion for Field branch.

draw out the tree also draws out new knowledge, ideas, and insights regarding the game, leading to better testing. It's very important that you eagerly include new (valid) ideas in your tests instead of keeping them to yourself because you are embarrassed or fear punishment for not having thought of them sooner.

Add a main Host branch to the tree. Fashion this new branch to follow the same structure as the major Field branch. Figure 13.14 shows the additional Host branch.

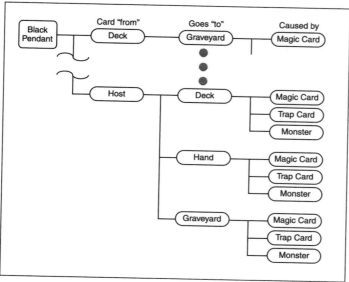

Figure 13.14 Host branch added to Black Pendant test tree design.

Go through the same pruning process that you did for the previous branches. The Host-Deck branch only has one node—the Morphing Jar #2 card for Monster-All. Similarly, the Host-Hand branch has two nodes resulting from the Crass Clown (Monster-One) and Penguin Soldier (Monster-Multiple) cards. These trimmed portions of the tree are shown in Figure 13.15.

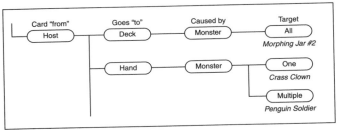

Figure 13.15 Host-Deck and Host-Hand branches of the Black Pendant test tree design.

The Host-Graveyard branch is completely populated. The game has at least one example for each of the Magic, Trap, and Monster scenarios represented in the tree, as shown in Figure 13.16.

Figures 13.17 and 13.18 show (in two parts) the complete structure of this test tree, with the specific card names removed. The result is that you found 31 tests to perform for verifying the proper behavior of the Black Pendant card.

In the same way that the test case tree was discussed in the "Test Case Trees" section earlier in this chapter—used to identify a narrow scope of tests to run for a given set of code changes—this test tree can pinpoint a narrow range of game behaviors to repair when a defect is found. For example, in the course of running the preceding tests, it turns out that the 500 points of damage are not applied when the monster equipped with Black Pendant is destroyed (removed from the Field) to pay for a monster's (Cannon Soldier) effect. This corresponds to the Host-Graveyard-Monster-Cost node in the test tree design. Once the game software is updated to fix this defect, it would make sense to re-run all of the Host-Graveyard-Monster tests as well as tests for each Cost node.

A second defect occurs when Morphing Jar #2's effect sends the Host monster back to the player's deck. This is on the Host-Deck-Monster-All node. Were this to occur by itself, you could plan on re-running Host-Deck-Monster and the *-All tests. Given the fact that there are now two bugs associated with Host-*-Monster branches, I would recommend re-running all Host-*-Monster tests once the bugs are fixed instead of just the Host-Deck Monster and Host-Graveyard-Monster tests.

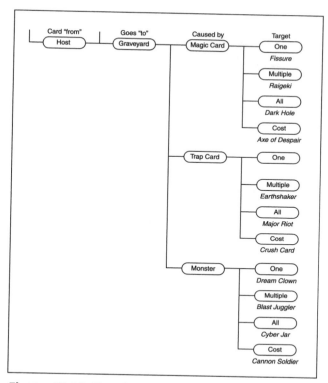

Figure 13.16 Host-Graveyard branch of the Black Pendant test tree design.

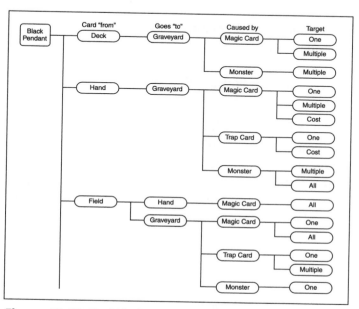

Figure 13.17 Final Black Pendant test tree design structure, Part 1.

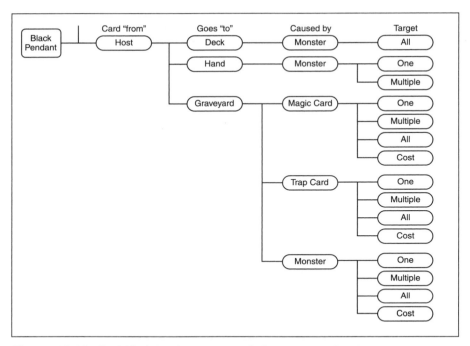

Figure 13.18 Final Black Pendant test tree design structure, Part 2.

One final caution. Be careful about trying to reuse test trees for sequels to previous titles. In the collectible card game example, the tree may not be complete for *Yu-Gi-Oh!* titles released after *Eternal Duelist Soul*. This is because new card mechanics, card types, card restrictions, and/or rule changes can be introduced as new cards are released to the public and included in subsequent videogames. Go back to the point prior to fitting specific cards to each branch and use that as your starting point for completing your test tree designs for newer titles.

This design technique is also useful to fill in the "whitespace" of any feature where you already have experience or intuition of what should be tested, but want to ensure more complete testing, especially concerning various interaction or situational possibilities. In addition to applying this technique to card battle games, you may also find test tree designs useful for testing things like computer opponent AI, networked game message processing, or spell interactions and combinations.

Summary

Tree structures are useful for organizing test cases so that the proper set of tests can easily be selected for a given set of changes to the game code. Each downstream node represents a set of tests with a more specific purpose and scope than the nodes above.

Additionally, tests can reflect tree-like relationships that exist between game functions and elements. The behavior of these structures is tested by exercising the values along the various possible paths from the start of the tree to each of the terminal nodes.

Finally, test trees can be designed to improve understanding of a complex game feature and bring order to a potentially chaotic function, especially regarding interactions with other game rules, elements, and functions. The tree is constructed by progressively decomposing the feature until the bottom nodes identify specific actions to perform or elements to use during testing.

Exercises

1. From the test case tree in Figure 13.2, which test branch(es) should you re-run for a new release of the game that fixes a bug with the sound effect used for the Orks "Big Shoota" weapon?

2. There are actually four Multiplayer game modes in *Dawn of War*: LAN, Online, Direct Host, and Direct Join. Furthermore, the same choices available in Skirmish mode—Maps, # of Players, Race, Game Options, and Win Conditions—apply to the LAN and Direct Host multiplayer modes. Describe how you would update the test case tree in Figure 13.2 to include these two additional levels of depth.

3. (a) Draw a tree for the FFTA Summoner job (Viera race) that requires two White Mage abilities and two Elementalist abilities. The Elementalist job requires one Fencer ability and one White Mage ability. The Fencer and White Mage abilities have no prerequisites.

   (b) List the test cases you should use to determine that the Summoner job is properly restricted or enabled.

4. Besides going to the Deck, Hand, or Graveyard, *Yu-Gi-Oh!* cards can also be "Removed from play." Create an updated version of the Host branch of the Black Pendant to account for this possibility.

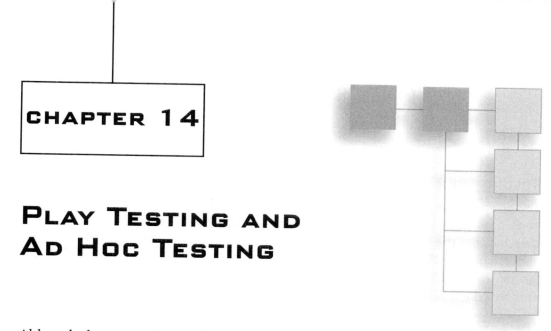

CHAPTER 14

PLAY TESTING AND AD HOC TESTING

Although the vast majority of this book is designed to help you take a methodical, structured approach to testing a game, this chapter focuses on a more chaotic, unstructured—yet no less crucial—approach to game testing.

Ad hoc testing, sometimes referred to as "general" testing, describes searching for defects in a less structured way. *Play* testing describes playing the game to test for such subjective qualities as balance, difficulty, and the often-elusive "fun factor." Because ad hoc testing is closer to the more traditional structured testing described in earlier chapters, this chapter examines it first.

Ad Hoc Testing

Ad hoc is a Latin phrase that can be translated as "to this particular purpose." It is, in its purest form, a single test improvised to answer a specific question.

Despite the most thorough and careful test planning and test design, or the most complex test suite you may have designed, even after being reviewed carefully by other test leads or the project manager, there is always something you (and they) might have missed.

Ad hoc testing allows you as an individual tester to explore investigative paths that may have occurred to you, even subconsciously or unconsciously, in the course of performing structured test suites on the game. During the course of testing a game you will have almost daily thoughts along the lines of "I wonder what happens if I do... ?"

Ad hoc testing gives you the opportunity to answer those questions. It is the mode of testing that best enables you to explore the game, wandering through it as you would a maze.

There are two main types of ad hoc testing. The first is *free testing*, which allows the professional game tester to "depart from the script" and improvise tests on-the-fly. The second is *directed testing*, which is intended to solve a specific problem or find a specific solution.

Testing from the Right Side of Your Brain

Because it is a more intuitive and less structured form of testing, I sometimes call free testing "right-brain testing." Nobel prize-winning psychobiologist Roger W. Sperry asserted that the two halves of the human brain tend to process information in very different ways. The left half of the brain is much more logical, mathematical, and structured. The right half is more intuitive, creative, and attuned to emotions and feelings. It is also the side that deals best with complexity and chaos.

Note

> For a good summary of Sperry's ideas on this topic, especially as it applies to creativity, see Chapter 3 of Edwards, *Drawing on the Right Side of the Brain* (Tarcher/Perigee, 1989).

As the videogame industry continues to grow, there is continued pressure to offer bigger, better, and more in every aspect of a game's design—more features, more user customization, more content, and more complexity. At its best, ad hoc testing allows you as a tester to explore what at times can appear to be an overwhelmingly complex game design.

Ad hoc testing also presents you with an opportunity to test the game as you would play it. What type of gamer are you? Do you like to complete every challenge in every level and unlock every unlockable? Do you like to rush or build up? Do you favor a running game or a passing game? Do you rabbit through levels or explore them leisurely? Ad hoc testing allows you to approach the game as a whole and test it according to whatever style of play you prefer (for an expanded description of player types, see Chapter 12, "Cleanroom Testing").

"Fresh Eyes"

Just as familiarity breeds contempt, it can also breed carelessness on the part of testers forced to exercise the same part of the game over and over. Battle fatigue often sets in over the course of a long project. It's very easy to become "snowblind," a condition in which you've been looking at the same assets for so long that you can no longer recognize anomalies as they appear. You need a break.

Ad hoc testing can allow you to explore modes and features of the game that are beyond your primary area of responsibility. Depending on the manner in which your project is managed, you as a tester may be assigned to one specific area, mode, feature, or section of the game. All the test suites you perform on each build may focus on that specific area. Ad hoc testing allows you to move beyond to other areas, and allows other testers to explore your area, without a test suite to guide them.

By using ad hoc testing, you can put fresh eyes on various parts of the game and find previously overlooked issues.

This method can include the following:

- Assigning members of the multiplayer team to play through the single-player campaign.

- Assigning campaign testers to skirmish (or multiplayer) mode.

- Assigning the config/compatibility/install tester to the multiplayer team.

- Assigning testers from another project entirely to spend a day (or part of a day) on your game.

- Asking non-testers from other parts of the company to play the game (see the section "Play Testing" later in this chapter).

- Performing ad hoc testing early will quickly help to reveal any lingering deficiencies in your test plans, combinatorial tables, and test flow diagrams (see the following sidebar).

Who Turned the Lights On?

A venerable PC games publisher operated a handful of test labs in its various studios around the country, and the local test managers often would send builds of their current projects to each other for ad hoc testing and "idiot checking."

When one test manager handed the latest build of another studio's *PC Formula One* racing game to two of his testers, he was surprised to see them back in his office minutes later. "Crashed it already," they reported proudly.

"How?" the manager cried. "You've barely had time to get past the main menu!"

"We turned the headlights on!"

As you might expect, the default time in the default track in the default mode was "day." When the two testers started their race in this mode, they turned the headlights on "just to see what happens." The game crashed instantly.

Needless to say, this counterintuitive pair of settings (time = day and headlights = on) was added to the combinatorial tables by the chastened but wiser test lead.

Tip

The "fresh eyes" concept is applicable to structured testing as well. It's wise to have testers rotate the specific suites they're responsible for periodically—even every build.

Making Order Out of Chaos

Ad hoc testing is a natural complement to structured testing, but it is by no means a substitute for it. Whether you have been given a specific assignment by your test lead or you're playing through the single-player campaign "just to see what happens," your testing should be documented, verifiable, and worthwhile.

Set Goals and Stick to Them

Before you begin, you should have a goal. It need not (and should not) be as complex or as well thought out as the test cases and test suites discussed earlier. But you need to know where you're going so you don't wind up wasting your (and the project's) time. Briefly write out your test goal before you launch the game.

(Whether you actually achieve the goal of your free testing is less important. If, in the course of trying to reach your goal, you stumble upon a defect you hadn't intended to find, that's great. That is what free testing is all about.)

This goal can be very simple, but it must be explicit. Here are some examples:

- How far can I play in story mode?
- Can I play a full game by making only three-point shots?
- Is there a limit to the number of turrets I can build in my base?
- Can I deviate from the strategy suggested in the mission briefing and still win the battle?
- Is there anywhere in the level I can get my character stuck in the geometry?

If you're leading a multiplayer test, let every other tester know the purpose of the game session before it starts. Successful multiplayer testing requires communication, coordination, and cooperation, even if it seems that the testers are merely running around the level trying to shoot each other. In most circumstances, one tester should direct all of the other players in order to reach an outcome successfully. This can often be as difficult as herding kittens. If one tester in a multiplayer test loses sight of the aim of the test, the amount of time wasted is multiplied by the number of testers in the game. Don't let your team fall into this trap.

Tip

In your testing career, avoid the use of the verb "to play" when you refer to game testing. This will help to counter the widely held notion that your department "just plays games for a living." It will also help to reinforce to your test team that your work is just that, *work*. I've taken to correcting people who refer to testing as playing with the following observation: "The first time you play through a game, you're playing. The fortieth time, you're working."

If You're Not Taping, You're Not Testing

You should constantly take notes as you're testing through the game. Game designer Will Wright (*The Sims*) has said that gameplay is made up of "interesting decisions." It is imperative that you keep track of these decisions—writing down which options you choose, paths you take, weapons you equip, plays you call, and so on—in a very meticulous and diligent manner. In so doing, when you encounter a defect, you will better be able to come up with a reproducible path (see the following sidebar, "How to be a Repro Man (or Woman)").

Documentation may be difficult when you're in the middle of a 12-trick chain in a *Tony Hawk*-style stunt game. That's where videotape becomes an almost indispensable test tool. Every tester should have console, a TV, and a VCR with a tape to record every move they make in the game. (PC testers will need a video card with a TV output.)

Taping should not become a crutch, or an excuse for less-than-diligent work on the part of the tester. It should serve as a research tool and a last-resort means of reporting a defect. Use the following steps as a guide when you are taping:

1. Start the VCR and press the record button before you start the game. (It's too easy to forget, otherwise.)

2. When you come to a defect you can't reproduce, rewind the tape, study the tape, then show it to your test lead and colleagues to discuss what may have caused the bug and whether anyone else has seen the same behavior in similar circumstances.

3. If you absolutely, positively cannot reproduce the defect, rip a clip of the video to an .AVI file or other digital format. This will allow you to attach the video to a bug report, email it to the developer, or even keep it on your computer for reference.

4. Once you've filled up a videotape, replace it with a fresh one in your VCR. Keep the old tape in a safe spot for a couple of days, however, in case you need to refer back to it.

It's generally safe to record over the old tape once the next build enters test.

Free testing should have clear goals. The work done should be documented (via video-tape) and documentable (through clear, concise, reproducible bug reports). It should also be worthwhile. The following are but a few of the common pitfalls you should avoid when free testing:

- Competing with other testers in multiplayer games. It's not about your individual score or win/loss record, it's about delivering a good product.

- Competing against the AI (or yourself) in single-player games.

- Spending a lot of time testing features that may be cut. You may be made aware that a certain mode or feature is "on the bubble," that is, in danger of being eliminated from the game. Adjust your focus accordingly.

- Testing the most popular features of the game. Communicate frequently with your test lead and colleagues so you can stay current with what areas, features, and modes have been covered (and re-covered) already. Focus on the "unexplored territory."

- Spending a disproportionate amount of time testing features that are infrequently used. You're wasting your (and the project's) time spending day after day exploring every nook and cranny of the map editor in your RTS, for example. Only about 15% of all users typically ever enter a map editor, and fewer than 5% actually use it to create maps. You want those folks to have a good experience, but not if it places the other 85% of your players at risk.

Avoid Groupthink

Because ad hoc testing depends on the instincts, tastes, and prejudices of the individual tester, it's important as a test manager to create an environment where testers think differently from one another. Gamers are not a uniform, homogenous group; your test lab shouldn't be, either. If you've staffed your lab with nothing but hardcore gamers, you won't find all the bugs, nor will you ship the best product.

Groupthink is a term coined by social psychologist Irving Janis to describe a situation in which flawed decisions or actions are taken because a group under pressure often sees a decay in its "mental efficiency, reality testing and moral judgment." One common aspect of groupthink is a tendency toward self-censorship—where individuals within a group fail to voice doubts or dissent out of a fear of being criticized, ostracized, or worse. This is a danger in game testing because the majority of people who aggressively seek game tester jobs are men in their early 20s—young enough that pressure to conform to the peer group is still very strong.

Note

For more information on groupthink, see Janis, *Victims of Groupthink* (Houghton Mifflin, 1972).

Tip

Turn your hardcore gamers into hardcore testers. Hardcore gaming is not the same as hardcore testing. So-called "hardcore" gamers are generally a masochistic lot—they willingly pay for games weeks and months before they're even released; they gladly suffer through launch week server overload problems; they love to download patches. Use the methods described in this book to get them to understand that bug-fixing patches can be the exception, rather than the rule. All it takes is careful test planning, design, and execution.

You may encounter attitudes in your test lab such as

- "Everybody has broadband, so we don't need to test modem play."
- "Nobody likes the L.A. Clippers, so I won't test using them as my team."
- "Everybody played *StarCraft*, so we don't need to test the tutorial in our own RTS."
- "Nobody likes CTF (capture the flag) mode, so we don't need to spend a lot of time on it."
- "Nobody uses melee weapons, so I'll just use guns."

Your job as a tester, and test manager, is to be aware of your and your team's pets and pet peeves, and to create an atmosphere in which a variety of approaches are discussed and respected freely and frequently. Cultivate and encourage different types of play styles. Recruit sports gamers. Recruit casual and non-gamers. Foster diversity.

Testing as Detective Work

The second broad category of ad hoc testing is directed testing. You could best describe this method as "detective testing" because of its specific, investigative nature. The simplest form of directed testing answers a very specific question, such as

- Does the new compile work?
- Can you access all the characters?
- Are the cut-scenes interruptible?
- Is saving still broken?

The more complex type of directed testing becomes necessary when testers find a major defect that is difficult or seemingly impossible to reproduce. The tester has "broken the game," but can't figure out how she or he did it. Like a good homicide case, the tester finds himself with a body (the bug) and an eyewitness (himself or other testers). Unlike a homicide case, the focus is not on "whodunnit." The perpetrator is a defect in the code. The focus is "howdithappen."

How to Be a Repro Man (or Woman)

One of the most critical bits of information in any bug report is the *rate of reproduction*. In a defect tracking database, this field may be called (among other things) *frequency, occurrence rate, "happens,"* or *repro rate*. All these various terms are used to describe the same thing. *Reproduction rate* can be defined as *the rate at which, following the steps described in the bug report, anyone will be able to reproduce a defect.*

This information is generally expressed as a percentage ranging from 100% to "once," but this can be misleading. Assume, for example, that you find a defect during the course of your free testing. After a little research, you narrow down the steps to a reproducible path. You follow those steps and get the bug to happen again. You could, reasonably, report the defect as occurring 100% of the time—you tried the steps twice and it happened both times. However, it may be just as likely that the bug is only reproducible 50% of the time or less, and you just got lucky, as though you had flipped a penny and got it to land heads up twice in a row.

For this reason, many QA labs report the repro rate as the number of attempts paired with the number of observed occurrences, (for example, "8 occurrences out of 10 attempts"). This information is far more useful and accurate, because it allows your test lead, the project manager, and anyone else on the team to evaluate how thoroughly the bug has been tested. It also serves to keep you honest about the amount of testing you've given the defect before you write your report. How likely are you to report that a crash bug happens "once" if you only tried to reproduce it once? If you want to maintain your credibility as a member of the test team, you won't make a habit of this.

On the other hand, with certain defects, even a relatively novice tester can be certain that a bug occurs 100% of the time without iterative testing. Bugs relating to fixed assets, such as a typo in in-game text, can safely be assumed to occur 100% of the time.

The word "anyone" is critical to the definition above, because a defect report is not very helpful if the tester who found the bug is the only one able to re-create it. Because videogame testing is often skill-based, it is not uncommon to encounter a defect in a game (especially a sports, fighting, platform jumper, or stunt game) that can only be reproduced by one tester, but that tester can reproduce the bug 100% of the time. In an ideal situation, that tester will collaborate closely with other members of the team so that they can zero in on a path that will allow the others to re-create the bug.

If this is not possible due to time or other resource constraints, be prepared to send a videotape or .AVI clip of the defect to the development team or, in the worst cases, send the tester to the developer to do a live demonstration of the bug. This is very costly and time consuming because, in addition to any travel expenses, the project is also paying for the cost of having the tester away from the lab (and not testing) for a period of time.

In summary, the more reproducible a bug is, the more likely it is that it will be fixed. So always strive to be a true "repro man."

Directed testing commonly begins when one or more testers report a "random" crash in the game. This is a very frustrating experience, because it often delays running complete test suites and a significant amount of time may be spent restarting the application and re-running tests. Unstable code, especially in the later phases of the project, can be very stressful. Again, remember Rule 1: *Don't panic.*

Tip

"Random" crashes are seldom random. Use directed testing and the scientific method to eliminate uncertainty along your path to being able to reproduce the bug often enough so that you can get the development team to find and fix it.

The Scientific Method

It's no coincidence that the department where game testers work is often called the *lab.* Like most laboratories, it's a place where the scientific method is used both to investigate and to explore. If, like most of us, you've forgotten this lesson from middle school science class, here's a review of the steps in the scientific method:

1. Observe some phenomenon.
2. Develop a theory—a *hypothesis*—as to what caused the phenomenon.
3. Use the hypothesis to make a prediction; for example, *if I do this, it will happen again.*
4. Test that prediction by retracing the steps in your hypothesis.
5. Repeat steps 3 and 4 until you are reasonably certain your hypothesis is true.

These steps provide the structure for any investigative directed testing. Assume you've encountered a quirky defect in a PC game that seems very hard to reproduce. It may be a condition that breaks a script, gets your character stuck in the geometry of the level, causes the audio to drop out suddenly, or that favorite of game testers and players alike, a crash to your PC's desktop. Here's what you do:

First, review your notes. Quickly jot down any information about what you were doing when the defect occurred, while it's still fresh in your mind. Review the videotape. Determine as best you can the very last thing you were doing in the game before it crashed.

Second, process all this information and make your best educated guess as to what specific combination and order of inputs may have caused the crash. Before you can retrace your steps, you have to determine what they were. Write down the input path you think most likely caused the crash.

Third, read over the steps in your path until you are satisfied with them. You guess that if you repeat them, the defect will occur again.

Fourth, reboot your computer, restart the game, and retrace your steps. Did you get the crash to occur again?

Fifth, if you did, great! Write it up. If you didn't, change one (and only one) step in your path. Try the path again, and so on, until you successfully re-create the defect.

Unfortunately, games can be so complex that this process can take a very long time if you don't get help. Don't hesitate to discuss the problem with your test lead or fellow testers. The more information you can share, the more brainstorming you can do, the more "suspects" you can eliminate, and the sooner you'll nail the bug.

Play Testing

Play testing is entirely different from the types of testing discussed so far in this book. The previous chapters have concerned themselves with the primary question of game testing: *Does the game work?*

Play testing concerns itself with a different but arguably more important question: *Does the game work well?*

The difference between these two questions is obvious. The word "well" implies an awful lot in four little letters. The answer to the first question is binary; the answer is either yes or no. The answer to the second question is far from binary because of its subjective nature. It can lead to a lot of other questions:

Is the game too easy?

Is the game to hard?

Is the game easy to learn?

Are the controls intuitive?

Is the interface clear and easy to navigate?

And the most important question of all:

Is the game fun?

Unlike the other types of testing covered so far, play testing concerns itself with matters of judgment, not fact. As such, it is some of the most difficult testing you can do.

A Balancing Act

Balance is one of the most elusive concepts in game design, yet it is also one of the most important. *Balance* refers to the game achieving a point of equilibrium between various, usually conflicting, goals:

- Challenging, but not frustrating
- Easy to get into, but deep enough to compel you to stay
- Simple to learn, but not simplified
- Complex, but not baffling
- Long, but not too long

Balance can also refer to a state of rough equality between different competing units in a game:

- Orcs vs. humans
- Melee fighters vs. ranged fighters
- The NFC vs. the AFC
- The Serpent Clan vs. the Lotus Clan
- Paul vs. Yoshimitsu
- Sniper rifles vs. rocket launchers
- Rogues vs. warlocks
- Purple triangles vs. red squares

The test team may be asked by the development team or project manager for balance testing at any point in the project life cycle. It is often prudent to suggest delaying any serious consideration of balance until at least Alpha, because it is hard to form useful opinions about a game if key systems are still being implemented.

Once the game is ready for gameplay testing, it is important for test feedback to be as specific and presented in as organized and detailed a manner as any other defect report. Some project managers may ask you to report balance issues as bugs in the defect-tracking database; others may ask the test lead to keep gameplay and balance feedback separate from defects. In either case, express your gameplay observations so that they seem fact-based, and hence authoritative.

Let's examine some feedback I collected from my testers when we conducted balance testing on *Battle Realms*, a PC RTS developed by Liquid Entertainment. It became clear very early in the course of play testing that the Lotus Warlock unit may be over-powered. One tester wrote:

```
Lotus Warlocks do too much damage and need to be nerfed.
```

If you've ever spent any time on Internet message boards, comments like this should look very familiar. The tester is not specific. How much damage is too much? Relative to what? If *nerfed* means "made less powerful," how much less? 50%? 50 points? The development team is not very likely to take this comment seriously, thinking it's an impulsive, emotional reaction. (And it was. The tester had just been on the receiving end of a warlock rush.)

```
Lotus Warlocks should have a 5-second cooldown added to their attack.
```

This tester is overly specific. He has identified a problem (overpowered warlocks) and gone too far by appointing himself game designer and declaring that the solution is a five-second cooldown (that is, a delay of five seconds between the end of a unit's attack and the beginning of its next attack). This comment presumes three things: that the warlocks are indeed overpowered, that the designers agree that the best solution is to implement a cooldown, and that the code has been written (or can be written) to support a cooldown between attacks. The development team is likely to bristle at this presumption (even if it is a viable solution).

```
Lotus Warlocks are more powerful than the other three races' highest-level units. Their
attack does approximately 10% more damage than the Dragon Samurai, Serpent Ronin and
Wolf Clan Werewolf. They get three attacks in the same time it takes the other clans'
heavy units to do two attacks. Players who choose to play as the Lotus Clan win 75% of
their games.
```

This comment is specific and fact-based. It gives the producers and designers enough information for them to start thinking about rebalancing the units. It does not, however, suggest how the problem should be solved.

Sometimes, however, testers may have suggestions to make…

"It's Just a Suggestion"

Play testing occurs constantly during defect testing. Because testers are not robots, they will always be forming opinions and making judgments, however unconscious, about the game they are testing. Occasionally, a tester may feel inspired to suggest a design change. In some labs, these are called "suggestion bugs," and are frequently ignored. Because bugs stress out programmers, artists, and project managers, they rarely appreciate the bug list being cluttered up with a lot of suggestion, or "severity S," defects.

A far more successful process of making your voice heard as a tester, if you're convinced you've got a valuable (and reasonable) idea for a design change, is the following:

- Ask yourself whether this is a worthwhile change. "Zorro's hat should be blue," is not a worthwhile change.

- Express your idea in the positive. "The pointer color is bad," is a far less helpful comment than, "Making the pointer green will make it much easier to see."

- Sleep on it. It may not seem like such a good idea in the morning.

- Discuss it with your fellow testers. If they think it's a good idea, then discuss it with your test lead.

- Ask your test lead to discuss it with the project manager or lead designer.

- If your test lead convinces the development team that your idea has merit, at that point you may be asked to enter the suggestion into the defect database as a bug so that it can be tracked like any other change. Only do this if you are asked to.

I know this process works. As a tester, I have had design tweaks I suggested incorporated into more than a dozen games; yet I've never written a single suggestion bug.

It's Hard Work Making a Game Easy

One element of game balance that becomes the most difficult to pin down late in the development cycle is, ironically, *difficulty*. Games take months and years to develop. By the time a game enters full-bore testing, the game testers will likely have completed the game more often that even the most ardent fan. The design and development team may have been playing the game for more than a year. Over the course of game development, the following take place:

- Skills improve with practice. If you couldn't grind a rail for more than 10 feet when you got the first test build of a stunt game, you can now grind for hours and pull off 20-trick chains without breaking a sweat.

- AI patterns, routes, and strategies are memorized. The behavior of even the most sophisticated AI opponents becomes predictable as you spend weeks playing against them.

- Puzzles stop being puzzling. In adventure games or other types of games with hide-and-seek puzzle elements, once you learn how to solve a puzzle or where an item is hidden, it's impossible to unlearn it.

- Tutorials stop tutoring. It's very difficult to continue to evaluate how effective a lesson is if you've already learned the lesson.

- Jokes become stale.

- What was once novel becomes very familiar. And familiarity breeds contempt.

The upside of all this is that, on release day, the development and test teams are the best players of their own game on the planet. (This won't last long, though, so you should enjoy "schooling" new players online while you can.)

The downside is that you (and the rest of the project team) lose your ability to objectively evaluate difficulty as the game approaches release. Nothing of what is supposed to be fresh and new to a player seems fresh and new to you. That is why you need another set of fresh eyes: outside gameplay testers.

External Gameplay Testing

External testing begins with resources outside of the test and development teams, but still inside your company. These opinions and data can come from the marketing department, as well as other business units. It's a good idea to have everyone who is willing, from the CFO to the part-time receptionist, to play test the game if there are questions that remain to be answered.

Here we must be careful to keep in mind Dr. Werner Heisenberg's warning that the act of observing something changes the reality observed. Even small children are aware they're participating in a focus group or play test. Because they (or their adult counterparts) are often eager to please, they may tell you what they think you want to hear. Entire books have been written on how to manage this problem with consumer research.

Note

For more information on managing problems with consumer research, see Sudman and Wansink, *Consumer Panels* (South-Western, 2002).

Although outside gameplay testing and opinion gathering is an effort typically initiated by the development or design teams, it is often implemented and managed by the test team.

Subject Matter Testing

If your game takes place in the real world, past or present, the development team may wisely choose to have subject matter experts review the game for accuracy.

During the development of the PC jet fighter simulator *Flanker*, producers at the publisher, SSI, used the Internet to pull together a small group of American and Russian fighter pilots who were given Beta builds of the game. Their feedback about the realism of the game, from the feel of the planes to the Russian-language labels on the cockpit dials, proved invaluable.

These experts posted their comments to a closed message board, and their feedback was carefully recorded, verified, and passed on to the development team. The game was released to very good reviews and was given high marks for its realistic creation of Soviet-era fighter planes.

Such an expert panel tends to be relatively small and easy to manage. It's much more challenging to manage a mass Beta test effectively.

Beta Testing

External Beta testing can give you some very useful data. It can also give you a ton of useless data if the testing is not managed properly.

As mentioned in Chapter 5, there are two types of Beta testing: closed and open. *Closed* Beta occurs first and is carefully controlled. Closed Beta testers are screened carefully and usually have to answer a lot of questions before they are accepted into the Beta test. These questions can range from the technical specifications of their computer to which specific games they've played recently.

The simplest type of closed Beta testing occurs on console or other offline platforms. Testers are recruited to come into the publisher's or developer's offices, review and play the game, and then fill out a questionnaire or participate in a focus group discussion.

Open Beta occurs after closed Beta concludes. Open Beta is open to all who are interested in participating. Although developers will still solicit some level of gameplay feedback from this much larger group, their role may be primarily to load test the network code and shake out such items as the login system, matchmaking, overall network stability, lag, and so on.

Although Beta testers won't run test cases, they will report defects, in addition to providing gameplay feedback. Most Beta test managers email a bug reporting form or host a bug reporting site that allows Beta testers to report defects, make comments, and ask questions.

Besides playing the game the way it would "normally" be played, here are some other strategies you can adopt as an individual Beta tester:

- Try to create infinite point-scoring, money-making, or experience-producing strategies.
- Try to find ways to get stuck in the game environment, such a pinball bouncing forever between two bumpers or an adventurer who falls into the river and can't get out.
- Spend some time in every feature, mode, or location provided in the game.
- Spend all of your time in one feature, mode, or location and fully explore its options and functions.
- Try to find ways to access prohibited modes or locations such as locked race tracks.

- See what happens when you try to purchase, acquire, or use items and abilities that were designed for characters at a level much higher than yours.
- Try to be the first one to accomplish something "first" in the game, such as becoming the first level 2 character, the first to enter a particular town, the first to win a match, the first to form a clan, and so on.
- Wear, wield, and/or activate as many stat-increasing items as you can at one time, such as armor or powerups.
- Try to be the one with the "most" of something in the game, such as wins, points, money, trophies, or vassals.

Likewise, you can conspire with other Beta testers to create situations that might not have been foreseen by the game developers, or were impossible for them to test, such as:

- Get as many people as you can to show up in the same location in the game.
- Get as many people as you can to log into the game at the same time.
- Get as many people as you can to join the same match at the same time.
- Get as many people as you can to send you an in-game message at the same time.
- Create an in-game chat/message group with as many people as possible.
- Get multiple people to try to give you items at the same time.
- Get as many people as you can to stand within range of your "area of effect" spell.
- Get as many people as you can to cast stat increasing or decreasing spells on you.

Who Decides?

Ultimately, decisions that relate to changing the design, rebalancing, adding (or cutting) features, even delaying the release to allow more time for "polish" are not made by game testers. The testers' role is to supply the appropriate decision-makers and stake-holders with the best opinions and information they can, so that the best decisions can be made.

Summary

In this chapter, you learned that ad hoc testing is the mode of testing that best enables you to explore the game, wandering through it as you would a maze. There are two main types of ad hoc testing. The first is *free testing*, which allows the professional game tester to "depart from the script" and improvise tests on the fly. The second is *directed testing*, which is intended to solve a specific problem or find a specific solution.

Exercises

1. True or False: It's a good idea to keep the same tester performing the same test cases for the length of the assignment.

2. Why is it unwise for game testers to refer to their work as "playing"?

3. Discuss the differences (in both method and results) between free testing and gameplay testing.

4. What are two methods of expressing a defect's reproduction rate?

5. You and seven other testers jump into a deathmatch session of the online shooter you're testing. Once the game starts, it's a free-for-all, with each tester competing to win the session. Is this play testing or ad hoc testing? Why?

6. You've been assigned to test the gameplay of a *Tekken*-style fighting game and suspect that one of the fighters seems significantly weaker than the others. What ad hoc tests can you perform in order to confirm and quantify your suspicion?

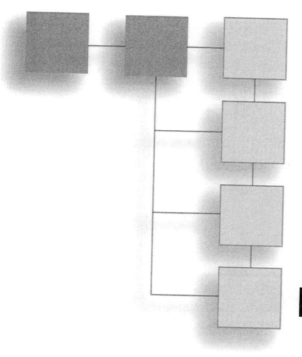

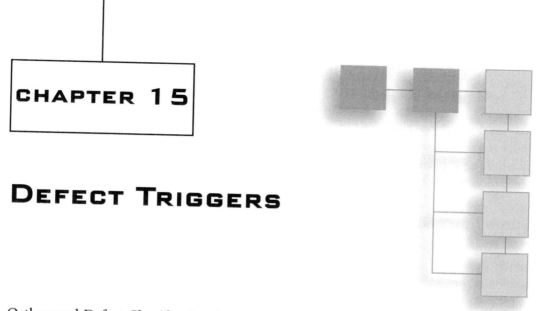

CHAPTER 15

DEFECT TRIGGERS

Orthogonal Defect Classification (ODC) includes a set of Defect Triggers to categorize the way defects are caused to appear. These same triggers can be used to classify tests as well as defects. Test suites that do not account for each of the triggers will be incapable of revealing all of the defects in the game.

Operating Regions

Game operation can be broken down into three stages: Game Start, In-Game, and Post-Game. These regions don't just apply to the game as a whole. They can also be mapped to discrete experiences within the game, such as new missions, seasons, or levels. There is also a Pre-Game region in which the game environment—hardware, operating system, and so on—is operational but the game has not been started. Figure 15.1 shows the relationship of these operating regions.

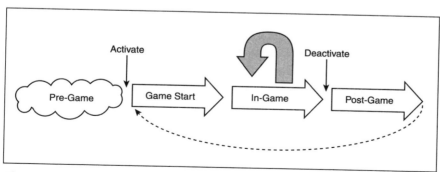

Figure 15.1 Game software operating regions.

Pre-Game Operating Region

The Pre-Game region represents the period that precedes the use of the game. For consoles, this would be the time prior to inserting the game disk. On PCs and mobile phones this is the period in time before you start the game app. Cartridge-based hand-helds may also have an operational mode prior to inserting the game cartridge. In each of these cases, the user can change settings and do things with the device that potentially impact the subsequent operation of your game.

Game Start Operating Region

The Game Start region accounts for operations that are performed from the time the player starts the game until the time the game is actually ready to be played. Some activities that take place during this time can be interrupted, such as cinematic sequences that provide an introduction or highlights of the game's features. Other activities, such as a screen displaying the "loading" progress, cannot be accelerated or interrupted. The game software also performs activities that are essential to the proper operation of the game but are not visible to the player. At the very end of this process the game may be in a "ready" state, during which it is waiting for the player to hit a button or key in order to enter the game.

In-Game Operating Region

The In-Game region covers all of things you could possibly do when playing the game. Some functions can only be performed once during the course of the game, whereas others can be repeated throughout the game. There are also functions that depend on the player meeting some condition before they can occur. Games that incorporate non-player characters (NPCs) also manage and control these resources during this operating period.

Post-Game Operating Region

The player can end the game or a gaming session a number of ways. Quitting without saving requires less processing than when saving. The player is often given the opportunity to save character data and progress before the game terminates itself. Games played on portable devices can be ended by turning off the device. If the device's Off switch is under software control, the game software can perform save and shutdown operations prior to killing power.

Story-based games treat the user to a final cinematic sequence and roll credits when users reach the end of the story. Some games unlock new experiences for the player who reaches the end so he can continue to enjoy the game when going back through it a second time. This may activate code that is not exercised at all until the game is completed the first time.

The Triggers

Six Defect Triggers span the four game operating regions. These triggers describe ways to cause distinct categories of game defects to show up during testing. Together, these triggers account for all of the possible defects that can occur.

The Configuration Trigger

Some game configuration takes place in the Pre-Game region, prior to running the game. This includes device or environment settings that are established before running the game, such as game platform software versions. Date and time, screen resolution, system audio volume, operating system version, patches, and language settings are all examples of Configuration triggers.

Configuration also involves external devices that are associated with the game platform. Game controllers, keyboards, mice, speakers, monitors, network connections, headsets, and so on are also part of the test configuration. As shown in Figure 15.2, such devices are attached to various external connectors on the Sega Dreamcast or any other modern game hardware platform.

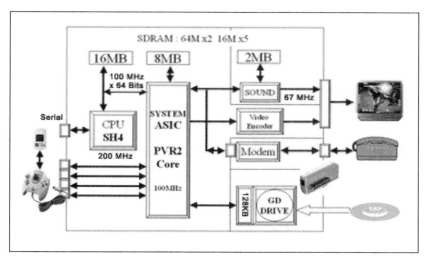

Figure 15.2 Sega Dreamcast block diagram.

The nature of these external devices is that they each have their own settings, properties (for example, version), and physical connection. Some of these devices can even have additional devices attached to them, such as the Nyko® Xbox game controller shown in Figure 15.3, which can have lights, fans, vibration, memory, and microphone and/or speaker capabilities depending on the models and add-ons that are used.

Memory Unit

SpeakerCom™

Figure 15.3 Nyko® multifunction Xbox game controller configuration.

Disconnecting one or more devices during gameplay is a type of configuration change. Unfortunately for developers, the game software is unable to do anything to prevent the user from connecting or disconnecting external devices during gameplay, or from changing settings or software versions on the game platform. Configuration changes can occur in any of the game software operating regions.

Connecting a device could be done to correct an accidental disconnection ("The dog kicked the phone cable out of the wall!"), change out a faulty device, or add a new capability, such as a headset for voice control. This too should be anticipated by the game design and incorporated into the game tests.

These possibilities shouldn't be excluded from testing just because your initial response might be "Why would anyone ever do that?" Recognize when you have this kind of reaction that you should test that area vigorously. It is likely that other people would have had reacted similarly and didn't bother to find out what would happen in that case.

Configuration failures might show up immediately as a result of the configuration operation or at some later time when a game operation relies on the new configuration. Seemingly unrelated capabilities might also fail as a side-effect of a configuration change.

The Startup Trigger

The Startup trigger is utilized by attempting operations while some game function is in the process of starting up or immediately after that while code values and states are in their initial conditions. This could be a highly noticeable activity, such as a "Loading please wait…" screen or something that's behind the scenes such as loading data for a room you've just entered.

Particular code vulnerabilities exist during the startup period. These do not present themselves at any other time in the game. Code variables are being initialized. Graphics information is being loaded, buffered, and rendered. Information is read from and/or written to disk.

As an example, here is a summary of the events that take place in the Unreal engine in order to start up a new level:

1. The GameInfo's `InitGame()` event is called
2. The GameInfo's `SetGrammar()` event is called
3. All Actors' `PreBeginPlay()` events are called
4. All Actors' `BeginPlay()` events are called
5. All Actors' zones are set
6. All Actors' volumes are set
7. All Actors' `PostBeginPlay()` events are called
8. All Actors' `PostNetBeginPlay()` events are called
9. All Actors' `SetInitialState()` events are called
10. All Actors either with `bShouldBaseAtStartup = True` and `Physics` set to `PHYS_None` or `PHYS_Rotating` or with an Attach Tag get their base set

Startup defects are triggered by operations that take place during the Game Start period. These operations can be user-initiated or caused by the game platform. Interrupting any part of this sequence could mean that some essential operation will not complete its work or may not get to run at all. The Startup trigger accounts for bugs that will only show up as a result of the initial conditions that result from the game's initialization and startup processes. That means that defects that occur the very first time you use a game capability—a new map, item, powerup, or spell, for example—should also be classified as Startup defects.

The Exception Trigger

Special portions of the game code are exercised by the Exception trigger. Exception handling in a game is normally recognized by the player. Audio "bonks" or alert boxes are common ways in which an in-game problem is communicated. Some exceptions are under the control of the game, such as restricting user input choices. Other exceptions are caused by external conditions that are not under the control of the game software, such as network connection problems. Figure 15.4 shows the special alert you get when trying to play *Dawn of War* in multiplayer online mode when your game PC is not connected to the Internet. Exceptions can occur in any of the game operating regions.

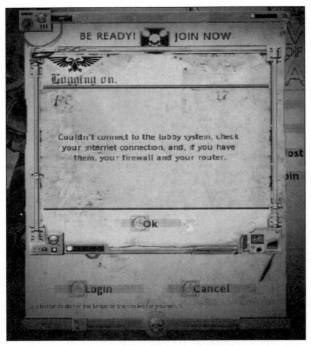

Figure 15.4 *Dawn of War* online game mode connection exception alert.

The Stress Trigger

The Stress trigger tests the game under extreme conditions. These could be conditions imposed on either hardware or software resources. Memory, screen resolution, disk space, file size, and network speed are all examples of game conditions that could be stressed by users or through testing. Simply reaching a limit does not constitute a stress condition. Once stressed, the resource must be used or operated in some way for the stress behavior to reveal itself.

The Normal Trigger

Normal game operation takes place in the In-Game operating region. This refers to using the game apart from any stress, configuration, or exception conditions, kind of like the way you would script a demo or show how the game should be played in the user manual. The "normal" code is distinct from the code that handles the exceptions, the code that processes configuration changes and the code that takes over under stressful conditions.

Most of the testing that is done uses Normal triggers. That is okay because that is how the game will be used the vast majority of the time and testing is not just about finding defects; it also demonstrates that the game functions the way it is supposed to.

However, testing that almost exclusively uses Normal triggers is only training the code to follow a script. It will not detect many user faults that will occur in real-life situations.

The Restart Trigger

The Restart trigger classifies a failure that occurs as a result of quitting, ending the game, turning off the game device, ejecting the game disk, or terminating the game's operation in any other way. Some games are nice about this and prompt you to save vital information before allowing you to exit a game scenario, mission, or battle in progress. When ending the game, some information needs to be remembered and some forgotten. If either is done incorrectly, the player can gain an advantage or lose precious progress.

Sometimes you can notice the effects of a Restart defect during the End Game period, or you may have to wait until the next time you use the game. For example, there is a bug in *All Star Baseball*™ 2004 where you can Quit and Save a game while you are pitching, restart the game system, and then reload your saved game to fully recover your pitcher's energy. This kind of defect goes unnoticed if your test doesn't go back into the game after saving, so remember to do that whenever you apply a Restart trigger.

Classifying Defects

You don't have to wait for your next project to start using Defect Triggers in your tests. Use keywords to help classify new or existing tests and defects. With that information you can identify where the defects are coming from and what testing is missing. Not surprisingly, a lot of bugs that get released belong to Defect Triggers that received little attention, if any, during game testing. When defects of a certain trigger start to show up, that's your cue to beef up the tests to use that trigger even more. Table 15.1 provides lists of keywords you can use to classify your defects and tests according to each of the six defect triggers.

Here are some examples taken from the *Star Trek Elite Force II* version 1.10 patch readme file. Remember, missing capabilities are defects as well as functionality that is in the game but doesn't work properly.

> *"Mouse 4 and 5 are now key-bindable in the Configure menu"*

This is an easy one to start off with. The bug description mentions that the problem is with the Configure menu, so classify this as a Configuration defect.

> *"The sniper rifle now reloads automatically in all game modes. It no longer waits for the player to let go of the fire button."*

Table 15.1 Defect Trigger Keywords

Trigger	Keywords
Configuration	configure, model, type, version, environment, connect, disconnect, add, remove
Startup	startup, initial, first, un-initialized, creation, boot, warm up, wakeup, loading, setup, entry, transition, delay
Exception	exception, error, violation, exceeds, NULL, unexpected, recover, prevented, blocked, prohibited, unavailable
Stress	stress, load, rate, slowest, fastest, low, high, speed, capacity, limit, long, short, few, many, empty, full
Normal	normal, typical, common, usual, expected, planned, basic, allowed, available
Restart	restart, reset, cleanup, eject, power down, ctrl-alt-del, quit

In this situation, holding down the fire button prevented the reloading of the rifle. This should be considered an undesirable behavior of the weapon Restart process.

> *"Saved game issues with long computer names fixed."*

The Stress keyword "long" is used here and it is in reference to a problem that occurs when trying to perform a function (saving the game) with the long computer name, so this is a Stress defect.

> *"The Ultridium Explosive damage has been increased."*

Here is a function that wasn't quite operating the way it was intended. The damage increase is not limited to a particular configuration or condition and affects something that happens during gameplay (the In-Game operating region). This is simply a Normal defect.

> *"Death will no longer break chat in MultiMatch."*

In this context, "death" is part of a player's life cycle: Spawn-Fight-Die-Spawn and so on. Death's place in this life cycle is to initiate a "restart" of the player's character. This restart breaks the chat function. The defect is a Restart defect.

> *"The visual graphic indicating that you have the flag in MultiMatch Capture the Flag matches has been enhanced."*

Problems don't just have to happen in game logic to be considered bugs. Here one of the graphics effects was improved. The solution is not related to a particular condition or configuration of the game. This is a Normal defect.

> *"Teams are no longer automixed on map restart in MultiMatch."*

Game maps can also have a life cycle: Start Map-Use Map-Change/Restart Map and so on. An undesirable function—the automixing of teams—takes place as a result of the map restart. Therefore, this defect is triggered by that Restart.

> "When playing a Disintegration match in MultiMatch, the reload delay for the sniper rifle is now shorter."

Yet another "life cycle" reveals itself here. The cycle of shooting a weapon: a round of ammunition is ready to be fired, shoot weapon, wait for shooting effects to occur (shooting sound, projectile launched, cartridge ejected, ammo count decreased, and so on). Then the next round is ready, and so on. The problem is noticed ("triggered") when the player tries to shoot the weapon but the gun is spending too much time in the "ammunition is ready to be fired" part of the sequence. Think of the "loading" keyword and map this to the Startup trigger.

> "The server will now inform the player if they vote to switch to a map that doesn't exist on the server."

This is a case where the player is referencing an "unavailable" resource by making a request that the game can't comply with. Apparently it was permitted prior to the patch without notifying the player that she was throwing away her vote. This is an Exception trigger defect.

> "The point of view for demo recording will now follow the direction in which the player is looking."

Don't confuse a game "mode" with "configuration." Think of a mode as another feature or function of the game. Even though this bug only had to be fixed for demo recording, the problem was in the In-Game operating region and not dependent on any configuration or condition. It is another Normal trigger defect.

Sometimes you will come across defects that may seem to belong to more than one trigger category. An example might be the case where an exception is not handled properly during startup. What you must resolve is which situation was mostly responsible for triggering the defect. If the situation is only considered an "exception" during startup, then it is the exception that is triggering the fault. The rationale is that there is a particular piece of code that should exist to handle the exception during startup. The exception condition causes that code to execute and finds that it is missing or faulty. On the other hand, if the handling of that exception is common throughout the game and it only fails to operate properly during startup, then it is the fact that you tried it at startup that triggered the exception code not to run or to run improperly. Your responsibility as a tester is to test the handling of this exception in all operating regions of the game to help make this kind of determination.

Defect Triggers and Test Designs

Each element in the test design represents one of the Defect Triggers. Using one or more test design technique will not by itself guarantee that all of the Defect Triggers will be sufficiently represented in your tests. It takes an explicit effort to identify appropriate triggers and incorporate them into whatever type of test designs you produce. All of the Defect Triggers should be included either in a single test design or a set of test designs related to a specific game feature, function, or capability. If you have data from previous projects, see which triggers have been effective at finding defects and include those in your designs as well as any others you can think of.

The effectiveness of each trigger can be measured in terms of defects per test. You can also think of this as the sensitivity of the game code to each trigger. A large defects/test number relative to other triggers tells you how to find bugs economically and may also hint at an underlying flaw in the game platform design or implementation. If you only have time or resources to run a given number of tests, running the tests for the most effective triggers will yield more defects than the trigger that produces the fewest defects per test (usually the Normal trigger). As you continue to create and run more tests for the most effective triggers, you will saturate them and no longer be able to find new bugs. Repeat this process to establish saturation for all of the triggers.

Combinatorial Design Trigger Examples

Let's go back to the *HALO* Advanced Controls combinatorial design, shown in Chapter 10 in Figure 10.26, to see if any triggers need to be added. Look Sensitivity is tested for its default, minimum, and maximum values. The minimum and maximum values could be considered Stress values since the game is supposed to respond ("process") as slowly or as quickly as it can to the movement of the joystick. The remaining parameters have values that determine whether a capability is either on or off. None of these address a particular configuration or a situation that would apply to Startup, Restart, Exception, or Stress conditions. As a result, the majority of test values represent Normal behavior. For this test to be more effective, incorporate the missing triggers as well as any other possible Stress values.

Start by identifying Configuration resources related to the Advanced Controls options. All of these parameters affect the use of the game controller. There are different types of game controllers, such as those with or without vibration and those that are wireless or wired. The controller can be inserted into any of the slots provided on the game console. It is also possible to remove the controller during the process of selecting the options, and subsequently re-insert it in the same position or a different one. These possibilities create new parameters and values to add to the combinatorial table.

The updated table is shown in Figure 15.5. Because of the added complexity introduced by the new parameters and values, the Allpairs tool was used to generate this table.

Test	Look Sensitivity	Invert Thumbstick	Controller Vibration	Invert Flight Control	Auto-Center	Remove Controller	Replace Controller	Vibration Equipped	Controller Connection
1	1	YES	YES	YES	YES	1	1	YES	WIRED
2	3	NO	NO	NO	NO	1	2	NO	WIRELESS
3	3	NO	YES	YES	NO	2	1	YES	WIRELESS
4	1	YES	NO	NO	YES	2	2	NO	WIRED
5	10	NO	YES	NO	YES	3	3	YES	WIRED
6	10	YES	NO	YES	NO	3	4	NO	WIRELESS
7	1	NO	NO	YES	NO	4	3	YES	WIRELESS
8	3	YES	YES	NO	YES	4	4	NO	WIRED
9	10	NO	NO	NO	YES	1	1	NO	WIRELESS
10	10	YES	YES	YES	NO	2	2	YES	WIRED
11	3	YES	NO	YES	YES	3	3	NO	WIRED
12	1	NO	YES	NO	NO	3	4	YES	WIRELESS
13	10	YES	NO	NO	NO	4	1	YES	WIRED
14	1	YES	YES	YES	NO	1	3	NO	WIRELESS
15	3	NO	NO	YES	YES	2	4	YES	WIRED
16	1	NO	YES	YES	YES	4	2	NO	WIRELESS
17	10	NO	YES	NO	YES	2	3	NO	WIRELESS
18	10	YES	NO	YES	NO	1	4	YES	WIRED
19	3	YES	YES	NO	NO	3	1	NO	WIRELESS
20	1	NO	NO	NO	YES	3	2	YES	WIRED

Figure 15.5 Advanced Controls combinatorial table with Configuration triggers.

As an alternative, create a separate table to cover the configuration-related parameters and value pairs. This kind of approach enables you to use the mostly "Normal" table as a sanity test and then proceed with the tables for the other triggers once the game passes the sanity tests. The Advanced Options game controller configuration table is shown in Figure 15.6.

As it turns out, no matter which slot the controller is removed from, the game prompts you to "Please reconnect #1 controller" as shown in Figure 15.7. Additionally, your ability to modify the settings is restored no matter which slot you replace the controller in. Another side effect or removing the controller is that the changes you made prior to its removal are lost—the settings revert to their last stored values. This might not be so bad on a screen where you only have a few values to keep track of, but if you are updating dozens of values to customize an RPG character, this loss of data can be frustrating. In contrast, *Tony Hawk's Underground* identifies the specific controller that was removed, requires the controller to be replaced into the same slot in order to continue, and preserves the changed option values.

Test	Remove Controller	Replace Controller	Vibration Equipped	Controller Connection
1	1	1	YES	WIRED
2	1	2	NO	WIRELESS
3	1	3	YES	WIRELESS
4	1	4	NO	WIRED
5	2	1	NO	WIRELESS
6	2	2	YES	WIRED
7	2	3	NO	WIRED
8	2	4	YES	WIRELESS
9	3	1	YES	WIRED
10	3	2	NO	WIRELESS
11	3	3	YES	WIRELESS
12	3	4	NO	WIRED
13	4	1	NO	WIRELESS
14	4	2	YES	WIRED
15	4	3	NO	WIRED
16	4	4	YES	WIRELESS

Figure 15.6 Advanced Option game controller configuration table.

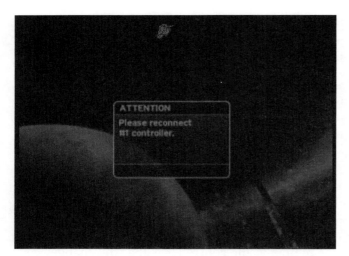

Figure 15.7 *HALO* "game controller removed" attention notice.

The next step is to seek out Exception trigger opportunities. Since the option values are selected by scrolling, there is no opportunity to enter a "wrong" value. However, it may be possible to disrupt the selection mechanism itself. The A and B buttons are used for accepting the options or going back to the previous screen. Try holding down X, Y, the Left Trigger ("L"), or Right Trigger ("R") during the selection of the test values.

Again, one of your options is to add a column for these values plus the "None" choice into a single table, as shown in Figure 15.8. Although the table has grown again, these 28 cases represent pairwise coverage of 15,360 total possible combinations of these values!

Test	Look Sensi-tivity	Invert Thumb-stick	Controller Vibration	Invert Flight Control	Auto-Center	Remove Controller	Replace Controller	Vibration Equipped	Controller Connection	Simul-taneous Key
1	1	YES	YES	YES	YES	1	1	YES	WIRED	NONE
2	3	NO	NO	NO	NO	2	2	NO	WIRELESS	NONE
3	10	YES	NO	NO	YES	1	2	NO	WIRED	X
4	1	NO	YES	YES	NO	2	1	YES	WIRELESS	X
5	3	NO	YES	YES	YES	3	3	NO	WIRED	Y
6	10	YES	YES	NO	NO	4	4	YES	WIRELESS	Y
7	1	NO	NO	NO	YES	3	4	YES	WIRELESS	L
8	3	YES	NO	YES	NO	4	3	NO	WIRED	L
9	10	NO	NO	YES	NO	1	3	YES	WIRELESS	R
10	3	YES	YES	NO	YES	2	4	NO	WIRED	R
11	10	YES	NO	NO	NO	3	1	NO	WIRELESS	Y
12	1	NO	YES	YES	YES	4	2	YES	WIRED	L
13	1	YES	YES	NO	NO	1	3	NO	WIRELESS	NONE
14	10	NO	NO	YES	YES	2	4	YES	WIRED	NONE
15	3	NO	YES	NO	YES	3	1	YES	WIRELESS	X
16	1	NO	NO	YES	NO	1	2	YES	WIRED	Y
17	3	YES	NO	NO	NO	1	1	NO	WIRED	L
18	1	NO	NO	NO	YES	4	1	NO	WIRELESS	R
19	10	YES	YES	YES	NO	3	2	NO	WIRED	X
20	10	YES	NO	YES	YES	2	3	YES	WIRED	R
21	10	NO	YES	YES	NO	2	4	NO	WIRELESS	L
22	3	NO	NO	NO	YES	4	3	YES	WIRELESS	X
23	1	YES	NO	NO	NO	3	2	YES	WIRELESS	R
24	3	YES	YES	YES	YES	1	4	YES	WIRELESS	Y
25	10	YES	NO	YES	NO	4	4	NO	WIRED	NONE
26	1	NO	YES	NO	YES	3	3	NO	WIRED	NONE
27	1	YES	NO	NO	NO	2	4	NO	WIRED	X
28	3	NO	YES	NO	YES	2	2	NO	WIRELESS	Y

Figure 15.8 Advanced game options with Configuration and Exception triggers.

A potential danger in doing this is that most of your test cases will result in an exception behavior that may prevent you from observing the effects of the other test values. In Figure 15.8, only six tests—1, 2, 13, 14, 25, and 26—avoid an input exception. A way around this is to create a separate table to isolate the exception effects, as shown in Figure 15.9. The "NONE" value for the Simultaneous Key parameter is not included because it is not an Exception trigger and it is already implicitly represented in the non-exception table for this feature.

The extreme Look Sensitivity values were identified as Stress triggers, but is there any other "stressful" operation that can be done during option selection? For this particular game, both the left analog stick and the D-Pad on the game controller can be used to scroll through the options (vertically) and choices (horizontally). Operating them simultaneously could produce interesting results. Add this to the test table by defining the Scroll Control parameter with the values of LEFT STICK, D-PAD, and BOTH. Follow the same rationale as for the previous triggers when deciding whether to add these parameters and values to a single table for this screen versus creating a separate table for this trigger.

Test	Look Sensi- tivity	Invert Thumb- stick	Controller Vibration	Invert Flight Control	Auto- Center	Simul- taneous Key
1	1	YES	YES	YES	YES	X
2	3	NO	NO	NO	NO	X
3	1	NO	YES	NO	YES	Y
4	3	YES	NO	YES	NO	Y
5	10	YES	YES	NO	NO	L
6	10	NO	NO	YES	YES	L
7	1	YES	NO	NO	NO	R
8	3	NO	YES	YES	YES	R
9	10	YES	YES	YES	NO	X
10	10	NO	NO	NO	YES	Y
11	1	NO	NO	YES	NO	L
12	3	YES	YES	NO	YES	L
13	10	YES	NO	YES	YES	R

Figure 15.9 Original Advanced Controls table with only Exception triggers added.

All that's left now is to identify Startup and Restart triggers for your Advanced Controls tests. These particular settings are tied to individual player profiles. This presents the opportunity to test the settings for a brand new profile versus one that has already been in use. The new profile behavior is your Startup trigger. Add this to the tests as a "Profile" parameter with NEW (Startup) or EXISTING (Normal) choices.

The advanced controls selection process can be restarted in a variety of ways: go back to the previous screen without saving, eject the game disk from the console, or turn the console off. Follow up these operations by going back into the Advanced Controls screen to check for any abnormalities. Since these settings can be stored in either internal or removable memory, another way to do a "restart" is to load information previously saved to external memory back on top of your internally saved modified values. Represent these possibilities in your table with a "Re-Enter" parameter that has a possible value of NONE for the Normal trigger and BACK, EJECT, OFF, and LOAD EXTERNAL for the Restart trigger.

TFD Trigger Examples

TFD triggers are located along the flows. The Ammo TFD template, provided in Appendix D, will be used to illustrate how to incorporate all of the Defect Triggers into a TFD. It has a few more flows than the TFD you constructed in Chapter 11, but is it "complete" in terms of triggers? Use it in a specific context—*Unreal Tournament 2004* for the PC—and see what you can dig up.

To begin with, the template includes plenty of Normal trigger flows such as GetGun and GetAmmo when you have neither (NoGunNoAmmo). However, the same event can represent different triggers depending on its context with respect to the states it's leaving and entering. For example, GetAmmo when you already have the maximum amount is a case of performing a function when a resource (ammo) is at its maximum. This qualifies as a Stress trigger. Shooting a gun with no ammo falls on the other end of the spectrum where the ammo resource is at a minimum (0). Figure 15.10 shows the Ammo TFD template with these Stress triggers highlighted.

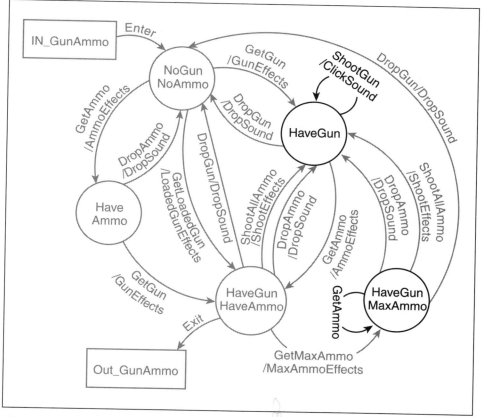

Figure 15.10 Ammo TFD template with Stress flows highlighted.

Now how about adding a Startup trigger? The TFD Enter flow jumps right to the point where the player is active in the match. In reality, there is a "pre-game" period where the player can run around the arena before hitting the "fire" button (usually the left mouse button) to initiate the match. This is relevant to the purpose of the test because a player who runs over weapons or ammo during this time should not accumulate any items as a result.

Represent this startup process on the TFD by performing "mitosis" on the NoGunNoAmmo state. That is, split it into two connected states. One state retains the original name and connections (except for the Enter flow) while the other captures the dry run and countdown behavior. Figure 15.11 shows the process of splitting this portion of the TFD.

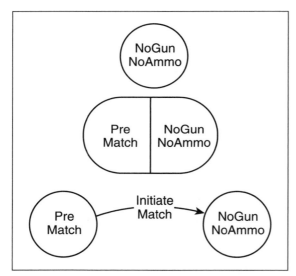

Figure 15.11 NoGunNoAmmo state mitosis.

The new PreMatch state can be introduced to the TFD. Start by disconnecting the Enter flow from NoGunNoAmmo and attaching it to PreMatch. Then add flows to attempt GetAmmo and GetGun during the PreMatch period. These flows are Startup triggers. Figure 15.12 shows how this looks.

Next add the Restart trigger to the diagram. It's possible to change your status to Spectator in the middle of a match and then Join back in as a participant. Spectator mode takes your character out of the game and lets you follow players in the game while you control the camera angle. Any guns or ammo picked up prior to entering Spectator mode should be lost when you Join to return to the same match in progress. Rejoining the game from Spectator mode is done instantly without the countdown timer that you get when you start the match for the very first time. Suspending and rejoining can be done at any time during the match after the initial countdown timer has expired. Add a SpectateAndJoin flow from each of the in-game states on the TFD and tie it back to NoGunNoAmmo. Don't forget the loop flow from NoGunNoAmmo back to itself. A TFD with these updates is shown in Figure 15.13.

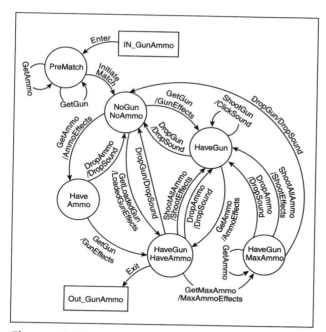

Note how more "pressure" is being put on the NoGunNoAmmo state with all of the flows entering and exiting. It's like a busy intersection; they tend to be much more dangerous than the ones that aren't so busy. This reflects the importance of this state to the well-being of the feature and its potential sensitivity to changes.

Figure 15.12   PreMatch state and Startup trigger flows added to Ammo TFD.

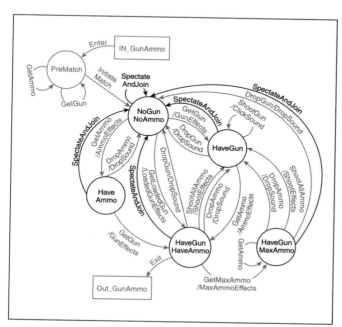

The TFD is getting cozy but there are a still a few more triggers to consider. For the Exception trigger, there is an operation available to use a weapon's alternate fire mode. Typically, the left mouse button is used for normal firing and the right mouse button for alternate firing. Some weapons, such as the Grenade Launcher, do not have an alternate firing mode. They should not fire nor decrement their ammo count when the user attempts alternate firing.

Figure 15.13   Ammo TFD with SpectateAndJoin Restart flows highlighted.

This is something you can use as an Exception trigger. Since this "Unsupported AltFire" operation will not change the ammo status of the weapon, add it as a loop on the TFD states where there is both a gun and ammo. Your result should look like Figure 15.14.

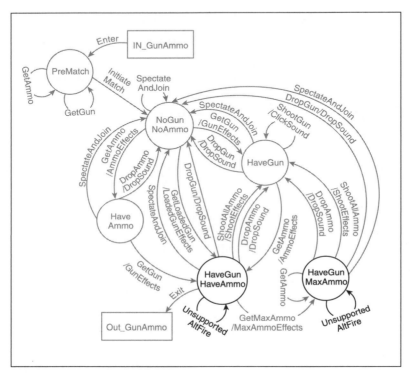

Figure 15.14 Ammo TFD with AltFire Exception flows highlighted.

Finally, the Configuration must be included. One of the weapon settings in the game allows the player to select an older style rendering of certain weapons. While this is appealing to players who owned earlier titles in this series, it also creates an additional test responsibility. You can check that changing the weapon rendering while the game is in progress does not affect the amount of ammo loaded in that weapon or produce unwanted artifacts such as unexpected audio or "shadow" (duplicate) weapons. Add a ToggleWeaponSkin flow at all of the states where the player has the weapon. Since this should not affect the ammo, these flows will loop back into the states from which they originated. Figure 15.15 shows the TFD with these Configuration flows.

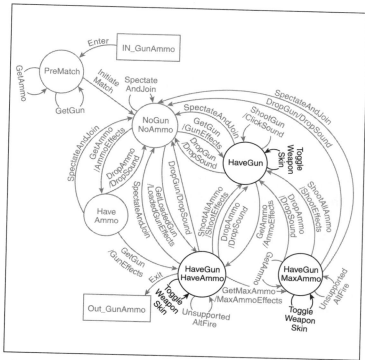

Figure 15.15 Ammo TFD with weapon skin Configuration flows.

Now the TFD is getting really crowded! Just remember that the same option that was presented for combinatorial tests is applicable to TFDs, test tree designs, or any other formal or informal means you use to come up with test cases. You can incorporate the triggers into a single design or create companion test designs that work together as a suite of tests to provide the trigger coverage you need.

You may also find it useful to document the intended triggers for each test element. One easy way is to provide a letter code in parentheses after the event name on each TFD flow, parameter value for combinatorial tests, or branch node for test tree designs. You can count the number of times each letter appears to see how many times each trigger is being used. It also helps you classify defects you find when running the tests. Just be aware that this carries a maintenance burden to re-evaluate the trigger designation whenever you move or add new test elements to the design.

Summary

What a difference the extra triggers make in the test design! Is it more work? Yes. But it's also better. You have improved the capability of this test to find defects and you will have more confidence in your game when it passes tests that use all of the triggers. Defect Triggers were not created with any one particular test methodology in mind. They are effective whether you are testing at the beginning or the end of the project and whether you have meticulous test designs or you are just typing in test cases as you go along. If you choose not to use them, you are adding to the risk of important defects escaping into your shipping game.

Exercises

Having come this far in the book, you may find yourself being asked to offer your opinion and contribute to your team's test strategies. The following exercises are designed to give you practice at this.

1. Which is your favorite Defect Trigger? Why? Which one would be the most difficult for you to include in your tests, both in terms of test execution and test design?

2. Earlier in this chapter it was mentioned that both the D-Pad and Analog joystick could be used to make the *HALO* option selections. Describe how you would incorporate these choices into your test suite. Do you prefer adding them to a large single table for the feature or creating a separate smaller table focused on the option selection means? Describe what factors would cause you to change your answer.

3. It would also be interesting to start an *Unreal Tournament* match while standing on one of the gun or ammo items. The game automatically snaps you back to the original starting point after a three-second countdown before the action starts. Describe how you would update the Ammo TFD to include this possibility.

4. Again, for the Ammo TFD, describe how you would add or change flows to represent a player firing the gun using a joystick rather than the left mouse button, which is typically used for firing. Treat this as a case where both the mouse and joystick are connected during the game. Also indicate which triggers are represented by this possibility.

5. Texas Hold 'Em poker has become very popular recently and many video-games on various platforms are popping up to take advantage of the present level of interest in this card game. Make a list or outline of how you would include each trigger in your testing of a hypothetical or actual Texas Hold 'Em videogame. Don't stop at one example—list at least three values, situations, or cases for each of the non-Normal triggers. Remember to include tests of the betting rules—not just the mechanics and winning conditions for the hand. If you are not familiar with the rules of this card game, do a search online and read a few descriptions before you build your trigger lists.

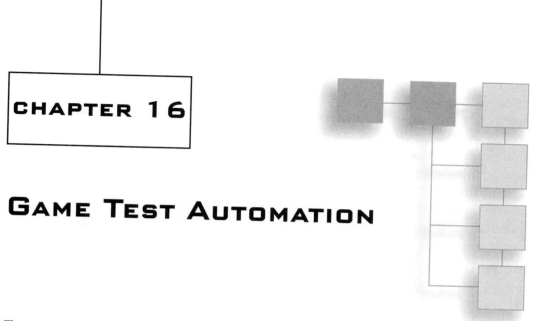

CHAPTER 16

GAME TEST AUTOMATION

Test automation is a hotly debated topic in the game industry. At one extreme are those who argue that all aspects of game testing should be automated. At the other, many remain unconvinced that test automation in the game industry is viable other than in certain, specific instances. That said, a surprisingly large number of game developers and publishers have made little or no use of test automation nor have they explored its uncharted potential.

Can Automated Testing Work for Me?

The potential advantages of automating game testing are

- Improved game reliability
- Greater tester and machine efficiency
- Greater consistency of results
- Repetition, repetition, repetition
- Faster testing
- The ability to simulate tremendously large numbers of concurrent players for stress and load testing without having to use large pools of human testers

In order to enjoy these benefits, you need to deal with a number of factors that can get in the way of successful game test automation if they aren't handled properly.

Production Costs

The cost of hiring new developers to write additional lines of code into a game to support automation (as well as writing scripts and other test utilities, interfaces, and so on) can be more than it would cost to pay human testers. Furthermore, the reality is that code written for the purposes of automating testing is like any other code. It may not work right and comes with its own set of bugs. It's very possible for automated testing to add significantly to both the cost and development time of a game. Cost overruns and missed deadlines are common in the game industry. The threat of higher costs and further delays without any guarantee (some would argue) of clear benefits makes it hard for many managers to approve a large-scale automated testing program. To have a fighting chance, your test automation strategy must address the areas of the game that can provide the best return on the automation labor and code investment.

Reusability

Reusability of automated test code from one game to another is also a factor that has deterred many managers from approving automated testing programs in their company. Unlike other software businesses, the game industry is famous for creating new code with each new title. Even when the "same" engine or core code is reused for a new game, that engine or code is often modified, repaired, and improved upon. Those changes could prevent some or all of the automated test code from working with the new title. Maximize your automated test reusability by providing functions that hide the game code details from the automated tests. For each new or revised game, only a few functions should have to change in order to re-enable the use of your existing automated test library.

The Human Factor

It is extremely unlikely that even the most cleverly written test automation code will ever replace the need for actual human testers playing your game. For instance, it would be an impressive algorithm indeed that could automatically determine whether a given part of a game was sufficiently "fun" to play. Similarly, human focus group testing is going to remain crucial to gaining key feedback about a game's playability and balance. Even aspects of game mechanics, personal opinions about the design of interfaces, and so on are all likely to be determined by human testers for some time to come. In addition, human testers are likely to continue to out-perform even the most cleverly written test scripts when it comes to the creative "let's see if I can find a way to break this" mentality. The knack or instinct for finding new ways to break the game sets good testers apart from the merely average ones. It is a uniquely human characteristic to think of new and ingenious ways to press a combination of keys and buttons in a way the designer and programmers of the game never thought of to find that the code can crash in the most spectacular of ways and on the most unpredictable of occasions! However, once this has been accomplished, the operations that lead to these crashes can themselves be automated, freeing up time for humans to find more of the playability, balance, and "fun" issues in the game.

Scale Matters

A fundamental decision you need to make is whether your automation is going to be done on a large or small scale. If your vision is to automate virtually all aspects of testing in your company, you will have to take a great many factors into account.

First, large-scale automation will involve a fundamental shift in the way the entire company operates. And for some, this factor alone will mean large-scale test automation is not feasible.

Second, large-scale automation is a long-term investment that may not pay off in the first few games you create once the system is in place. Very long game projects can be an exception, as well a single titles that must be ported to multiple platforms. All key people in the company will need to understand that the payoff may be far off in the future.

Third, test automation is a form of software development. Although this is widely agreed upon, it is also surprisingly frequently overlooked when companies discuss the topic. Automation is not going to be a simple matter of buying an off-the-shelf product or tool that is simply thrown into the development mix and "magically" reduces the time it takes to identify and fix bugs, or to improve playability.

If you intend to go large-scale, you are clearly going to need somebody in your company who can act as a key evangelist for test automation. Without someone at a sufficiently high level who can act as the visionary for the process and who can get behind it and make sure that interest in the idea doesn't wane when there are no immediate "upfront" advantages, the automatic testing program is likely to fail and fall into disuse.

If you are considering a small-scale roll-out of automatic testing tools and programs, your risks are considerably smaller. Start the process by selecting test automations that are likely to give fairly immediate rewards, thereby buoying up support for automation within the company, while only incrementally increasing cost or development time.

Tip

If you are not committed to a long-term investment, large-scale test automation is probably not right for your company.

Great Expectations

Adding automatic testing tools creates a heightened expectation in upper management. Suddenly, the fact that automatic testing tools are being used can lead managers to have unrealistic expectations about lower production costs, reduced development times, and so on. Indeed, this exact point is a key hurdle facing any test automation advocate in a company. How do you introduce something to management that in the near term might significantly add to cost and production time, but that holds out the promise of potential gains down the road in titles that may not see the light of day for some seasons to come? If there is sufficient stability and commonality in your typical game code or the types of games you produce, then perhaps you will have a clear argument. If your automated test code, scripts, and tools need to be extensively rewritten for each new game, your argument about the long-term payoff will be greatly diminished.

It is vital that you set management expectations accurately and reasonably when proposing to automate even a small part of your testing process. In doing so, you may find you are up against ingrained beliefs about automated testing, the result of media hype, misconceptions of many kinds, and more. Here are some of the false expectations you may face:

- **Everything will be automated.** For the vast majority of companies it just will not make sense to automate everything.

- **Automation will lead to lower costs and greater efficiency.** While greater efficiency is hopefully gained where automation is used properly, the fact is that, in the near term at least, costs will rise as extra lines of code and scripts need to be written, management of code increases, greater volume of data is generated that has to be managed and considered, and so on.

- **All manual tests will be automated.** Much of what is being done manually will not be suitable for automation.

- **Tools will be purchased off the shelf.** In reality, if your company uses a lot of proprietary game code, your test code and test scripts will probably be custom written too.

- **No ramp-up time will be needed.** For some reason, automation seems to carry with it the connotation for some of no ramp-up, but the opposite is the case.

- **Financial benefits will be immediate.** There will be an expectation of instant payback, when in fact it may be several titles down the road before the full positive effects of automation are realized.

- **Automated defect reporting will remove the need for human staff.** Without human involvement, teams soon discover that automated systems can generate a staggering amount of data. Much of that data should not be sent to the team, because it consists of false positives, false negatives, or merely duplicate data.

"We currently have five machines constantly building and validating data; one for each platform, including the PC, and the "monkey" machine, which runs a test script that loads each portion of the game while mashing controller buttons. The "monkey" machine so far has not been as effective as I hoped; usually somewhere there's a crash bug in the game that takes many hours to solve and the monkey is sitting idle during those hours.

Getting these autobuild scripts built isn't free. It takes a few weeks of coder time, and then requires regular maintenance. Frequently our autobuild machines will fail for one reason or another; a human has to check on them on a semi-regular basis (daily isn't often enough; hourly is too often) to make sure they're still churning away."

Jamie Fristrom, programmer on *Spider-Man* 2

http://www.gamasutra.com/features/20031212/fristrom_01.shtml#

Infrastructure

If you are intent on bringing automated testing to your company, a key consideration is to first build a solid infrastructure onto which the automatic testing programs can be placed, selected, and tracked. This will be essential if the test department hopes to keep up with changes that must be made to the test code whenever there is any significant change to a game build, a game's functionality, or its feature set.

Putting this infrastructure in place is software development involving the introduction of extensive database-driven systems to implement and track the test program. Time, resources, and funding need to be allocated to ensure the system is well designed and bulletproof before the necessary step of integrating it with game development. Here is a very important point: The way that all your company's games are written may have to change significantly to incorporate the test code, the hooks, the harnesses, and the frameworks that will enable test automation to be integrated into your company's game-creation process. This is especially true if you decide to go for a large-scale deployment of test automation.

Team Work

Game test automation involves a combination of software development and database management skills. Automating your testing doesn't require a whole new set of skills or a significant change in fundamental company procedures, other than the obvious fact that automation must now be inherent in all steps of the process of creating a title.

Still, you are likely to need a new game team structure that can focus on the needs of creating and rolling out your test automation program. You will need to have key positions on the test team for programmers who fully understand game code. They need to be able to write test code and scripts that fully integrate with the game code or they need to be able to convey clearly and succinctly their needs to the game code developers who can add the necessary hooks and lines of code that automatic testing requires.

Any effort to introduce test automation into a project needs the new test automators to be staffed in addition to the existing game developers and the balance of your testing department. It will be vital for the "automators" to remain uninvolved in the day-to-day issues of either the game code development or manual testing. This sub-team will need to be a well-managed one that works harmoniously and cooperates within itself, as well as being capable of working smoothly with the development team and the rest of the testing department. If you use staff that is already assigned to other testing tasks, you run the risk of significant conflicts between the needs of the "regular" testers and those doing automation. When the demands of manual testing get overloaded (and depending on where in the development cycle your title is, this is likely), the manager, testers, or programmers will find it harder and harder to justify keeping the automatic testing up to date. Potentially, automatic testing can get so far out of synch that it will get put aside in favor of using only human testers. Once the automation is up and running, manual testers can gradually shift their efforts to executing, maintaining, and creating new automated tests. Ideally, over time, every tester should be capable of contributing to both manual and automated testing. This transition period may span many releases or even multiple game projects.

Maturity Test

Is your test department a mature, well-developed organism comprised of well-trained individuals with a clear testing system? Or, do you still tend to undertake game testing on a rather ad hoc basis? Do you use entirely external testers? These factors will determine whether it is advisable for you to introduce automated testing, let alone seek to go entirely automatic. As a rule, adding automation may either be a significant boon to your company or a major disaster depending on the skill set of your team and the existing systems that you have (or do not have) in place. If your projects already tend to go substantially past due and over budget, you may decide that you are an ideal candidate for test automation, believing that it will shorten your development times and lower your costs by increasing your efficiency. Sadly, this is almost the opposite of what usually takes place. If your organization is already running at lower than peak efficiency, adding automation to your testing department could, and probably will, add significant new headaches. It can substantially increase the code that your team has to deal with (potentially hundreds of test scripts that have to be constantly maintained and updated, tracked, and so on) and appreciably increase the amount of test data that your team has to process, store, and analyze. Imagine you are already inundated with thousands of bug reports coming in from your internal and external testers. How will you, your team, and your system cope if an automated program generates tens of thousands of lines of data, much of which can be ignored but none of which can you assume is unimportant?

Introducing test automation in the middle of a project will not help a poorly run test effort. As Figure 16.1 suggests, it's a bad time to automate when your test department is overwhelmed and having trouble keeping up with the demands of development and marketing to get the game completed and bug free. Yet this is exactly the mistake that often occurs. Testers at the end of their wits recommend automation as a way to lessen their workload, not realizing it is (at least in the near term) likely to substantially increase the workload of both testers and programmers.

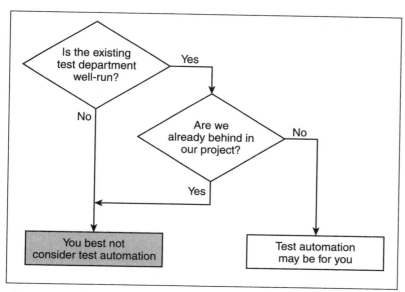

Figure 16.1 Should you automate?

Types of Games to Automate

Clearly some games are better suited to full-scale test automation than others, although most would benefit from at least some degree of automation.

Massively Multiplayer Games

One key genre that has had reported success with test automation is that of massively multiplayer (MMP) games like *The Sims Online* and *World of Warcraft*. It is precisely these massively multiplayer, persistent state world games or sizable role-playing games that have been such a challenge to code and test prior to retail launch. The sheer scale of these systems and their distributed nature makes them inherently difficult to test. Yet, the stability of these worlds at launch is clearly desirable, given the negative impact that a lack of stability will have on customer service calls, player experience, and your company's reputation. Here, then, is an ideal opportunity for automatic testing to shine. Even with MMPs, automated testing is not for all parts of the game, but generally more for those elements that

- Have a high number of repetitive actions
- Must simulate a very large number of players connected at once
- Are synchronized among a large number of servers and clients simultaneously

Simulating server load, for instance, has been a key use of automated scripts. Simply having large, open Beta tests cannot always consistently or reliably give you the stress/load data you are seeking—at least not in a repeatable and consistent fashion that is ideally sought after if you want to launch a stable product.

Another key use for automatic testing scripts in massively multiplayer games is that of repetitive behaviors and their effects on the game code and lag issues. Complete testing of such games can include picking up and dropping any given object thousands (if not tens of thousands) of times, or entering, leaving, and re-entering rooms thousands of times. For human testers to undertake this form of testing is not only extremely tedious, but also unreliable and unscalable. Surprisingly, as many obvious advantages as this approach seems to have, many companies building MMP games have not written such scripts and have relied on Beta testers to return the data they seek. If they do create such scripts, they often limit them to certain classes or races of characters instead of creating them for the entire game. This undoubtedly reflects the lack of upper-level management commitment to test automation in today's games industry. But if these tools are to be created, the testing management needs to ensure that they are not only easy to integrate into current game code, but also flexible enough to be reused in future games.

Clearly, automated techniques are going to be of significantly less use for MMPs where code is highly complex and often changed, or where there has historically been a low incidence of errors. Similarly, as described earlier, it is probably best left to manual testing to discover small bugs in interfaces, individual game loop logic, characters getting stuck in the environment, minor graphical clipping issues, and so on.

Ideally with an MMP, whether you are testing highly repetitive tasks or seeking to emulate server load, you will want to create test scripts that mimic actual players as closely as possible. For this reason you will likely want to have the actual main game code run the scripts and, where possible, use prerecorded actions of real players as templates upon which to build your automated scripts (another reason that even with test automation, human testing is unlikely to entirely disappear!). Furthermore, where possible you will want to have test clients speaking to the same server that live players speak to, so that the main game server cannot tell whether it is receiving input from live players or your automated script-based client. To achieve this, you can create a simple scripting language that sends common commands to the game server, such as `pickup_object`, `buy_object`, `open_door`, and so on. Ideally, you will also provide a simple interface so testers can easily set up scripts to automate a series of repetitive actions by indicating how often a given loop must be repeated, for example.

Other Types of Games

Many other types of games can benefit from automated testing, too. Level-based games such as first-person shooters could have sequences of play tested by well-written scripts that imitate a player repeatedly shooting in a certain pattern. Additional tests could be automated to randomly test paths through a level. Such tests would seek out instances where clipping occurs, check if the game hangs, or find where players can pass through walls and floors. Although automated tests are unlikely to be of much use on level balancing or the subjective elements of playing a level (how much "fun" it is), any aspect of the design that can be tested by repeated action is optimal for automated testing. For instance, it can be highly tedious to have to test the entire GUI of a game over and over again with every new build. This is traditionally an area where human testers are—or can be—inefficient. Simple scripts that automatically test each combination of button press or menu item selection can significantly increase the early detection of bugs in the game code and lessen the chance that any bug will persist to retail release of the game.

On the face of it, simple puzzle games might seem to be the least likely candidates for automatic testing. In fact, testing can be extremely useful for such titles. Many early EDGE games produced in the 1980s were puzzle games in which the clear danger faced by testers was that they knew the solution to the game and the players did not. Thus, automated scripts were used in even simple puzzle games to specifically test what would happen if players made moves the programmers had not expected them to make. These were moves that the human testers tended to miss. The result of that approach was that not a single error of this kind was reported in any of the puzzle games released during that period. Needless to say, this is a good way to make your manager a fan of game test automation!

Mobile phone games are another genre potentially well-suited to test automation. A developer can be required to have any given game run on many tens or hundreds of mobile phone handsets over the life of the title. Most handsets differ only slightly from each other, but some differ substantially in annoyingly disparate ways. Automating the testing of game screen displays, key press actions, and menu selections for each phone is advantageous over purely manual testing. Very modular test code is essential to cost-effective automation of these mobile phone games.

Five Habits of Effective Automated Testing

Establishing the five practices described in the following sections will positively impact the effectiveness and success of your test automation initiatives.

Filter Automated Test Results

If you decide to move ahead with some degree of automated testing, a key element to put in place early on is some form of filter or prescreening process for the data your test scripts generate. This process should include both human and automated filters to ensure that the same bug is not being reported over and over, or that trivial bugs are being passed on through the system and accorded the same level of priority as important bugs. Indeed, you would do well to implement a tiered system of bug importance, because it will relate specifically to the potentially immense amount of data your test scripts may produce. A high incidence of a particular bug can be an indicator of how important it is to fix it, so your system cannot merely assume that frequently reported bugs are trivial. You will also want to introduce a feedback loop in your internal system to ensure that erroneous "bugs" your scripts turn up are not continuously generated and flooding the system with unnecessary data. Also, see to it that the test scripts are rewritten as necessary to enhance their hit rate on significant bugs—bugs worth noting and eliminating. It is common for the introduction of automated testing to go hand-in-hand with excessive numbers of error email reports that get widely disseminated throughout the company. These take precious time from team members who have to wade through trying to decide which bug report they should attend to and which they can safely ignore. Designating a specific member of the team—an ombudsman or ombugsman?—whose job it is to act as a filter can save tens upon tens of wasted person-hours as you go automatic.

What Happens in Testing Stays in Testing

For very practical reasons, you definitely want to ensure that all hooks and additional code you've added to your game code for testing purposes are removed prior to launch.

Keep the game code clean for launch right from the early stages of development by ensuring that any comments placed in the code or any functions that are introduced for testing (infinite life, invulnerability, hooks for automatic test scripts, and so on) can be easily and reliably removed. Nothing can be more embarrassing than to let code ship with comments like "remember to remove this prior to shipping!" These comments suggest that the code was not in a true release state when it went to retail, which is hardly the image most companies want to project. Where possible, consider whether such code or hooks can be placed in separate DLL files. Clearly label test files separately from the release version of the same files to reduce the risk that the commercial code will enable people to cheat or flood the game servers with simulated players just as you did in your stress test phase of automated testing. Although all of this may sound obvious, a book could be written on code and comments that have been left in games when they were never meant to be there at retail!

Manage Builds

Test procedure automation will be substantially impeded if your company does not have good build management procedures in place. Once you set up scripts to test certain parts of the game code with each new build, any builds that slip through with those parts of the code omitted will throw your automated system into disarray. Your tests will generate a sizable amount of false data in the belief they have found errors. As mentioned earlier, if you have a good filter in place, this need not disrupt your entire project. Nonetheless, it will introduce unnecessary headaches for the person responsible for filtering the automated test output.

Poor build management can also lead to immense confusion with automated scripts if the changes made in a given build should have been accompanied by revised test hooks written into the new game code or revised test programs and tools written to accommodate the new changes in the code. Continue implementing your best configuration management practices in conjunction with automated testing and also consider how they might be impacted by the introduction of automation.

Test Game Code Prior to Committing

In the rush to get a title completed, programmers can be tempted to commit code that is not tested. This can bring the entire project to a grinding halt. Here is one area where test automation can flourish and become integral to the build-management system upon which the rest of the test automation program relies. Building into your system the requirement that every programmer must submit his or her new code for testing before it can be committed is just good sense. This is also something that can be highly automated. By setting up a procedure whereby the route to committing new code is via a test machine, and by automating the tests that the machine carries out before clearing new code for a commit, you can trap just about all common errors well before they have any chance of tainting your main game code. The test scripts you run on this test machine can look for common errors and automate an email notice program that notifies all key personnel of the new code, its new features, and so on—using the notes that each programmer is required to attach to new code they submit to the test machine. Another advantage of automating this system is that you can track the mistakes that are being made and take steps to prevent them going forward.

> "One rule you have to have when you allow sloppy submits is this: don't submit if you're going to leave work soon. It's very tempting when you get to the end of the day, and you've put the finishing touch on that feature you were implementing, to submit it and go home. But then you might break the build and someone else is going to have to fix it. Either be willing to wait until the auto-build machines have validated your submit, or wait until the next morning to submit."
>
> Jamie Fristrom, programmer on *Spider-Man 2*
>
> http://www.gamasutra.com/features/20031212/fristrom_01.shtml#

Integrate Testing with Building

The practice of ensuring that all new code gets submitted for testing before a coder can make a commit is a significant step in the right direction. It's also essential to a well-ordered system that you ensure your team is working on the same build version and that at any given time the build version is as stable and bug-free as possible. You can achieve this by doing the following:

- At least once a day, automate the creation of a build that also coordinates all new and existing assets and executables. Automated testing can be used to ensure that new assets do not break the existing code and to test new code snippets, audio, and so on.

- Make sure the system embeds version numbers and any other meta-data that might prove useful in the smooth running of the development cycle, such as asset and code source data and so on.

- Make sure the system runs automated regression tests.

- Once a day, have someone run the latest version of the game to check for obvious errors the automated system may have missed.

The potential negative effects of adding test automation to your procedures was mentioned earlier in this chapter. Nevertheless, basic automation of source version control, running automated tests on daily builds, running daily regression tests, and insisting that all new code at least have basic tests run on it before it is committed are just plain good-sense practices. You can save many person-hours simply by keeping obviously buggy code out of the system and by ensuring everyone is working on the same version. Limit the basic test scripts in the automated system by testing just for obvious crashes, omissions, and so on. This will not introduce any significant new test code to the overall system that itself then would need constant debugging and management. Given that it is usually easy to find stable change points in your code, you can write a script that ensures that everyone is automatically synchronized to the latest known stable release that your automatic test system has validated.

> "What finally did help is the end-to-end autobuild, or, as we call it, "churning". As soon as one build completes and is successful, the testing machine gets the next change. If there is no new changelist yet, the testing machine idles until another change is submitted. Then it syncs to the new change, rebuilds the data, and emails the team if there are any failures. We've accepted that people are going to make mistakes—giving up on Steve Maguire's claim that it's possible to keep bugs out of the master sources—what we have now is a system that catches those mistakes within minutes of when they're made."
>
> Jamie Fristrom, programmer on *Spider-Man 2*
>
> http://www.gamasutra.com/features/20031212/fristrom_01.shtml

Cost Analysis

Your company is going to want to undertake its own cost analysis before embarking on the introduction of any significant automated testing. Too often managers will see the introduction of automated testing as some kind of "silver bullet" that should cure all their cost overruns and late product releases. While significant success stories are starting to appear in the game industry following various companies' deployment of automated test systems, there are far more tales of woe where companies tried to automate and got badly burned. The reality is that there are many costs to consider before taking the step to automate.

Setting clear expectations to upper management is crucial in presenting the concept of test automation. Clearly the need is to keep clear in your mind where you feel test automation will definitely impact your company positively and where it may have either a minimal or insufficient impact. And then when presenting to management, be sure to make clear what the realistic benefits of automation are likely to be and when those benefits are likely to be realized. If introducing large-scale test scripts is not likely to significantly benefit the current title in development, or even the ensuing two, but is expected to start showing benefits from the third project onward, then be sure to present this picture clearly rather than promote the frequent misconception that automation will yield immediate and tangible financial benefits. Here are some of the factors your management team will need to consider:

- No hands-on testing. It's easy to factor in how much an additional human tester will cost and what his/her likely value will be, but how do you factor computer control and testing?

- Assumed increase in productivity. The mere fact you have decided to automate will give the expectation of increased efficiency and lower costs.

- Reduction of perceived productivity. Ironically, your department will seem less productive due to the time it takes to implement and use automatic tools.

- Deeper levels of test issues. Because automation brings new opportunities to test, it will often introduce deeper levels of testing, which can be a good or bad thing.

- Fundamental changes in how software is developed. The ramifications of introducing automated testing can reach company-wide.

- Test cycles performed. Because automatic testing runs so much faster than human testing, it can lead to greater churning, which in turn may encourage productivity or lead to laziness.

- Improved professionalism. Automating testing can often motivate the team if it is done well and lead to improved morale and professionalism.

In computing the likely ROI on the company's proposed investment in automating its testing program, you have to consider many more variables than management is expecting to have to look at. You'll also have to argue that all the benefit ultimately gained will not be realized for some time, and this is in itself going to be a hard sell. Not least because you need to be clear the extent to which automating the testing will impact company-wide operations and change the way that the development team codes its games, the way game engines are written, and so forth. However, you have some convincing weapons in your arsenal to persuade that automating at least part of your testing program will make a lot of sense: If you produce massively multiplayer online games, for instance, your "pitch" can be substantially assisted by the well-publicized reports that automation has greatly benefited many developers when it comes to regression and load/stress tests on massive online environments. But even if online MMP games are not your company's main output, you will still be on solid logical ground arguing that highly repetitive testing is well suited to being replaced with automated testing. You will also be on firm ground arguing that to some degree, at least, automated "sniff test" testing should be introduced, which ensures that new code does not contain obvious flaws before a commit is permitted.

Some of the predictable fixed costs when converting to automation are as follows:

- Additional hardware (or at the least upgrades to existing hardware)
- Middleware and tool licenses (you are likely to need at least some)
- Scripting tool creation
- New game code to add hooks, framework, and so on for automation
- Tool training
- Management software and support
- Ramp-up costs
- Additional team members who are devoted to automation

You will face some variable costs, too:

- Test case implementation
- Test case designs specific to automation
- Maintenance
- Results analysis
- Defect reporting
- Night-time system runtime

It should be straightforward to calculate the costs of these factors. They are based on well-known variables and cost bases that already exist in some (at least similar) form within your company, either in relation to existing manual testing or to game code development.

Test Automation in Action: *The Sims Online*

In their 2003 presentation to the Game Developer's Conference in San Jose, Greg Kearney, Larry Mellon, and Darrin West detailed their implementation of game test automation in the development of *The Sims Online* (http://serious-code.net/moin.cgi/AutomatedTestingInMmpGames). The problem they identified was that developing and deploying massively multiplayer Permanent State Worlds (PSWs) has proven to be very difficult due to the distributed nature and large scale of the system.

Their goal was to significantly reduce costs, appreciably stabilize the game, and reduce errors in *The Sims Online* (TSO) by automating their testing program. They wanted the tools they created to increase the efficiency of the initial development of the game, provide early load testing, and carry over to central company operations as long-term aids in the maintenance and testing of extensions of TSO and future games.

The TSO test team focused its automation efforts on game aspects involving highly repetitive actions and scenarios that would require large numbers of connected players. For this reason, the team identified regression and load testing as the ideal candidates for automation, because a roadblock in the client connection process could make the entire game grind to a halt. Other less mission-critical elements could be tested by hand and would not have as great an effect on the gameplay. Additionally, the team wanted to add further automated code to assist in game development, game tuning, and marketing.

SimScript

The TSO team used a subset of the main game client to create a test client in which the GUI is mimicked via a script-driven control system. To the main game server these test clients look identical to actual connected game player clients. Test scripts produce in-game actions in place of human players. This is enabled by a Presentation Layer inserted between the TSO client's GUI and the supporting client-side portions of the game code. Their scripting system—which they dubbed *SimScript*—is attached to this Presentation Layer. Simulated user play sessions are generated by a series of scripted actions such as "Create Avatar," "Use Object," or "Buy House."

SimScript is an extremely simple scripting system. As it is intended to mimic or record a series of user actions, it supports no conditional statements, loop constructs, or arithmetic operations. Stored procedures and const-style parameters are used to support reusable scripts for common functionality across multiple tests.

Two basic flow control statements exist in SimScript: `WaitFor` and `WaitUntil`. These provide the ability to simulate the time gaps between mimicked user actions "wait_for 5 seconds", "wait_until reading _skill:100", to block until a process enters a particular state ("wait_until client_state:in_a_house"), and to synchronize actions across the distributed system ("wait_until avatar_two:arrives"). `WaitUntil` commands simply block script execution until the condition is met, or a timeout value is exceeded.

http://serious-code.net/moin.cgi/AutomatedTestingInMmpGames

Here's an example of SimScript code:

```
# this script brings an avatar directly into a testable condition inside the game: a
quick skill test is then performed

wait_until       game_state      selectasim
pick_avatar      $alpha_chimp
wait_until       game_state      inlot

chat             Hi. I'm in and running.
log_message      Testing object placement
log_objects
place_object     chair           10 10
log_objects

# invoke a command on a different client
remote_command   $monkey_bo.                  use_object chair sit

# and do some skill increase for self
set_data         avatar                       reading_skill 0
use_object       bookshelf                    read
wait_until       avatar                       reading_skil 100
```

Load Testing

Load-testing using the TSO system was a significant challenge because they wanted to simulate realistic loads accurately on a continual basis to stabilize their system prior to going live. To this effect, they created a series of test clients. Each client acts independently and is controlled either by a scripted series of individual user interface actions or by an event generation algorithm. The system was set up to collect data from all clients and from the main server cluster and to start up and shut down the system automatically, while also fully automating the metrics collection. To control the load testing they used LoadRunner, a commercially available load generation system. Bridge code hooks LoadRunner into the TSO test client and enables LoadRunner to control up to thousands of simulated users against a given candidate server cluster. Configuring the client to run without a GUI (NullView) significantly reduces the memory footprint and allows many more test clients per load generation box.

Regular Regression

Because of the nature of distributed systems, new code will regularly break old code. For this reason, the TSO automated test system had to be able to validate every game feature to ensure stability of the release game. Its regression engine was linked closely to the outcome of normal QA procedures, ensuring that wherever a new defect was observed, the regression test client would focus on suspected trouble spots and generate useful data to completely eradicate the bug. Thus, critical path roadblocks were quickly identified and removed. Interestingly, the team noted a large number of false positives and false negatives generated by the system, so the importance of human viewing of test result data was emphasized to ensure there would be no wasted time chasing items that could be overlooked.

New Use for Old Code

Surprisingly, the team reported that relatively little new C++ code was required to support their testing system. This was largely achieved by utilizing the existing game code—the game client code in particular—and reformatting it as test code. Similarly, reusing the actual game GUI and reconfiguring it for test purposes kept new coding to a minimum. Indeed, the basis for the test code was found in existing code already in the game that had been put there to enable normal testers and programmers to "cheat."

All for One and One for All

Many of the TSO test scripts are relatively short. Scripting all required test conditions by hand was not realistic, so an extensible series of algorithms was used to generate events wherever possible. Random and deterministic strategies were used to generate scripts on-the-fly to replace the otherwise lengthy hand coding that would have been required. For instance, the TSO team introduced an algorithm they called `TestAll` that would walk through the list of all objects currently in a location, build a list of all possible interactions, and then execute all possible actions using a deterministic strategy. They were then able to generalize the results by having the system place the objects in various locations throughout the game world and retest the objects in a host of new terrain or location configurations. Using this approach, the team had 230 game objects under regression and about 40% of the game's supporting infrastructure under automated regression within a month of starting.

Lessons Learned

The TSO team learned a number of important lessons from automating the testing of their game. See which ones you can apply to your own:

- Use automated regression tests to ensure that once a feature works it should never be allowed to stop working.

- Get solid support from management to prevent even minor deviations from the test procedures. This could defeat much of what you are trying to accomplish with your automation.

- Identify the critical path elements and protect them. Basic infrastructure tests need to precede any specific scripted feature tests.

- Build testability into the core design of a game. The team soon discovered that many elements of TSO were not well suited to automated testing, but they could have been if testing had been a concern from the genesis of the design process.

- Develop or acquire new tools to help organize and track the information the original test tools generate. Creating and maintaining hundreds of automated test cases can quickly become unmanageable.

- Automate the noise reduction aspect of the system, filtering out data that the system doesn't need to process. Otherwise, information overload can quickly become a problem.

- Run a basic low-level "sniff test" of the code before it gets into the main release of the game. This is immensely useful in avoiding substantial roadblocks in the development process.

- Automate full-scale load testing, running constant tests of thousands of active clients. These tests significantly reduce problems that you would otherwise face at launch.

- Abstract test commands to maximize their re-use. The SimScript language can be used to automate single or multiplayer modes and titles, and is independent of which platform the game is being tested on.

The TSO team succeeded by not trying to automate everything, focusing the automation where it was of best use and, where possible, using game code and existing game clients that minimized the need to create new code that itself would need to be debugged.

The Future of Test Automation

There are increasing trends in game design toward procedurally written code and algorithmic approaches to game design. This suggests that in moving forward, it may become easier and easier to integrate automated testing into game code because the code will often be generated by algorithms that may be modified to perform self-detection of errors and self-healing of errors identified. For instance, if the on-screen experience (path-finding, collision detection, clipping, and so on) is being generated algorithmically, then logically the same algorithmic substructure can be used to test the outcomes and self-cure any errors that are detected.

Beyond the advantages that game design trends may bring, the game industry is likely to remain one where test automation, while desirable, is going to remain difficult to deploy on a wide-scale basis simply because so much game code is custom written for each game. There is likely to remain a fundamental problem that large-scale test automation will be only justifiable if a company can envision ways in which automation will eventually pay off because the test system is reusable for all games they produce over the course of many years. This, however, is unlikely to happen unless the idea of testing the code is built into the game design practices of the company at a very deep level and deployed across all games that the company works on.

Finally, once the practice of designing tests becomes more prevalent, they can be integrated into an automated test generation process. As features evolve during the course of the project, you would only need to update the design and regenerate a new set of automated tests. Here's a small SimScript test that checks that when a player with 0 money bashes a piñata his money total will go up:

```
set_data      avatar    skill    10
set_data      avatar    money    0
use_object    piñata    bash
wait_until    piñata    broken
log_message   Money should go up after breaking the piñata
log_dat       avatar    money
```

This test case might appear in a combinatorial test design, as shown in Figure 16.2. The test parameters are starting skill, money, and what kind of item to bash. The values for this test are 0, 10, and piñata, respectively.

Test	Skill	Money	Item to Bash	Result
2	10	0	Piñata	Player gets money

Figure 16.2 Bash testing combinatorial table excerpt.

Each of the test values has a small piece of test code associated with it.

Starting Money = 0 is coded as

```
set_data     avatar    money    0
```

Skill = 10 is coded as

```
set_data     avatar    skill    10
```

Item to Bash = Piñata is coded with two lines:

```
use_object   piñata    bash
wait_until   piñata    broken
log_message  Money should go up after breaking the piñata
```

Finally, the code that checks the result is

```
log_dat      avatar    money
```

Using basic test design principles, you can imagine what might be in the rest of the test table. Besides a skill of 10, what about 0 or the maximum possible skill? What if the player's money is maximum before breaking the piñata—is the money lost or does it lie on the ground for other players to pick up? What other items besides the piñata can be broken to provide money to the player? These questions may already be answered in the game's design or they might not. All it takes is a few extra pieces of code to incorporate additional test values. For example, the code for 0 skill would not be much different from the code for skill = 10:

```
set_data     avatar    skill    0
```

You can generate code for each row in your combinatorial table by substituting the test code for each value that appears in the row. If a new "bashable" item is introduced in an expansion set, just add it to the test table, define new code for it, and regenerate the automated tests.

The same test code generation approach can be applied to test flow diagrams. In this case, test code is associated with each state, event, and action. Once the paths are generated, substitute the test code for each primitive to compose the equivalent automated test. A TFD excerpt for the piñata bashing test might look like Figure 16.3.

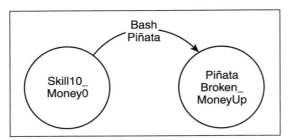

Figure 16.3 TFD excerpt for piñata bashing test.

The TFD design principles raise some different questions than the previous combinatorial test. Once the piñata is bashed, what happens if you try to bash it again, creating a "loop" flow at the PiñataBroken_MoneyUp state? Is there a way to repair the piñata so it is no longer broken, creating a flow back to the Skill10_Money0 state? As with combinatorial test code generation, you just need to update the design, add new test code for added or changed elements, and regenerate the test paths. Moving or removing existing flows will not cost you anything in terms of new coding. In fact, it's also "free" to add new flows to the diagram that use primitives that already have their test code defined.

Summary

Game test automation is a hotly debated topic in the game industry. Some believe that all aspects of testing should be automated, while others say that, apart from certain specific automated testing, using human testers can cost less and have less of a negative impact on the development process. There are, however, clear potential advantages to be gained from automating your test process. It can save many person-hours, lead to better game quality, and be more efficient than manual testing.

Although at present test automation is typically employed in the later stages of development, there is a strong argument for starting as early as possible and automating testing of game code throughout the development cycle.

If you are considering large-scale deployment of test automation, you need to realize it is a long-term investment that will fundamentally alter how your company creates games. Implementing any degree of automated testing will require the full support of your management. It will also be vital to have strong foundations in place that govern all aspects of your testing program before you begin to automate.

Exercises

1. What are the top two factors that would help you decide whether your company should automate its game testing?

2. What are the main reasons you may not wish to automate testing?

3. What are the main reasons you may wish to automate testing?

4. Which types of games are best suited for test automation?

5. Which aspects of game testing are best suited to automation?

6. Using the SimScript commands presented in this chapter, write an automated test to move a guitar from coordinate (10, 10) to coordinate (40, 40), "play" it to increase your "music_skill," and then move the guitar back to (10,10). Be sure to verify the success of each operation you attempt.

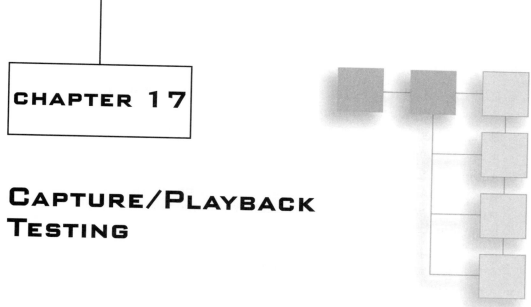

CHAPTER 17

CAPTURE/PLAYBACK TESTING

Test automation enables you to get more testing done with the precious time you have. By leaving repetitive testing tasks to machines, testers can spend more time on creating new test designs, improving existing tests, and keeping up with the game code as it changes throughout the project life cycle. Choosing the right projects, people, and automation tools will prevent individual frustration and organizational rejection. Capture/playback testing is one automation approach that you can start working with right away. Ideally, testers should implement automation as a regular part of their job instead of treating it as a project of its own that requires additional effort and budget. Capture/playback automation will come "naturally" to testers who have practice, skill, and more practice.

Capture/Playback Automation Characteristics

Capture/playback test automation is not terribly suited for making "touchy feely" assessments of a game. Automated tests excel at comparing stored information against what occurs during the test, but they cannot judge ease of use, playability, or how fun a game is.

Most off-the-shelf test automation solutions are not suited for random events such as mob spawns, AI opponents, or dealing shuffled cards. To support capture/playback automation in these cases you need access to tools that give you control of the random number seed(s) or other mechanisms that drive the random behavior in a deterministic and repeatable manner. For example, a value can be provided in the game data file for testers to specify which seed to use for the AI, or a special pop-up in-game control panel can be provided for the same purpose. This kind of support needs to be identified —in your test plan or through some other means—early in the project so your automated tests can be developed in time for test execution.

Following are some real benefits to utilizing capture/playback automation:

- Retesting is faithfully repeated exactly as it was done the first time. You will discover intentional and unintentional changes to software this way.
- Problems get noticed and recorded every time, no matter how late in the day it is or how long the test machine has been working.
- Automated tests produce documentation of the test results every step along the way, every time the test is run. Typically other pertinent information is recorded as well, such as date, time, and identification of the software build being tested.
- Different automated tests can run concurrently on multiple computers. One person can easily manage two machines running automated tests.
- Automated tests can be run during non-working days and hours. In some game projects there is no such thing as "non-working days and hours," but perhaps automated testing can re-introduce that concept to your project....

On the other hand, capture/playback testing has some limitations and drawbacks:

- Capture/playback automation requires some overhead to keep automation scripts up to date with the game code.
- Capture/playback automation won't notice if something goes wrong outside of what is specifically checking for. A test that is checking one part of the UI may not notice when your health suddenly goes to zero or your sword disappears.
- You can't just grab anyone who says they do testing and expect them to be immediately successful at capture/playback test automation. Programming training and experience will make a difference, as will reading and working through this chapter.

Achieving even modest automation goals can have a big impact. If you expend the effort to get just 20% of your tests automated, that could save up to one extra work day a week for each tester.

Capture/Playback Test Automation

Some automated test solutions involve special hardware, software, programming languages, or all three. These are not always a good fit for testers who may not have heavy hardware and/or software engineering backgrounds. These solutions also tend to be expensive because of their special-purpose nature. A preferable approach is one that is light on programming and keeps the tester focused on the art and science of testing.

Capture/playback test automation is like using a digital video recorder while you test.

Your inputs are recorded as you play the game and at various points you designate, screen images are captured for comparison whenever you "replay" the test in the future. This is well suited to the graphical nature of videogames.

Capture/playback testing adds a slight overhead to running the test manually the first time. At various points during your manual testing you will need to guide the test tool to capture the game data and screen elements that must be checked by the test. This investment pays off when you can automatically play back the tests every time after that. Maintaining the tests is expensive when the game features being tested are unstable. Time is wasted on implementing, reviewing, and managing changes that are only good for a few test runs. In that case, you should postpone automation until the requirements, design, and code are stable.

Vermont HighTest™ (VHT) is a capture/playback test product that was used for the examples in this chapter. The book's CD-ROM includes a link to the VHT Web site where you can download a 30-day demo of VHT as well as a User's Guide. Each VHT "test" consists of database files containing data captured during recording and a document file containing the test code. Log files (documents) are created each time the test is run.

Recording

You should have some idea of what you are going to record and test for before you start automating. You can use tests that are produced by the various design methodologies described elsewhere in this book or test scripts that have been in your family for generations. In either case, you need to define or plan ahead of time which screen or window elements you are going to check (capture) in order to establish that the game is working right.

You start recording a test in VHT by selecting New from the Record menu or by pressing F11. During recording, a Record Bar window appears on your screen as shown in Figure 17.1. The icons in the first row of this window are used to capture various types of screen contents such as the entire screen, a specific window, or a region that is defined by the tester during recording. The icons in the second row are used to add comment or control statements to the test as it is being recorded. The stop sign icon in the third row is used to suspend recording.

Another way you can use the capture function is to record ad hoc and playability testing. The test can't detect problems it's not programmed to look for, but you can pause at any time to capture interesting windows or screen images to show to skeptical developers. The recording can be used to see what steps got you to the problem spot.

Figure 17.1 Control panel with test recording controls.

This is sort of like the airplane black box recorder that's always on, so that when an accident occurs analysts can work backward from the data to draw conclusions about what caused the accident.

Here is a breakdown of what a recorded test looks like:

```
;FileName: c:\documents and settings\administrator\desktop\vht test files\test1.inb
;
;Created: Tue Dec 21 15:51:46 2004
;Author:
;
;Product:
;Abstract:
;
```

This part is the header that is automatically added by VHT. It includes the filename and path of the test file and the creation date of the file. There are also placeholders to provide the author's name, a product identifier, and an abstract description of the test.

```
ActivateWindow("Progman", "Program Manager", NULL, 10.0)
ActivateWindow("SysListView32", "FolderView", 1, 10.0)
ClickListView(1, "Dawn of War", DBLCLK, 0.0)
ActivateWindow("Plat::Window {DB3DC0D7-BBA3-4d06-BCD8-40CD448B4AE3}", "Warhammer 40,000:
Dawn of War", NULL, 10.0)
```

Here the recording begins to capture your test actions. It shows that the test starts by launching the game window. As you can see from the data in the test commands, you are testing *Dawn of War*. The ClickListView command captures and plays back the act of double-clicking on the game's icon. It will find the game icon no matter where it is located on your desktop, even if it has moved since the time when you recorded the test.

```
Keys("[Esc][Esc][Esc]", 0.0, 1.04, 1.07)
```

This is a recording of the three times I hit the Esc key to skip over the introductory splash screens.

```
MouseClick(540, 396, INTEL, LEFT, 19.59)
```

This is the left mouse click to select the Army Painter from the main menu. The INTEL parameter specifies "Intelligent" mode (did you think it was some sort of advertising for a chip maker?). This will adjust the mouse coordinates for the current window.

```
CompareScreen("Region 1")
```

This line is added after you select the Compare Region icon from the Record Bar. It's the fourth one from the left on the first row of icons. The recording pauses while you drag a rectangle around the area of the screen you want to capture. VHT automatically names the region and inserts the CompareScreen command into the test file.

```
MouseClick(216, 406, INTEL, LEFT, 0.0)
MouseDoubleClick(216, 406, INTEL, LEFT, 0.5)
MouseDoubleClick(216, 406, INTEL, LEFT, 0.78)
MouseDoubleClick(216, 406, INTEL, LEFT, 0.56)
MouseDoubleClick(216, 406, INTEL, LEFT, 0.51)
MouseClick(216, 406, INTEL, LEFT, 0.46)
```

These steps click an up arrow on the screen to increment the red color palette setting 10 times. Depending on how fast you click, VHT will record either a single MouseClick or a MouseDoubleClick. The two MouseClick commands plus the four MouseDoubleClick commands produces a total of 10 clicks.

```
MouseDoubleClick(230, 420, INTEL, LEFT, 2.14)
MouseDoubleClick(230, 420, INTEL, LEFT, 0.51)
MouseDoubleClick(230, 420, INTEL, LEFT, 0.46)
MouseDoubleClick(230, 420, INTEL, LEFT, 0.5)
MouseDoubleClick(230, 420, INTEL, LEFT, 0.5)
```

This series of five double-clicks decrements the green color palette setting by 10.

```
MouseClick(81, 6, INTEL, LEFT, 5.12)
CompareScreen("Region 2")
```

Finally, these two lines move the cursor off of the down arrow and then compare the updated portion of the screen (captured using the Record Bar again) to the one that was originally recorded. The images captured for Region1 (left) and Region2 (right) are shown in Figure 17.2.

Editing

VHT produces a test file during recording. It also inserts a header at the top of the test file that includes the filename of the test and the date and time it was captured. This header also has placeholders for you to enter "Author:", "Product:", and "Abstract:" information. You can edit this file using the tool's own editor or export it to a text file that can be imported back in after you are done with your editing.

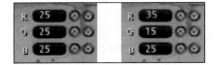

Figure 17.2 Region1 and Region2 images captured during recording.

Once the test is recorded, you can make changes to it. For example, you can add an in-line comment to any of the commands in the file by entering a semicolon followed by your comment text. Here's a comment explaining the three Esc keys:

```
Keys("[Esc][Esc][Esc]", 0.0, 1.04, 1.07)   ;Skip splash screens
```

You may also find that you want to delete commands from the test after you've already made a recording. You can, for example, remove an accidental key press or mouse click that is not meant to be part of the test. These can be removed by deleting the offending line from the test file. If you want to be more cautious, you can comment out any line by inserting a leading semicolon.

If you left something out and want to add it without going through the capture process all over again, the same commands available from the Record Bar can be typed directly into your test file, or altered to fit your needs. Appendix B of the Vermont HighTest User's Guide lists the available commands along with details of their syntax and parameters.

VHT also provides control and function statements. These can be used to create chunks of automation that you can add to your scripts without having to recapture those sequences. You can even use variables to alter the number of times you perform various operations during the test, such as multiple mouse button clicks. Details of these commands are provided in Appendix A of the VHT User's Guide.

If you are so inclined, you can create automated tests entirely from scratch with the commands available to you. If you are savvy with the automated command syntax, you could even automate the automation by using your tests to generate text files that can be imported and run by the automated test tool.

Test editing is also useful for automating a set of tests that only vary slightly from one another. Capture the "master" test normally, and then make copies of the recorded file. Edit the recordings as desired. This can save a lot of time versus trying to repeat the same capture process over and over again for each new test.

Playback

The Run (F12) option in the playback menu runs the test that is open in the VHT editor or prompts you to select a test file if none is open. Running the test produces a log file.

The log file consists of three parts: the header, the body, and the footer. Information within the body consists of your recorded test commands on the left side of the page and the results of each command to the right. The possible result values are Success or Failure. The following listing shows a successful playback—all of the operations return a Success result.

```
**************************************************************
* FileName:        c:\documents and settings\administrator\desktop\vht test
files\test1.inb
* Log Created on:  Wed Dec 22 06:26:43 2004
*
* Playback Options:
*      Play Speed: 50
*      Terminate on Failure:
*

*      Ignore During Compare:
**************************************************************

ActivateWindow --> "Progman", "Program Manager", NULL, 10.0......Result: Success
ActivateWindow --> "SysListView32", "FolderView", 1, 10.0.......Result: Success
ClickListView --> 1, "Dawn of War", DBLCLK, 0.0.................Result: Success
ActivateWindow --> "Plat::Window {DB3DC0D7-BBA3-4d06-BCD8-40CD448B4AE3}", "Warhammer
40,000: Dawn of War", NULL, 10.0...Result: Success
Keys --> "[Esc][Esc][Esc]", 0.0, 1.04, 1.07.....................Result: Success
MouseClick --> 540, 396, INTEL, LEFT, 19.59.....................Result: Success
CompareScreen --> "Region 1"....................................Result: Success
MouseClick --> 216, 406, INTEL, LEFT, 0.0.......................Result: Success
MouseDoubleClick --> 216, 406, INTEL, LEFT, 0.5.................Result: Success
MouseDoubleClick --> 216, 406, INTEL, LEFT, 0.78................Result: Success
MouseDoubleClick --> 216, 406, INTEL, LEFT, 0.56................Result: Success
MouseDoubleClick --> 216, 406, INTEL, LEFT, 0.51................Result: Success
MouseClick --> 216, 406, INTEL, LEFT, 0.46......................Result: Success
MouseDoubleClick --> 230, 420, INTEL, LEFT, 2.14................Result: Success
MouseDoubleClick --> 230, 420, INTEL, LEFT, 0.51................Result: Success
MouseDoubleClick --> 230, 420, INTEL, LEFT, 0.46................Result: Success
MouseDoubleClick --> 230, 420, INTEL, LEFT, 0.5.................Result: Success
MouseDoubleClick --> 230, 420, INTEL, LEFT, 0.5.................Result: Success
MouseClick --> 81, 6, INTEL, LEFT, 5.12.........................Result: Success
CompareScreen --> "Region 2"....................................Result: Success


**************************************************************
* Log Ended on:  Wed Dec 22 06:28:06 2004
**************************************************************
```

Not all test runs will be so clean. The playback is very unforgiving. Failures can occur due to minute problems in the position of an item on the screen or the slightest variation in any of its attributes, such as color, font, or value, for example.

Playback Options

Playback options are independent of the recorded test file. This allows you to "turn the knobs" for the tests you've already recorded without having to recapture the results.

Speed is an important playback option. In Vermont HighTest the playback speed ranges from 1 to 100, where a value of 50 represents the real-time speed of the test recording. Running the test back at a higher speed can improve your automated test throughput. However, running at too fast a rate can cause new test failures. You will have to analyze the results to distinguish between failures caused by improper test speed versus actual game code failures.

Another way to utilize the Speed value is to check the game against potential user speed "profiles." Do elements of the game time out too soon if the player takes a long time to respond to a dialog or complete a mission? Do game input buffers overflow if they are bombarded with rapid clicks, buttons, or key presses? These can be real defects in the game code.

Running the *Dawn of War* test at maximum speed does produce some failures. Look for the entries in the following log file that have a Failure result:

```
*************************************************************
* FileName:        c:\documents and settings\administrator\desktop\vht test
files\playspeedmax\test1.inb
* Log Created on:  Tue Dec 21 19:17:02 2004
*
* Playback Options:
*     Play Speed: 100
*     Terminate on Failure:
*
*
*     Ignore During Compare:
*************************************************************


ActivateWindow --> "Progman", "Program Manager", NULL, 10.0......Result: Success
ActivateWindow --> "SysListView32", "FolderView", 1, 10.0.......Result: Success
ClickListView --> 1, "Dawn of War", DBLCLK, 0.0................Result: Success
ActivateWindow --> "Plat::Window {DB3DC0D7-BBA3-4d06-BCD8-40CD448B4AE3}", "Warhammer
40,000: Dawn of War", NULL, 10.0...Result: Success
```

```
Keys --> "[Esc][Esc][Esc]", 0.0, 1.04, 1.07.....................Result: Success
MouseClick --> 540, 396, INTEL, LEFT, 19.59....................Result: Success
CompareScreen --> "Region 1"..................................Result: Failure
MouseClick --> 216, 406, INTEL, LEFT, 0.0.....................Result: Success
MouseDoubleClick --> 216, 406, INTEL, LEFT, 0.5...............Result: Success
MouseDoubleClick --> 216, 406, INTEL, LEFT, 0.78..............Result: Success
MouseDoubleClick --> 216, 406, INTEL, LEFT, 0.56..............Result: Success
MouseDoubleClick --> 216, 406, INTEL, LEFT, 0.51..............Result: Success
MouseClick --> 216, 406, INTEL, LEFT, 0.46....................Result: Success
MouseDoubleClick --> 230, 420, INTEL, LEFT, 2.14..............Result: Success
MouseDoubleClick --> 230, 420, INTEL, LEFT, 0.51..............Result: Success
MouseDoubleClick --> 230, 420, INTEL, LEFT, 0.46..............Result: Success
MouseDoubleClick --> 230, 420, INTEL, LEFT, 0.5...............Result: Success
MouseDoubleClick --> 230, 420, INTEL, LEFT, 0.5...............Result: Success
MouseClick --> 81, 6, INTEL, LEFT, 5.12.......................Result: Success
CompareScreen --> "Region 2"..................................Result: Failure


**************************************************************
* Log Ended on:  Tue Dec 21 19:17:32 2004
**************************************************************
```

The failures occurred in the two places where a portion of the Army Painter screen was checked by the CompareScreen function. One way to diagnose the cause of this type of problem is to run the automated test again and carefully watch what happens on the screen. In this case, all of the mouse clicks happened while the game was still loading, so they were ignored. After that the game just sat in the main menu, shown in Figure 17.3, because all of the recorded test steps had already been played back.

You can also try to manually verify that there's no problem with the main menu timing by clicking the Army Painter choice as soon as the menu comes up on the screen. If that works correctly, you should be able to run the test faster than it was captured in real time. It's a matter of making the right changes to the test file. VHT provides a Delay function that you can add during capture by selecting it from the Record Bar. You can also edit the test file to insert this command. An important feature of this command is that it will delay for the specified number of second regardless of what the playback Speed is set to. For this case select a relatively long delay, such as 15 seconds, to account for target machines with slow CPUs or disk access times. Here's the portion of the test code with a commented Delay command inserted:

```
ClickListView(1, "Dawn of War", DBLCLK, 0.0)
ActivateWindow("Plat::Window {DB3DC0D7-BBA3-4d06-BCD8-40CD448B4AE3}", "Warhammer 40,000:
Dawn of War", NULL, 10.0)
Keys("[Esc][Esc][Esc]", 0.0, 1.04, 1.07)  ;Skip splash screens
```

```
Delay(15) ;Wait for game to load and bring up main menu
MouseClick(540, 396, INTEL, LEFT, 2.43)
CompareScreen("Region 1")
```

Figure 17.3 *Dawn of War* main menu screen with Army Painter highlighted.

Now the test passes when it runs at maximum speed.

Once one of the test steps fails it might be a waste of time for the test to continue running through the rest of its commands. This is especially true for a test file with hundreds or thousands of lines of code. You could also waste time looking through the log file pages to find the place where the test originally failed. You can save time by adjusting the VHT playback preferences to specify one or more categories of commands that will halt test execution immediately if they fail. Figure 17.4 shows the CompareScreen function added to the list of commands that will cause playback to Terminate on Failure.

When the test fails on any of its Terminate on Failure operations, a special pop-up window appears and the test playback stops. Figure 17.5 shows the terminate pop-up you get when a CompareScreen operation fails.

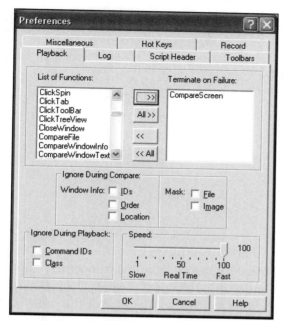

Figure 17.4 Playback options set to Speed = 100 and Terminate on Failure of CompareScreen.

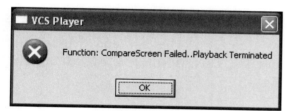

Figure 17.5 Terminate on Failure pop-up window.

Once you specify which commands will cause Terminate on Failure, VHT will automatically list them in the log file header. You can also see in the following code how test logging and playback stopped once CompareScreen("Region1") failed.

```
**************************************************************
* FileName:        c:\documents and settings\administrator\desktop\vht test
files\toftest1.inb
* Log Created on:  Tue Dec 21 19:40:56 2004
*
* Playback Options:
*     Play Speed: 100
*     Terminate on Failure:
*          CompareScreen,
```

```
*     Ignore During Compare:
***********************************************************

ActivateWindow --> "Progman", "Program Manager", NULL, 10.0......Result: Success
ActivateWindow --> "SysListView32", "FolderView", 1, 10.0.......Result: Success
ClickListView --> 1, "Dawn of War", DBLCLK, 0.0................Result: Success
ActivateWindow --> "Plat::Window {DB3DC0D7-BBA3-4d06-BCD8-40CD448B4AE3}", "Warhammer
40,000: Dawn of War", NULL, 10.0...Result: Success
Keys --> "[Esc][Esc][Esc]", 0.0, 1.04, 1.07.....................Result: Success
MouseClick --> 540, 396, INTEL, LEFT, 19.59....................Result: Success
CompareScreen --> "Region 1"....................................Result: Failure
```

Capture/Playback Example

Now it's your turn to sit in the driver's seat. Check to see if you have the *Minesweeper* game on your PC. In Windows XP, go to All Programs\Games\Minesweeper. This game tests your skill at identifying the locations of mine placed on a grid. The random placement of mines on the field is not under your control, so that part of the game is not a good candidate for capture/playback testing. However, you can change some game options that affect the size of the game board. Those will be the subject of this automation example.

Before starting the automation process, put a *Minesweeper* shortcut (icon) on your Desktop. You can probably find one to copy at Documents and Settings\All Users\Start Menu\Programs\Games on your PC. This will make it easy to launch *Minesweeper* during recording and playback.

Note

It's not a good idea to have your automated test launch applications from the Windows "All Programs" menu. If any apps have been added or deleted since the time you made the test recording, the menu order will be different and the mouse will be happily clicking away at whatever is there. Nothing ruins your day like having apps uninstalled by an automated test.

If you haven't done so already, get the demo version of Vermont HighTest from their Web site and install it on your PC. After installation is successful, double-click the "Vermont Hightest" icon and you're ready to continue.

Minesweeper Test Capture

Before you start recording, review the following steps. Then select New from the Record menu or hit F11 to begin recording.

Your automated test should follow these steps:

1. Double-click the *Minesweeper* icon to start the game. Do a window capture of the initial minefield, shown in Figure 17.6.

Figure 17.6 Initial *Minesweeper* game field.

2. Click the Game menu and select Custom…. Capture the region containing the three numeric boxes, as illustrated in Figure 17.7.

Figure 17.7 Custom Field value area to capture.

3. Click inside each of the CustomField value boxes and change them to 20, 20, and 2. You can backspace to erase the existing digits and then type in your own. Do a capture of the new values. It's okay if you don't trace the region in exactly the same place you did the first time. The important thing is to get all of the boxes and their values. Figure 17.8 shows how the window should look prior to capturing the image of your new values.

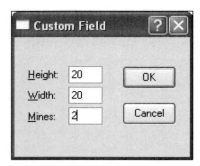

Figure 17.8 New custom values to be captured.

4. Click OK. This should take you back to an updated minefield window that uses your custom height and width values. Your minefield should look exactly like Figure 17.9. Capture this as a window.

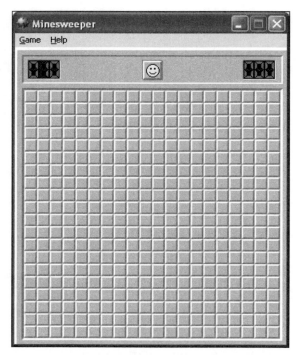

Figure 17.9 Updated minefield using new custom values.

5. Now go back to the Game menu and select Custom... again. Your window should look like Figure 17.10. Once again, capture a region containing the three custom values.

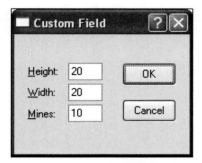

Figure 17.10 Revisited Custom Field window.

At this point you can click on the "stop" icon in the Record Bar. Go back to Vermont HighTest and finish recording by clicking the End selection from the Record menu. Update the test header information and save your file.

When you are done, your test file should look something like this:

```
;FileName: c:\documents and settings\administrator\desktop\vht test files\minetest1.inb
;
;Created: Thu Dec 23 01:11:26 2004
;Author: Me
;
;Product: Game Testing All In One
;Abstract: Minesweeper automation example
;
ActivateWindow("Shell_TrayWnd", "", NULL, 10.0)
ActivateWindow("Progman", "Program Manager", NULL, 10.0)
ActivateWindow("SysListView32", "FolderView", 1, 10.0)
ClickListView(1, "Minesweeper", DBLCLK, 0.0)
CompareScreen("Window 1")
ActivateWindow("Minesweeper", "Minesweeper", NULL, 10.0)
ClickMenu("&Game", 0.09)
ClickMenu("&Game;&Custom...", 2.67)
CompareScreen("Region 1")
ActivateWindow("#32770", "Custom Field", NULL, 10.0)
ClickEdit(141, 1, 0, 0.09)
Keys("[Backspace]", 0.82)
Keys("20", 0.37, 0.1)
ClickEdit(142, 1, 0, 1.74)
Keys("[Backspace]", 0.62)
Keys("20", 0.51, 0.06)
ClickEdit(143, 2, 0, 1.64)
```

```
Keys("[Backspace][Backspace]", 0.64, 0.18)
Keys("2", 0.79)
CompareScreen("Region 2")
ClickButton("OK", 1, 22.25)
CompareScreen("Window 2")
ActivateWindow("Minesweeper", "Minesweeper", 51249669, 10.0)
ClickMenu("&Game", 0.13)
ClickMenu("&Game;&Custom...", 1.94)
CompareScreen("Region 3")
```

Minesweeper Test Playback

Reset the *Minesweeper* field back to its original state—in Beginner mode—and close it. Select Run from the VHT playback menu or hit F12 to play your newly recorded test. Sit back and watch the magic. When you see the final window that you captured, you have reached the end of the playback. VHT will also pop up and have a log file available for you to analyze.

Your log of the playback should look similar to this:

```
*************************************************************
* FileName:         c:\documents and settings\administrator\desktop\vht test
files\minetest1.inb
* Log Created on:  Thu Dec 23 01:11:44 2004
*
* Playback Options:
*     Play Speed: 50
*     Terminate on Failure:
*

*     Ignore During Compare:
*************************************************************

ActivateWindow --> "Shell_TrayWnd", "", NULL, 10.0..............Result: Success
ActivateWindow --> "Progman", "Program Manager", NULL, 10.0......Result: Success
ActivateWindow --> "SysListView32", "FolderView", 1, 10.0........Result: Success
ClickListView --> 1, "Minesweeper", DBLCLK, 0.0.................Result: Success
CompareScreen --> "Window 1"...................................Result: Failure
ActivateWindow --> "Minesweeper", "Minesweeper", 51249669, 10.0..Result: Failure
ClickMenu --> "&Game", 0.09....................................Result: Success
ClickMenu --> "&Game;&Custom...", 2.67.........................Result: Success
CompareScreen --> "Region 1"...................................Result: Success
ActivateWindow --> "#32770", "Custom Field", NULL, 10.0.........Result: Success
```

```
ClickEdit --> 141, 1, 0, 0.09....................................Result: Success
Keys --> "[Backspace]", 0.82.....................................Result: Success
Keys --> "20", 0.37, 0.1.........................................Result: Success
ClickEdit --> 142, 1, 0, 1.74....................................Result: Success
Keys --> "[Backspace]", 0.62.....................................Result: Success
Keys --> "20", 0.51, 0.06........................................Result: Success
ClickEdit --> 143, 2, 0, 1.64....................................Result: Success
Keys --> "[Backspace][Backspace]", 0.64, 0.18...................Result: Success
Keys --> "2", 0.79...............................................Result: Success
CompareScreen --> "Region 2".....................................Result: Success
ClickButton --> "OK", 1, 22.25...................................Result: Success
CompareScreen --> "Window 2".....................................Result: Success
ActivateWindow --> "Minesweeper", "Minesweeper", 51249669, 10.0..Result: Failure
ClickMenu --> "&Game", 0.13......................................Result: Success
ClickMenu --> "&Game;&Custom...", 1.94...........................Result: Success
CompareScreen --> "Region 3".....................................Result: Success


****************************************************************
* Log Ended on:  Thu Dec 23 01:13:03 2004
****************************************************************
```

Minesweeper Test Editing and Debugging

Hmm. All of the CompareScreen commands succeeded, but all of the ActivateWindow commands failed! After applying Rule 1, look up the syntax for ActivateWindow in the VHT User's Guide. You will find out that the third parameter is the window ID. Well, this number is created anew each time the *Minesweeper* application is started. The IDs recorded in your test are probably different than the ones listed in the preceding code. To ignore the ID value during playback, use your editing skills to change the IDs to NULL in all of the ActivateWindow commands. Here's what each one should look like:

```
ActivateWindow("Minesweeper", "Minesweeper", NULL, 10.0)
```

Now rerun the test and you should get a Success result for every command.

If you need help debugging, consult the VHT User's Guide for the syntax and operational details of any commands that fail. Chapter 6 specifically describes the debugging capabilities of VHT. If you're not sure why screen comparisons are failing, you can select Screenshot... under the Compare menu in VHT. This gives you a list of the images that were captured for your test. The ones with a red X, like Window 1 shown in Figure 17.11, are the comparisons that failed. Click a failed item to see the image captured during playback of the test. Clicking the displayed image will toggle between the recently captured image and the test's reference image.

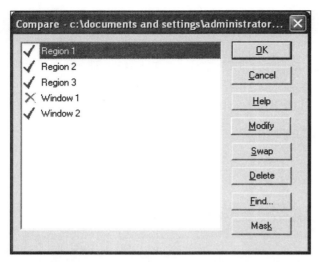

Figure 17.11 Screenshot compare list for failed *Minesweeper* test.

Minesweeper Test Modularity and Reuse

Isn't it annoying that you have to manually reset the *Minesweeper* game back to its initial state after running each automated test? You will waste time if you re-run the test and forget to reset and close the game. If many tests need to be run in sequence, the manual activity time would add up and defeat the whole purpose of automation. A way to deal with this is to automatically return the game to the proper state after you run each test. You could add a chunk of code at the end of every test, but a more efficient solution is to create a separate module that performs the cleanup. That module would get called by each of your *Minesweeper* tests. This approach costs only one additional line per test to call the cleanup routine.

The steps you need to implement in the cleanup module are as follows:

1. Click OK to close the custom options window that was left open at the end of the original test (see Figure 17.10).
2. Activate the *Minesweeper* window.
3. Select the Game options and click Beginner.
4. Close the *Minesweeper* window.

This is a good situation in which to use a `LogComment` statement at the beginning of the module. It will leave behind a textual note in the log file to explain what is happening.

In this case, explain that what is happening is only for the purposes of cleaning up and is not intended to test any particular functionality. Here's an example you can put at the beginning of your cleanup file:

```
LogComment("Nothing more to check, just shutting down for next test...")
```

That part was easy, but what about implementing the four cleanup steps? One strategy would be to capture the cleanup steps and then add the LogComment statement. You already know how to do that, so think about another possibility. Okay, time's up! You could enter the test code directly into the file. Take a look at what you have already captured and see if any of those operations are similar to the cleanup activities.

First, there's an example of clicking the OK button in the main test routine. The command is

```
ClickButton("OK", 1, 12.25)
```

Next, there are also commands to activate the *Minesweeper* window. These are the ones you edited to use NULL instead of a specific window ID:

```
ActivateWindow("Minesweeper", "Minesweeper", NULL, 10.0)
```

There is no exact match for cleanup step 4 in the main test file, but there is something that is close. In the main test file there are commands that choose the Custom option from the Game menu. This requires two steps: selecting the Game menu and then selecting Custom... from the option list. Since you want the Beginner option, change "Custom" to "Beginner" like so:

```
ClickMenu("&Game", 0.11)
ClickMenu("&Game;&Beginner", 1.13)
```

Last but not least, you need to provide some way to close the *Minesweeper* window. Since you've seen the ActivateWindow command, it may not be too much of a leap to guess that there is a CloseWindow command. A quick check of the VHT User's Guide reveals that indeed there is. Just add the window name and you're all set to go. Here's what the complete cleanup should look like, after filling in your header information:

```
;FileName: c:\documents and settings\administrator\desktop\vht test files\minesweepercp\cleanmine.inb
;
;Created: Thu Dec 23 10:58:57 2004
;Author: Me
;
;Product: Game Testing All in One
;Abstract: Reusable script to shutdown Minesweeper after each test
;
```

```
LogComment("Nothing more to check, just shutting down for next test...")
ClickButton("OK", 1, 12.25)
ActivateWindow("Minesweeper", "Minesweeper", NULL, 10.0)
ClickMenu("&Game", 0.11)
ClickMenu("&Game;&Beginner", 1.13)
CloseWindow("Minesweeper")
```

To use this routine, `Call` it from the main test file. Since it's in its own file, use the file-name as the call parameter. You should add this line to the end of the main test. Don't forget the `.inb` file extension.

```
Call("cleanmine.inb")
```

Now you can run the main test file and it will call the cleanup file. When your auto-mated test ends, *Minesweeper* has been put back into Beginner mode and closed up for the next test. The test produces a single test log that incorporates the results of the main test file and the external `cleanmine` routine. Your results should look like the following:

```
***************************************************************
* FileName:        c:\documents and settings\administrator\desktop\vht test
files\minesweepercp\minetest3.inb
* Log Created on:  Thu Dec 23 13:14:43 2004
*
* Playback Options:
*      Play Speed: 50
*      Terminate on Failure:
*


*      Ignore During Compare:
***************************************************************


ActivateWindow --> "Shell_TrayWnd", "", NULL, 10.0..............Result: Success
ActivateWindow --> "Progman", "Program Manager", NULL, 10.0.....Result: Success
ActivateWindow --> "SysListView32", "FolderView", 1, 10.0.......Result: Success
ClickListView --> 1, "Minesweeper", DBLCLK, 0.0.................Result: Success
CompareScreen --> "Window 1"....................................Result: Failure
ActivateWindow --> "Minesweeper", "Minesweeper", NULL, 10.0.....Result: Success
ClickMenu --> "&Game", 0.09.....................................Result: Success
ClickMenu --> "&Game;&Custom...", 2.67..........................Result: Success
CompareScreen --> "Region 1"....................................Result: Success
ActivateWindow --> "#32770", "Custom Field", NULL, 10.0.........Result: Success
ClickEdit --> 141, 1, 0, 0.09...................................Result: Success
Keys --> "[Backspace]", 0.82....................................Result: Success
```

```
Keys --> "20", 0.37, 0.1..........................................Result: Success
ClickEdit --> 142, 1, 0, 1.74.....................................Result: Success
Keys --> "[Backspace]", 0.62......................................Result: Success
Keys --> "20", 0.51, 0.06.........................................Result: Success
ClickEdit --> 143, 2, 0, 1.64.....................................Result: Success
Keys --> "[Backspace][Backspace]", 0.64, 0.18....................Result: Success
Keys --> "2", 0.79................................................Result: Success
CompareScreen --> "Region 2".......................................Result: Success
ClickButton --> "OK", 1, 12.25....................................Result: Success
CompareScreen --> "Window 2".......................................Result: Success
ActivateWindow --> "Minesweeper", "Minesweeper", NULL, 10.0......Result: Success
ClickMenu --> "&Game", 0.13.......................................Result: Success
ClickMenu --> "&Game;&Custom...", 1.94............................Result: Success
CompareScreen --> "Region 3".......................................Result: Success
Call --> C:\Documents and Settings\Administrator\Desktop\VHT TEST
FILES\MinesweeperCP\cleanmine.inb ...Result: Success
Nothing more to check, just shutting down for next test...
LogComment --> "Nothing more to check, just shutting down for next test..."...Result:
Success
ClickButton --> "OK", 1, 12.25....................................Result: Success
ActivateWindow --> "Minesweeper", "Minesweeper", NULL, 10.0......Result: Success
ClickMenu --> "&Game", 0.11.......................................Result: Success
ClickMenu --> "&Game;&Beginner", 1.13.............................Result: Success
CloseWindow --> "Minesweeper".....................................Result: Success


****************************************************************
* Log Ended on:  Thu Dec 23 13:15:37 2004
****************************************************************
```

Summary

Automated testing is not free, it's profitable. Capture/playback testing is a good way to start. It produces reusable recordings of the tests you are already performing manually. Look beyond PC games. Many console, handheld, and mobile games can be developed, controlled, and/or emulated on a PC. Be creative about using capture/playback through these interfaces to automate controller, keypad, or network inputs and check screen, audio, and network responses. Automating only small portions of your testing will provide noticeable benefits in the long run. Testers should get into the habit of automating.

Exercises

1. Did the last window in the *Minesweeper* test appear the way you expected it to? Explain.

2. Pretend that the last *Minesweeper* window is wrong and should actually match the one shown in Figure 17.8, which you stored after you changed the initial custom values. How would you change the automated test code to check for the "expected" screen instead of the "actual" one? How do you think the log file will change as a result? Make the change(s) and re-run your test to find out.

3. Another way to run the test with *Minesweeper* in the proper state is to set it up before your test runs instead of afterwards. Discuss the pros and cons of each approach. Create updated versions of your test to implement both solutions and run them. Did you change your mind about which is best? Describe any new insights you gained from this.

4. Are you happy or sad that you reached the end of this book? Elaborate.

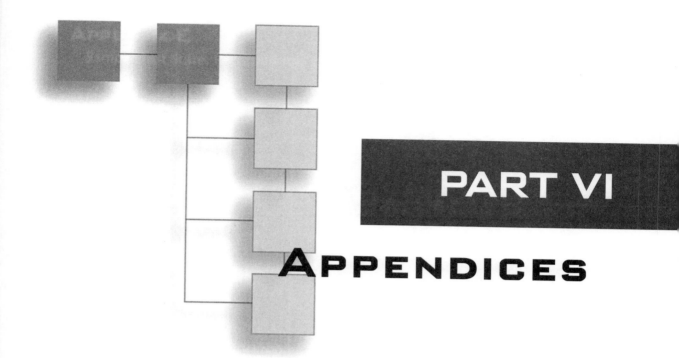

APPENDICES

APPENDIX A

ANSWERS TO EXERCISES

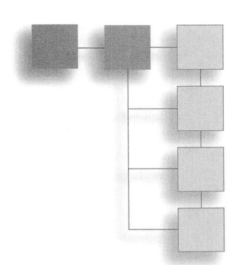

Chapter 1

1. Don't panic.

2. The answer is specific to the reader.

3. Trust no one.

4. The answer is specific to the reader.

5. d

6. "Don't Panic" is from Douglas Adams' *The Hitchhiker's Guide to the Galaxy* (www.douglasadams.com/creations/infocom.html) and "Trust No One" is originally from *The X-Files* (www.thexfilesgame.com). You can claim extra credit if you also recognized "Trust No One" as a tagline from the game *Ice Nine*.

Chapter 2

1. Trust no one.

2. a-J, b-P, c-J, d-P

3. c

4. e

5. Check if the megazooka ammo is still in your inventory and if anything else you were carrying is gone. Check if this problem occurs on other levels, with other character types, and while wearing other armor. Check if this occurs when you are not carrying a weapon other than the knife, and with no weapon at all—just the megazooka ammo. Check if this bug occurs when the ammo is in different inventory slots. Drop the megazooka and pick it up again while you still have the ammo to see if it still reads 0 ammo. Try manually reloading the megazooka. Try picking up more megazooka ammo while you are using the empty megazooka. Get two megazooka ammo packs and then pick up the empty megazooka.

6. Some potential problems are: Male Scoundrel picture or title might not get highlighted at the appropriate time, wrong picture could be shown for Male Scoundrel, scoundrel description might be wrong or contain an error, scoundrel description might not get shown at the right time, X or Y buttons could affect the selection or display of the scoundrel, right analog stick could affect the selection or display of the scoundrel, X or Y buttons could affect the subsequent operation of the B (back) button, right analog stick could affect the subsequent operation of the B button.

7. Outline Test:

   Main Menu

   New Game

   Character Selection

   Scoundrel

   Scout

   Scoundrel

   Invalid controls

   Main Menu

   > Advantages:

   >> Shorter

   >> Less chance of making an error when writing the test

   >> Easier to reuse across different game platforms

   >> May get run different ways by different testers

   > Disadvantages:

   >> Does not specify "Invalid controls"

   >> Does not draw tester's attention to what item to check at each step

   >> A developer may have trouble reproducing a defect found this way

   > May not get repeated exactly the same way by another tester

   Note that the 4th advantage and disadvantage are the same. By running it differently, someone else could find a defect that didn't show up the first time. But running it differently each time, a tester could miss a defect that was the target of the original test.

Chapter 3

1. Yes.

2. The answer is specific to the reader.

3. Correct answers to this question should be along the lines of: when you are placed in a particular location in the game world, when you type in a name for something in the game (a player, town, pet, etc.), when you change a game option (language, difficulty, etc.), when you gain a new ability (skill, level, job, unlocked item, etc.), when you set the selling price of an item.

4. Correct answers should relate to dynamic processes in the game, such as: aging (people, creatures, the environment, etc.), movement of objects in the environment (due to wind, gravity, etc.), the formation and effects of disasters (earthquakes, fire, flood, etc.), population growth (people, animals, plants, etc.), planetary cycles (sun, moon, meteors, etc.), weather (rain, snow, lightning, etc.).

5. `RespawnItem` defect type opportunities:

> Function—1 through 19 (random selection), 20-24 (setup and use flags), 25-26 (play respawn sound)
>
> Assignment—9, 10 (2), 12 (2), 15 (2), 17 (2), 20, 27
>
> Checking—2, 6, 11, 16
>
> Timing—26
>
> Build/Package/Merge—21
>
> Algorithm—14, 22, 23
>
> Documentation—7 (a literal string is used to report an error)
>
> > Interface—0, 7, 24, 26

6. And again for `G_SpawnItem`:

> Function—2-8 (spawn item), 9-10 (make sound), 15-20 (apply damage). The other lines, such as 11, set values but don't perform the function in this routine.
>
> Assignment—1 (possible missing initialization of local variable), 4, 8, 10, 13, 19
>
> Checking—9, 12, 15, 18
>
> Timing—7 (if this line is not there, spawn timing could be wrong)
>
> Build/Package/Merge—none
>
> Algorithm—7
>
> Documentation—none (strings passed to functions in this routine are not intended to be displayed as text)
>
> > Interface—0, 2, 3, 8, 9, 10, 13, 16, 17

Chapter 4

1. Development Teams, Test Teams, Art Teams, Sound Teams, and Matrixed Teams

2. a) Start Game to Front-End

   b) Front-End to Starting Grid

   c) Front-End to End Game

   d) Starting Grid to Racing

   e) Racing to Race Wrap-Up

   f) Racing to Pause

   g) Pause to Front-End

   h) Pause to Starting Grid

i) Pause to Racing

j) Pause to End Game

k) Race Wrap-Up to Front-End

l) Race Wrap-Up to Starting Grid

m) Race Wrap-Up to End Game

3. a) Start to Starting Grid

b) Start to Racing

c) Start to Race Wrap-Up

d) Start to Pause

e) Start to End Game

f) Front-End to Pause

g) Front-End to Racing

h) Front-End to Race Wrap-Up

i) Starting Grid to Front-End

j) Starting Grid to Pause

k) Starting Grid to Race Wrap-Up

l) Starting Grid to End Game

m) Racing to Front-End

n) Racing to Starting Grid

o) Racing to End Game

p) Pause to Race Wrap-Up

q) Race Wrap-Up to Racing

r) Race Wrap-Up to Pause

4. Some rotating vehicle view tests:

a) From first vehicle: click right arrow once, wait for new vehicle to rotate past 360 degrees. Check for smooth rotation, cracks or flicker in the graphics. Repeat until you arrive back at first vehicle.

b) From first vehicle: click left arrow once, wait for new vehicle to rotate past 360 degrees. Check for smooth rotation, cracks, or flicker in the graphics. Repeat until you arrive back at first vehicle.

c) From first vehicle: click right arrow once, wait for new vehicle to rotate past 360 degrees. Check for smooth rotation, cracks, or flicker in the graphics. Click left arrow once. Check that first vehicle is shown and rotating properly.

d) From first vehicle: click left arrow once, wait for new vehicle to rotate past 360 degrees. Check for smooth rotation, cracks, or flicker in the graphics. Click right arrow once. Check that first vehicle is shown and rotating properly.

e) From first vehicle: rapidly click right then left arrow, check first vehicle is shown and is rotating properly.

f) From first vehicle: rapidly click left then right arrow, check first vehicle is shown and rotating properly.

g) From first vehicle: rapidly click right arrow until you arrive back at first vehicle. Check that first vehicle is promptly shown and is rotating properly.

h) From first vehicle: rapidly click left arrow until you arrive back at first vehicle. Check that first vehicle is promptly shown and is rotating properly.

5. Example for an office building lobby containing marble floors, front and rear glass doors, guard station with guard, and two central steel-door elevators.

   A. Check placement and behavior of objects

      i) check left and right front doors open and close from both directions

      ii) check left and right rear doors open and close from both directions

      iii) check guard station placed inside rear door to the right as you enter

      iv) check elevators located in center of lobby, one on either side. Each should have its own call button in the Up direction only.

      v) check elevator call buttons light when pressed and remain lit when pressed again.

      vi) check that when an elevator arrives at the first floor, its doors open and the call button light goes out if it was lit

   B. Check the behavior and placement of NPCs

      i) check that the guard is standing at the guard station

      ii) check that the guard greets you when you enter through either rear door

   C. Check the fit and form of each unique tile mesh and texture used in the level

      i) check glass door fit, transparency, and reflective factor for front and rear doors

      ii) check metal door handle color, reflectivity, and fit with glass door

      iii) check texture and shine of marble floor and wall tiles

      iv) check fit of marble floor tile edges with walls and elevator doors

      v) check steel elevator door texture and reflectivity for each elevator

   D. Check the functions and load times of transitions from one level to another

      i) check that there is no noticeable break or flicker in gameplay when entering through either front door

      ii) check that there is no noticeable break or flicker gameplay when entering through either rear door

      iii) check that there is no noticeable break or flicker gameplay when entering either elevator door

Chapter 5

1. *Star Wars: Knights of the Old Republic*—Ordinary guy finds out he's extraordinary

   HALO—Can one man save the universe?

   Unreal Tournament—*Mortal Kombat* with guns

Zoo Tycoon—*SimCity* set in a zoo

True Crime: Streets of LA—*Grand Theft Auto* in reverse

Wario Ware, Inc.—Rapid-fire games without rules

2. Art Bible—Preproduction

Competitive Analysis—Concept Development

Game Prototype—Preproduction

New maps—Upgrades

Risk Analysis—Concept Development

Game Design Document—Preproduction

Test Lead on-board—Development

Technical Design Document—Preproduction

Code submitted for compliance testing—Beta

Celebrate—Release to Manufacture

Concept document—Concept Development

Volunteer testers participate—Beta

3. High Concept—Low detail

Estimated Budget—Low detail

Story in Concept Doc—Low detail

Game Design Doc—High detail

Development Schedule in Project Plan—High detail

Game Prototype—Low detail

Beta Release—High detail

Manpower Plan in Project Plan—High detail

Asset List in Pre-Production Plan—Low detail

4. Game Design Document—Yes

Prototype—No

Project Plan—Yes

Art Production Plan—Yes

Patches—No

Chapter 6

1. Your total released defects are 35 + 17 = 52. The table in Figure 6.1 has a column for 100,000 but not for 200,000 so double the defect count values in the 100,000 column. A defect count of 66 indicates a 4.9 sigma level and 48 is 5 sigma. Your 52 defects don't reach the 5 sigma level, so your game code is at 4.9 sigma.

2. The Fagan Inspection Moderator has the extra responsibility of scheduling and conducting an Overview meeting prior to the actual peer review of the work. The walkthrough Leader actively presents the material during the peer review, while the inspection Moderator's main purpose is to see that the meeting is conducted properly and collect inspection metrics. The walkthrough Leader is not well-suited to take notes during the meeting, while the inspection Moderator typically has enough bandwidth to do so.

3. New PCEs: Requirements = 0.69, Design = 0.73, Code = 0.66.

4. Your Control Chart should look like Figure A.1.

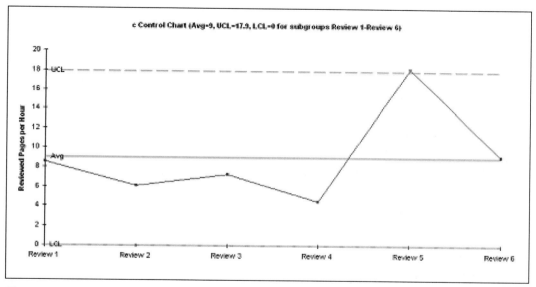

Figure A.1 Control Chart for review rates.

The value for Review 5 falls outside the Upper Control Limit (UCL). This rate is considered "too high." Reviewing material too quickly can be an indication of any of the following:

- poor preparation
- lack of participation and interaction during the review
- lack of understanding of the material being reviewed
- schedule pressures which "encourage" reviewers not to spend "too much" time on reviews

Whatever the reasons, the potential consequence of a high review rate is missed faults.

On the other hand, going too slow could be the result of:

- Too much debate over disagreements during the review
- Spending time discussing issues not related to the review material
- Lack of understanding of the material being reviewed

The consequences of low review rates are that the team should have covered more material during the same time which would have caught more faults. Managers will take quick notice when reviews become unproductive and too many bad experiences can jeopardize the use of reviews for the remainder of the project or water down the process to the point where it is ineffective.

Chapter 7

1. The main responsibilities of a Lead Tester are: managing the test team, designing and implementing the overall project test plan, "owning" the bug database.

2. The primary tester should be allowed to modify all fields in the bug database except for Priority, Status, Assigned To, and Developer Comments.

3. False

4. a) is appropriate, as it is a "feature question" to understand how the feature and its tests should really work.

   b) is appropriate as "test improvement" subject matter.

   c) is not appropriate.

   d) is appropriate as "test improvement" subject matter.

   e) is appropriate as it deals with the "recent defect history" of the feature.

   f) is appropriate, as it relates to gathering "equipment, files, and programs needed for test."

   g) is appropriate as "test improvement" subject matter.

5. False

6. True

7. False

8. False

9. Put briefly, a test plan defines the overall structure of the testing cycle. A test case is one specific question or condition the code is operated and evaluated against.

Chapter 8

1. The Expected Result is the way the game should work according to its design specification. The Actual Result is anomalous behavior observed when you used the game, caused by a software defect.

2. Regression testing verifies that fixes have been properly implemented in the code.

3. Remove the old build, and all related saved data. Verify and amend your hardware setup to meet the spec of the new build. Install the new build.

4. The "knockdown list" is the regression set—that is, the list of defects that the development team believes it has fixed in the current build.

5. False

6. False

7. False

8. False

9. True

10. False

11. Your answer should look something like the following sequence. Check for any steps or details you missed in your answer.

    a. Look on the table next to the bed. You will see an odd plastic box with a coiled cord looped on one side. This is a "telephone."

    b. Looped cord is connected to a bracket-shaped piece on the top of the telephone. The brackets end in two round cups. This is the "receiver."

    c. Pick up the receiver and notice that one cup has many more holes than the other. Put the cup with the fewest number of holes to your ear. You should hear a loud, steady hum.

    d. Push the numbered buttons in the following order: 5-5-5-1-2-3-4. When you hear a voice answer, begin talking.

Chapter 9

1. The original two testers, B and Z, were progressing at a steady rate which was not quite enough to keep up with the goal. Tester D was added in January but the team's total output was not improved. This could be due to effort diverted from testing to provide support to D or to verify his tests were done properly. On January 8, C and K were thrown into the mix while B took a day off. We can presume C and K knew what they were doing as the group output went up and they almost caught up with the goal line. K and Z did not participate after that and the output went back down even as B returned. Ultimately only D was left on the project as presumably the others were reassigned to more vital testing. D completed seven tests on the 12th but it remains to be seen if he can sustain this output and hold the fort until this project can get its testing staff back up to where it should be. The two important observations here are that you can't treat every tester as an identical plug-in replacement for any other tester—they each have their own strengths and skill sets—and adding more testers does not guarantee a proportional increase in team output, especially during the first few days.

2. Test execution is currently 22 tests behind the goal. In ten working days, the team needs to complete 10 * 12 tests to match the planned rate, plus the 22 tests needed to catch up. This means 142 tests in ten days. Strictly going by the average rate of about four tests per day provided in Figure 9.3, three testers would only complete 120 tests in that time, but four testers could complete 160 (4 testers * 4 tests/day * 10 days). There is currently one tester, so three more need to be added. In a situation like this, it's good to staff a little above what's needed to account for startup and learning curve time. The extra 18 staff days between the need (142) and the projection (160) will come in handy.

3. Tester C made the best use of her test opportunity to find the most defects per test. However, other testers such as B and Z were able to perform many more tests and find a few more defects. Since "Best Tester" is based on the combined overall contribution to tests completed and defects found, C is not in the running. It's still important to identify C's achievements and recognize them. If B and Z could have been as "effective" as C, they could have found about six more defects each; a very significant amount.

4. Tester's X 130 tests puts the total tests run for the project at 700. Since Z is the current title holder, X has to have better numbers than Z. Z's new test contribution is 169/700 = 24%. X's test contribution is 130/700 = 18.5%. X needs to contribute 7% more of the defects found than Z. Let "x" be the number of defects X needs to find. Prior to X's defects, the defect total is 34. When X's defects are found, the new defect total will be 34 + x. X's defect contribution will be x / (34 + x) and Z's contribution is 9 / (34 + x). Since X's contribution must be 7% (0.07) higher than Z's, the equation to solve is x / (34 + x) = (9 / (34 + x)) + 0.07. Eliminate the fractions by multiplying the equation by (34 + x). This gives you x = 9 + (34 * 0.07) + (x * 0.07). Subtract 0.07x from both sides of the equation and add the constants remaining on the right side to get 0.93x = 11.38. Divide by 0.93 to solve for x, which is 12.23. Since you can only have whole numbers of defects, X needs to find 13 defects to grab the "Best Tester" crown.

5. Some positive aspects of measuring participation and effectiveness: some people will do better if they know they are being "watched," some people will use their own data as motivation to improve on their numbers during the course of the project, provides a measurable basis for selecting "elite" testers for promotion or special projects (as opposed to favoritism for example), testers seeking better numbers may interact more with developers to find out where to look for defects.

Some negative aspects: effort is required to collect and report this tester data, it can be used as a "stick" against certain testers, may unjustly lower the perceived "value" of testers who make important contributions in other ways such as mentoring, could lead to jealousy if one person constantly wins, testers may argue over who gets credit for certain defects (hinders collaboration and cooperation), some testers will figure a way to exceed at their individual numbers without really improving the overall test capabilities of the team (such as choosing easy tests to run).

Chapter 10

1. Full combinatorial tables provide all possible combinations of a set of values with each other. The size of such a table is calculated by multiplying the number of choices being considered (tested) for each parameter. A pairwise combinatorial table does not have to incorporate all combinations of every value with all other values. It is "complete" in the sense that somewhere in the table there will be at least one instance of any value being paired up in the same row with any other value. Pairwise tables are typically much smaller than full combinatorial tables; sometimes hundreds or thousands of times smaller.

2. A parameter represents a function that can be performed by the game or the game player. Values are the parameter (function) choices that are available, possible or interesting from a test perspective.

3. Use the template for 7 params to arrive at the table in Figure A.2. The cells with "*" can have either a "Yes" or "No" value and your table will still be a correct pairwise combinatorial table.

4. In the three new rows, just add one instance of each of the remaining parameters. The order is not important since they have already been paired with the other parameters in the original portion of the table. Your new table should resemble the one in Figure A.3. The cells with "*" can have either a "Yes" or "No" value and your table will still be a correct pairwise combinatorial table.

Test	Quarter Length	Play Calling	Game Speed	Challenges	Coach Mode	Multiple Routes	Performance EQ
1	1 min	Package	Slow	Yes	Yes	Yes	Yes
2	5 min	Formation	Normal	No	No	Yes	Yes
3	15 min	Coach	Fast	Yes	No	No	Yes
4	1 min	Formation	Fast	No	Yes	No	No
5	5 min	Coach	Slow	No	Yes	No	*
6	15 min	Package	Normal	No	Yes	No	*
7	1 min	Coach	Normal	Yes	No	Yes	No
8	5 min	Package	Fast	Yes	No	Yes	No
9	15 min	Formation	Slow	Yes	No	Yes	No

Figure A.2 *ESPN NFL 2K5* game options test table with seven parameters.

Test	Quarter Length	Play Calling	Game Speed	Challenges	Coach Mode	Multiple Routes
1	1 min	Package	Slow	Yes	Yes	Yes
2	5 min	Formation	Normal	No	No	Yes
3	15 min	Coach	Fast	Yes	No	No
4	1 min	Formation	Fast	No	Yes	No
5	5 min	Coach	Slow	No	Yes	No
6	15 min	Package	Normal	No	Yes	No
7	1 min	Coach	Normal	Yes	No	Yes
8	5 min	Package	Fast	Yes	No	Yes
9	15 min	Formation	Slow	Yes	No	Yes
10	2 min	Package	Slow	Yes	Yes	Yes
11	2 min	Coach	Normal	No	No	No
12	2 min	Formation	Fast	*	*	*

Figure A.3 *ESPN NFL 2K5* game options test table with 2 min value combinations.

case	Body Type	Skin Tone	Face	Height	Weight
1	Skinny	Lightest	Type 1	6'0"	220
2	Normal	Light	Type 1	5'6"	150
3	Large	Light Medium	Type 1	7'0"	405
4	Normal	Lightest	Type 2	7'0"	220
5	Skinny	Light	Type 2	6'0"	405
6	Extra Large	Light Medium	Type 2	5'6"	220
7	Large	Lightest	Type 3	5'6"	150
8	Extra Large	Light	Type 3	7'0"	220
9	Skinny	Light Medium	Type 3	6'0"	150
10	Normal	Dark Medium	Type 4	6'0"	405
11	Large	Dark	Type 4	5'6"	220
12	Extra Large	Darkest	Type 4	7'0"	150
13	Extra Large	Dark Medium	Type 5	5'6"	405
14	Skinny	Dark	Type 5	7'0"	150
15	Large	Darkest	Type 5	6'0"	220
16	Skinny	Dark Medium	Type 6	5'6"	220
17	Extra Large	Dark	Type 6	6'0"	405
18	Normal	Darkest	Type 6	5'6"	405
19	Large	Lightest	Type 6	7'0"	150
20	Large	Dark Medium	Type 7	7'0"	150
21	Extra Large	Lightest	Type 7	6'0"	405
22	Skinny	Light	Type 7	5'6"	220
23	Normal	Dark	Type 2	~6'0"	150
24	Skinny	Darkest	Type 3	~7'0"	405
25	Large	Light	Type 1	~6'0"	~405
26	Normal	Light Medium	Type 1	~7'0"	~220
27	Extra Large	Dark Medium	Type 1	~6'0"	~150
28	Large	Dark Medium	Type 2	~7'0"	~405
29	Normal	Dark	Type 3	~5'6"	~405
30	Skinny	Lightest	Type 4	~5'6"	~405
31	Normal	Light	Type 5	~7'0"	~150
32	Normal	Light Medium	Type 7	~6'0"	~150
33	~Skinny	Darkest	Type 2	~5'6"	~150
34	~Normal	Dark Medium	Type 3	~6'0"	~220
35	~Large	Light Medium	Type 4	~6'0"	~220
36	~Extra Large	Light	Type 4	~7'0"	~150
37	~Extra Large	Light Medium	Type 5	~5'6"	~405
38	~Normal	Lightest	Type 5	~6'0"	~220
39	~Large	Light	Type 6	~6'0"	~220
40	~Skinny	Light Medium	Type 6	~7'0"	~150
41	~Large	Dark	Type 7	~7'0"	~220
42	~Extra Large	Darkest	Type 7	~5'6"	~220
43	~Large	Darkest	Type 1	~5'6"	~150
44	~Skinny	Dark	Type 1	~7'0"	~405

5. You should have used all of the values available for Body Type, Skin Tone, and Face. For this solution they were each listed in order from lowest to highest in the input table. It is sufficient to only use the default, minimum, and maximum values for Height and Weight. They were specified in that same order in the input table. If you correctly fed Allpairs, you should get the tests shown in Figure A.4. The "pairings" column has been left off. If your input table had the parameters in a different order than was used for this solution, check that you have the same number of test cases. 1512 full combinations have been reduced to 44 pairwise tests. If your result doesn't seem right, redo the input table with the ordering described here and try again.

Figure A.4 *ESPN NFL 2K5* Create Player pairwise combinatorial table.

Chapter 11

1. Your answer should at least describe the following kinds of changes:

   a) Change "Ammo" to "Arrows" and "Gun" to "Bow".

   b) "DropSound" would be different for the arrows (rattling wood sound) than for the bow (light "thud" on grass, "clank" on cobblestone), so need two distinct events for "DropArrowsSound" and "DropBowSound."

   c) If you have both the bow and some arrows, dropping the bow will not cause you to lose your arrows, so flow 8 should connect to the "HaveAmmo" state.

   d) It's not really possible to pick up a loaded bow, so eliminate the "GetLoadedGun" flow (9).

   e) "ShootGun" (now "ShootBow") may make more of a "twang" or "whoosh" sound if there is no arrow, so change "ClickSound" to "NoArrowSound" or something similarly descriptive.

   f) Firing a bow requires more steps than shooting a gun. You could add some or all of the states and flows for the steps of taking an arrow from the quiver, loading the arrow onto the bowstring, pulling the string, aiming, and releasing the arrow. Your reason for doing this should remain consistent with the purpose of the TFD. For example, with a bow and arrows, you could load the arrow to go to an ArrowLoaded state, but then unload the arrow to go back to HaveBowHaveArrows to make sure the arrow you didn't fire was not deducted from your arrow count.

2. Your updated TFD should at least have a GetWrongAmmo flow going from HaveGun to a new HaveGunWrongAmmo state. From that state you would have a DropWrongAmmo flow going back to HaveGun and a ShootGun flow with a ClickSound action looping back to HaveGunWrongAmmo the same way flow 3 does with the HaveGun state.

3. Using the added event and actions names from answer 2, you need new Data Dictionary entries for GetWrongAmmo, HaveGunWrongAmmo, and DropWrongAmmo. Your Minimum path must include all of the new flows, passing through the HaveGunWrongAmmo state. For Baseline path generation, you may choose the same baseline that applies to Figure 11.13 or define a different one. At some point, you need to have a derived path that get to the HaveGunWrongAmmo state and passes through the ShootGun loop. Swap your test case with a friend and check each other's results step by step. It may help to read out loud as you go along and trace the flows that are covered with a highlighter.

4. You need to represent the phone prior to playing, when the game is active, when a game is suspended while in a call and when the game is suspended with the flip closed. Be sure to have a flow that closes the flip when you are in a call. Depending on the phone, this can also end the call. Make sure you include return flows for "reversible" actions such as getting a call and ending the call, or closing and opening the flip. Also check that the game is not playable or adversely affected if you try to use it during the call. Your TFD should include states and flows similar to those shown in Figure A.5.

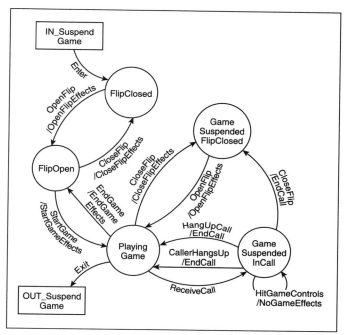

Figure A.5 Mobile game suspension TFD.

Chapter 12

1. The answer is specific to the reader.

2. All of the pairs for Look Sensitivity = 1 are missing. For Look Sensitivity = 10, it's missing pairs with Invert Thumbstick = YES, Controller Vibration = NO, Invert Flight Control = YES, and Auto-Center = NO. Invert Thumbstick = YES is missing pairs with Controller Vibration = NO, Invert Flight Control = YES, and Auto-Center = NO. Lastly, Controller Vibration is unpaired with Invert Flight Control = YES and Auto-Center = NO.

   When you choose to do Cleanroom testing, you aren't concerned about covering all of the pairs. The purpose is to represent the frequency at which various game features are going to be used by your customers. If you try to use Cleanroom test generation to get pairwise coverage, you will have to keep trying over and over again, checking each new table to see if it covers all of the pairs. This could take many cycles and/or many time more tests than you need to generate if you just focus on pairwise coverage. If you want to use both approaches, use them separately.

3. It is possible to have the same exact test case appear more than once in a Cleanroom test set. This would typically involve values that have high usage frequencies but, like the lottery, it's also possible that infrequent value combinations will be repeated in your Cleanroom table.

4. Using the process described in Chapter 14, you should have calculated the following casual player inverted usages for each of the Advanced Settings parameters:

Look Sensitivity: 1 = 32%, 3 = 4%, 10 = 64%

Invert Thumbstick: YES = 90%, NO = 10%

Controller Vibration: YES = 20%, NO = 80%

Invert Flight Control: YES = 75%, NO = 25%

Auto-Center: YES = 70%, NO = 30%

5. The random number set used to produce the table in Figure 12.14 produces the following inverted usage tests:

a) Look Sensitivity = 1, Invert Thumbstick = YES, Controller Vibration = NO, Invert Flight Control = YES, Auto-Center = YES

b) Look Sensitivity = 10, Invert Thumbstick = YES, Controller Vibration = NO, Invert Flight Control = YES, Auto-Center = YES

c) Look Sensitivity = 1, Invert Thumbstick = YES, Controller Vibration = NO, Invert Flight Control = YES, Auto-Center = YES

d) Look Sensitivity = 10, Invert Thumbstick = YES, Controller Vibration = NO, Invert Flight Control = YES, Auto-Center = YES

e) Look Sensitivity = 3, Invert Thumbstick = YES, Controller Vibration = NO, Invert Flight Control = NO, Auto-Center = NO

f) Look Sensitivity = 10, Invert Thumbstick = YES, Controller Vibration = YES, Invert Flight Control = YES, Auto-Center = YES

6. Figure A.6 shows how your TFD with inverted usage values should look.

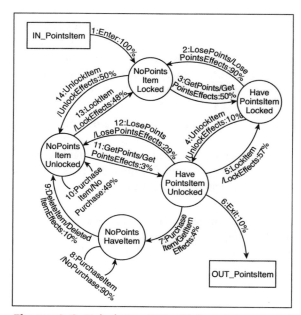

Figure A.6 Unlock Item TFD with inverted usage values.

7. The path produced from the inverted usage values will depend on the random numbers that you generate. Ask a friend or classmate to check your path and offer to check theirs in return.

Chapter 13

1. The bug fix affects "sound," "Orks", and "weapon" so you should run the collection of tests associated with to the following nodes on the tree:

> Options—Sound
>
> Game Modes—Skirmish—Races (Orks)
>
> Races—Orks

2. Start by creating four branches—LAN, Online, Direct Host, and Direct Join—from the Multiplayer node. Then, reproduce the set of branches attached to the Skirmish node and attach them to both the new LAN and Direct Host nodes. The affected portion of the tree should look like Figure A.7.

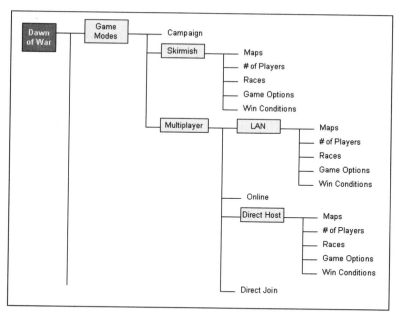

Figure A.7 Expanded Multiplayer portion of test tree.

3. (a) The Summoner job tree is shown in Figure A.8.

   (b) Based on the nodes in the Summoner job tree, you should have the following test cases:

   > 2 Elementalist abilities and 2 White Mage abilities: Summoner job is available
   >
   > 2 Elementalist abilities and 1 White Mage ability: Summoner job is not available
   >
   > 1 Elementalist ability and 2 White Mage abilities: Summoner job is not available

1 Fencer ability and 1 White Mage ability: Summoner job is not available

0 Fencer abilities and 1 White Mage abilities: Summoner job is not available

1 Fencer ability and 0 White Mage abilities: Summoner job is not available

4. Figure A.9 shows the initial Host branch expansion to include the "Removed from play" possibility. From there you would check which cards available in the game can produce each of the effects represented. Any effects which are not possible should be removed from the tree.

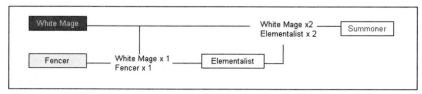

Figure A.8 Summoner job tree.

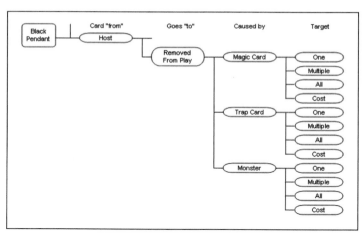

Figure A.9 Initial "Removed from Play" portion of the Black Pendant "Host" branch.

Chapter 14

1. False

2. Game testing is very hard and often tedious work. If the work of game testing is going to be valued (and compensated) fairly, game testers must do all they can to reinforce to non-testers the serious nature of their contribution to the production of games.

3. Free testing is an unstructured search for software defects. It results in additional bugs being discovered. Play testing is a structured attempt to judge the quality, balance, and fun of a game. It results in suggestions and feedback that the designers can use to tweak and polish the design of the game.

4. Either as a percentage or as X occurrences out of Y attempts.

5. This is play testing. The testers are playing the game, not testing the game.

6. Run the following series of tests in two-player mode. The tester should control only one character, so the other character just stands there and doesn't fight back.

   a) Count the number of punches it takes for the suspect character to kill the default character.

   b) Count the number of kicks it takes for the suspect character to kill the default character.

   c) Count the number of punches it takes for the default character to kill the suspect character.

   d) Count the number of kicks it takes for the default character to kill the suspect character.

   Repeat these tests several times, using three or four different characters against the suspect character. If the suspect character consistently needs more punches or kicks to kill an opponent that the average of the other characters, the suspect character may be underpowered.

Chapter 15

1. The answer is specific to the reader.

2. Incorporating the different control possibilities into a single table minimizes the total number of tests. While separating the controller functions from the option parameter tests would produce more test cases, it may cost less in terms of test execution. If the team is incrementally adding features, the separate tables would be useful to establish the functionality of the game parameters and then when the controller functions are expanded, you could start running the controller tests. If these two concepts are blended into a single table from the start of the project, many tests might be blocked and you would be unable to provide valuable feedback for certain pairs in the test table.

3. Representing the "snap back" behavior on the TFD requires a state to represent you avatar at the starting location and another state to represent you standing at a gun or ammo location. A MoveToGun flow would take you from the PreMatch location to the "standing" location. A flow with a PrematchTimerExpires event would take you from your standing location to the NoGunNoAmmo state, accompanied by an action describing the "snap back" to the starting position. For the case where you don't move from the initial spawning location, add a PrematchTimerExpires flow from the PreMatch location to NoGunNoAmmo but without the snap back action.

4. Different firing methods would be represented by additional flows in parallel with the existing ShootGun and ShootAllAmmo flows. They would simply need distinct names and flow numbers. With more than one shooting control connected at the same time, it would be possible for a player to use both simultaneously. If this is blocked by the game code, then simultaneous shooting flows would loop back to their present states. If it is permitted, then another parallel flow is required wherever shooting flows already exist. The possibility of different controls provides Configuration trigger coverage. The ability to fire simultaneously from multiple controls provides a Stress situation.

5. Besides the Normal trigger testing, which you are accustomed to, here are some ways to utilize other defect triggers for this hypothetical poker game:

Startup: Do stuff during the intro and splash screens, try to bet all of your chips on the very first hand, try to play without going through the in-game tutorial

Configuration: Set the number of players at the table to the minimum or maximum, set the betting limits to the minimum or maximum, play at each of the difficulty settings available, play under different tournament configurations

Restart: Quit the game in the middle of a hand and see if you have your original chip total when you re-enter the game, create a split pot situation where one player has wagered all of his chips but other players continue to raise their bets, save your game and then reload it after losing all of your money

Stress: Play a hand where all players bet all of their money, play for long periods of time to win ridiculous amounts of cash, take a really long time to place your bet or place it as quickly as possible, enter a long player name or an empty one (0 characters)

Exception: Try to bet more money than you have, try to raise a bet by more than the house limit, try using non-alphanumeric characters in your screen name

Chapter 16

1. The two factors are how well your department is run and whether or not you are behind on your project.

2. You may not wish to automate testing if you are unwilling to invest in the staffing and game infrastructure changes that are necessary to make test automation successful.

3. Improved game reliability, greater tester and machine efficiency, consistency of results, faster testing, and the ability to simulate tremendously large numbers of concurrent players for stress and load testing without having to use large pools of human testers are good reasons to automate.

4. Online multiplayer games, first-person shooters, puzzle games, and mobile games are all suitable candidates for at least some degree of test automation.

5. Play sequences, repeating actions, user interfaces, and randomly walking through game worlds are all useful applications of test automation.

6. Whenever an object or player attribute or property changes, make sure you are checking (logging) before and after then change. The following SimScript-like sequence implements the test described for this exercise:

```
# guitar test
log_objects
place_object    guitar      10 10
log_objects
move_object     guitar      40 40
log_objects
set_data        avatar              guitar_skill 0
use_object      guitar              shred
```

```
wait_until     avatar              guitar_skill 100
log_objects
place_object   guitar        10 10
log_objects
```

Chapter 17

1. The test put a "2" the Mines field, but when the Custom Field window was opened at the end of the test (see Figure 17.10) the Mines value was 10. Typically, the user would be warned about entering an invalid value.

2. The captured results produce code that must be manually updated if you want to check for a "desired" result which is different from what was actually captured. Change the VHT code to check for the Mines value of 2 instead of 10. If you scan through the generated code, you will find that after entering the "2" a check is made for "Region 2":

```
Keys("[Backspace][Backspace]", 0.64, 0.18)
Keys("2", 0.79)
CompareScreen("Region 2")
```

At the end of the session, the window with the wrong Mines value is captured, represented by the following code:

```
ClickMenu("&Game;&Custom...", 1.94)
CompareScreen("Region 3")
```

In order to check for the screen with Mines = 2 instead of Mines = 10, replace the "Region 3" check with a check for "Region 2" as follows:

```
ClickMenu("&Game;&Custom...", 1.94)
CompareScreen("Region 2")
```

From then on, when you play this script back you will get a Failure on the final comparison until the defect gets fixed.

3. Establishing the correct game state prior to each test is helpful when you are picking and choosing tests from different features and running them one after another. Each test carries the responsibility to set itself up properly. Establishing the correct game state after your test can also serve this purpose once a proper game state is established by some other means prior to running the first test. The post-test cleanup has the benefit of leaving the test machine in some kind of usable state. Tests that only "clean up" before they run could leave a mess behind if someone needs to use the machine for manual testing purposes. In either case it's important to have a consistent policy. Doing a pre-test cleanup after the previous test has done a post-test cleanup is a slight waste of time. What's worse is when a test that doesn't clean up after itself is followed by one that does not do a pre-test cleanup.

4. Ideally, you are happy because you have learned much from this book that you will put into practice, and you are sad that there aren't any more fun testing things to learn from this book.

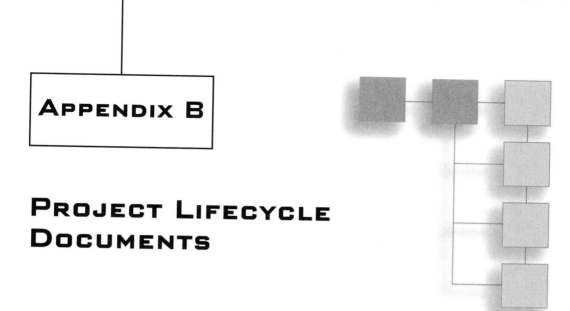

APPENDIX B

PROJECT LIFECYCLE DOCUMENTS

This appendix contains guidelines, outlines, or templates for creating most of the documents used in the course of a game project.

Lack of good communication is the single biggest obstacle to efficient software development, so it's worthwhile to think carefully about how these documents can best be developed and maintained.

The larger a document is, the less likely people are to read it. In paper form, large documents are almost impossible to maintain. A good solution is to maintain your documents on an internal Web page where everyone on the team can modify the information. Go to www.openwiki.com for a very powerful *no-cost* solution to this problem.

The rest of this appendix will assume that you're maintaining your documents online.

Index to Documents

The "home page" of your internal Web page should contain a list of the major project-related documents. In turn, these documents may contain links to other sub-documents that are maintained by the teams working on particular areas of the game.

1. Index to Documents
2. High Concept
3. Pitch Doc
4. Concept Doc
5. Game Design Doc (GDD)
6. Art Production Plan
7. Technical Design Doc (TDD)

8. Test Plan
9. Project Plan
    a. Manpower Plan
    b. Resource Plan
    c. Project Tracking Doc
    d. Budget
    e. P&L
    f. Development Schedule
    g. Milestone Definitions
10. External Events
11. Current Risks
12. Credits List
13. Change List & Project Archives

High Concept Document

This is a very short document, no more than a few sentences, which answers the question, "What is your game about?" See Chapter 5 for more details and examples. It may seem strange to devote an entire document to this brief topic, but it's important to do so.

Like a company's mission statement, it's useful to print this up and post it around the office so everyone has a visible reminder of what they're trying to create. It should also be maintained in a prominent place on the organization's internal Web.

If the high concept changes while the game is in development, that's a major event that should receive a lot of attention. If this happens, make sure to update this document and post new copies where everyone can be reminded how the basic course of the project has changed.

Game Proposal ("Pitch Doc")

This is the one- or two-page executive summary of the game that you give to prospective publishers during your pitch meeting. Ideally, it would be accompanied by a playable prototype of the game, as well as a more complete concept doc (see next section).

The game proposal document should have the following sections:

1. High Concept. The one- or two-sentence statement of the experience you're trying to create.

2. Genre. A single sentence that places the game within a genre or a hybrid of genres.

3. Gameplay. A paragraph that describes what kinds of actions the player can perform during the game.

4. Features. A list of the major features that set this game apart, including anything from technical advancements to artistic style.

5. Setting. A paragraph about what makes the game world and its occupants unique and interesting.

6. Story. If the game has a story, summarize it here in a paragraph.

7. Target Audience. A single sentence that describes the demographic you're trying to reach.

8. Hardware Platforms. A list of devices your game can be played on.

9. Estimated Schedule and Budget. Your estimate of how long the game will take to develop and how much it will cost.

10. Competitive Analysis. A list of existing and planned games that will compete with yours.

11. Team. Names and credentials of the design, tech, and art leads. Also, list the games the organization has shipped.

12 Summary. A restatement of why this will be a great game, and why your team is the one to develop it.

Concept Document

As discussed in Chapter 5, this is a more detailed version of the pitch document. It's too large to use in a presentation meeting, but you should leave it for the publishing team to give them a more in-depth understanding of your game.

1. High Concept. The one- or two-sentence statement of the experience you're trying to create. This shouldn't change from the pitch doc.

2. Genre. A discussion of the genre your game falls under. This section should include comparisons to other titles in the genre.

3. Gameplay. A description of the kinds of actions the player can perform during the game, along with some examples.

4. Features. The pitch doc listed the features that set this game apart. Here, you should go into more detail about why each of these features is important, and how you'll implement them.

5. Setting. Describe the game world in detail, and explain what makes it and its occupants unique and interesting.

6. Story. If the game has a story, describe it here in greater detail than in the pitch doc. Include the major characters, their motivations, and how they achieve (or fail to achieve) their goals.

7. Target Audience. Explain why the game will appeal to the target demographic you've identified.

8. Hardware Platforms. A list of devices your game can be played on. If you plan to develop different features for the various platforms, use this section to explain how the game will be different on each one.

9. Estimated Schedule and Budget. Break out the major phases of development, and the level of effort associated with each, to show how you arrived at the estimates in the pitch doc. Also include a P&L estimate if you have one.

10. Competitive Analysis. List the games you'll be competing with for sales, and explain how your game will stack up against them.

11. Team. List the names and credentials of the design, tech, and art leads, as well as other key team members. Also, list the games the organization has shipped. Publishers place as much importance on the team as on the concept, so make sure this section convinces them that your organization is capable of delivering the product you're proposing.

12. Risk Analysis. Explain the risks the project faces, and how you plan to minimize them.

13. Summary. End on a high note. Emphasize again why this will be a great game, and why the publisher should have confidence in your team's ability to deliver it.

Game Design Document (GDD)

This is the document that everyone involved with the game comes to for an understanding of the game's details.

Different parts of the document will take shape over time. You won't be ready to write final dialogue on the first day of product development, for example, but you should know how many characters you'll be asking the art team to create. Similarly, you won't have a detailed level walkthrough on day one, but you should know what will happen in each level, what equipment the player will start with, and what new toys he'll acquire.

What's important for you to realize is that at some point, you'll need to document all the following information. Keep it current. Failure to maintain an up-to-date game design document (or, more accurately, *set* of documents) will cause team members to waste their time creating features whose specifications have been altered, or that may no longer be needed at all.

You'll notice that a change list is not included as part of this document. While it's important to keep a change list for many documents (especially formal agreements between companies), it's hard enough to get people to read the *current* design document, much less slog through information that's out-of-date. Instead, see the final document in this appendix, which contains a separate change list and project archives.

The following game design doc template can be used for an action game, and it can be modified for games in other genres as needed. Please note that many of the "lists" should actually be maintained as linked spreadsheets or tables. Also note that the order of the sections is somewhat arbitrary; you should order the sections in your own GDD in the way that makes most sense to you.

See Chapter 5 for additional notes about developing and maintaining the game design document.

1. Game Name
    a. Copyright Information
2. Table of Contents

3. SECTION I: PROJECT OVERVIEW
    a. Team Personnel (with contact information for each individual)
        i. Production Team
            1. Producer
                a. Office phone
                b. Home phone
                c. Cell phone
                d. Email
            2. Assistant Producer
                a. Same contact info as above
            3. Etc.
        ii. Design Team
            1. Design Lead
            2. Level Designer #1
            3. Writer #1
            4. Etc.
        iii. Programming Team
            1. Tech Lead
            2. Additional Programmers

      iv. Art Team
         1. Art Lead
         2. Additional Artists
      v. QA Team
         1. QA Lead
         2. Additional Testers
      vi. External Contractors
         1. Mocap Company
            a. Contact Name
            b. Contact Phone Number
            c. Company Address
         2. Composer
         3. Sound Effects House
         4. CGI house
         5. Voice Director
         6. Etc.

b. Executive Summary
    i. High Concept
    ii. The Hook
    iii. Story Synopsis and Setting
    iv. Genre & Scope (such as number of missions or levels)
    v. Visual Style (2D? 3D? Isometric? etc.)
    vi. Engine (and editor?)

c. Core Gameplay (What does the player *do*?)
    i. Single-player
    ii. Co-op?
    iii. Multiplayer?

d. Game Features
    i. Gameplay innovations
    ii. Advances in AI
    iii. Artistic techniques and achievements
    iv. License tie-ins (if applicable)
    v. Other features that will make this game better than others like it on the market

e. Project Scope
    i. Number of distinct locations
    ii. Number of levels/missions
    iii. Number of NPCs
    iv. Number of weapons
    v. Number of vehicles
    vi. Etc.

f. Target Audience

g. Delivery Platform(s)

4. SECTION II: STORY, SETTING, AND CHARACTER
   a. Story
      i. Back story
      ii. In-game story (What happens during the game)
   b. Environments
      i. Area #1
         1. General description
         2. Physical characteristics
         3. List of levels that take place in this area
      ii. Area #2
      iii. Etc.
   c. Characters
      i. Player Character(s)
         1. Personality
         2. Back story
         3. "Look"
         4. Special abilities
            a. Ability #1
               i. When it's acquired
               ii. How the player invokes it
               iii. Effect it has on the world
               iv. Graphic effect that accompanies it
            b. Ability #2
            c. Etc.
         5. Weapon set
         6. Regular animations
            a. Walk, run, climb, roll, swim, crouch, crawl, idle, etc.
         7. Situation-specific animations
         8. Statistics (if applicable)
      ii. Allies
         1. Ally #1
            a. Personality
            b. Relationship to player character
            c. Back story
            d. "Look"
            e. Special abilities
            f. Weapon set
            g. Regular animations
            h. Situation-specific animations
            i. Statistics
         2. Ally #2
         3. Etc.

       iii. Bad Guys
- 1. Ultimate bad guy
  - a. Personality
  - b. Relationship to player character
  - c. Back story
  - d. "Look"
  - e. Special abilities
  - f. Weapon set
  - g. Regular animations
  - h. Situation-specific animations
  - i. Statistics
- 2. Sub-bosses
- 3. Grunts

       iv. Neutrals
- 1. World NPCs
  - a. NPC#1
    - i. Attitude towards player character
    - ii. Function in the game
    - iii. Animation set
  - b. NPC#2
  - c. Etc.
  - d. Level Flow (A flowchart that summarizes the action of each level, and the cutscenes or mission briefings [if any] that take place between them)

5. SECTION III: COMBAT

  a. Weapons

    i. Weapon #1
- 1. General description and most effective use
- 2. When it is first acquired
- 3. Art (if available)
- 4. Statistics (for both primary and secondary fire)
  - a. Type of ammunition
  - b. Shots per clip
  - c. Fire rate
  - d. Reload rate
  - e. Damage inflicted
  - f. Range

    ii. Weapon #2

    iii. Etc.

  b. Spells

    i. Spell #1
- 1. Description
- 2. When it is first acquired

      3. How the player invokes it

      4. Statistics

        a. Range

        b. "Refire rate"

        c. Damage

        d. Area of effect

  ii. Spell #2

  iii. Etc.

c. Inventory Items/Gadgets

  i. Item #1

      1. Brief physical description of the object

      2. When it is first acquired

      3. What it does

      4. Art (if available)

      5. How the player equips it

      6. Statistics

  ii. Item #2

  iii. Etc.

d. Powerups

  i. Powerup #1

      1. Brief physical description of how the object is represented in the world

      2. When it is first acquired

      3. Art (if available)

      4. What it does

      5. Statistics

        a. Effect

        b. Duration

  ii. Powerup #2

  iii. Etc.

e. Melee (hand-to-hand) combat (if applicable)

  i. Attacks

  ii. Defensive moves

  iii. Combos

f. Vehicles (if applicable)

  i. Capacity

  ii. Speed

  iii. Armor

  iv. Weaponry

  v. Combat statistics

  vi. Etc.

6. SECTION IV: CONTROLS
   a. PC Keyboard/Mouse Commands
      i. Default keys for movement controls
         1. Move forward
         2. Move backward
         3. Strafe left
         4. Strafe right
         5. Jump
         6. Etc.
      ii. Default keys for using weapons
         1. Primary fire
         2. Alt-fire
         3. Reload
         4. Previous weapon
         5. Next weapon
         6. Etc.
      iii. Inventory access and manipulation
      iv. Menu access
   b. Console Platform #1
      i. A picture of the controller explaining what each button does
      ii. Movement controls
      iii. Weapon controls
      iv. Action controls
      v. Combos
      vi. Force-feedback options
   c. Console Platform #2
   d. Etc.

7. SECTION V: INTERFACE
   a. The Camera
      i. Standard view
      ii. Alternate views
      iii. Player-controllable options
   b. HUD
      i. Worldview (what the player sees)
      ii. Status information
         1. Health
         2. Energy
         3. Armor
         4. Weapon equipped
         5. Ammo remaining
         6. Mission objectives?
      iii. Crosshairs (targeting reticule)
      iv. Radar or proximity map?

    c. Menus
       i. Game screen flow diagrams (schematic of how all the game's various screens are accessed)
      ii. Start Menu
          1. Install
          2. Play game
          3. Explore CD (bonus features)
          4. Uninstall
          5. Quit
     iii. Main Menu
          1. Single-Player
             a. Load game
             b. Save game
             c. Play training level
             d. Set difficulty level
          2. Co-op
          3. Multiplayer
             a. Connection instructions
             b. Character/team selection
     iv. Game Menus
          1. Remap player controls
          2. Display (video)
          3. Audio
          4. Music
          5. Map
          6. Advanced
          7. Help screen
          8. Quit
      v. Inventory Menu
     vi. Credits

8. SECTION VI: ARTIFICIAL INTELLIGENCE (AI)
    a. NPC #1
       i. Statistics
          1. Field of view
          2. Range of view
          3. Etc.
      ii. Internal states & the triggers that change them
          1. Idle
          2. Guarding an area
          3. Patrol
          4. Follow
          5. Search
          6. Etc.

      iii. Movement
         1. Pathing
      iv. Combat decisions
         1. Friend/foe recognition
         2. Targeting decisions
         3. Attack with ranged weapon
         4. Attack with melee weapon
         5. Take cover
         6. Team-based decisions
         7. Etc.
   b. NPC #2
   c. Etc.

9. SECTION VII: DETAILED LEVEL/MISSION DESCRIPTIONS
   a. Level #1
      i. Synopsis
      ii. Introductory material (Cutscene? Mission briefing?)
      iii. Mission objectives (player goals)
      iv. Physical description
      v. Map
      vi. Enemy types encountered in-level
      vii. Weapons/powerups available
      viii. Level walkthrough, including scripted sequences and non-interactive scenes. This should also include any puzzles the player must solve, as well as the solutions to those puzzles.
      ix. Closing material (Cutscene? Debriefing? Statistics menu?)
   b. Level #2
   c. Etc.

10. SECTION VIII: CUTSCENES
   a. Cutscene #1
      i. List of actors
      ii. Description of setting
      iii. Storyboard thumbnails
      iv. Script. This should be done in screenplay format, as if you were writing a movie. Include the action, suggested camera angles, location descriptions, etc. You must also include all lines of dialogue that are to be recorded or displayed on the screen.
   b. Cutscene #2
   c. Etc.

11. SECTION IX: SCORING, CHEATS, EASTER EGGS, & BONUSES
   a. Score
      i. How score is tracked
      ii. How score is communicated to the player

    b. Cheats (God mode, all weapons, etc.)
       i. Cheat #1
         1. What it does
         2. How it's activated by the developer
         3. How it's unlocked by the player
       ii. Cheat #2
      iii. Etc.
    c. Easter Eggs/Bonus Material
       i. Easter Egg #1
         1. What it is
         2. How it's activated/unlocked
       ii. Easter Egg #2
      iii. Etc.

12. SECTION X: GAME MODES
    a. Single-player
    b Split-screen/coop (if applicable)
    c. Multiplayer game types (if applicable)
       i. Gametype #1 (such as "Capture the Flag")
         1. Description of gameplay
         2. Min/max # of Players
         3. Rules
         4. Respawning
            a. Delay
            b. Respawn locations
            c. Default weapons
         5. Victory conditions
         6. Scoring
         7. Maps
       ii. Gametype #2
      iii. Etc.

13. SECTION XI: ASSET LIST
    a. Art
       i. Model & Texture List
         1. Characters
            a. Player character
               i.   Undamaged
               ii.   Damaged
            b. Allies
            c. Bad guys
            d. Neutrals

2. Weapons
   a. Weapon #1
   b. Weapon #2
   c. Etc.
3. Equipment/Gadgets
   a. Item #1
   b. Item #2
   c. Etc.
4. Environmental Objects
   a. Object #1
   b. Object #2
   c. Etc.

ii. Animation list
1. Characters
   a. Character #1
      i. Move #1
      ii. Move #2
      iii. Etc.
   b. Character #2
   c. Etc.
2. Weapons
   a. Weapon #1
      i. Firing animation
      ii. Reload animation
      iii. Projectile in flight animation (if appropriate)
3. Destructible or animated objects in the world
   a. Object #1
   b. Object #2
   c. Etc.

iii. Effects list
1. Weapon effects list
   a. Firing effects
   b. Hit effects
   c. Etc.
2. Environmental effects
   a. Decals
   b. Smoke
   c. Sparks
   d. Fire
   e. Explosions
   f. Etc.

    iv. Interface Art List
1. Icons
2. Buttons
3. Menus
4. Windows
5. Etc.

b. Sound
    i. Environmental Sounds
1. Walking/running sounds on different surfaces
2. Foley sounds of character actions within the game
3. Explosions
4. Doors opening and closing
5. Etc.

    ii. Weapon Sounds
1. Weapon #1
    a. Firing sound
    b. Hit sound
    c. Reload sound
2. Weapon #2
3. Etc.

    iii. Interface Sounds
1. Various clicks, beeps, etc., as the player maneuvers through the menus.
2. Alert/acknowledgment sounds as the player picks up objects or his game state changes.

c. Music
    i. Ambient
1. Loop #1 + duration
2. Loop #2
3. Etc.

    ii. "Action"
1. Loop #1 + duration
2. Loop #2
3. Etc.

    iii. "Victory" loops
    iv. "Defeat" loops
    v. Cutscene music
1. Piece #1
    a. General description of mood and accompanying action
    b. Duration
2. Piece #2
3. Etc.

    d. Voice
       i. Actor #1 lines
          1. Line #1. Each line in the game must have a unique identifying filename. This will help both the recording process and localization. Don't forget to include various screams, yells, grunts, laughs, and other "non-word" lines.
          2. Line #2
          3. Etc.
       ii. Actor #2 lines
      iii. Etc.

14. SECTION XII: LOCALIZATION PLAN
    a. Languages with full text and voice localization
    b. Languages with text localization only
    c. Text to be localized
       i. In-game text
      ii. Game interface text
    d. Voice to be localized
       i. (See "Voice" section of asset list above)

15. SECTION XIII: MAJOR EVENT PLANNING
    a. Trade Shows
       i. Trade Show #1
          1. Date
          2. Materials needed for event
          3. Demo description and specifications
      ii. Trade Show #2
      iii. Etc.
    b. Special Publicity Events
       i. Event #1 (such as "Editors Day" to show off game)
          1. Date
          2. Description of event
          3. Materials needed for event
          4. Demo description and specifications
      ii. Event #2
      iii. Etc.
    c. PR/Marketing Support
       i. Date when concept art will be available
      ii. Date when first screenshots will be available
      iii. Plan for creating additional screenshots throughout project
      iv. Plan for making team available for interviews
      v. Etc.
    d. Sales Team Support
       i. Projected date of first "sell-sheet"
      ii. Demo loop for retail outlets

iii. Other materials
iv. Etc.
e. Prerelease Demo
i.   Date
ii. Scope
iii. Content

16. SECTION XIV: TECHNICAL SUMMARY
a. Single-Player
i. PC
1. Minimum system requirements
2. Recommended system requirements
3. Number of characters viewable at once
4. Max # polys per character
5. Max # polys per level
ii. Console Platform #1
iii. Etc.
b. Multiplayer
i.   Type of connectivity (Splitscreen? LAN? Online?)
ii. Max # simultaneous players
iii. Client-server? Peer-to-peer?
iv. Etc.

17. SECTION XV: MISCELLANEOUS
a. Acronyms used in this document
b. Definition of terms

18. SECTION XVI: REFERENCES
a. Games
b. Movies
c. Books
d. Art

Art Production Plan

This document plus the GDD and TDD are the trio of content-creation documents that must be maintained throughout the project. This is where people will look not only for concept pieces, but also for detailed visuals on all aspects of the game.

1. Game Name
a. Copyright Information
2. Table of Contents

3. SECTION I: ART TEAM (including areas of responsibility and contact info for each individual)
   a. Art Director
      i. Office phone
      ii. Home phone
      iii. Cell phone
      iv. Email
   b. Animators
   c. Modelers
   d. Texture Artists
   e. Effects Artists
   f. CGI Artists
   g. GUI Artists
   h. External Resources
   i. Etc.

4. SECTION II: EXECUTIVE SUMMARY
   a. Project Overview from the Art Creation Perspective
   b. Delivery Platforms
      i. PC
         1. Content creation/conversion plan
      ii. Console Platform #1
      iii. Etc.

5. SECTION III: BUDGETS (Poly/memory limits for each delivery platform)
   a. Characters
      i. Main character
         1. PC
         2. Console Platform #1
         3. Console Platform #2
         4. Etc.
      ii. Allies
      iii. Bad Guys
         1. Ultimate Bad Guy
         2. Bosses
         3. Grunts
      iv. Other World NPCs
   b. Levels
   c. Weapons
   d. Other Equipment
   e. GUI

6. SECTION IV: PRODUCTION PATH (A description of how art will be integrated in the game through the following steps)
   a. Requirements
   b. Concept
   c. Model
   d. Skin/Texture
   e. Animation
   f. Integration into the Game
   g. Porting Across Different Delivery Platforms

7. SECTION V: ART BIBLE (CONCEPT ART/STYLE GUIDE)
   a. Overview
      i. Reference Material
   b. Characters
   c. Environments
   d. Weapons
   e. Equipment
   f. GUI

8. SECTION VI: FINAL ART (as it becomes available)
   a. Characters
   b. Environments
   c. Weapons
   d. Equipment
   e. GUI
   f. Screenshots, along with a tracking doc that records when each shot was made available, and to whom. This will be especially useful when magazines are requesting exclusive shots that haven't been used before.

9. SECTION VII: CUTSCENES
   a. Cutscene #1
      i. Storyboard thumbnails
      ii. Selected shots from final game
   b. Cutscene #2
   c. Etc.

10. SECTION VIII: ASSET LIST (This should be maintained in parallel with the list in the game design document)
    a. Model & Texture List
       i. Characters
          1. Player character
             a. Undamaged
             b. Damaged
          2. Allies

        3. Bad Guys

        4. Neutrals

    ii. Weapons

        1. Weapon #1

        2. Weapon #2

        3. Etc.

    iii. Equipment/Gadgets

        1. Item #1

        2. Item #2

        3. Etc.

    iv. Environmental Objects

        1. Object #1

        2. Object #2

        3. Etc.

b. Animation list

    i. Characters

        1. Character #1

            a. Move #1

            b. Move #2

            c. Etc.

        2. Character #2

        3. Etc.

    ii. Mocap List (if applicable)

        1. Actor #1

            a. Move #1

            b. Move #2

            c. Etc.

        2. Actor #2

        3. Etc.

    iii. Weapons

        1. Weapon #1

            a. Firing animation

            b. Reload animation

            c. Projectile in flight animation (if appropriate)

        2. Destructible or animated objects in the world

            a. Object #1

            b. Object #2

            c. Etc.

c. Effects list

    i. Weapon effects list

        1. Firing effects

        2. Hit effects

        3. Etc.

      ii. Environmental effects
1. Decals
2. Smoke
3. Sparks
4. Fire
5. Explosions
6. Etc.

   d. Interface Art list
      i. Icons
      ii. Buttons
      iii. Menus
      iv. Windows
      v. Etc.

11. SECTION IX: SCHEDULING
   a. Task Lists
   b. Man-Month Scheduling
   c. Calendar Month Scheduling
   d. Milestone Schedule & Deliverables
   e. Major Event Planning
      i. Trade Shows
1. Trade Show #1
   a. Date
   b. Materials needed for event
   c. Demo description and specifications
2. Trade Show #2
3. Etc.
      ii. Special Publicity Events
1. Event #1 (such as "Editors Day" to show off game)
   a. Date
   b. Description of event
   c. Demo description and specifications
2. Event #2
3. Etc.
      iii. PR/Marketing Support
1. Date when first screenshots will be available
2. Plan for creating additional screenshots throughout project
3. Plan for making team available for interviews
4. Etc.
      iv. Sales Support/Team Support
1. Demo loop for retail outlets
2. Other materials
3. Etc.

    v. Prerelease Demo
     1. Date
     2. Scope
     3. Content

12. SECTION X: RECRUITMENT
  a. Current Personnel
  b. Additional Team Members Needed
  c. Schedule for Hiring Additional Personnel
  d. Risk Plan for Handling Delays in Acquiring Additional Resources

13. SECTION XI: EQUIPMENT BUDGET AND COSTS
  a. Team Personnel with Hardware and Software Toolset
   i. Team Member #1
    1. Hardware
     a. Development PC
      i. Specs
     b. Console Dev Kit
      i. Add-ons (TV, controllers, memory cards, hubs, etc.)
     c. Debug Kit
    2. Software Tools Needed
     a. 2D Art Package
     b. 3D Art Package (+ support?)
     c. Plug-Ins and Add-Ons
     d. Tools and Utilities
     e. Mocap Editing Suite
     f. Other Specialized Software
     g. Etc.
   ii. Team Member #2
   iii. Etc.
  b. Equipment Acquisition Schedule and Costs (Summary of who needs what, when they will need it, and how much it will cost.)

14. SECTION XII: LOCALIZATION PLAN (Every effort should be made to keep text that must be localized from creeping into graphics. Even so, some territories may require the development of different art packages.)
  a. Territory #1
   i. Customized models, textures, etc.
  b. Territory #2
  c. Etc.

Technical Design Document (TDD)

The technical design document is a companion piece to the game design document and the art bible. Like the other docs, the TDD should be maintained on an internal Web site and kept up to date throughout the project.

1. Game Name
   a. Copyright Information
2. Table of Contents

3. SECTION I: TECHNICAL TEAM (including areas of responsibility and contact info for each individual)
   a. Tech Lead
      i. Office phone
      ii. Home phone
      iii. Cell phone
      iv. Email
   b. AI Programmers
   c. Gameplay Programmers
   d. Graphics Programmers
   e. Tools Programmers
   f. Scripters
   g. Etc.

4. SECTION II: EXECUTIVE SUMMARY
   a. Project Overview from a Technical Perspective
   b. Delivery Platforms
      i. PC
         1. Minimum specifications
         2. Recommended specifications
         3. Disk budget
      ii. Console Platform #1
         1. Disk budget
      iii. Etc.

5. SECTION III: ENGINE EVALUATION
   a. Internal solutions
   b. External solutions from affiliated organizations
   c. Middleware

6. SECTION IV: PLATFORM-SPECIFIC ISSUES
   a. Delivery Platform #1
      i. Strategy and comments
      ii. Platform-specific processes
      iii. Memory management scheme and budgets

          iv. Risks

      b. Delivery Platform #2

      c. Etc.

7. SECTION V: DEVELOPMENT PLAN

      a. Use Cases

      b. Game Mechanics

      c. Main Loop

      d. Data Structures

      e. Data Flow

      f. Physics

      g. Artificial Intelligence

          i. Pathing

          ii. Scripting

      h. Graphics

          i. Rendering

               1. Geometry

               2. Textures

          ii. Animation

          iii. Particle System

          iv. Effects

          v. Lighting

          vi. Camera

      i. Collision

      j. GUI

          i. HUD

          ii. Menu Flow Diagram

      k. Fonts

      l. Audio/Video

      m. Special Requirements for Multiplayer Support

8. SECTION VI: CODING STANDARDS

      a. Programming Standards

      b. Style Guide

      c. Code Review Procedures

      d. Profiling Plan

9. SECTION VII: SCHEDULING

      a. Preliminary Task Lists

          i. Programming Tasks

               1. Core Libraries

               2. Object System

               3. Object System, AI

               4. Engine

       5. Tool Creation
       6. Mapping System
       7. Special Effects
       8. GUI
       9. Game Mechanics
          a. Movement
          b. Inventory
          c. Camera
          d. Weapons
      10. Conversion Support
    ii. Art Task Summaries (Taken from art plan)
    iii. Design Task Summaries (Taken from game design doc)
b. Man-Month Scheduling
c. Calendar Month Scheduling
d. Milestone Schedule & Deliverables
e. Major Event Planning
    i. Trade Shows
       1. Trade Show #1
          a. Date
          b. Materials needed for event
          c. Demo description and specifications
       2. Trade Show #2
       3. Etc.
    ii. Special Publicity Events
       1. Event #1 (such as "Editors Day" to show off game)
          a. Date
          b. Description of event
          c. Demo description and specifications
       2. Event #2
       3. Etc.
    iii. PR/Marketing Support
       1. Date when first screenshots will be available
       2. Plan for creating additional screenshots throughout project
       3. Plan for making team available for interviews
       4. Etc.
    iv. Sales Support/Team Support
       1. Demo loop for retail outlets
       2. Other materials
       3. Etc.
    v. Prerelease Demo
       1. Date
       2. Scope
       3. Content

10. SECTION VIII: RECRUITMENT
    a. Current Personnel
    b. Additional Team Members Needed
    c. Schedule for Hiring Additional Personnel
    d. Risk Plan for Handling Delays in Acquiring Additional Resources

11. SECTION IX: EQUIPMENT BUDGET AND COSTS
    a. Team Personnel with Hardware and Software Toolset
        i. Team Member #1
            1. Hardware
                a. Development PC
                    i.   Specs
                b. Console Dev Kit
                    i.   Add-ons (TV, controllers, memory cards, hubs, etc.)
                c. Debug Kit
            2. Software Tools Needed
                a. Development environment (compiler/editor/debugger)
                b. 2D art package
                c. 3D art package (+ support?)
                d. Etc.
        ii. Team Member #2
        iii. Etc.
    b. Teamwide Tools
        i. Network/infrastructure requirements
        ii. Version control system
        iii. Asset management package
        iv. QA tracking package
    c. Summary Table of Equipment and Software
        i.   PCs
        ii.   DVD burners
        iii. DevKits
        iv. Debug kits
        v.   Network/infrastructure
        vi. Seats for 3D software
        vii. Seats for 2D software
        viii. Plug-ins and add-ons
        ix. Other specialized software
        x.   Level editors
        xi. Mocap editing suite
        xii. Sound processing software
        xiii. Tools and utilities
        xiv. Version control system
        xv. Asset management package

        xvi. QA tracking system
       xvii. Etc.
    d. Equipment Acquisition Schedule and Costs

12. SECTION X: LOCALIZATION PLAN
    a. Languages with Full Text and Voice Localization
    b. Languages with Text Localization Only
    c. Text to Be Localized
      i. In-game text
      ii. Game interface text
    d. Voice to Be Localized
      i. (See "Voice" section of asset list)
    e. Art to Be Localized
      i. See art production plan

13. SECTION XI: DATA SECURITY PLAN
    a. Network Security
    b. Onsite Backup Plan
    c. Offsite Backup Plan

14. SECTION XII: MISCELLANEOUS
    a. Acronyms Used in This Document
    b. Definition of Terms

Test Plan

1. Game Name
    a. Copyright Information
2. Table of Contents

3. SECTION I: QA TEAM (and areas of responsibility)
    a. QA Lead
      i. Office phone
      ii. Home phone
      iii. Cell phone
      iv. Email
    b. Internal Testers
    c. External Testers

4. SECTION II: TESTING PROCEDURES
    a. General Approach
      i. Basic Responsibilities of Test Team
        1. Bugs
          a. Detect them as soon as possible after they enter the build
          b. Research them

      c. Communicate them to the dev team

      d. Help get them resolved

      e. Track them

  2. Maintain the Daily Build

  3. Levels of Communication. There's no point in testing unless the results of the tests are communicated in some fashion. There are a range of possible outputs from QA. In increasing levels of formality, they are:

      a. Conversation

      b. ICQ

      c. EMail to Individual

      d. EMail to Group

      e. Daily Top Bugs List

      f. Stats/Info Dump Area on DevSite

      g. Formal Entry into Bug Tracking System

 b. Daily Activities

  i. The Build

    1. Generate a daily build.

    2. Run the daily regression tests, as described in "Daily Tests" which follows.

    3. If everything is okay, post the build so everyone can get it.

    4. If there's a problem, send an email message to the entire dev team that the new build cannot be copied, and contact whichever developers can fix the problem.

    5. Decide whether a new build needs to be run that day.

  ii. Daily Tests

    1. Run through a predetermined set of single-player levels, performing a specified set of activities.

      a. Level #1

        i.   Activity #1

        ii.   Activity #2

        iii.   Etc.

        iv.   The final activity is usually to run an automated script that reports the results of the various tests and posts them in the QA portion of the internal Web site.

      b. Level #2

      c. Etc.

    2. Run through a predetermined set of multiplayer levels, performing a specified set of activities.

      a. Level #1

        i.   Activity #1

        ii.   Activity #2

        iii.   Etc.

        iv.   The final activity is usually for each tester involved in the multiplayer game to run an automated script that reports the results of the various tests and posts them in the QA portion of the internal Web site.

        b. Level #2

        c. Etc.

    3. Email showstopper crashes or critical errors to the entire team.

    4. Post showstopper crashes or critical errors to the daily top bugs list (if one is being maintained).

c. Daily Reports

    i. Automated reports from the preceding daily tests are posted in the QA portion of the internal Web site.

d. Weekly Activities

    i. Weekly tests

        1. Run through every level in the game (not just the preset ones used in the daily test), performing a specified set of activities and generating a predetermined set of tracking statistics. The same machine should be used each week.

            a. Level #1

                i. Activity #1

                ii. Activity #2

                iii. Etc.

            b. Level #2

            c. Etc.

        2. Weekly Review of Bugs in the Bug Tracking System

            a. Verify that bugs marked "fixed" by the development team really are fixed.

            b. Check the appropriateness of bug rankings relative to where the project is in the development.

            c. Acquire a "feel" for the current state of the game, which can be communicated in discussions to the producer and department heads.

            d. Generate a weekly report of closed-out bugs.

    ii. Weekly Reports

        1. Tracking statistics, as generated in the weekly tests.

e. Ad Hoc Testing

    i. Perform specialized tests as requested by the producer, tech lead, or other development team members.

    ii. Determine the appropriate level of communication to report the results of those tests.

f. Integration of Reports from External Test Groups

    i. If at all possible, ensure that all test groups are using the same bug tracking system.

    ii. Determine which group is responsible for maintaining the master list.

    iii. Determine how frequently to reconcile bug lists against each other.

    iv. Ensure that only one consolidated set of bugs is reported to the development team.

g. Focus Testing (if applicable)

    i. Recruitment methods

    ii. Testing location

    iii. Who observes them?

    iv. Who communicates with them?

    v. How is their feedback recorded?

      h. Compatibility Testing
         i. Selection of external vendor
        ii. Evaluation of results
      iii. Method of integrating filtered results into bug tracking system

5. SECTION III: HOW TESTING REQUIREMENTS ARE GENERATED
    a. Some requirements are generated by this plan.
    b. Requirements can also be generated during project meetings, or other formal meetings held to review current priorities (such as the set of predetermined levels used in the daily tests).
    c. Requirements can also result from changes in a bug's status within the bug tracking system. For example, when a bug is marked "fixed" by a developer, a requirement is generated for someone to verify that it has been truly killed and can be closed out. Other status changes include "Need More Info" and "Can't Duplicate," each of which creates a requirement for QA to investigate the bug further.
       1. Some requirements are generated when a developer wants QA to check a certain portion of the game (see "Ad Hoc Testing").

6. SECTION IV: BUG TRACKING SOFTWARE
    a. Package name
    b. How many seats will be needed for the project
    c. Access instructions (Everyone on the team should have access to the buglist)
    d. "How to report a bug" instructions for using the system

7. SECTION V: BUG CLASSIFICATIONS
    a. "A" bugs and their definition
    b. "B" bugs and their definition
    c. "C" bugs and their definition

8. SECTION VI: BUG TRACKING
    a. Who classifies the bug?
    b. Who assigns the bug?
    c. What happens when the bug is fixed?
    d. What happens when the fix is verified?

9. SECTION VII: SCHEDULING AND LOADING
    a. Rotation Plan. How testers will be brought on and off the project, so that some testers stay on it throughout its lifecycle while "fresh faces" are periodically brought in.
    b. Loading Plan. Resource plan that shows how many testers will be needed at various points in the life of the project.

10. SECTION VIII: EQUIPMENT BUDGET AND COSTS
    a. QA Team Personnel with Hardware and Software Toolset
       i. Team Member #1
         1. Hardware

        a. Testing PC
          i.   Specs
        b. Console Debug Kit
          i.   Add-ons (TV, controllers, memory cards, hubs, etc.)
    2. Software Tools Needed
        a. Bug tracking software
        b. Other
  ii. Team Member #2
  iii. Etc.
b. Equipment Acquisition Schedule and Costs (summary of who needs what, when they will need it, and how much it will cost)

Project Plan

The project plan is a suite of documents that the producer uses to estimate costs, track progress, maintain the schedule, and estimate profitability.

1. Manpower plan. This is a spreadsheet that lists when all the internal people connected to the project come on board, and when they finish up. Here is a drastically simplified version:

	January	February	March	April	May	June	Total
Designer	0.5	1	1	1	1	1	5.5
Tech Lead		0.5	1	1	1	1	4.5
Programmer #2			1	1	1		3
Art Lead		0.5	1	1	1	1	4.5
Artist #2			1	1	1		3
QA Lead			1	1	1	1	4
Tester #2				1	1	1	3
Total Man-months	0.5	2	6	7	7	5	27.5

2. Resource plan. This spreadsheet lists all the external costs of the project and when they will be incurred. The external costs appropriate to the preceding manpower plan might look something like this:

	January	February	March	April	May	June	Total
3 DevKits	10000	10000	10000				30000
2 Debug Kits			1000	1000			2000
Art Tool #1 (2)		5000	5000				10000
Art Tool #2 (4)		1000	1000				2000
Bug Tracking Tool			5000	150			5150
							0
Composer					5000		5000
Voice				5000	5000		10000
Total Ext Costs	10000	16000	22000	6150	10000	0	54150

3. Project tracking doc. This is usually a Gantt chart generated by the producer using project management software. Each department head supplies a list of tasks, along with the people assigned to them and how long they think the tasks will take. With this information, the producer can see if the project is on schedule, what the critical path to completion is, which resources are overloaded, etc.

4. Budget. This is a spreadsheet of all the costs associated with the project. Line items will include the following.

5. Internal personnel costs (salaries of people applied to the project)
   a. Hardware costs
   b. Software licenses
   c. External contractor fees
   d. Engine royalties
   e. IP acquisition costs (license fee)
   f. Marketing & PR costs
   g. An overhead multiplier that applies fixed costs (building rent, utilities, travel, personnel benefits, etc.) to the project
   h. Profit-and-Loss (P&L) statement. This is another spreadsheet that the publisher uses to estimate the profitability of each project. The projected lifecycle sales estimates from the sales team are compared to the costs from the preceding budget to determine if the game will make enough money to justify the investment.

6. Development schedule. This table breaks out the stages of development, with significant events along the way:

Event	Date
Concept phase	00/00/00 – 00/00/00
Start preproduction	00/00/00
Start development	00/00/00
Milestone #1	00/00/00
Milestone #2	00/00/00
… (Additional milestones)…	00/00/00
Alpha	00/00/00
Beta	00/00/00
Localization deliverable #1	00/00/00
Pre-submission (console only)	00/00/00
First submission (console only)	00/00/00
Second submission (console only)	00/00/00
Code freeze	00/00/00
Release to manufacture (RTM)	00/00/00
Shelf date	00/00/00

7. Milestone definitions. Here, the deliverable for each milestone is specified in detail, along with the date it's due.

Milestone	Date
Milestone #1. General description	
Deliverable #1	
Deliverable #2	
Deliverable #3	
	00/00/00
Milestone #2. General description	
Deliverable #1	
Deliverable #2	
Deliverable #3	
	00/00/00
Milestone #3. General description	
Deliverable #1	
Deliverable #2	
Deliverable #3	
	00/00/00
Etc.	Etc.

External Events

In the course of development, predictable interruptions will occur. These must be included in the project plan from the start. Here is a sample list of events and the team involvement that may be needed to support them:

Description	Date	Team Involvement and Materials Needed
Trade show #1	00/00/00	Producer. Designer. Show off non-interactive demo in backroom.
Trade show #2	00/00/00	Producer. Designer. LDs. Interactive demo on show floor.
Trade show #3 (overseas)	00/00/00	No one from the team. Supply "leave-behind" demo to PR crew. Also screenshots for press kit.
PR event #1 (Onsite Editor's Day)	00/00/00	Entire team. Interviews. Working game on several machines. New screenshots.
PR event #2 (License launch by content partner)	00/00/00	Corp. Executives. Screenshots for press kit.
Internal sales team presentation	00/00/00	Producer. Designer. "Highlights" demo. One-page features summary.
Other corporate events	Etc.	Etc.

Current Risks

The current risks document is an assessment by the project manager of the top risks to the project, and how they're being mitigated. Usually this takes the form of a "Top Ten" list, but the number is arbitrary and will change over time.

1. Risk #1
   a. Description
   b. Potential impact
   c. Possible ways to mitigate the risk
   d. Current course of action
2. Risk #2
3. Etc.

Risk	Impact	Mitigation & Current Course
Staffing: Our AI programmer's visa is due to expire in two months.	1) The AI programmer is distracted from his work. 2) If he leaves, the project schedule will slip by at least one month.	1) We are working with the INS to request an expedited visa. 2) We have paired another programmer with the AI lead to minimize the impact of his departure, if that happens.
Infrastructure: Our build server has crashed three times in the past week.	The entire team's progress is slowed when they don't have access to the daily build.	1) Our MIS manager is reviewing the server's security to check for attacks from the outside. 2) We have ordered a new hard drive for the server and will install it next week. 3) In the meantime, we have dedicated another machine to "mirror" the server.
External Resources: The contractor creating the CGI cutscenes missed their last deliverable.	1) No current impact to the schedule. (These cutscenes are not on the critical path.) 2) The movies must be received eventually, however, because most of them are integral to advancing the story.	1) The contractor claims this is a one-time failure due to the illness of a key employee. 2) We have reprioritized the cutscene list to have the contractor complete the essential ones first. 3) We are evaluating other contractors as a fallback in the event that this failure continues.
Etc.	Etc.	Etc.

Credits

This is a document that should be maintained from the very start of the project. On long projects, people come and go, and it's hard to remember everyone who has contributed.

There's no industry standard for assigning project credits. The following format is used quite frequently, but each team may develop its own approach.

1. Production
   a. Executive Producer
   b. Associate Producer
   c. Assistant Producer
2. Design
   a. Lead Designer
   b. Level Designers (alphabetical)
3. Technical
   a. Tech Lead
   b. Programmers (alphabetical)
4. Art
   a. Art Lead
   b. Artists (alphabetical)
5. QA
   a. QA Lead
   b. Testers (alphabetical)
6. Localization Team
   a. Localization Lead
   b. Language #1
      i. Personnel
   c. Language #2
   d. Etc.
7. Executive Team
   a. VP Production
      i. Team
   b. Sales Director
   c. Marketing Director
      i. Brand Manager
   d. PR Director
      i. Project Manager
8. Voice Talent
   a. Character #1—Actor Name
   b. Character #2—Actor Name
9. Mocap Actors
   a. Actor #1
   b. Actor #2
   c. Etc.
10. External Companies & Contractors
    a. Company #1 Name
       i. Person #1
       ii. Person #2
       iii. Etc.
    b. Company #2 Name
    c. Etc.

Change List and Project Archives

The advantage of maintaining "live" documentation is that whenever a team member looks something up, she'll see the current specification.

You can't rely on team members to constantly check the documents, however, so it's wise to set up a change notification alert system. Whenever someone changes a document, it should trigger an email to the appropriate team members with a summary of the change.

A list of these emails should be maintained so that everyone can see the change history. This list takes the place of "revision history" or "change list" section that used to be at the top of the project documents. (Note, however, that changes that affect milestones or deliverables are important enough to be tracked separately, most often as formal amendments to the development contract.)

From time to time, the project manager (or his designee) should go through the Web site to ensure that everything is current. If too much old information is cluttering things up, it's best to archive it in a separate area.

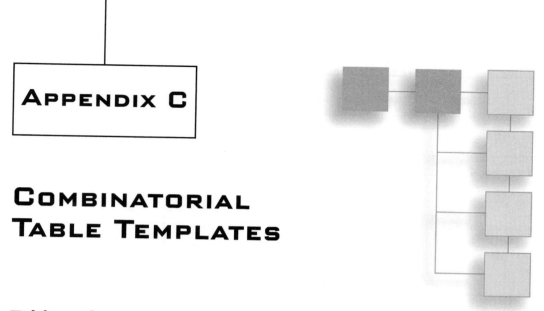

APPENDIX C

COMBINATORIAL TABLE TEMPLATES

Tables of Parameters with Two Test Values

Test	ParamA	ParamB	ParamC
1	A1	B1	C1
2	A2	B1	C2
3	A1	B2	C2
4	A2	B2	C1

Figure C.1 Three parameters, two values each.

Test	ParamA	ParamB	ParamC	ParamD
1	A1	B1	C1	D1
2	A2	B1	C2	D1
3	A1	B2	C2	D2
4	A2	B2	C1	D1
5	A2	B1	C1	D2

Figure C.2 Four parameters, two values each.

Test	ParamA	ParamB	ParamC	ParamD	ParamE
1	A1	B1	C1	D1	E1
2	A2	B1	C2	D1	E1
3	A1	B2	C2	D2	E2
4	A2	B2	C1	D1	E2
5	A2	B1	C1	D2	E2
6	A*	B2	C*	D2	E1

Figure C.3 Five parameters, two values each.

Test	ParamA	ParamB	ParamC	ParamD	ParamE	ParamF
1	A1	B1	C1	D1	E1	F1
2	A2	B1	C2	D1	E1	F1
3	A1	B2	C2	D2	E2	F1
4	A2	B2	C1	D1	E2	F2
5	A2	B1	C1	D2	E2	F2
6	A1	B2	C2	D2	E1	F2

Figure C.4 Six parameters, two values each.

Test	ParamA	ParamB	ParamC	ParamD	ParamE	ParamF	ParamG
1	A1	B1	C1	D1	E1	F1	G1
2	A2	B1	C2	D1	E1	F1	G2
3	A1	B2	C2	D2	E2	F1	G2
4	A2	B2	C1	D1	E2	F2	G2
5	A2	B1	C1	D2	E2	F2	G1
6	A1	B2	C2	D2	E1	F2	G1

Figure C.5 Seven parameters, two values each.

Test	ParamA	ParamB	ParamC	ParamD	ParamE	ParamF	ParamG	ParamH
1	A1	B1	C1	D1	E1	F1	G1	H1
2	A2	B1	C2	D1	E1	F1	G2	H2
3	A1	B2	C2	D2	E2	F1	G2	H1
4	A2	B2	C1	D1	E2	F2	G2	H2
5	A2	B1	C1	D2	E2	F2	G1	H1
6	A1	B2	C2	D2	E1	F2	G1	H2

Figure C.6 Eight parameters, two values each.

Test	ParamA	ParamB	ParamC	ParamD	ParamE	ParamF	ParamG	ParamH	ParamJ
1	A1	B1	C1	D1	E1	F1	G1	H1	J1
2	A2	B1	C2	D1	E1	F1	G2	H2	J2
3	A1	B2	C2	D2	E2	F1	G2	H1	J2
4	A2	B2	C1	D1	E2	F2	G2	H2	J1
5	A2	B1	C1	D2	E2	F2	G1	H1	J2
6	A1	B2	C2	D2	E1	F2	G1	H2	J1

Figure C.7 Nine parameters, two values each.

Test	ParamA	ParamB	ParamC	ParamD	ParamE	ParamF	ParamG	ParamH	ParamJ	ParamK
1	A1	B1	C1	D1	E1	F1	G1	H1	J1	K1
2	A2	B1	C2	D1	E1	F1	G2	H2	J2	K2
3	A1	B2	C2	D2	E2	F1	G2	H1	J2	K1
4	A2	B2	C1	D1	E2	F2	G2	H2	J1	K1
5	A2	B1	C1	D2	E2	F2	G1	H1	J2	K2
6	A1	B2	C2	D2	E1	F2	G1	H2	J1	K2

Figure C.8 Ten parameters, two values each.

Tables of Parameters with Three Test Values

Test	ParamA	ParamB	ParamC
1	A1	B1	C1
2	A2	B2	C2
3	A3	B3	C3
4	A1	B2	C3
5	A2	B3	C1
6	A3	B1	C2
7	A1	B3	C2
8	A2	B1	C3
9	A3	B2	C1

Figure C.9 Three parameters, three values each.

Test	ParamA	ParamB	ParamC
1	A1	B1	C1
2	A2	B2	C1
3	A3	B3	C1
4	A1	B2	C2
5	A2	B3	C2
6	A3	B1	C2
7	A1	B3	C*
8	A2	B1	C*
9	A3	B2	C*

Figure C.10 Two parameters with three values, one parameter with two values.

Test	ParamA	ParamB	ParamC
1	A1	B1	C1
2	A2	B2	C1
3	A3	B1	C1
4	A1	B2	C2
5	A2	B1	C2
6	A3	B2	C2

Figure C.11 One parameter with three values, two parameters with two values.

Test	ParamA	ParamB	ParamC	ParamD
1	A1	B1	C1	D1
2	A2	B2	C2	D1
3	A3	B3	C3	D1
4	A1	B2	C3	D2
5	A2	B3	C1	D2
6	A3	B1	C2	D2
7	A1	B3	C2	D3
8	A2	B1	C3	D3
9	A3	B2	C1	D3

Figure C.12 Four parameters, three values each.

Test	ParamA	ParamB	ParamC	ParamD
1	A1	B1	C1	D1
2	A2	B2	C2	D1
3	A3	B3	C3	D1
4	A1	B2	C3	D2
5	A2	B3	C1	D2
6	A3	B1	C2	D2
7	A1	B3	C2	D*
8	A2	B1	C3	D*
9	A3	B2	C1	D*

Figure C.13 Three parameters with three values, one parameter with two values.

Test	ParamA	ParamB	ParamC	ParamD
1	A1	B1	C1	D1
2	A2	B2	C2	D1
3	A3	B3	C1	D1
4	A1	B2	C1	D2
5	A2	B3	C2	D2
6	A3	B1	C2	D2
7	A1	B3	C2	D*
8	A2	B1	C1	D*
9	A3	B2	C*	D*

Figure C.14 Two parameters with three values, two parameters with two values.

Test	ParamA	ParamB	ParamC	ParamD
1	A1	B1	C1	D1
2	A2	B2	C2	D1
3	A3	B1	C2	D2
4	A1	B2	C2	D2
5	A2	B1	C1	D2
6	A3	B2	C1	D1

Figure C.15 One parameter with three values, three parameters with two values.

Test	ParamA	ParamB	ParamC	ParamD	ParamE
1	A1	B1	C1	D1	E1
2	A2	B2	C2	D2	E2
3	A3	B3	C3	D1	E2
4	A1	B2	C3	D2	E1
5	A2	B3	C1	D2	E1
6	A3	B1	C2	D2	E1
7	A1	B3	C2	D1	E2
8	A2	B1	C3	D1	E2
9	A3	B2	C1	D1	E2

Figure C.16 Three parameters with three values, two parameters with two values.

Test	ParamA	ParamB	ParamC	ParamD	ParamE
1	A1	B1	C1	D1	E1
2	A2	B2	C2	D2	E1
3	A3	B3	C1	D2	E2
4	A1	B2	C2	D1	E2
5	A2	B3	C2	D1	E2
6	A3	B1	C2	D1	E2
7	A1	B3	C1	D2	E1
8	A2	B1	C1	D2	E1
9	A3	B2	C1	D2	E1

Figure C.17 Two parameters with three values, three parameters with two values.

Test	ParamA	ParamB	ParamC	ParamD	ParamE
1	A1	B1	C1	D1	E1
2	A2	B2	C2	D1	E1
3	A3	B1	C2	D2	E1
4	A1	B2	C2	D2	E2
5	A2	B1	C1	D2	E2
6	A3	B2	C1	D1	E2

Figure C.18 One parameter with three values, four parameters with two values.

Test	ParamA	ParamB	ParamC	ParamD	ParamE	ParamF
1	A1	B1	C1	D1	E1	F1
2	A2	B2	C2	D2	E2	F1
3	A3	B3	C3	D1	E2	F2
4	A1	B2	C3	D2	E1	F2
5	A2	B3	C1	D2	E1	F2
6	A3	B1	C2	D2	E1	F2
7	A1	B3	C2	D1	E2	F1
8	A2	B1	C3	D1	E2	F1
9	A3	B2	C1	D1	E2	F1

Figure C.19 Three parameters with three values, three parameters with two values.

Test	ParamA	ParamB	ParamC	ParamD	ParamE	ParamF	ParamG
1	A1	B1	C1	D1	E1	F1	G1
2	A2	B2	C2	D2	E2	F1	G1
3	A3	B3	C3	D1	E2	F2	G1
4	A1	B2	C3	D2	E1	F2	G2
5	A2	B3	C1	D2	E1	F2	G*
6	A3	B1	C2	D2	E1	F2	G*
7	A1	B3	C2	D1	E2	F1	G2
8	A2	B1	C3	D1	E2	F1	G2
9	A3	B2	C1	D1	E2	F1	G2

Figure C.20 Three parameters with three values, four parameters with two values.

APPENDIX D

TEST FLOW DIAGRAM (TFD) TEMPLATES

Powerups

Powerups are items that give your character some kind of temporary bonus. You might need to drive over them, run over them, trigger a special item in a puzzle, or hit a special sequence on your game controller or keypad. The TFD template in Figure D.1 covers acquiring the powerup, using its abilities, canceling the powerup, checking for powerup expiration, and stacking powerups. This same template could also be used for RPG and adventure games where a player can trigger temporary effects from a weapon, get a temporary boost from an item, or receive temporary "buff" spells from other characters.

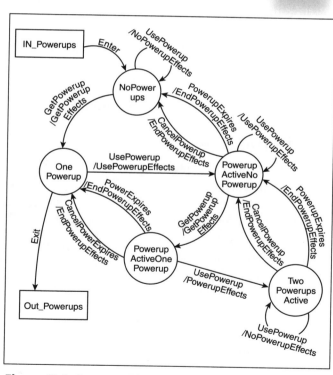

Figure D.1 Powerups TFD template.

Craft Item

Crafting an item in a game world requires the player to have the ingredients and the skill to craft that particular type of item. In addition to being trained in the right skill, the character must also have raised his skill to a sufficient level to make a crafting attempt of the target item. Some or all of ingredients are normally consumed whether or not the crafting attempt was successful. These factors are incorporated into the TFD template in Figure D.2.

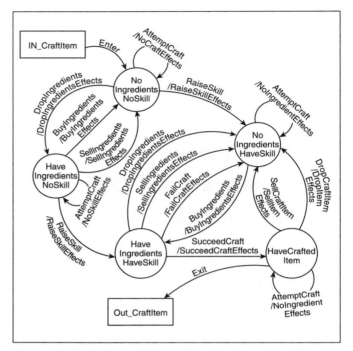

Figure D.2 Craft Item TFD template.

Heal Character

Whether its medics, magic, or a well-deserved nap, nothing beats a timely heal to get you through a tough mission, level, or battle. Get a friend to resurrect you or respawn to start over. You can also change "Heal" to "Repair" and use the TFD template in Figure D.3 when it's your car or robot that's taking a beating.

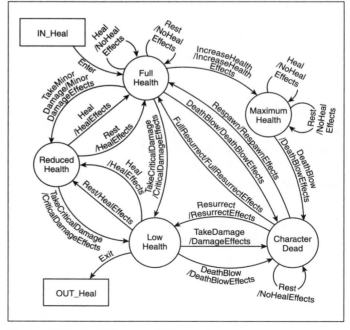

Figure D.3 Heal Character TFD template.

Create/Save

Games are full of custom elements. You can create characters, teams, playbooks, song lists, and skateboards. You also need to save them if you want to see them the next time you fire up the game. The TFD template in Figure D.4 handles creating, deleting, and filling up your save slots and restarting the game without saving your changes. If you're using this for something besides character creation, replace "Character" with the name of the type of element you are testing.

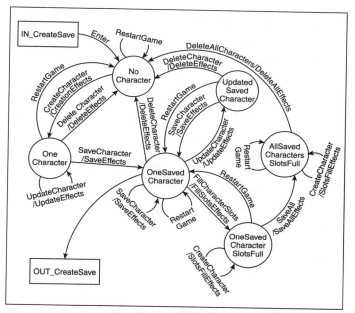

Figure D.4 Create/Save TFD template.

Unlock and Buy Item

Simulation, RPG, adventure, and even sports games tend to have featured items that you can purchase once you have unlocked the ability to purchase the item and have enough points to actually buy it. The "items" could be weapons, spells, clothing, furniture, mini-games, new vehicles, or new levels. To unlock them you may have to complete a specific task or mission, defeat a particular opponent, raise your character's level, or achieve a result under special circumstances. Test your purchasing power using the TFD template in Figure D.5. Some of these criteria are documented in the game and some are hidden. Shhhh...

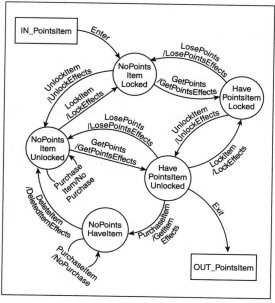

Figure D.5 Use Points Buy Unlocked Item TFD template.

Update Song List

It's a big deal for games to incorporate popular music. You might find today's hits blasting from a car radio or a street basketball court. Music can also be a more integral part of gameplay such as in a dancing or karaoke game. The TFD template in Figure D.6 reflects the player's ability to add and delete songs, order them, map them to game events, and trigger them from within the game. Depending on the game, triggering could be user controlled—such as tuning to a particular in-game radio station—or event-driven like the music played when the home team scores a touchdown. Just remember that "New Order" on the TFD refers to the order of songs in the list, not the electronica supergroup.

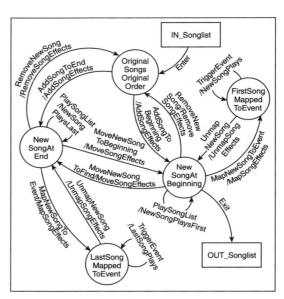

Figure D.6 Update Song List TFD template.

Complete a Mission or Quest

Many games will reward points, money, items, or access to new parts of the game if you can complete a particular mission, quest, or other designated goal. It's common for these missions to be broken into multiple objectives that must be completed individually to achieve success and earn the reward. These objectives could be things like capturing a set of territories or villains, winning a series of competitions, or completing a set of bonus words. This TFD template in Figure D.7 is constructed for goals with three objectives, but you can also use it for two objectives by knocking out the states and flows that deal with Objective3.

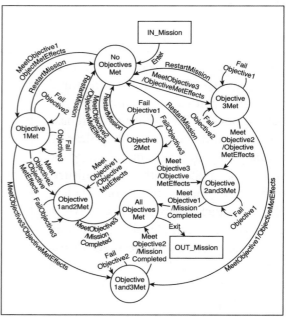

Figure D.7 Complete a Mission or Quest TFD template.

Get Weapon and Ammo

The TFD template in Figure D.8 is an enhancement of the diagram from the walkthrough in Chapter 11. A state and flows have been added for handling the case where the weapon has maximum ammo. You can also apply this TFD structure to game elements that have a similar relationship, such as cars and fuel or spells and mana. Just replace "Gun" and "Ammo" with the corresponding elements.

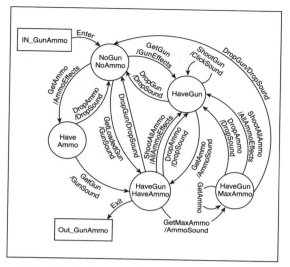

Figure D.8 Weapon and Ammo TFD template.

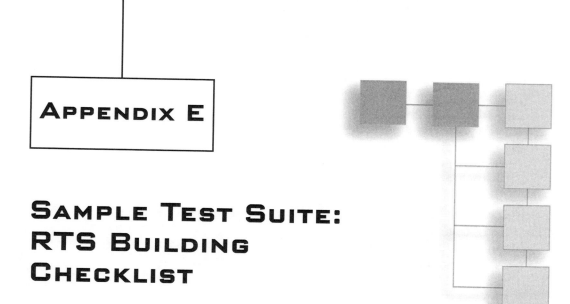

APPENDIX E

SAMPLE TEST SUITE: RTS BUILDING CHECKLIST

The following is a test suite written to test all the building functionality for one faction of a 3D real-time strategy game. It attempts to isolate each graphic and audio asset associated with each building, as well as the individual functions of each. Note that each question is written such that a "yes" answer means a pass condition and a "no" answer means a fail—and a possible defect.

```
Dragon Building Checklist
Name _____        Build No. _____
(NOTE:  Start all buildings with one peasant.)
Peasant Hut
      Select a Peasant.  Choose Peasant Hut.
      Building cost ok?
      Text ok?
      Can't build if price not met?
      Building footprint graphic ok?
      Can't place building if footprint is red?
      Can rotate building 360 degrees?
      Right-click places building?
      Building site appears in Peasant's LOS (line of sight)?
      Peasant constructs building?
      Construction animation ok?
      Phase one graphic ok?
      Phase two graphic ok?
      Phase three graphic ok? (if present)
      Completed building graphic ok?
      "Building Finished" audio ok?
```

Select building.

    Toolbar graphics ok?

    Text ok?

    Can destroy building?

    Can cancel building destruction?

    Confirming destroys building?

    Animation ok?

    Audio ok?

Build new building of the same type.

Place it away from first building.

    Alt+right-click makes peasant run to building site?

Select new building. Right-click on ground nearby to set rally point.

    Flag appears?

    Spawning units walk to rally point?

Select building again. Alt+right-click to set new rally point farther away.

    Flag appears?

    Spawning units run to rally point?

Select building again. Set rally point on rice field.

    Spawning units gather rice?

Select building again. Set rally point on water source.

    Spawning units gather water?

Create second Peasant Hut. Select first Peasant Hut.

    Peasant toggle icon okay?

    Text ok?

    Stops peasants from spawning from this building?

Select building again. Right-click on any barracks.

    Spawning units enter barracks for training?

Have fire-damaging enemies attack building. (Serpent Raiders are good for this.)

    Building burns?

    Animation ok?

    Audio ok?

    Building is destroyed in stages?

    Stage one graphics okay?

    Audio ok?

    Stage two graphics okay?

    Audio ok?

    Stage three graphics okay (if present)?

    Audio ok?

    Building leaves rubble when destroyed?

    Rubble disappears after a while?

```
Well
Select a Peasant.  Choose Well.
     Building cost ok?
     Text ok?
     Can't build if price not met?
     Can't build if prerequisites not met?
     Building footprint graphic ok?
     Can't place building if footprint is red?
     Can rotate building 360 degrees?
     Right-click places building?
     Building site appears in Peasant's LOS?
     Peasant constructs building?
     Construction animation ok?
     Phase one graphic ok?
     Phase two graphic ok?
     Phase three graphic ok? (if present)
     Completed building graphic ok?
     "Building Finished" audio ok?
Select building.
     Toolbar graphics ok?
     Text ok?
     Can destroy building?
     Can cancel building destruction?
     Confirming destroys building?
     Animation ok?
     Audio ok?
Select Peasant.  Click Well.
     Peasant gathers water?
Have fire-damaging enemies attack building.  (Serpent Raiders are good for this.)
     Building burns?
     Animation ok?
     Audio ok?
     Building is destroyed in stages?
     Stage one graphics okay?
     Audio ok?
     Stage two graphics okay?
     Audio ok?
     Stage three graphics okay (if present)?
     Audio ok?
     Building leaves rubble when destroyed?
     Rubble disappears after a while?
```

Dojo
Select a Peasant. Choose Dojo.
    Building cost ok?
    Text ok?
    Can't build if price not met?
    Can't build if prerequisites not met?
    Building footprint graphic ok?
    Can't place building if footprint is red?
    Can rotate building 360 degrees?
    Right-click places building?
    Building site appears in Peasant's LOS?
    Peasant constructs building?
    Construction animation ok?
    Phase one graphic ok?
    Phase two graphic ok?
    Phase three graphic ok? (if present)
    Completed building graphic ok?
    "Building Finished" audio ok?
Select building.
    Toolbar graphics ok?
    Text ok?
    Can destroy building?
    Can cancel building destruction?
    Confirming destroys building?
    Animation ok?
    Audio ok?
Build new building of the same type.
Place it away from first building.
    Alt+right-click makes peasant run to building site?
Select new building. Right-click on ground nearby to set rally point.
    Flag appears?
Send unit in for training.
    Exiting units walk to rally point?
Select building again. Alt+right-click to set new rally point farther away.
    Flag appears?
Send unit in for training.
    Exiting units run to rally point?
Select building again. Right-click on any other barracks.
    Flag appears?
Send unit into Dojo for training.
    Exiting units enter second barracks for training?
Select a peasant, then hover cursor over building.
    "Train _____" hotspot is entire building footprint?

Send unit into building.
    Cancel button graphics ok?
    Text ok?
    Unit exits building when you click Cancel?
    Resource cost recovered?
Have fire-damaging enemies attack building. (Serpent Raiders are good for this.)
    Building burns?
    Animation ok?
    Audio ok?
    Building is destroyed in stages?
    Stage one graphics okay?
    Audio ok?
    Stage two graphics okay?
    Audio ok?
    Stage three graphics okay (if present)?
    Audio ok?
    Building leaves rubble when destroyed?
    Rubble disappears after a while?
Build four of this building.
Send a peasant in to train in the first building; buy one each of
the building's three techniques in the other three buildings.
(Do this as close to simultaneously as you can.
Use the yinyang cheat to get enough yin or yang points.)
    Peasant enters building?
    Peasant progress meter ok?
    Technique 1 progress meter ok?
    Technique 2 progress meter ok?
    Technique 3 progress meter ok?
    First-level unit exits building?
Exit game. Create new game.
Build four of this building.
Send a first-level unit in to train in the first building; then buy one each of
the building's three techniques in the other three buildings.
(Do this as close to simultaneously as you can.
Use the yinyang cheat to get enough yin or yang points.)
    First-level unit enters building?
    First-level unit progress meter ok?
    Technique 1 progress meter ok?
    Technique 2 progress meter ok?
    Technique 3 progress meter ok?
    Second-level unit exits building?
Exit game. Create new game.

Build four of this building.
Send a Second-level unit in to train in the first building; then buy one each of
the building's three techniques in the other three buildings.
(Do this as close to simultaneously as you can.
Use the yinyang cheat to get enough yin or yang points.)
  Second-level unit enters building?
  Second-level unit progress meter ok?
  Technique 1 progress meter ok?
  Technique 2 progress meter ok?
  Technique 3 progress meter ok?
  Third-level unit exits building?
Now, send a peasant into the first building, a first-level unit into the
second building, and a second-level unit into the third.
(Do this as close to simultaneously as you can.)
  Peasant enters building?
  Progress meter ok?
  First-level unit enters building?
  Progress meter ok?
  Second-level unit enters building?
  Progress meter ok?
  New units exit buildings?
Archery Range
Select a Peasant. Choose Archery Range.
  Building cost ok?
  Text ok?
  Can't build if price not met?
  Can't build if prerequisites not met?
  Building footprint graphic ok?
  Can't place building if footprint is red?
  Can rotate building 360 degrees?
  Right-click places building?
  Building site appears in Peasant's LOS?
  Peasant constructs building?
  Construction animation ok?
  Phase one graphic ok?
  Phase two graphic ok?
  Phase three graphic ok? (if present)
  Completed building graphic ok?
  "Building Finished" audio ok?
Select building.
  Toolbar graphics ok?
  Text ok?
  Can destroy building?

```
        Can cancel building destruction?
        Confirming destroys building?
        Animation ok?
        Audio ok?
    Build new building of the same type.
    Place it away from first building.
        Alt+right-click makes peasant run to building site?
    Select new building.  Right-click on ground nearby to set rally point.
        Flag appears?
    Send unit in for training.
        Exiting units walk to rally point?
    Select building again.  Alt+right-click to set new rally point farther away.
        Flag appears?
    Send unit in for training.
        Exiting units run to rally point?
    Select building again.  Right-click on any other barracks.
        Flag appears?
    Send unit into Archery Range for training.
        Exiting units enter second barracks for training?
    Select a peasant, then hover cursor over building.
        "Train _____" hotspot is entire building footprint?
    Send unit into building.
        Cancel button graphics ok?
        Text ok?
        Unit exits building when you click Cancel?
        Resource cost recovered?
    Have fire-damaging enemies attack building.  (Serpent Raiders are good for this.)
        Building burns?
        Animation ok?
        Audio ok?
        Building is destroyed in stages?
        Stage one graphics okay?
        Audio ok?
        Stage two graphics okay?
        Audio ok?
        Stage three graphics okay (if present)?
        Audio ok?
        Building leaves rubble when destroyed?
        Rubble disappears after a while?
    Build four of this building.
    Send a peasant in to train in the first building; buy one each of
    the building's three techniques in the other three buildings.
```

(Do this as close to simultaneously as you can.
Use the yinyang cheat to get enough yin or yang points.)
     Peasant enters building?
     Peasant progress meter ok?
     Technique 1 progress meter ok?
     Technique 2 progress meter ok?
     Technique 3 progress meter ok?
     First-level unit exits building?
Exit game. Create new game.
Build four of this building.
Send a first-level unit in to train in the first building; then buy one each of
the building's three techniques in the other three buildings.
(Do this as close to simultaneously as you can.
Use the yinyang cheat to get enough yin or yang points.)
     First-level unit enters building?
     First-level unit progress meter ok?
     Technique 1 progress meter ok?
     Technique 2 progress meter ok?
     Technique 3 progress meter ok?
     Second-level unit exits building?
Exit game. Create new game.
Build four of this building.
Send a second-level unit in to train in the first building; then buy one each of
the building's three techniques in the other three buildings.
(Do this as close to simultaneously as you can.
Use the yinyang cheat to get enough yin or yang points.)
     Second-level unit enters building?
     Second-level unit progress meter ok?
     Technique 1 progress meter ok?
     Technique 2 progress meter ok?
     Technique 3 progress meter ok?
     Third-level unit exits building?
Now, send a peasant into the first building, a first-level unit into the
second building, and a second-level unit into the third.
(Do this as close to simultaneously as you can.)
     Peasant enters building?
     Progress meter ok?
     First-level unit enters building?
     Progress meter ok?
     Second-level unit enters building?
     Progress meter ok?
     New units exit buildings?

```
Alchemist Hut
    Select a Peasant.  Choose Alchemist Hut.
        Building cost ok?
        Text ok?
        Can't build if price not met?
        Can't build if prerequisites not met?
        Building footprint graphic ok?
        Can't place building if footprint is red?
        Can rotate building 360 degrees?
        Right-click places building?
        Building site appears in Peasant's LOS?
        Peasant constructs building?
        Construction animation ok?
        Phase one graphic ok?
        Phase two graphic ok?
        Phase three graphic ok? (if present)
        Completed building graphic ok?
        "Building Finished" audio ok?
    Select building.
        Toolbar graphics ok?
        Text ok?
        Can destroy building?
        Can cancel building destruction?
        Confirming destroys building?
        Animation ok?
        Audio ok?
Build new building of the same type.
Place it away from first building.
        Alt+right-click makes peasant run to building site?
Select new building.  Right-click on ground nearby to set rally point.
        Flag appears?
Send unit in for training.
        Exiting units walk to rally point?
Select building again.  Alt+right-click to set new rally point farther away.
        Flag appears?
Send unit in for training.
        Exiting units run to rally point?
Select building again.  Right-click on any other barracks.
        Flag appears?
Send unit into Alchemist Hut for training.
        Exiting units enter second barracks for training?
Select a peasant, then hover cursor over building.
        "Train _____" hotspot is entire building footprint?
```

Send unit into building.
        Cancel button graphics ok?
        Text ok?
        Unit exits building when you click Cancel?
        Resource cost recovered?
Have fire-damaging enemies attack building. (Serpent Raiders are good for this.)
        Building burns?
        Animation ok?
        Audio ok?
        Building is destroyed in stages?
        Stage one graphics okay?
        Audio ok?
        Stage two graphics okay?
        Audio ok?
        Stage three graphics okay (if present)?
        Audio ok?
        Building leaves rubble when destroyed?
        Rubble disappears after a while?
Build four of this building.
Send a peasant in to train in the first building; buy one each of
the building's three techniques in the other three buildings.
(Do this as close to simultaneously as you can.
Use the yinyang cheat to get enough yin or yang points.)
        Peasant enters building?
        Peasant progress meter ok?
        Technique 1 progress meter ok?
        Technique 2 progress meter ok?
        Technique 3 progress meter ok?
        First-level unit exits building?
Exit game. Create new game.
Build four of this building.
Send a first-level unit in to train in the first building; then buy one each of
the building's three techniques in the other three buildings.
(Do this as close to simultaneously as you can.
Use the yinyang cheat to get enough yin or yang points.)
        First-level unit enters building?
        First-level unit progress meter ok?
        Technique 1 progress meter ok?
        Technique 2 progress meter ok?
        Technique 3 progress meter ok?
        Second-level unit exits building?
Exit game. Create new game.

Build four of this building.

Send a Second-level unit in to train in the first building; then buy one each of the building's three techniques in the other three buildings.

(Do this as close to simultaneously as you can.

Use the yinyang cheat to get enough yin or yang points.)

      Second-level unit enters building?

      Second-level unit progress meter ok?

      Technique 1 progress meter ok?

      Technique 2 progress meter ok?

      Technique 3 progress meter ok?

      Third-level unit exits building?

Now, send a peasant into the first building, a first-level unit into the second building, and a second-level unit into the third.

(Do this as close to simultaneously as you can.)

      Peasant enters building?

      Progress meter ok?

      First-level unit enters building?

      Progress meter ok?

      Second-level unit enters building?

      Progress meter ok?

      New units exit buildings?

Bathhouse

Select a Peasant. Choose Bathhouse.

      Building cost ok?

      Text ok?

      Can't build if price not met?

      Can't build if prerequisites not met?

      Building footprint graphic ok?

      Can't place building if footprint is red?

      Can rotate building 360 degrees?

      Right-click places building?

      Building site appears in Peasant's LOS?

      Peasant constructs building?

      Construction animation ok?

      Phase one graphic ok?

      Phase two graphic ok?

      Phase three graphic ok? (if present)

      Completed building graphic ok?

      "Building Finished" audio ok?

Select building.

      Toolbar graphics ok?

      Text ok?

      Can destroy building?

       Can cancel building destruction?

       Confirming destroys building?

       Animation ok?

       Audio ok?

Build new building of the same type.

Place it away from first building.

       Alt+right-click makes peasant run to building site?

Select new building. Right-click on ground nearby to set rally point.

       Flag appears?

Send unit in for training.

       Exiting units walk to rally point?

Select building again. Alt+right-click to set new rally point farther away.

       Flag appears?

Send unit in for training.

       Exiting units run to rally point?

Select a peasant, then hover cursor over building.

       "Train Geisha" hotspot is entire building footprint?

Send unit into building.

       Cancel button graphics ok?

       Text ok?

       Unit exits building when you click Cancel?

       Resource cost recovered?

Have fire-damaging enemies attack building. (Serpent Raiders are good for this.)

       Building burns?

       Animation ok?

       Audio ok?

       Building is destroyed in stages?

       Stage one graphics okay?

       Audio ok?

       Stage two graphics okay?

       Audio ok?

       Stage three graphics okay (if present)?

       Audio ok?

       Building leaves rubble when destroyed?

       Rubble disappears after a while?

Build four of this building.

Send a peasant in to train in the first building; buy one each of

the building's three techniques in the other three buildings.

(Do this as close to simultaneously as you can.

Use the yinyang cheat to get enough yin or yang points.)

       Peasant enters building?

       Peasant progress meter ok?

       Technique 1 progress meter ok?

Technique 2 progress meter ok?

Technique 3 progress meter ok?

Nurse unit exits building?

Now, send a peasant each into the first two buildings,

(Do this as close to simultaneously as you can.)

Peasant enters first building?

Progress meter ok?

Peasant enters second building?

Progress meter ok?

Nurse units exit buildings?

Shrine

Select a Peasant. Choose Shrine.

Building cost ok?

Text ok?

Can't build if price not met?

Can't build if prerequisites not met?

Building footprint graphic ok?

Can't place building if footprint is red?

Can rotate building 360 degrees?

Right-click places building?

Building site appears in Peasant's LOS?

Peasant constructs building?

Construction animation ok?

Phase one graphic ok?

Phase two graphic ok?

Phase three graphic ok? (if present)

Completed building graphic ok?

"Building Finished" audio ok?

Select building.

Toolbar graphics ok?

Text ok?

Can destroy building?

Can cancel building destruction?

Confirming destroys building?

Animation ok?

Audio ok?

Build new building of the same type.

Place it away from first building.

Alt+right-click makes peasant run to building site?

Select new building. Right-click on ground nearby to set rally point.

Flag appears?

Send unit in for battle gear.

Exiting units walk to rally point?

Select building again. Alt+right-click to set new rally point farther away.
    Flag appears?
Send unit in for battle gear.
    Exiting units run to rally point?
Select any barracks, then right-click on Shrine to set rally point.
    Flag appears?
    Units exiting barracks walk into Shrine?
Select any barracks, then Alt+right-click on Shrine to set rally point.
    Flag appears?
    Units exiting barracks run into Shrine?
Select a unit, then hover cursor over building.
    Hotspot is entire building?
    Text ok?
    Cost ok?
Send unit into building.
    Cancel button graphics ok?
    Text ok?
    Unit exits building when you click Cancel?
    Resource cost recovered?
Have fire-damaging enemies attack building. (Serpent Raiders are good for this.)
    Building burns?
    Animation ok?
    Audio ok?
    Building is destroyed in stages?
    Stage one graphics okay?
    Audio ok?
    Stage two graphics okay?
    Audio ok?
    Stage three graphics okay (if present)?
    Audio ok?
    Building leaves rubble when destroyed?
    Rubble disappears after a while?
Make two of this building.
Send same unit type into both buildings simultaneously.
    Progress meters ok?
    Units emerge with battle gear?
Send a different unit type into each building simultaneously.
    Progress meters ok?
    Units emerge with battle gear?
Fireworks Factory
Select a Peasant. Choose Fireworks Factory.
    Building cost ok?

   Text ok?

   Can't build if price not met?

   Can't build if prerequisites not met?

   Building footprint graphic ok?

   Can't place building if footprint is red?

   Can rotate building 360 degrees?

   Right-click places building?

   Building site appears in Peasant's LOS?

   Peasant constructs building?

   Construction animation ok?

   Phase one graphic ok?

   Phase two graphic ok?

   Phase three graphic ok? (if present)

   Completed building graphic ok?

   "Building Finished" audio ok?

Select building.

   Toolbar graphics ok?

   Text ok?

   Can destroy building?

   Can cancel building destruction?

   Confirming destroys building?

   Animation ok?

   Audio ok?

Build new building of the same type.

Place it away from first building.

   Alt+right-click makes peasant run to building site?

Select new building. Right-click on ground nearby to set rally point.

   Flag appears?

Send unit in for battle gear.

   Exiting units walk to rally point?

Select building again. Alt+right-click to set new rally point farther away.

   Flag appears?

Send unit in for battle gear.

   Exiting units run to rally point?

Select any barracks, then right-click on Fireworks Factory to set rally point.

   Flag appears?

   Units exiting barracks walk into Fireworks Factory?

Select any barracks, then Alt+right-click on Fireworks Factory to set rally point.

   Flag appears?

   Units exiting barracks run into Fireworks Factory?

Select a unit, then hover cursor over building.

   Hotspot is entire building?

```
        Text ok?
        Cost ok?
Send unit into building.
        Cancel button graphics ok?
        Text ok?
        Unit exits building when you click Cancel?
        Resource cost recovered?
Have fire-damaging enemies attack building.  (Serpent Raiders are good for this.)
        Building burns?
        Animation ok?
        Audio ok?
        Building is destroyed in stages?
        Stage one graphics okay?
        Audio ok?
        Stage two graphics okay?
        Audio ok?
        Stage three graphics okay (if present)?
        Audio ok?
        Building leaves rubble when destroyed?
        Rubble disappears after a while?
Make two of this building.
Send same unit type into both buildings simultaneously.
        Progress meters ok?
        Units emerge with battle gear?
Send a different unit type into each building simultaneously.
        Progress meters ok?
        Units emerge with battle gear?
Watchtower
Select a Peasant.  Choose Watchtower.
        Building cost ok?
        Text ok?
        Can't build if price not met?
        Can't build if prerequisites not met?
        Building footprint graphic ok?
        Can't place building if footprint is red?
        Can rotate building 360 degrees?
        Right-click places building?
        Building site appears in Peasant's LOS?
        Peasant constructs building?
        Construction animation ok?
        Phase one graphic ok?
        Phase two graphic ok?
```

```
        Phase three graphic ok? (if present)
        Completed building graphic ok?
        "Building Finished" audio ok?
        Tower LOS ok?
  Select building.
        Toolbar graphics ok?
        Text ok?
        Can destroy building?
        Can cancel building destruction?
        Confirming destroys building?
        Animation ok?
        Audio ok?
Build new building of the same type.
Place it away from first building.
        Alt+right-click makes peasant run to building site?
Select new building.  Right-click on ground nearby to set rally point.
        Flag appears?
Send unit into tower.
        Tower LOS increases when unit reaches top?
Send enemy unit(s) near tower.
Click "Daze" icon on tower.
        Animation ok?
        Audio ok?
        Enemies dazed?
Order unit from tower.
        Exiting unit walks to rally point?
Select building again.  Alt+right-click to set new rally point farther away.
        Flag appears?
Select any barracks, then right-click on Tower to set rally point.
        Flag appears?
        Units exiting barracks walk into Tower?
Select any barracks, then Alt+right-click on Tower to set rally point.
        Flag appears?
        Units exiting barracks run into Tower?
Select a unit, then hover cursor over building.
        Hotspot is entire building?
        Text ok?
Have fire-damaging enemies attack building.  (Serpent Raiders are good for this.)
        Building burns?
        Animation ok?
        Audio ok?
        Building is destroyed in stages?
```

Stage one graphics okay?
Audio ok?
Stage two graphics okay?
Audio ok?
Stage three graphics okay (if present)?
Audio ok?
Building leaves rubble when destroyed?
Rubble disappears after a while?

Town Hall
Select a Peasant. Choose Town Hall.
Building cost ok?
Text ok?
Can't build if price not met?
Can't build if prerequisites not met?
Building footprint graphic ok?
Can't place building if footprint is red?
Can rotate building 360 degrees?
Right-click places building?
Building site appears in Peasant's LOS?
Peasant constructs building?
Construction animation ok?
Phase one graphic ok?
Phase two graphic ok?
Phase three graphic ok? (if present)
Completed building graphic ok?
"Building Finished" audio ok?
Rice limit increased?
Water limit increased?
Select building.
Toolbar graphics ok?
Text ok?
Can destroy building?
Can cancel building destruction?
Confirming destroys building?
Animation ok?
Audio ok?
Have fire-damaging enemies attack building. (Serpent Raiders are good for this.)
Building burns?
Animation ok?
Audio ok?
Building is destroyed in stages?
Stage one graphics okay?

Audio ok?

Stage two graphics okay?

Audio ok?

Stage three graphics okay (if present)?

Audio ok?

Building leaves rubble when destroyed?

Rubble disappears after a while?

Build new building of the same type.

Place it away from first building.

Alt+right-click makes peasant run to building site?

"Upgrade to Royal Academy" button on toolbar?

Text ok?

Button graphics ok?

Click upgrade button.

Upgrade animation ok?

Upgrade audio ok?

Royal Academy appears?

Graphics ok?

Toolbar graphics ok?

Text ok?

Select Royal Academy.

Toolbar graphics ok?

Text ok?

Can destroy building?

Can cancel building destruction?

Confirming destroys building?

Animation ok?

Audio ok?

Build a new Town Hall and upgrade it to a Royal Academy.

Select new building. Right-click on ground nearby to set rally point.

Flag appears?

Select a peasant, then hover cursor over building.

"Train Guardian" hotspot is entire building footprint?

Send unit into building.

Cancel button graphics ok?

Text ok?

Unit exits building when you click Cancel?

Resource cost recovered?

Send unit in for training.

Exiting units walk to rally point?

Select building again. Alt+right-click to set new rally point farther away.

Flag appears?

Send unit in for training.
    Exiting units run to rally point?
Select building again. Right-click on any other barracks.
    Flag appears?
Select a geisha, then hover cursor over building.
    "Train Battle Maiden" hotspot is entire building footprint?
Keep
Select a Peasant. Choose Keep.
    Building cost ok?
    Text ok?
    Can't build if price not met?
    Can't build if prerequisites not met?
    Building footprint graphic ok?
    Can't place building if footprint is red?
    Can rotate building 360 degrees?
    Right-click places building?
    Building site appears in Peasant's LOS?
    Peasant constructs building?
    Construction animation ok?
    Phase one graphic ok?
    Phase two graphic ok?
    Phase three graphic ok? (if present)
    Completed building graphic ok?
    "Building Finished" audio ok?
Select building.
    Toolbar graphics ok?
    Text ok?
    Monk progress meter ok?
    Text ok?
    Meter stops after four monks?
    Text ok?
    Can destroy building?
    Can cancel building destruction?
    Confirming destroys building?
    Animation ok?
    Audio ok?
Build new building of the same type.
Place it away from first building.
    Alt+right-click makes peasant run to building site?
Select new building. Right-click on ground nearby to set rally point.
    Flag appears?
    Exiting units walk to rally point?

Select building again. Alt+right-click to set new rally point farther away.

    Flag appears?

    Exiting units run to rally point?

Have fire-damaging enemies attack building. (Serpent Raiders are good for this.)

    Building burns?

    Animation ok?

    Audio ok?

    Building is destroyed in stages?

    Stage one graphics okay?

    Audio ok?

    Stage two graphics okay?

    Audio ok?

    Stage three graphics okay (if present)?

    Audio ok?

    Building leaves rubble when destroyed?

    Rubble disappears after a while?

Dragon's Monument

Select a Peasant. Choose Dragon's Monument.

    Building cost ok?

    Text ok?

    Can't build if price not met?

    Can't build if prerequisites not met?

    Building footprint graphic ok?

    Can't place building if footprint is red?

    Can rotate building 360 degrees?

    Right-click places building?

    Building site appears in Peasant's LOS?

    Peasant constructs building?

    Construction animation ok?

    Phase one graphic ok?

    Phase two graphic ok?

    Phase three graphic ok? (if present)

    Completed building graphic ok?

    "Building Finished" audio ok?

Select building.

    Toolbar graphics ok?

    Text ok?

    Can destroy building?

    Can cancel building destruction?

    Confirming destroys building?

    Animation ok?

    Audio ok?

Build new building of the same type.
Place it away from first building.
    Alt+right-click makes peasant run to building site?
Link three barracks to create Samurai.
Select last barracks (from which Samurai will emerge) and right-click Dragon's Monument.
    Samurai exit barracks and enter Dragon's Monument?
    Samurai portrait appears?
    Portrait ok?
    Text ok?
    Samurai appears on platform?
    Clicking portrait makes Samurai exit?
Select a Samurai, then hover cursor over building.
    "Sacrifice _____" hotspot is entire building footprint?
    Building full at four Samurai?
    Text ok?
    Black Lightning icon highlights?
    Text ok?
Activate Black Lightning.
    Can target?
    Animation ok?
    Text ok?
    Damages enemy units?
    Damages enemy buildings?
Have fire-damaging enemies attack building. (Serpent Raiders are good for this.)
    Building burns?
    Animation ok?
    Audio ok?
    Building is destroyed in stages?
    Stage one graphics okay?
    Audio ok?
    Stage two graphics okay?
    Audio ok?
    Stage three graphics okay (if present)?
    Audio ok?
    Building leaves rubble when destroyed?
    Rubble disappears after a while?
Stables
Select a Peasant. Choose Stables.
    Building cost ok?
    Text ok?
    Can't build if price not met?
    Can't build if prerequisites not met?

Building footprint graphic ok?

Can't place building if footprint is red?

Can rotate building 360 degrees?

Right-click places building?

Building site appears in Peasant's LOS?

Peasant constructs building?

Construction animation ok?

Phase one graphic ok?

Phase two graphic ok?

Phase three graphic ok? (if present)

Completed building graphic ok?

"Building Finished" audio ok?

Select building.

Toolbar graphics ok?

Text ok?

Can destroy building?

Can cancel building destruction?

Confirming destroys building?

Animation ok?

Audio ok?

Build new building of the same type.

Place it away from first building.

Alt+right-click makes peasant run to building site?

Select new building. Right-click on ground nearby to set rally point.

Flag appears?

Send unit in to mount horse.

Exiting units walk to rally point?

Select building again. Alt+right-click to set new rally point farther away.

Flag appears?

Send unit in to mount horse.

Exiting units run to rally point?

Select a peasant, then hover cursor over building.

"Get Pack Horse" hotspot is entire building footprint?

Have fire-damaging enemies attack building. (Serpent Raiders are good for this.)

Building burns?

Animation ok?

Audio ok?

Building is destroyed in stages?

Stage one graphics okay?

Audio ok?

Stage two graphics okay?

Audio ok?

    Stage three graphics okay (if present)?

    Audio ok?

    Building leaves rubble when destroyed?

    Rubble disappears after a while?

Build four of this building.

Send a peasant in to train in the first building; buy one each of the building's three techniques in the other three buildings.

(Do this as close to simultaneously as you can.

Use the yinyang cheat to get enough yin or yang points.)

    Peasant enters building?

    Peasant progress meter ok?

    Technique 1 progress meter ok?

    Technique 2 progress meter ok?

    Technique 3 progress meter ok?

    First-level unit exits building?

Exit game. Create new game.

Build four of this building.

Send a first-level unit in to train in the first building; then buy one each of the building's three techniques in the other three buildings.

(Do this as close to simultaneously as you can.

Use the yinyang cheat to get enough yin or yang points.)

    First-level unit enters building?

    First-level unit progress meter ok?

    Technique 1 progress meter ok?

    Technique 2 progress meter ok?

    Technique 3 progress meter ok?

    Second-level unit exits building?

Exit game. Create new game.

Build four of this building.

Send a second-level unit in to train in the first building; then buy one each of the building's three techniques in the other three buildings.

(Do this as close to simultaneously as you can.

Use the yinyang cheat to get enough yin or yang points.)

    Second-level unit enters building?

    Second-level unit progress meter ok?

    Technique 1 progress meter ok?

    Technique 2 progress meter ok?

    Technique 3 progress meter ok?

    Third-level unit exits building?

Now, send a peasant into the first building, a first-level unit into the second building, and a second-level unit into the third.

(Do this as close to simultaneously as you can.)

```
Peasant enters building?
Progress meter ok?
First-level unit enters building?
Progress meter ok?
Second-level unit enters building?
Progress meter ok?
New units exit buildings?
```

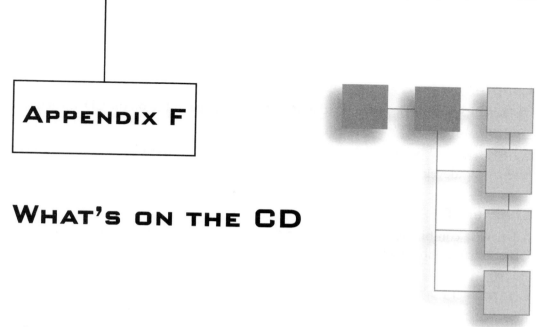

APPENDIX F

WHAT'S ON THE CD

Chapter Data

The CD accompanying this book contains various files which are separated according to the chapter they appear in. There are also links provided to connect you with online material that can be valuable to you when working in the particular chapters. The links are provided here, along with the chapter directories where there is content on this disc.

Chapter 4

"*Super Street Racer* Game Design" is a design document referenced in this chapter. As of January 20, 2005 it could be found at

http://sourceforge.net/project/showfiles.php?group_id=99297

Chapter 6

An Excel file containing software quality tables can be found on the CD at \chapter\ chapter06.

Additionally, an SQA Plan Template you can use to create your own Software Quality Assurance Plan can be found online at http://www.teraquest.com/resource/documents/ SQAPlanTemplateOne.doc

Chapter 7

The test kickoff checklists described in this chapter can be found on the CD at \chapter\chapter07.

You can create a Test Plan for your own project using the Test Plan Outline found at http://www.developsense.com/testing/TestPlanOutline.doc.

Chapter 10

A pairwise combinatorial test table constructed in this chapter can be found on the CD at \chapter\chapter10.

Chapter 11

Example Test Flow Diagrams constructed in this chapter can be found on the CD at \chapter\chapter11.

Chapter 12

Test designs and usage profile tables discussed in this chapter can be found on the CD at \chapter\chapter12.

Chapter 15

Combinatorial test tables utilizing defect triggers can be found on the CD at \chapter\chapter15.

Chapter 17

The logfile of a capture/playback test described in this chapter can be found on the CD at \chapter\chapter17.

Appendix C

Excel spreadsheets containing the combinatorial test templates shown in Appendix C can be found on the CD at \chapter\AppendixC.

Appendix D

The Test Flow Diagram templates shown in Appendix D can be found on the CD at \chapter\AppendixD.

Tools

In addition to the chapter data, the CD includes Web links to various tools that you need to use to follow the examples and complete some of the exercises in this book

DevTrack

DevTrack is a popular defect-tracking tool discussed in Chapter 2. Product and documentation downloads are available at http://www.techexcel.com/products/devtrack.html.

SPC for Excel

SPC for MS Excel provides macros which can be used to easily produce control charts and other quality-related graphs in an Excel document. Some of these charts are described and illustrated in Chapter 6. A demo version with limited capabilities can be downloaded from http://www.spcforexcel.com/demo.htm.

Allpairs

The Allpairs tool automatically generates a pairwise combinatorial table from an input data specification. This tool is used in Chapters 10, 12, and 15. A full-featured free version can be downloaded from http://www.satisfice.com/tools.shtml.

SmartDraw 6 Trial Edition

SmartDraw 6 is used to produce the Test Flow Diagrams in Chapter 11, Chapter 12, Chapter 15, and Appendix D of this book. As of January 20, 2005, you can download a free trial version of this software from ftp://ftp.ttp.co.uk/smartdraw_6_full_trial.exe.

Alternatively, you can download a free trial of the latest version of SmartDraw at http://www.smartdraw.com/downloads/.

Vermont High Test

Vermont High Test is a capture/playback test automation tool featured in Chapter 17. A free trial version can be downloaded from http://www.vtsoft.com/vcsdemos/index.html.

INDEX

Gamedev.net

The most comprehensive game development resource

- The latest news in game development
- The most active forums and chatrooms anywhere, with insights and tips from experienced game developers
- Links to thousands of additional game development resources
- Thorough book and product reviews
- Over 1,000 game development articles!
  Game design
  Graphics
  DirectX
  OpenGL
  AI
  Art
  Music
  Physics
  Source Code
  Sound
  Assembly
  And More!

Gamedev.net